LEARNING Microsoft® WORD 2000

Suzanne Weixel

275 Madison Avenue, New York, NY 10016

Acknowledgements

The author would like to thank everyone at DDC Publishing for their hard work putting this book together, especially Jen Frew and Chris Katsaropoulos. And, of course, she wants to thank her family—Rick, Nathaniel, and Evan for their patience.

Suzanne Weixel

Managing Editor	English Editor	Technical Editors	Design and Layout
Jennifer Frew	Cheryl Ralston	Cheryl VegaRyan	Shu Chen
		Allan Wyatt	Maria Kardasheva
			Midori Nakamura

Acquisitions Manager — Chris Katsaropoulos

Editorial Assistants — Emily Hay, Jacinta O'Halloran

Cover Design — Amy Capuano

Contents

Contents

Contents

Introduction

Microsoft Word 2000 is Microsoft's word processing application. Using Word 2000 you can create business letters, memos, Web pages, newsletters, and more. Using formatting features, such as tables or drawing, you can improve the appearance of your word processing documents.

How We've Organized the Book

Learning Microsoft Word 2000 is made up of fourteen lessons:

- **Lesson I: Basics**
  This short lesson introduces essential Word 2000 skills—including how to start Word, how to use the mouse and keyboard, screen elements, and an overview of features in the Word application.

- **Lesson 2: Create, Save, and Print Documents**
  In this lesson, you will create and work with Word documents. You will also learn how to format business letters, envelopes, and labels. You will also use the Internet simulation provided on the CD-ROM that accompanies this book to go to Web sites to get information.

- **Lesson 3: Open and Edit Documents**
  Essential editing skills are introduced in this lesson. You will also send a Word document as an e-mail.

- **Lesson 4: Text Formatting**
  For documents to be effective, they must be formatted properly. Formatting skills are introduced in this lesson.

- **Lesson 5: Document Formatting**
  Work with alignment, line and paragraph spacing, and hyperlinks in this lesson. You will also create and format a one-page report.

- **Lesson 6: Manage Documents**
  In this lesson, you will preview files and work with document properties. You will also learn to locate a file—even if you're not sure of the file name or exact location.

- **Lesson 7: Tables**
  Use Word tables to organize information more clearly.

- **Lesson 8: Merge**
  Merge is used to create form letters, envelopes, and labels. You will learn how to do a mass mailing quickly and easily using Word's Merge feature.

- **Lesson 9: Multiple-Page Documents**
  Work with multiple-page documents, headers and footers, and outlines in this lesson.

- **Lesson 10: Desktop Publishing and Automation**
  Learn to use many of Word's desktop publishing features, such as columns, borders and shading, and text boxes. Also included in this lesson are templates and macros.

- **Lesson 11: Graphics**
  Enhance Word documents with graphics objects, clip art, and AutoShapes. In this lesson, you will also use the Internet simulation to download clip art from the Internet.

- **Lesson 12: Integration**
  If you are using Word as part of the Office 2000 suite, it is import to know how to integrate the applications. Learn to copy information between programs, embed an Excel worksheet in a Word document, and merge a Word document with an Access Database

- **Lesson 13: Challenge Exercises**
  This lesson combines critical thinking, application integration, and Internet skills. In the Challenge Lesson, you will retrieve data from the Internet, send Web documents via e-mail, download clip art, create a Web page, and more. In each exercise, only basic step directions are given—you need to rely on your own skills to complete the exercise.

- **Lesson 14: Bonus Lesson on CD**
  This lesson includes advanced skills such as creating table of contents, indexes, and forms.

Each lesson in **Learning Microsoft Word 2000** is made up of short exercises designed for using Word 2000 in real-life business settings. Every application exercise is made up of seven key elements:

- **On the Job.** Each exercise starts with a brief description of how you would use the features of that exercise in the workplace.

- **Exercise Scenario.** The Word tools are then put into context by setting a scenario. For example, you may be an assistant to the organizer of a Web page design conference creating a Web page advertising the conference.

- **Terms.** Key terms are included and defined at the start of each exercise, so you can quickly refer back to them. The terms are then highlighted in the text.

- **Notes.** Concise notes for learning the computer concepts.

- **Procedures.** Hands-on mouse and keyboard procedures teach all necessary skills.

- **Application Exercise.** Step-by-step instructions put your skills to work.

- **On Your Own.** Each exercise concludes with a critical thinking activity that you can work through on your own. You may have to create a personal Web page or compose a business letter. You are challenged to come up with data and then additionally challenged to use the data in a document. The *On Your Own* sections can be used as additional reinforcement, for practice, or to test skill proficiency.

- In addition, each lesson ends with a **Critical Thinking Exercise.** As with the *On Your Owns,* you need to rely on your own skills to complete the task.

Working with Data and Solution Files

As you work through the exercises in this book, you'll be creating, opening, and saving files. You should keep the following instructions in mind:

- Many exercises instruct you to open a file from the CD-ROM that comes with this book. The data files are used so that you can focus on the skills being introduced—not on keyboarding lengthy documents. The files are located in the **Datafiles** folders on the CD-ROM.

    ✓ See **What's on the CD** for more information on the data files.

- When the application exercise includes a file name and a CD icon ⊚, you should open the file provided on CD.

- The Directory of Files lists the exercise file (from the CD-ROM) you will need to open to complete each exercise and the name that you are directed to save the file as.

- Unless the book instructs otherwise, use the default settings for text size, margin size, and so on when creating a file. If someone has changed the default software settings for the computer you're using, your exercise files may not look the same as those shown in this book. In addition, the appearance of your files may look different if the system is set to a screen resolution other than 800 x 600.

- All the exercises instruct you to save the files created or to save the exercise files under a new name. You should verify the name of the hard disk or network folder to which files should be saved.

What's on the CD

We've included on the CD:

- **Data files** for many of the exercises. This way you don't have to type lengthy documents from scratch. The data files are all Word 2000 files.

- **Internet simulation** so that you can go to real Web sites to get information—without an Internet connection or modem. Following the steps in the book, you will experience going "online" to locate facts, data, and clip art. You will then use the information in Word documents.

- **Bonus Lesson** of advanced skills. The bonus lesson are provided in .pdf format. You must first install Adobe Acrobat (provided on the CD) before you can open, view, or print the files. Once Adobe Acrobat is installed, you simply double-click the file to open it. Exercises can be printed out and distributed.

- **Typing tests with automatic scoring** can be used to test typing speed and accuracy.

- **Computer Literacy Basics** include information on computer care, computer basics, and a brief history of computers. Once Adobe Acrobat is installed, these exercises can be printed out and distributed.

To access the files:

Data Files

Copy data files to a hard drive:

1. Open Windows 95 Explorer. (Right-click the **Start** button and click **Explore**.)

2. Be sure that the CD is in your CD-ROM drive. Select the CD-ROM drive letter from the Folders pane of the Explorer window.

3. Click to select the **Datafiles** folder in the Name pane of the Explorer window.

4. Drag the folder onto the letter of the drive to which you wish to copy the data files (usually **C:**) in the Folders pane of the Explorer Window.

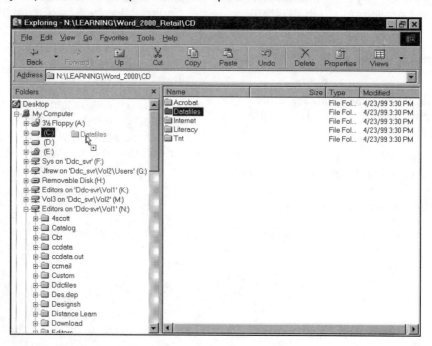

✓ *Be aware that if you copy the files to a network drive the file names may be truncated to eight characters. Some networks do not allow the long file names permitted by Windows 95.*

OR

Access data files directly from CD:

1. Be sure that the CD is in your CD-ROM drive. Select the CD-ROM drive letter from the Folders pane of the Explorer window.
2. Click to select the **Datafiles** folder in the Name pane of the Explorer window.
3. Double-click directly on the file to open it or open the file through the application using a File, Open command.

✓ *Opening and working with files is covered in the Lesson Three of the text. The data files do not need to be installed.*

Internet Simulation

Copy Internet simulation to a hard drive:

1. Open Windows 95 Explorer. (Right-click the **Start** button ![Start] and click **Explore**.)
2. Be sure that the CD is in your CD-ROM drive. Select the CD-ROM drive letter from the Folders pane of the Explorer window.
3. Click to select the **Internet** folder in the Name pane of the Explorer window.
4. Drag the folder onto the letter of the drive to which you wish to copy the data files (usually **C:**) in the Folders pane of the Explorer Window.

✓ *If you copy the Internet simulation to your hard drive, be sure to substitute the correct drive letter in the exercise directions.*

✓ *Important note about HTML files: The Internet simulation is made up of HTML files. If you copy the Internet simulation to your hard drive, be sure to **copy the entire HTML folder from the CD**; otherwise the HTML files will not display correctly.*

OR

Access Interment simulation directly from CD:

1. Be sure that the CD is in your CD-ROM drive. Select the CD-ROM drive letter from the Folders pane of the Explorer window.
2. Follow the directions in the Internet activities using the file path provided in the Internet exercises.

✓ *If your CD-ROM drive is not D:, you will have to substitute the correct drive letter in the exercise directions.*

✓ *The Internet simulation does not need to be installed. The HTML files are simply opened as directed in the Internet exercises.*

Bonus Lesson

To access the Bonus Lesson:

1. Locate the Acrobat Reader folder on the CD. (If you have already installed Adobe Acrobat, you do not need to go through these steps.)
2. Double-click the Setup icon.
3. Respond to the prompts to install Acrobat Reader 3.0.

After installing Acrobat Reader, you may either:

- Leave the Bonus Lesson files on the CD and open, view, and print them from the CD. These files are in a folder called **Bonus**.

- Copy some or all of the exercises to your hard drive using Windows Explorer (see directions for copying data files above). Once on your hard drive you can open, view, and print the files. These files are in a folder called **Bonus**.

Automated Typing Program

System Requirements

Software	Windows 95, Windows 3.1 (or higher), or Windows NT 3.51 (or higher)
Hardware	386/33MHZ or higher (486 or higher recommended), 8 MB RAM, 256 color monitor, and CD-ROM Drive
Disk Space	10 MB available hard disk space for a "Typical" installation.

1. Click **START** on the desktop, Click RUN and then type: **(CD-ROM drive letter):\TIMINGS\SETUP**.

2. Click **NEXT** twice to proceed to the Choose Directory Location screen.

3. Click **NEXT** to accept the default directory (or click **BROWSE** to select another directory) for installing program files.

   ✓ *TYPICAL is recommended for most users.*

4. At the Setup Type screen, click a setup option based on your system needs and click **NEXT**.

5. At the Select Program Folder screen, click **NEXT** to accept the default folder (or select another folder) for storing the program icons.

6. At the Setup Complete screen, click **FINISH**.

Start Automated Typing Program

✓ *Steps 3, 6, and 7 are only necessary the first time you log into the program or if you wish to make any program adjustments.*

1. If program and program icons were installed to the default locations, click **START** on the desktop, click **PROGRAMS**, then click **All the Right Type DDC Edition.**

2. When the introductory screen appears, click anywhere to continue.

3. At the Sign On screen, click **EDIT USERS**, then click **ADD**, type your name, click **OK**, and then click **DONE** to add it to the program.

4. Click your name in the User list and click **SELECT**.

5. Click **CONTINUE** at the welcome screen.

6. Click **Options** on the menu bar and select **Set Options**.

7. **TO SET A SPEED GOAL:**

   (a) Click Speed Goal.

   (b) Select a speed goal from the drop-down list and click **OK**.

   ✓ *The User Prompt option allows you to manually adjust the speed goal for each exercise with out returning to the Options screen.*

   OR

TO SET A TIME GOAL:

(a)   Click Timed Writing.

(b)   Select a time goal from the drop-down list.

✓ *The User Prompt option allows you to manually adjust the timing goal for each exercise without returning to the Options screen. However, the User Prompt option does not enable you to select 30-second timings, whereas the Timed Writing drop-down option does. THE TIMED WRITING, USER PROMPT OPTION IS THE RECOMMENDED SETTING FOR THIS PROGRAM.*

8.   At the FACULTY OF A.R.T. main campus screen, click the **TESTING CENTER** to access the timed writing exercises that accompany this book.

9.   Double-click the exercise for which you wish to be timed.

10.   Follow the online instructions.

Computer Literacy

To access the Computer Literacy Basics files:

1.   Locate the Acrobat Reader folder on the CD. (If you have already installed Acrobat Reader, you do not need to go through these steps.)

2.   Double-click the Setup icon.

3.   Respond to the prompts to install Acrobat Reader 3.0.

After installing Acrobat Reader, you may either:

- Leave the Computer Literacy files on the CD and open, view, and print them from the CD. The Computer Literacy files are located in the **Literacy** folder.

- Copy some or all of the exercises to your hard drive using Windows Explorer (see directions for copying data files above). Once on your hard drive, you can open, view, and print the files. The Computer Literacy files are located in the **Literacy** folder.

Support Material

A complete instructor support package is available with all the tools teachers need:

- Annotated Instructor's Guide includes entire student book with teacher notes, course curriculum guide, and lesson plans. (Catalog number Z37TE)

- Upgraded binder test bank includes pre- and post-assessment tests, mid-term exams, and final exams. Two kinds of tests for each lesson of the student book: conceptual (objective questions) and application (students do the work on their computers). All-new tests. (Catalog number BTZ37)

- Improved visual aids package includes 25 transparencies. (Catalog number F68)

- Visual aid on diskette—25 PowerPoint slides. (Catalog number VA37)

- CD of exercise solutions. (Catalog number SLZ35)

Directory of Files

Exercise #	File Name	Page #
Exercise 84	84MEMO.doc	434
Exercise 84	84XPENSE.xls	434
Exercise 84	84SHOW.ppt	434
Exercise 85	85MEMO.doc	438
Exercise 85	WD85	438
Exercise 85	85XPENSE.xls	438
Exercise 86	86MEMO.doc	443
Exercise 86	WD86-1.doc	443
Exercise 86	86XPENSE.xls	443
Exercise 86	WD86-2.xls	443
Exercise 87	87RETREAT.doc	448
Exercise 87	WD87-1	448
Exercise 87	87BUDGET.xls	448
Exercise 87	WD87-2.xls	448
Exercise 88	88MERGE.mdb	452
Exercise 88	WD88-1.mdb	452
Exercise 88	88SURVEY	452
Exercise 88	WD88-2	452
Exercise 88	WD88-3	452
Exercise 88	WD88-4	452
Exercise 88	WD88-5	452
Exercise 89	WD89-1	456
Exercise 89	89TRAIN.ppt	456
Exercise 89	WD89-2.ppt	456
Exercise 89	WD89-3.doc	456
Exercise 89	WD89-4.rtf	456
Exercise 90	WD90-1.doc	460
Exercise 90	90MONEY.xls	460
Exercise 90	WD90-2.xls	460
Exercise 90	WD90-4	460
Exercise 90	WD90-5	460
Exercise 91	WD91	464
Exercise 92	92BIKING.doc	467
Exercise 92	WD92-1.doc	467
Exercise 92	92COSTS.xls	467
Exercise 92	WD92-2.xls	467
Exercise 93	93BIKING	470
Exercise 93	WD93-1.doc	470
Exercise 93	WD93-2.htm	470
Exercise 93	93COSTS.xls	470
Exercise 93	WD93-3.xls	470
Exercise 94	94TRAVEL.doc	473

Exercise #	File Name	Page #
Exercise 94	WD94.htm	473
Exercise 94	94BIKE.htm	473
Exercise 94	94CANOE.htm	474
Exercise 94	WD96-2.doc	480
Exercise 95	95MEMO.doc	476
Exercise 95	WD95-1.doc	476
Exercise 95	95STOCKS.xls	476
Exercise 95	WD95-2.xls	476
Exercise 96	96MERGE.mdb	480
Exercise 96	WD96-1.mdb	480
Exercise 96	WD96-2.doc	480
Exercise 96	WD96-3.doc	480
Exercise 97	WD97-1.doc	482
Exercise 97	97SIDEB	482
Exercise 97	WD97-2.doc	482
Exercise 97	WD97-3.doc	483
Exercise 97	WD97-4.doc	483
Exercise 97	WD97-5.doc	483
Exercise 98	98TEMP	On CD
Exercise 98	WD98-1	On CD
Exercise 98	WD98-2	On CD
Exercise 99	99RPRT	On CD
Exercise 99	WD99	On CD
Exercise 100	100RPT	On CD
Exercise 100	WD100	On CD
Exercise 101	101MISS	On CD
Exercise 101	WD101-1	On CD
Exercise 101	101RPT	On CD
Exercise 101	WD101-2	On CD
Exercise 102	WD102	On CD
Exercise 102	102CHART.xls	On CD
Exercise 103	WD103-1	On CD
Exercise 103	WD103-2	On CD
Exercise 104	104TEMP	On CD
Exercise 104	WD104-1	On CD
Exercise 104	WD104-2	On CD
Exercise 104	104PLAN	On CD
Exercise 104	WD104-3	On CD
Exercise 104	104PACK	On CD
Exercise 104	WD104-4	On CD
Exercise 104	WD104-5	On CD

Lesson 1

Basics

Exercise 1

Skills Covered:

◆ **About Microsoft Word 2000** ◆ **Conventions Used in This Book**
◆ **Use the Mouse** ◆ **Use the Keyboard** ◆ **Start Word**
◆ **The Word Window** ◆ **Exit Word**

On the Job

Microsoft Word 2000 is a word-processing application you can use to prepare many different types of documents. Word 2000 makes it easy to create simple documents such as letters and memos, as well as more complex documents such as newsletters and brochures. You can use Word 2000 with only a keyboard, with only a mouse, or with a combination of the two.

You've just been hired as a marketing assistant at State-of-the-Art Solutions, a consulting firm. You want to become familiar with Microsoft Word and the Word window so you can use these skills on the job.

Terms

Format Arrange and enhance a document to improve its appearance.

Word processing The act of creating text based documents.

Internet A global network of computers.

Conventions Consistent organization and use of language that make it easy to understand the material in this book.

Font size The size of the characters typed in a document. Font size is measured in points, with approximately 72 points in an inch.

Mouse A device that allows you to select items on-screen by pointing at them with the mouse pointer.

Mouse pointer A marker on your computer screen that shows you where the next mouse action will occur. The mouse pointer changes shapes depending on the current action.

Toolbar A row of buttons used to select features and commands.

I-beam A mouse pointer shape resembling the uppercase letter I.

Mouse pad A smooth, cushioned surface on which you slide a mouse.

Window The area on-screen where an application is displayed.

Default A standard setting or mode of operation.

Elements Menus, icons, and other items that are part of Word's on-screen interface.

Keyboard shortcuts Key combinations used to execute a command without opening a menu.

Scroll To page through a document in order to view some part of its contents which is not currently displayed.

Zoom To increase (zoom in) or decrease (zoom out) the displayed size of the document on-screen.

Notes

About Word 2000

- Microsoft Word 2000 is designed to make it easy for you to create, edit, **format**, and distribute **word processing** documents.

- With Word 2000 you can easily include text and graphics in documents.

- You can transfer data between documents and between different applications running under the Windows operating environment.

- Word 2000 also provides tools for accessing the **Internet** and for creating documents for distribution on the Internet.

- If you have used previous versions of Microsoft Word, you will notice many similarities as well as many new features and enhancements.

- If you are using Word 2000 as part of the Microsoft Office 2000 Suite of applications, you will find it easy to transfer your knowledge of Word 2000 to any of the other Office programs.

Conventions Used in This Book

- **Conventions** are used throughout this book to make it simple for you to understand the concepts and the skills required to use Word 2000 effectively.

  - Definitions of new words are provided in the Terms sections.

  - Concepts are introduced in the Notes sections.

  - Actions are listed in the Procedures sections.

  - Exercise Directions provide step-by-step instructions for applying the new skills.

  - Illustrations are included to provide visual support for the text.

- Documents used to illustrate exercises are created using a 12-point **font size**, unless otherwise noted. If the default font size on your computer system is 10 points, your instructor may ask you to change it so your completed documents match the solution files provided with this book.

  ✓ *Changing fonts and font sizes are covered in Lesson 4, Exercise 25.*

- This book assumes you have installed all of the features covered. If necessary, run Word 2000 Setup again to install additional options.

Use the Mouse

- Use your **mouse** to point to and select commands and features of Word 2000.

- When you move the mouse on your desk, the **mouse pointer** moves on-screen. For example, when you move the mouse to the left, the mouse pointer moves to the left.

- When you click a mouse button, Word 2000 executes a command. For example, when you click on the Print **toolbar** button, Word prints the current document.

- A mouse may have one, two, or three buttons. Unless otherwise noted, references in this book are to the use of the left mouse button.

- The mouse pointer changes shape depending on the program in use, the object being pointed to, and the action being performed. Common mouse pointer shapes include an arrow, an **I-beam**, and a hand with a pointing finger.

- You should use a mouse on a **mouse pad** that is designed specifically to make it easy to slide the mouse.

  ✓ *You can move the mouse without moving the mouse pointer by picking it up. This is useful if you move the mouse too close to the edge of mouse pad or desk.*

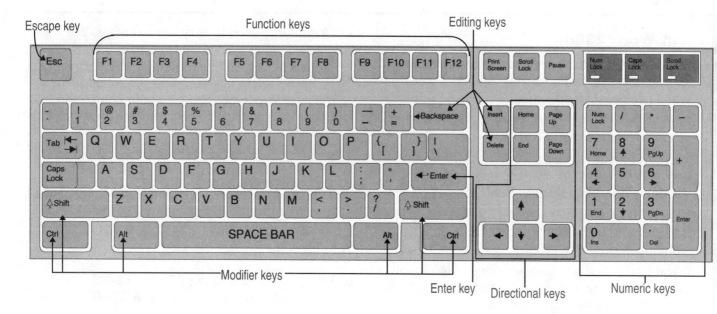

Use the Keyboard

- Use your keyboard to type text as well as to access Word commands and features.

- In addition to the regular text and number keys, computer keyboards have special keys used for shortcuts or for executing special commands.

  - Function keys (F1-F12) appear in a row above the numbers at the top of the keyboard. They can be used as shortcut keys to perform certain tasks.

  - Modifier keys (Shift, Alt, Ctrl) are used in combination with other keys or mouse actions to select certain commands or perform actions. In this book, modifier key combinations are shown as: the modifier key followed by a plus sign followed by the other key or mouse action. For example, Ctrl+S is the key combination for saving the current file.

  - The Numeric keys are made up of the 10-key keypad to the right of the main group of keyboard keys on an enhanced keyboard. When the Num Lock feature is on, the keypad can be used to enter numbers. When the feature is off, the keys can be used to move the insertion point in a document.

  - The Escape key (Esc) is used to cancel a task.

- Use the Enter key to apply a current dialog box selection or to close the dialog box.

- Directional keys are used to move the insertion point around a document.

- Editing keys (Insert, Delete, and Backspace) are used to insert or delete text.

Start Word

- To use Word 2000 you must first start it so it is running on your computer.

- You use Windows to start Word.

- When Word is running, it is displayed in a **window** on your screen.

- If you have Microsoft Office 2000, you can use Office to start Word

The Word Window

- The **default** Word window displays **elements** for creating, editing, formatting, and distributing a document.

- The following figure identifies the default elements of the Word window. The numbers denoting each element correspond to the numbers next to the descriptions.

The default Word window

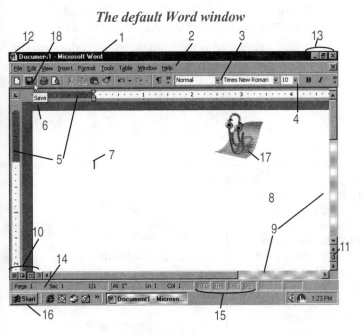

Title bar (1)
- Displays the program and document name.

Menu bar (2)
- Displays the names of the main menus. Select a menu name to drop down a list of commands or options.

Standard toolbar (3)
- Displays buttons for accessing common features and commands like saving, opening, and printing a file.

  ✓ *Available buttons change depending on the most recent selections. To see additional buttons, click More Buttons* ⏷.

Formatting toolbar (4)
- Displays buttons for accessing common formatting features and commands like centering text.

Rulers (5)
- Horizontal ruler measures width of the document page, and displays information such as left and right margins, tabs stops, and indents.
- Vertical ruler measures height of the document page and displays the top and bottom margins.

  ✓ *Vertical ruler is only displayed in Print Layout view and Print Preview.*

ScreenTip (6)
- Displays the name of the element on which the mouse pointer is resting.

Insertion point (7)
- A blinking vertical line displayed to the right of the space where characters are inserted in a document.

Document window (8)
- The area in which you type document text.

Scroll bars (9)
- Used with a mouse to shift the on-screen display up and down or left and right.

View buttons (10)
- Used to change to one of four available document views. These options are also available on the View menu.

Browse by object button (11)
- Used to shift the on-screen display according to a selected object, such as by page, by picture, or by heading.

Program Control icon (12)
- Used to display a menu with commands to control the Word window.

Document control buttons (13)
- Used to control the size and position of the document window.

Status bar (14)
- Displays document information, such as which page is displayed, where the insertion point is located, and which mode buttons are active.

Mode buttons (15)
- Used to change the way Word operates to make creating and editing documents easier.

  ✓ *Active mode buttons appear bold.*

Taskbar (16)
- A Windows feature used to start and switch among applications and documents.

Office Assistant (17)
- A tool for accessing Word's help program.

  ✓ *Using the Office Assistant is covered in Exercise 4.*

Mouse pointer (18)

- Marks the location of the mouse on-screen.

Exit Word

- When you are done using Word, you exit the Word application.

- If you try to exit Word without saving your documents, Word prompts you to do so.
- If you exit Word without closing your documents, Word closes them automatically.

Procedures

Conventions Used in This Book

Throughout this book, procedures for completing a task are documented as follows:

- **Keyboard shortcut** keys (if available) are included below the task heading.
- Mouse actions are numbered on the left
- Keystrokes are listed on the right.

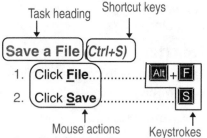

Change Font Size

1. Click **Font size** box on Formatting Toolbar.
2. Type new **font size**.
3. Press **Enter**.

Use the Mouse

Move the mouse pointer:

Right	Move mouse to right.
Left	Move mouse to left.
Up	Move mouse away from you.
Down	Move mouse toward you.

Mouse actions:

Point to	Move mouse pointer to touch specified element.
Click	Point to element then press and release left mouse button.

Right-click	Point to element then press and release right mouse button.
Double-click	Point to element then press and release left mouse button twice in rapid succession.
Drag	Point to element, hold down left mouse button, then move mouse pointer to new location.

✓ Element, or icon representing element, moves with mouse pointer.

Drop	Drag element to new location, then release mouse button.

IntelliMouse actions:

Scroll	Rotate center wheel backward to scroll down or forward to scroll up.
Pan	Press center wheel and drag up or down.
AutoScroll	Click center wheel to scroll down; move pointer up to scroll up.
Zoom	Hold down Ctrl and rotate center wheel.

Use the Keyboard

- Press specified key.

For key combinations:

1. Press and hold modifier key(s) ....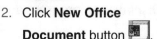
2. Press combination key.

✓ Remember, key combinations are written with a plus sign between each key. For example, Ctrl+Esc means press and hold Ctrl and then press Esc.

Start Word

1. Click **Start** button

   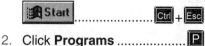

2. Click **Programs** .... P
3. Click **Microsoft Word** on Programs menu.

OR

1. Click **Start** button

2. Click **New Office Document** button.
3. Double-click **Blank Document** button.

OR

- Click **Microsoft Word** button on Office Shortcut bar.

Exit Word

- Click **Program Close** button X.

OR

- Double-click **Program Control** button X.

OR

1. Click **File** .... Alt+F
2. Click **Exit** X
3. Click **Yes** to save open documents .... Y

   OR

   Click **No** to close without saving .... N

6

Exercise Directions

1. Start your computer.
2. Move the mouse pointer around the Windows desktop.
   a. Point to the Start button.
      ✓ *A ScreenTip is displayed.*
   b. Point to the Recycle Bin icon.
3. Click the My Computer icon.
   ✓ *The icon is selected.*
4. Right-click the Recycle Bin icon.
   ✓ *A menu is displayed.*
5. Press Esc to cancel the menu.
6. Start Microsoft Word 2000.
   a. Click the Start button.
   b. Click Programs on the Start menu.
   c. Click Microsoft Word on the Programs menu.

7. Point to each button on the Standard and Formatting toolbars to see the ScreenTips.
8. Move the mouse pointer over the document window.
   ✓ *It changes from an arrow to an I-beam.*
9. Press Alt + F.
   ✓ *The File menu opens as shown in Illustration A. You learn about using menus in Exercise 2.*
10. Press Esc.
    ✓ *The File menu closes.*
11. Exit Word.
    • Click the Program Close button.
      ✓ *Do not save any changes to the document.*

Illustration A

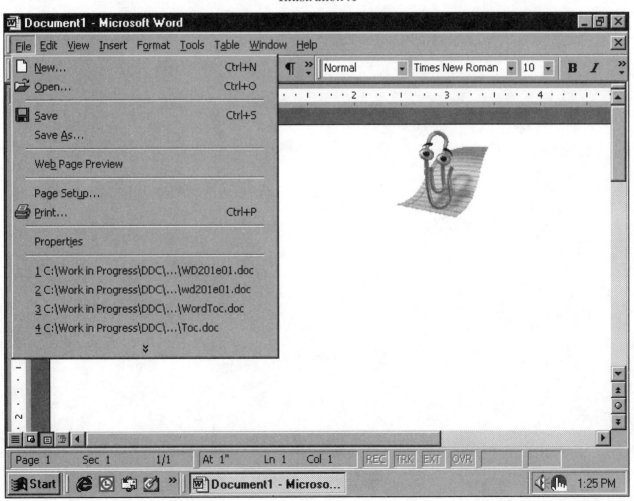

On Your Own

1. Practice starting and exiting Word using the mouse.

2. Practice moving the mouse around the Word window to identify different elements.

3. Point to the View buttons.

4. Point to the Close button.

5. Point to the Mode buttons.

6. Practice starting and exiting Word using the keyboard.

Exercise 2

On the Job

To accomplish a task in Word, you must execute a command. You select the commands using menus, toolbars, and dialog boxes. Once you learn to use these tools, you will be able to access the features you need to create documents with Word.

To get up to speed using Word 2000, you want to spend more time exploring the menus, toolbars, and dialog boxes. In this exercise, you will practice using toolbars, selecting menu commands, and choosing options in dialog boxes.

Terms

Command Input that tells the computer which task to execute.

Menu A list of commands.

Toolbar A row of buttons used to execute commands. Each button displays an icon (picture) representing its command.

Dialog box A window in which you select options that effect the way Word executes a command.

Icon A picture used to identify an element on screen, such as a toolbar button.

Toggle A command that can be switched off or on.

Ellipsis A symbol comprised of three periods that indicate more will follow (…).

Submenu A menu that is displayed when you select a command on another menu.

Hotkey The underlined letter in a command name.

ScreenTip A balloon containing information that is displayed when you rest your mouse pointer on certain screen elements.

Context menu A menu displayed at the location where the selected command will occur.

Notes

Commands

■ To accomplish a task in Word, you execute **commands**. For example, Save is the command for saving a document.

■ Commands are accessible in three ways:
  - **Menus**
  - **Toolbars**
  - **Dialog boxes**

■ You use the mouse and/or the keyboard to select and execute commands.

Menus

■ Word groups commands into nine menus, which are listed on the menu bar.

Menu bar

| File Edit View Insert Format Tools Table Window Help | ☒ |

- When you select—or open—a menu, a list of commands you use most often drops down into the window.

- You can expand the menu to see all commands in that group.

- Commands that are not available appear dimmed on the expanded menu.

- Command names are listed on the left side of a drop-down menu.

- If a toolbar button is available for a menu command, the button **icon** is displayed to the left of the command name.

- Some commands are **toggles** that can be either active or inactive. A check mark or bullet to the left of a toggle command means the command is already active.

- Shortcut keys and other symbols are listed on the right side of the menu
  - an **ellipsis** (…) indicates that the command opens a dialog box.
  - an arrowhead indicates that the command opens a **submenu**.

- Each menu and command has an underlined letter called a **hotkey**. Hotkeys are used to select commands with the keyboard.

Tools menu

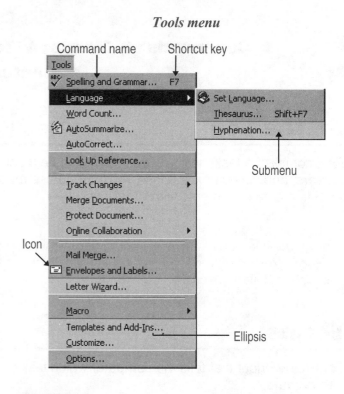

Toolbars

- Word comes with more than 16 toolbars, which provide quick access to common commands.

- By default, only the Standard and the Formatting toolbars are displayed.

- You can display or hide toolbars as needed.

- When you point to a toolbar button with the mouse, a **ScreenTip** displays the name of the button.

- Some buttons are toggles; they appear pressed in when active, or "on."

- Buttons representing commands that are not currently available are dimmed.

- Using the toolbar handle, you can drag a toolbar to any side of the Word window, or float it over the document window area.

- A *More buttons* button on the toolbar means that not all available buttons are currently displayed.

Toolbars

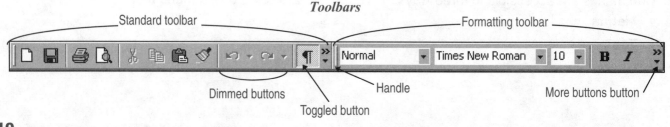

10

Dialog Box Options

■ Word displays a dialog box when you must provide additional information before executing a command. For example, in the Print dialog box, you can specify which pages to print.

■ You enter information in a dialog box using a variety of elements. Use the numbers to locate the corresponding element in the figures below.

Font dialog box

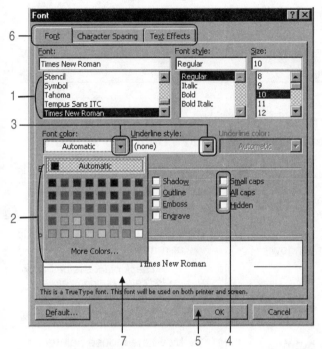

Print dialog box

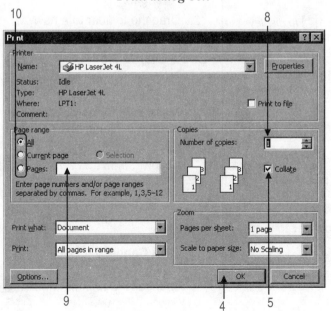

List box (1)

- A list of items from which selections can be made. If more items are available than can fit in the space, a scroll bar is displayed.

Palette (2)

- A display, such as colors or shapes, from which you can select an option.

    ✓ *Some commands (such as Backgrounds on the Format menu) and some toolbar buttons (such as Font Color on the Formatting toolbar) open palettes.*

Drop-down list box (3)

- A combination of text box and list box; type your selection in the box or click the drop-down arrow to display the list.

Check box (4)

- A square that you click to select or deselect an option. A check mark in the box indicates that the option is selected.

Command button (5)

- A button used to execute a command. An ellipsis on a command button means that clicking the button opens another dialog box.

Tabs (6)

- Markers across the top of the dialog box that display additional pages of options within the dialog box.

Preview area (7)

- An area where you can preview the results of your selections before executing the commands.

Increment box (8)

- A space where you type a value, such as inches. Increment arrows beside the box are used to increase or decrease the value with a mouse.

Text box (9)

- A space where you type variable information, such as a file name.

Option buttons (10)

- A series of circles; only one of which can be selected at a time. Click the circle you want to select one item or one control in the series.

Context Menus

■ **Context menus** are useful for quickly accessing commands pertaining to the current task using a mouse.

■ Context menus are sometimes referred to as shortcut menus.

■ Commands on context menus vary depending on the action being performed.

Context menu

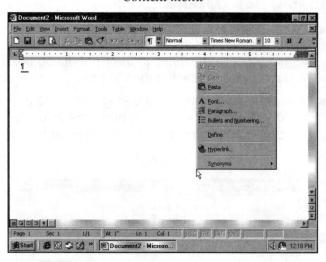

Procedures

Open a Menu with the Mouse

• Click the **menu name**.

Open a Menu with the Keyboard

1. Press and hold .... Alt

2. Press **hotkey** in menu name.
   OR
   a. Press **left and right arrow** keys to select menu name ....
   b. Press **Enter**.

Expand a Menu

• Click **expand arrows** at menu bottom .

OR

Click menu name and wait a few seconds.

Select a Menu Command

1. Click **menu name** .. Alt +hotkey

2. Click the desired **command** .... hotkey
   OR
   a. Press **up and down arrows** to highlight command ....
   b. Press **Enter** .... Enter

   ✓ *If a submenu is displayed, select the command from the submenu.*

Close a Menu without Making a Selection

• Click the menu name again.

   ✓ *If the menu expands instead of closing, click it again.*

OR
Click in the document window.
OR
Press Esc.

Select a Command from a Toolbar

1. Point to a **toolbar button**.

2. **Click**.

   ✓ *If the button you want is not displayed, click the More*

   Buttons button ▼ *to display additional buttons, and then click the button.*

Display/Hide Toolbars

1. Click **View** .... Alt + V

2. Click **Toolbars** .... T
   OR
   Right-click any **toolbar**.

   ✓ *A checkmark beside toolbar name indicates toolbar is already displayed.*

3. Click **desired toolbar** to display or hide.

Add a Button to a Toolbar

1. Click **More Buttons** button ▼

2. Click **Add or Remove Buttons** .... A

3. Click **button** you want to add or remove.

   ✓ *A check mark beside button indicates button is already available.*

Move a Toolbar

1. Move the mouse pointer so it touches toolbar handle.

   ✓ *The mouse pointer changes from an arrow to a cross with 4 arrows*

2. Drag the toolbar to a new location.

Use a Dialog Box

1. Select a **command** followed by an ellipsis (...).

2. Make **selections or type text entries** in dialog box.

3. Click **OK** command button .... Enter

   ✓ *Sometimes command button displays Close or Yes in place of OK.*

   OR

   Click **Cancel** to close dialog box without making changes ....

Dialog Box Options

Move from one option to the next:

- Click desired **option**.

OR

- Press **Tab** key .... `Tab`

OR

- Press .... `Alt`+hotkey

Select from a list box:

- Click desired **item** ... `↑↓`, `Enter`

Select from a drop-down list box:

1. Click **drop-down arrow** .... `Alt`+hotkey
2. Click desired **item** ... `↑↓`, `Enter`

Select/deselect check box:

- Click **check box** ..... `Alt`+hotkey

✓ *A check mark indicates box is selected. Repeat action to remove check mark and deselect box.*

Display tabbed pages:

- Click desired **tab** .... `Alt`+hotkey

✓ *If no hotkey is displayed, press Ctrl+Tab.*

Use a text box:

1. Click in **text box** ..... `Alt`+hotkey
2. Type **data**.

Use an increment box:

1. Click in **increment box** .... `Alt`+hotkey
2. Type **value**.

OR

Click **increment arrows** to change value.

Select option button:

- Click **option button** .... `Alt`+hotkey

✓ *A black dot indicates option is selected. Select alternative option button to change setting.*

Select palette option:

1. Click **palette** drop-down arrow.... `Alt`+hotkey

✓ *Some palettes are always open. If the palette is open, skip to step 2.*

2. Click desired **option** .... `↔`, `Enter`

Context Menus

1. Right-click **element** on screen.
2. Click **command** .... hotkey

✓ *If no hotkeys are available, use arrow keys to select command, then press Enter.*

Exercise Directions

1. Start Word.
2. Open the File menu using the mouse.
   - Click the word File on the menu bar.
3. Let the menu expand to show all commands.
4. Note the commands on the File menu.
5. Close the menu.
   - Click the word File on the menu bar, or press Esc.
6. Open the View menu using the mouse.
   - Click the word View on the menu bar.
7. Select the Toolbars commands.
   - Click the word Toolbars, or press the `T` key.
8. Look at the submenu of available toolbars.
   ✓ *Notice the check marks next to the toolbars that are currently displayed.*
9. Close the menu.
   - Click the word View on the menu bar, or press Esc twice.
10. Open the Format menu with the keyboard.
    - Press and hold `Alt`, and then press the `O` key.
11. Select the Font command.
    - Press the `F` key, or click the command name.
12. Select Bold in the Font style list box.

13. Select the Superscript check box.
14. Select the Text Effects tab to show another page of options.
15. Select the Font tab.
16. Open the Font Color palette.
    - Click the drop-down arrow, or press `Alt`+`C`.
17. Select the color red.
18. Open the Underline style drop-down list.
    - Click the drop-down arrow, or press `Alt`+`U`.
19. Cancel the dialog box without making any of the selected changes.
    - Click the Cancel command button, or press Esc twice.
20. Click the Bold button on the Formatting toolbar.
    - If the Bold button is not displayed, click the More buttons button to expand the toolbar, and then click the Bold button.
    ✓ *Bold is a toggle; it remains on (pressed in) until you turn it off.*
21. Click the Bold button again.
22. Right-click anywhere in the document window.
23. Select the Paragraph command.
    - Click the command.

24. Note that the Paragraph dialog box includes increment boxes, drop-down lists, and a preview area, as shown in Illustration A.

25. Cancel the dialog box without making any changes.
    - Click the Cancel command button or press Esc.

26. Exit Word.
    ✓ *If Word prompts you to save changes, select No.*

Illustration A

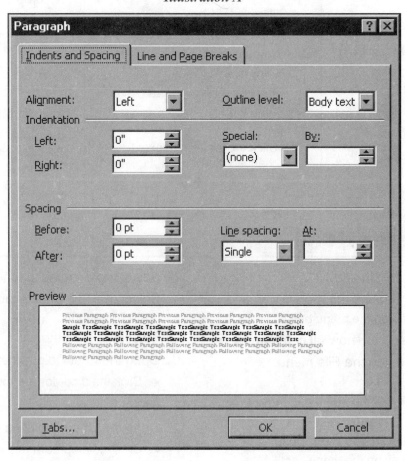

On Your Own

1. Start Word and explore the nine menus.
2. Look to see which commands are on each menu.
3. Notice which ones open dialog boxes, which open submenus, and which have corresponding toolbar buttons.
4. Select a command that opens a dialog box. For example, try opening the Options dialog box from the Tools menu.
5. If the dialog box has multiple pages, check out each page. Note the different options available on each page.
6. Use the More buttons button on the Standard and/or Formatting toolbars to see what other buttons are available.
7. Try moving the toolbars to other locations on the screen.
8. Move them back.
9. Exit Word without saving any changes.

Exercise 3

Skills Covered:

◆ **Window Controls** ◆ **Zoom** ◆ **Scroll**

On the Job

Controlling the way Word is displayed on your computer is a vital part of using the program successfully. For example, you can control the size and position of the program window on-screen, and you can control the size Word uses to display the document.

As you spend more time working with Word 2000, you'll find that there are many tools that help you do your job more efficiently. In this exercise, you will learn how to maximize, minimize, and restore the Word window on your screen, and you will experiment with the zoom level. You'll also practice scrolling through a document.

Terms

Default A standard setting or mode of operation.

Maximize Enlarge a window so it fills the entire screen.

Minimize Hide a window so it only appears as a button on the Windows taskbar.

Restore Return a window to its previous size and position on the screen.

Zoom in Increase the size of the document as it is displayed on-screen. This does not affect the actual size of the printed document.

Zoom out Decrease the size of the document as it is displayed on-screen. This does not affect the actual size of the printed document.

Scroll Shift the displayed area of the document up, down, left, or right.

Notes

Window Controls

■ Word starts using standard, or **default**, settings.

  ✓ *Some default settings control features of a new document, such as the margins, the line spacing, the character font, and the font size. You learn about these features in upcoming exercises.*

■ By default, the Word program window opens with a new blank document displayed in Print Layout view.

  ✓ *You learn more about views in Exercise 8.*

■ You can control the size and position of the Word window.

  • You can **maximize** the window to fill the screen.

  • You can **minimize** the window to a taskbar button.

  • You can **restore** the window to its previous size and/or position.

■ There are three ways to control the Word window:

  • With the Control buttons located on the right end of the title bar.

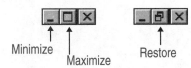

- With the Program Control icon drop-down menu.

Program Control icon

- With the taskbar button context menu.

Context menu

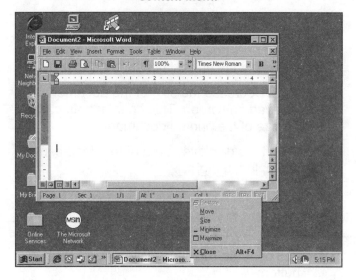

Zoom

- You can adjust the zoom magnification setting to increase or decrease the size Word uses to display a document on screen.

- Set the zoom using the Zoom drop-down list box on the Standard toolbar, or the Zoom dialog box.

Zoom dialog box

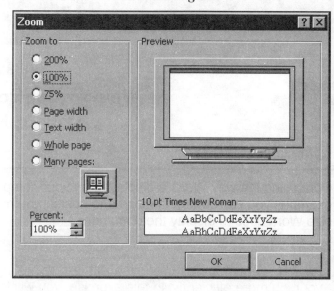

- **Zooming in** makes the document appear larger on screen. This is useful for getting a close look at text.

  ✓ *When you zoom in, only a small portion of the document will be visible on-screen at a time.*

Zoom in to display the document in a large size

Zoom drop-down list box

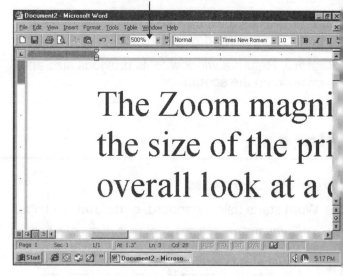

■ **Zooming out** makes the document appear smaller on screen. This is useful for getting an overall look at the document page.

Zoom out to display the entire page

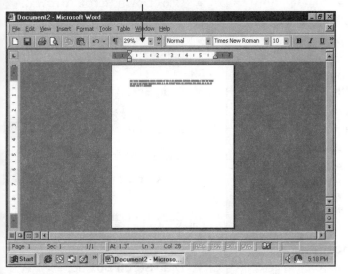

Zoom drop-down list box

■ You can set the zoom magnification as a percentage of the document's actual size. For example, if you set the zoom to 50%, Word displays the document half as large as the actual, printed document would appear. If you set the zoom to 200%, Word displays the document twice as large as the actual printed document would appear.

■ Alternatively, you can select from four preset sizes:

- Page width. Word automatically sizes the document so that the width of the page matches the width of the screen. You see the left and right margins of the page.

- Text width. Word automatically sizes the document so that the width of the text on the page matches the width of the screen. The left and right margins may be hidden.

- Whole page. Word automatically sizes the document so that one page is visible on the screen.

- Many pages. Word automatically sizes the document so that the number of pages you select can all be seen on the screen.

  ✓ Some options may not be available, depending on the current view. Options that are not available will appear dimmed

Scroll

■ When there is more text in a document than can be displayed on-screen at one time, you must **scroll** to see the hidden parts.

■ Scrolling is like flipping the pages of a book. You can scroll up, down, left, or right.

■ You can scroll using the directional keys on the keyboard, or using the scroll bars in the Word window.

Scroll in a document

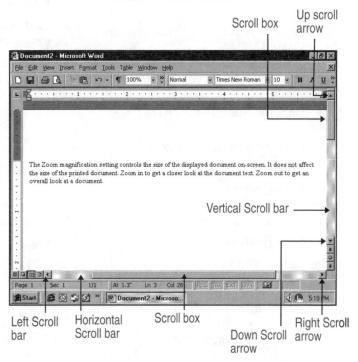

Scroll box   Up scroll arrow

Vertical Scroll bar

Left Scroll bar   Horizontal Scroll bar   Scroll box   Down Scroll arrow   Right Scroll arrow

✓ The size of the scroll boxes change to represent the percentage of the document visible on the screen. For example, in a very long document, the scroll boxes will be small, indicating that a small percentage of the document is visible. In a short document, the scroll boxes will be large, indicating that a large percentage of the document is visible.

Procedures

Control Windows

Minimize a Window:

- Click the **Minimize** button .

OR

1. Click the **Program Control** icon ![icon].
2. Click **Minimize**.

OR

1. Right-click the Word document taskbar button.
2. Click **Minimize**.

Restore a Window:

- Click the **Restore** button ![icon].

OR

1. Click the **Program Control** icon ![icon].
2. Click **Restore**.

OR

1. Right-click the taskbar button.
2. Click **Restore**.

Maximize a Window:

- Click the **Maximize** button ![icon].

OR

1. Click the **Program Control** icon ![icon].
2. Click **Maximize**.

OR

1. Right-click the taskbar button.
2. Click **Maximize**.

Adjust Zoom

Use zoom drop-down list:

1. Click **Zoom** button drop-down arrow ![icon] on Standard toolbar.
2. Click desired **percentage**.

OR

Click preset option:
- **Page Width**
- **Text Width**
- **Whole Page**
- **(Number of) Pages**
    - ✓ *The number of pages varies depending on how many pages are in the document.*

OR

a. Click in **Zoom** button ![88%] drop-down list box on Standard toolbar.
b. Type desired percentage.
c. Press **Enter** .... ![Enter]

Use Zoom dialog box:

1. Click **View** .... ![Alt]+![V]
2. Click **Zoom** .... ![Z]
3. Click desired **zoom option**:
    - **Page Width** .... ![Alt]+![P]
    - **Text Width** .... ![Alt]+![T]
    - **Whole Page** .... ![Alt]+![W]
    - **Many Pages** .... ![Alt]+![M]
        - ✓ *If you select Many Pages, click the computer icon to select the number of pages to display.*

OR

a. Click **Percent** increment box .... ![Alt]+![E]
b. Type **percentage**.

4. Click **OK** .... ![Enter]

Scroll

Scroll down:

- Click **Down Scroll Arrow** .... ![icon]

OR

- Click in **Vertical Scroll Bar** below Scroll box.

OR

- Drag **Scroll Box** down.

OR

- Press **Page Down** .... ![Page Down]

Scroll up:

- Click **Up Scroll Arrow** .... ![icon]

OR

- Click in **Vertical Scroll Bar** above Scroll Box.

OR

- Drag **Scroll Box** up.

OR

- Press **Page Up** .... ![Page Up]

Scroll left:

- Click **Left Scroll Arrow** .... ![icon]

OR

- Click in **Horizontal Scroll Bar** to left of Scroll Box.

OR

- Drag **Scroll Box** left.

Scroll right:

- Click **Right Scroll Arrow** .... ![icon]

OR

- Click in **Horizontal Scroll Bar** to right of Scroll Box.

OR

- Drag **Scroll Box** right.

Exercise Directions

1. Start Word
2. Minimize the Word window.
3. Maximize the Word window.
4. Restore the Word window.
5. Click in the document window and type your name.
   - ✓ *Do not worry about making errors while you type. This is just a practice exercise and you will not save the document. You learn more about typing and correcting errors in Exercise 6.*
6. Press Enter.
7. Type the first line of your address.
8. Press Enter.
9. Type the next line of your address.

10. Press Enter.
11. If necessary, type the next line of your address.
12. Set the Zoom to 25%.
13. Set the Zoom to 500%. It should look similar to the document shown in Illustration A.
14. Scroll down to the bottom of the document.
15. Scroll up to the top of the document.
16. Scroll to the right margin.
17. Scroll to the left margin.
18. Set the Zoom to Page Width.
19. Exit Word.
   - ✓ *When Word prompts you to save the changes, select No.*

Illustration A

On Your Own

1. Start Word.

2. Practice maximizing, minimizing, and restoring the Word window, using all three available methods.

3. Type some text in the Word document window.

4. Try different zoom magnifications to see how the display is affected.

5. When you are finished, leave the Word window maximized and the zoom set to page width.

6. Exit Word without saving the document.

Exercise 4

Skills Covered:

◆ **Office Assistant** ◆ **Help Program** ◆ **What's This?**
◆ **Microsoft Office on the Web**

On the Job

You can get help regarding any of Word's features while you work using a variety of methods. Type questions in the Office Assistant to quickly start Word's Help program and display specific information. Alternatively, use the Index or Contents in the Help program to locate the information you need. Microsoft also makes information about its programs and tips on using them available on the World Wide Web.

As a new employee at State-of-the-Arts Solutions, it's important to learn how to solve problems on your own. In this exercise, you will learn how to use the Help system to answer the questions you may have while working in Word 2000.

Terms

Office Assistant A feature of Microsoft Office Help program, designed to make it easy to locate helpful information when you need it.

Hyperlinks or links Text or graphics in a document set up to provide a direct connection with a destination location or document. When you click a hyperlink, the destination is displayed.

Internet A worldwide network of computers.

World Wide Web A system for finding information on the Internet through the use of linked documents.

Notes

Office Assistant

- If the **Office Assistant** is installed, it is displayed by default when you start Word and remains displayed until you hide it.

  ✓ *If Office Assistant is not installed, you can install it using Word's Setup program.*

- By default, the Office Assistant is represented by an animated paper clip, called Clipit. You can select a different animated figure.

- You can change the Office Assistant options to control when and how it is displayed.

- To locate information with the Office Assistant, you type a question, then select from a list of available topics.

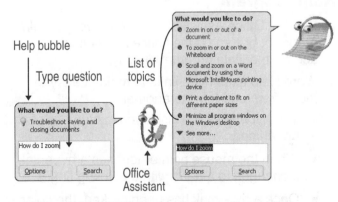

- The topics are linked to information in the Microsoft Word Help program.

- Help information is displayed in a Help program window and provides **hyperlinks** to other related topics.

  ✓ *See the next section for more information about using the Help program.*

- The Office Assistant is also set to display tips or suggestions about current features while you work. For example, if you start typing a letter, the Office Assistant will ask if you need help.

- If a light bulb appears above the Office Assistant, it means a tip is available. Click the light bulb to display the tip.

Help Program

- Use the Office Assistant to access Word's Help program, or turn off the Office Assistant to access the Help program directly.

- Word Help uses hyperlinks to make it easy to move from one topic to another.

  - The hyperlinks are displayed in blue and underlined.

  - When the mouse pointer touches a hyperlink, it changes to a hand with a pointing finger.

  - Once a hyperlink has been clicked, the color changes to violet.

    ✓ *You learn more about hyperlinks in Exercise 34.*

Word Help Window

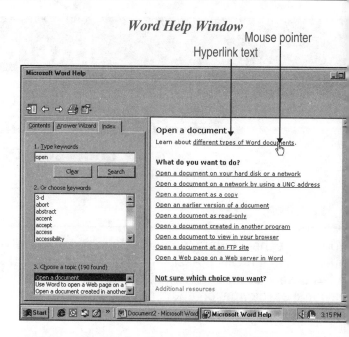

- Hyperlinks provide access to related topics, but if you want to look up a completely different topic without going back to the Office Assistant, you can use the Help window features.

- The Help window contains three tabs: Contents, Answer Wizard, and Index.

- The Contents tab is like a table of contents in a book.

  - Each topic in the table of contents appears with a small book icon.

  - Open the book to display its subtopics.

  - Close the book to hide its subtopics.

Word Contents page

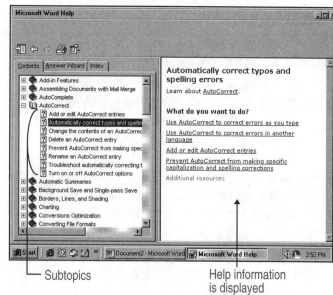

■ The Answer Wizard tab is similar to the Office Assistant.

- Type a question into the Wizard, and it displays a list of topics

Answer Wizard page

Select a topic
Type question
Help information is displayed

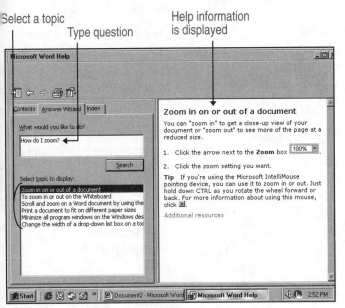

■ The Index tab allows you to locate a topic based on a keyword.

Word Index page

Type keyword
Help information is displayed

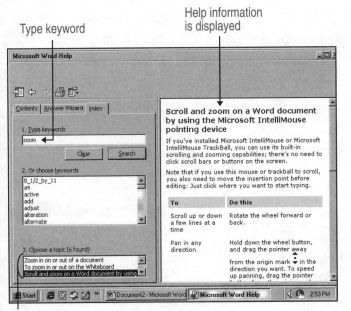

Select a topic

What's This?

■ Use the What's This? pointer to display help information in a ScreenTip.

What's This feature

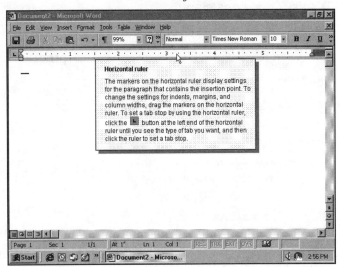

■ When you click a screen element or command with the What's This? pointer, a ScreenTip is displayed.

■ What's This? can be accessed from the Help menu or from within most dialog boxes.

Microsoft Office on the Web

■ If you have access to the **Internet**, you can connect to Microsoft on the **World Wide Web** and get up-to-date information and support for all the applications in Office, including Word 2000.

✓ *Internet Basics are covered in Exercise 13.*

Procedures

Office Assistant *(F1)*

Display Office Assistant:

- Click **Microsoft Word Help** button `[?]` on Standard toolbar.

OR

1. Click **Help** .... `Alt`+`H`
2. Click **Show the Office Assistant** .... `O`

   ✓ *If Office Assistant is covering information you want to see on-screen, drag it out of the way.*

Hide Office Assistant:

1. Right-click Office Assistant
2. Click **Hide** .... `H`

OR

1. Click **Help** .... `Alt`+`H`
2. Click **Hide the Office Assistant** .... `O`

Open Office Assistant Help bubble:

- Click **Microsoft Word Help** button `[?]` on Standard toolbar.

OR

- Click Office Assistant.

   ✓ *Repeat step to hide the bubble.*

Use Office Assistant:

1. Display **Office Assistant** and Help bubble `[?]` .... `F1`
2. Type question in text box.

   ✓ *Replace existing text if necessary.*

3. Click **Search** .... `Enter`
4. Click **See more** to see next page of topics .... `Tab`, `↑↓`, `Enter`
5. Click **See previous** to see previous page of topics .... `↑↓`, `Enter`
6. Click desired topic ... `↑↓`, `Enter`

   ✓ *Click See more to see next page of topics; Click See previous to see previous page of topics.*

7. Read information in **Help program window**.
8. Click **hyperlink** to display related topic.

OR

   Click Help window's

   Close button `X` .... `Alt`+`F4`

Change Office Assistant animation:

1. Display **Office Assistant** with Help bubble `[?]` .... `F1`
2. Click **Options** .... `Alt`+`O`
3. Click **Gallery** tab......... `Alt`+`G`
4. Click **Next** .... `Alt`+`N`
5. Repeat step 4 until desired animation is displayed.
6. Click **OK** .... `Tab`, `Enter`

   ✓ *If selected animation has not been installed, install it, or select a different animation.*

Change Office Assistant options:

1. Display **Office Assistant** with Help bubble `[?]` .... `F1`
2. Click **Options** .... `Alt`+`O`
3. Click **Options** tab .... `Alt`+`O`
4. Select or deselect options as desired.

   ✓ *If you want to turn the Office Assistant off so that you can access Help directly when you click the Help button or press F1, then turn off the Use the Office Assistant option.*

5. Click **OK** .... `Enter`

Turn Office Assistant off:

1. Display **Office Assistant** with Help bubble `[?]` .... `F1`
2. Click **Options** .... `Alt`+`O`
3. Click **Options** tab .... `Alt`+`O`

---

4. Deselect **Use the Office Assistant** check box ... `Alt`+`U`
5. Click **OK** .... `Enter`

   ✓ *Turning off Office Assistant makes Word Help program available directly from Help menu, by pressing F1, or by clicking Microsoft Word Help button.*

Use Microsoft Word Help *(F1)*

Start Help program and display Help window:

1. Use **Office Assistant** to locate a Help topic
2. Click **Show** button `Show` to expand Help window.

OR

1. Turn **Office Assistant** off.
2. Click **Microsoft Word Help** button `[?]` on Standard toolbar.

OR

   a. Click **Help** .... `Alt`+`H`
   b. Click **Microsoft Word Help** .... `H`

   ✓ *If Office Assistant was used to start Help program, it will be necessary to expand Help window as described. If Office Assistant is turned off, Help window is displayed by default.*

Use Contents:

1. Start **Help program** with Help window displayed.
2. Click **Contents** tab. ..... `Alt`+`C`
3. Double-click **book** to display subtopics .... `↑↓`, `Enter`

OR

   Click plus sign beside topic.

4. Click desired **subtopic** .... `↑↓`, `Enter`
5. Click **hyperlink** to see related topic.
6. Click Help window's

   Close button `X` .... `Alt`+`F4`

Use Answer Wizard:

1. Start **Help program** with Help window displayed.
2. Click **Answer Wizard** tab. .... `Alt`+`A`
3. Type a question or a **keyword** .... `Alt`+`W`, *text*
4. Click **Search** .... `Alt`+`S`
5. Click desired topic .... `Alt`+`T`, `↑↓`, `Enter`
6. Click **hyperlink** to see related topic.
7. Click Help window's Close button `X` .... `Alt`+`F4`

Use Index:

1. Start **Help program** with Help window displayed.
2. Click **Index** tab. .... `Alt`+`I`
3. Type **keyword** in Step 1 box.... `Alt`+`T`, *keyword*

OR

Click **keyword** in Step 2 box .... `Alt`+`K`, `↑↓`

   ✓ *To select new keywords, first clear the Step 1 box.*

4. Click **Search** .... `Alt`+`S`
5. Click desired topic in Step 3 box .... `Alt`+`H`, `↑↓`
6. Click **hyperlink** to see related topic.
7. Click Help window's Close button `X` .... `Alt`+`F4`

Use What's This? *(Shift+F1)*

1. Click **Help** .... `Alt`+`H`
2. Click **What's This?** .... `T`
3. Click any **screen element** or command.
4. Click **outside ScreenTip** to cancel What's This? .... `Esc`

Microsoft Office on the Web

1. Click **Help** .... `Alt`+`H`
2. Click **Office on the Web** ..... `W`
3. Follow steps to **connect** to Internet.
4. Click **hyperlinks** to display related topics
5. Follow steps to **disconnect** from Internet.

   ✓ *To connect to the Internet you must have a computer with a modem and an account with an Internet Service Provider. For more information, see Exercise 13.*

Exercise Directions

1. Start Word
2. Display the Office Assistant (if it is not already displayed).
3. Search for help topics about changing the Zoom magnification.
   a. Type Zoom in the Office Assistant Help bubble.
   b. Click Search.
4. Read the available topics.
5. Select the topic: *Zoom in on or out of a document*.
6. Read the Help topic.
7. Expand the Help window to show the dialog box tabs.
   • Click the Show button.
8. Display the Contents page.
9. Open the topic: *Creating, Opening, and Saving Document*.
10. Display the Index page.
11. Search for topics about ScreenTips.
    a. Type ScreenTip in the step 1 text box.
    b. Click Search.
12. Select the topic: *Display tips and messages through the Office Assistant*. The Help program should look similar to Illustration A.
13. Read the Help page.
14. Click the hyperlink for *Hide, show, or turn off the Office Assistant*.
15. Read the Help page.
16. Close the Help program.
    • Click the Close button in the upper right corner or press `Alt`+`F4`.
17. Turn on the What's This? pointer.
18. Click the Office Assistant.
19. Read the ScreenTip.
20. Turn off the What's This? pointer.
    • Click anywhere outside the ScreenTip or press Esc.
21. Hide the Office Assistant.
22. Exit Word.

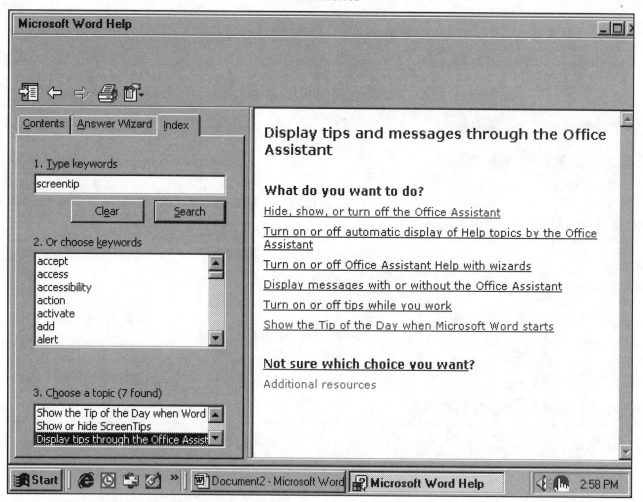

On Your Own

1. Start Word and display the Office Assistant.

2. Open the Office Assistant dialog box to see what other animations are available for use as the Office Assistant.

3. If you find one you like, select it.

4. Open the Office Assistant dialog box again to see the options available for controlling the Office Assistant.

5. Close the dialog box without making any changes.

6. Use the Office Assistant to search for help topics related to Menus.

7. Open any topic that sounds interesting.

8. Explore the topics on the Help Contents page.

9. Open any topic that sounds interesting.

10. Continue to explore the help topics as long as you want. When you are done, close the Help program and exit Word. Do not save the document.

Exercise 5

Critical Thinking

The marketing director has asked you to write a letter to a client. In this exercise, you will start writing the letter, and you will explore additional Help topics.

Exercise Directions

1. Start Word.
2. Exit Word using the keyboard.
3. Start Word again.
4. Open the Office Assistant if it is not already displayed.
5. Right-click the Office Assistant to display a context menu.
6. Click Choose Assistant from the context menu to open the Office Assistant dialog box.
7. Click the Options tab.
8. Deselect the Use Office Assistant checkbox.
9. Click OK.
   - ✓ *This turns off the Office Assistant.*
10. Select the Show Office Assistant command from the Help menu.
    - ✓ *This turns the Office Assistant back on.*
11. Minimize the Word window.
    - ✓ *Notice that the Office Assistant remains open on the Windows desktop.*
12. Maximize the Word window.
13. Set the zoom to 200%.
14. Type *Dear Mrs. Jones,*
15. Press Enter.
    - ✓ *The Office Assistant should offer help on typing a letter. If it doesn't, make sure you typed the comma after Jones.*

16. Click Cancel to close the Office Assistant Help bubble.
17. Display the Help bubble.
18. Type the question: *How do I use toolbars?* then click the Search button.
19. Look over the available topics, then select the topic *Move a toolbar*.
20. Hide the Office Assistant.
21. Read the topic.
22. Expand the Help window to show the dialog box.
23. On the Contents page, scroll down and open the topic: *Scrolling*.
24. Select the subtopic: *Scroll through a document*. The Help window should look similar to the one in Illustration A.
25. Click any hyperlink.
26. Close the Help program.
27. Set the zoom to Page width.
28. Exit Word. Do not save any changes when prompted.

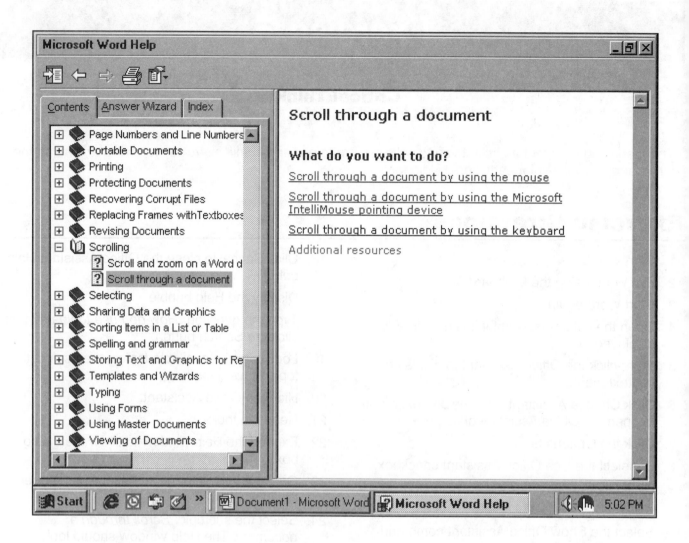

Lesson 2

Create, Save, and Print Documents

Exercise 6

Skills Covered:

◆ **Create a New Document** ◆ **Type in a Document** ◆ **Use Click and Type**
◆ **Correct Errors** ◆ **Save a New Document** ◆ **Close a Document**

On the Job

You use Word to create text-based documents such as letters, memos, reports, flyers, and newsletters. Now that you know how to get started with Word, the next step is learning how to create, save, and close documents.

The marketing director has asked you to create a mission statement explaining the goals for State-of-the-Art Solutions, a medium-sized consulting firm that advises clients interested in developing businesses on the World Wide Web. In this exercise, you will start Word and create and save a document.

Terms

Word wrap A feature that causes text to move automatically from the end of one line to the beginning of the next line.

Paragraph mark (¶) A nonprinting character inserted in a document to indicate where a paragraph ends.

Horizontal alignment The position of text on a line in relation to the left and right margins.

Save Store a file on a disk.

File type The format in which a file is saved. Some common file types include graphics files, text files, and word processing files.

Folder Location on a disk where Word and other Windows applications store files.

Notes

Create a New Document

- Word starts with a new blank document open.
- By default the new document is named Document1 until you save it and give it a new name.
- You can create additional new documents without closing and restarting Word.
  - ✓ *Each new document is named using consecutive numbers, so the second document is Document2, the third is Document3, and so on until you exit Word.*

Type in a Document

- By default, the insertion point is positioned at the beginning (left end) of the first line of a new document.
- You simply begin typing to insert new text.
- Characters you type are inserted to the left of the insertion point.
- **Word wrap** automatically wraps text at the end of a line to the beginning of the next line.
- When you press Enter, Word inserts a **paragraph mark** and starts a new paragraph.
- After you type enough text to fill a page, Word automatically starts a new page.

Use Click and Type

■ You can use the Click and Type feature to position the insertion point anywhere in a blank document to begin typing.

  ✓ *Click and Type is only active in Print Layout view and Web Layout view. Changing the view is covered in Exercise 8.*

■ With Click and Type, the mouse pointer changes to indicate the **horizontal alignment** of the new text.

  ✓ *You learn more about horizontal alignment in Exercise 24.*

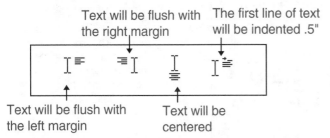

Text will be flush with the right margin

The first line of text will be indented .5"

Text will be flush with the left margin

Text will be centered

Correct Errors

■ You can erase characters to the left of the insertion point.

  ✓ *Deleting text is covered in more detail in Exercise 18.*

■ You can cancel commands before you execute them by pressing the Escape key or clicking a Cancel button.

■ You can use the Undo command to reverse actions.

  ✓ *The Undo command is covered in Exercise 18.*

■ Use the Help program to access information about how to accomplish a task or use a feature.

Save a New Document

■ If you want to have a file available for future use, you must **save** it on a removable disk or on an internal fixed disk.

■ When you save a new document, you must give it a name and select the location where you want it stored.

■ Word automatically adds a period and a three-character file extension to the end of the file name to identify the **file type**. By default, the file extension is .doc, which identifies a Word document file.

■ To specify a disk for storing the document, you select the disk drive letter. Floppy disk drives are usually drives A: and B:. A hard drive is usually drive C:.

■ You can store documents in a **folder** on your hard drive called My Documents, or you can select a different folder. You can also create new folders.

Close a Document

■ A document remains open on-screen until you close it.

■ Close a document when you are finished working with it.

■ If you try to close a document without saving it, Word prompts you to save it.

■ You can close a document without saving it if you do not want to keep it for future use or if you are not happy with changes you have made.

■ If only one document is open, the Close Window button used to close the active document is located on the menu bar and the Close Program button used to exit Word is on the title bar

■ If multiple documents are open, the Close button used to close the active document is located on the title bar.

Only one document is open

Close button

Close Window button

More than one document is open

Close button

Procedures

Create a New Document
(Ctrl+N)

- Click **New** button ☐ .

OR

1. Click **File** .... `Alt`+`F`
2. Click **New** .... `N`
3. Click **Blank**

   Document 🖼 Blank Document .... `Tab`
4. Click **OK** .... `Enter`

Click and Type

1. Move mouse pointer where you want to position insertion point.
2. Double-click.
3. Type new text.

Activate Click and Type

1. Click **Tools** .... `Alt`+`T`
2. Click **Options** .... `O`
3. Click **Edit** tab .... `Ctrl`+`Tab`
4. Select **Enable click and type** check box .... `C`
5. Click **OK** .... `Enter`

Correct Errors

- Press **Backspace** key .... `Backspace` to delete character to *left* of insertion point.
- Press **Delete** key .... `Del` to delete character to *right* of insertion point.
- Press **Escape** key .... `Esc` to cancel command or close dialog box.

   OR

   Click **Cancel**

   button .... `Cancel` .

Save a New Document
(Ctrl+S)

1. Click **Save** button 🖫 .

   OR

   a. Click **File** .... `Alt`+`F`
   b. Click **Save** .... `S`
2. Click **Save in** drop-down arrow .... `Alt`+`I`
3. Select **drive** and **folder**.
   a. Click **Create New Folder** button 📁 .

b. Type new folder name.

c. Click **OK** .... `Enter`
4. Double-click **File name** text box .... `Alt`+`N`
5. Type **file name**.
6. Click **Save** .... `Alt`+`S`

Close a Document *(Ctrl+W)*

- Click **Document Close Window** button ✕ .

   ✓ *If only one document is open, use the Close Window button located on the menu bar; if multiple documents are open, use the Close button located on the title bar.*

OR

1. Click **File** .... `Alt`+`F`
2. Click **Close** .... `C`
3. Click **Yes** to save document .... `Y`

   OR

   Click **No** to close without saving .... `N`

Exercise Directions

✓ *Note that the Word documents in the illustrations use a 12-point Times New Roman font, unless otherwise noted. The Word default font is 10-point Times New Roman. As a result, you may notice that the characters you type are smaller than the characters shown in the illustrations. If requested by your instructor, change the font size on your computer to 12. Changing fonts and font sizes are covered in Exercise 25.*

1. Start Word.
2. Hide the Office Assistant if it is displayed.
3. Starting at the beginning of the document, type the paragraph shown in Illustration A.

   ✓ *Remember that you do not have to press Enter at the end of each line.*

4. If you make a typing error, press Backspace to delete it, then type the correct text.

   ✓ *Word marks spelling errors with a red wavy underline and grammatical errors with a green wavy underline. If you see these lines in the document, proofread for errors.*

5. Close the document without saving it.
6. Create a new document.
7. Save the document with the name **WD06**.

   ✓ *Your instructor will tell you where to save the documents you create for use with this book.*

8. Use Click and Type to position the insertion point in the center of the first line of the document.

   ✓ *Click and Type is only active in Print Layout view, the default view. Changing views is covered in Exercise 8.*

a. Move the mouse pointer across the first line of the document until it changes to include lines of centered text.

b. Double-click.

9. Type the first line of text as shown in Illustration B.

10. Use Click and Type to leave a blank line and position the insertion point at the left side of the document.

a. Move the mouse pointer down and to the left until it changes to include lines of left-aligned text.

b. Double-click.

11. Type the first full paragraph shown in Illustration B.

12. Press Enter twice to start a new paragraph and insert a blank line.

13. Type the second paragraph shown in Illustration B.

14. Close the document and exit Word, saving all changes

Illustration A

At State-of-the-Art Solutions, our mission is to meet the needs of all of our clients. We aim to achieve nothing less than total satisfaction, and we vow not to rest until that goal is met. We firmly state that it is our corporate duty to pursue excellence, use intelligence, and produce quality results.

Illustration B

Mission Statement

Our company, State-of-the-Art Solutions, is committed to providing quality service to all clients. We strive for excellence at every level of our organization. We vow to maintain the highest standards, pursue success, and guarantee customer satisfaction.

At State-of-the-Art Solutions we respect our employees as well as our clients. We believe that fostering a strong community within the workplace strengthens our position in the marketplace. We are confident that our commitment will make us leaders in our industry.

On Your Own

1. Create a new document in Word.

2. Save the document as **OWD06**.

3. Type your own mission statement for this class into the blank document. Include information such as the goals you'd like to accomplish and the attitude you'd like to maintain.

4. Save your changes, close the document, and exit Word when you are finished.

Exercise 7

On the Job

Unless a document is designed to be read while displayed on screen, you must print it in order to distribute it. For example, you must print a letter in order to deliver it by mail. Preview a document before you print it to make sure the document is correct and looks good on the page. You save time and paper by correcting errors and adjusting layout before you print.

As a marketing assistant at State-of-the-Art Solutions, you have been asked to develop documents to send to prospective clients. In this exercise, you will create a document describing the company's background and experience to include in a marketing package. You will include the mission statement at the end of the document. When you have completed the document, you will preview it, and then print it.

Terms

Print Create a hardcopy of a document file on paper.

Notes

Preview a Document

- Use Print Preview to display a document as it will look when printed.
- By default, Word displays one full page of a document at a time in Print Preview.

Print Preview screen

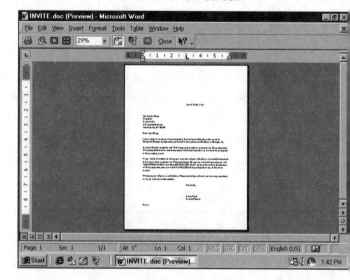

Print

- **Printing** creates a hard copy version of a document.
- Your computer must be connected to a printer in order to print.
- You can quickly print a single copy of the current document using the Standard toolbar, or you can use the Print dialog box to select Print options.

Print dialog box

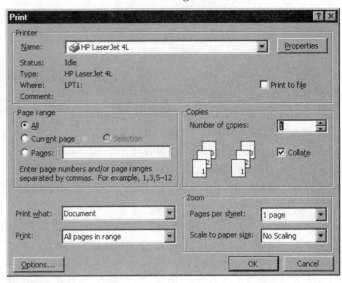

Procedures

Preview Document

1. Click **Print Preview** button 🔍.
   OR
   a. Click **File**.................Alt+F
   b. Click **Print Preview** V
2. Press **Page Down** to see next page.
3. Press **Page Up** to see previous page.
4. Click **Close** button
   Close ....Alt+C

Print *(Ctrl+P)*

- Click **Print** button 🖨.
OR
1. Click **File** ....Alt+F
2. Click **Print** ....P
3. Click **OK** ....Enter

Print Multiple Copies

1. Click **File**....................Alt+F
2. Click **Print**...........................P
3. Click **Number of copies**....................Alt+C
4. Type **number**.
5. Click **OK** ....Enter

Exercise Directions

1. Start Word.
2. Create a new document and save it as **WD07**.
3. Type the document shown in Illustration A.
   a. Use Click and Type to center lines as indicated.
   b. Use Click and Type to start the following paragraphs flush left as indicated.
   c. Press the Enter key twice between each paragraph to leave a blank line.

4. If you make typing errors, use Backspace or Delete to erase them.
5. Preview the document. It should look similar to the one shown in Illustration A.
6. Close Print Preview.
7. Print one copy of the document.
8. Close the document and exit Word, saving all changes.

Center ↓

Flush left State-of-the-Art Solutions

State-of-the-Art Solutions is dedicated to helping small businesses achieve profitability and growth. Originally founded to provide computer installation and maintenance, State-of-the-Art has evolved into one of the area's premier consulting firms specializing in the Internet and the World Wide Web. We are uniquely positioned to guide small companies looking for ways to take advantage of the global marketplace.

The experienced and savvy team of personnel at State-of-the-Art has experience in many aspects of technology, marketing, and international business. In addition to highly qualified engineers, our staff includes lawyers, educators, and financial analysts. When we sit down with a client, we bring a wealth of knowledge and expertise to the table.

At State-of-the-Art Solutions, we understand the concerns and needs of small businesses, because we have been a small business, too. We have faced the challenges of identifying a customer base, expanding to meet demand, and exploring new opportunities and technologies. We draw on our own past experiences to enhance the experiences of our clients. We use the lessons we have learned to help our clients avoid mistakes and pitfalls and to leap forward to success.

We have a proven track record for helping businesses locate new customers and tap into new sources of profit. Clients working with State-of-the-Art Solutions can expect only the highest quality service and results. Without exception, we guarantee satisfaction.

Some of Southern California's most successful Internet-based marketing and retail companies have sought advise from State-of-the-Art Solutions. Available for short-term or long-term contracts, we feel that no question is too insignificant, and no job is too small.

State-of-the Art Solutions is located in Brentwood, California.

Flush left *Center* → Mission Statement

Our company, State-of-the-Art Solutions, is committed to providing quality service to all clients. We strive for excellence at every level of our organization. We vow to maintain the highest standards, pursue success, and guarantee customer satisfaction.

At State-of-the-Art Solutions we respect our employees as well as our clients. We believe that fostering a strong community within the workplace strengthens our position in the marketplace. We are confident that our commitment will make us leaders in our industry.

On Your Own

1. Create a new document in Word.

2. Save the document as **OWD07**.

3. Type four or five paragraphs about the different types of documents you can create using Word 2000. For example, you can create letters, memos, reports, newsletters, and schedules.

4. Include information about why you would want to create each type of document, what you would include in each type of document, and whether or not you would need to print each type of document.

5. Preview the document.

6. Print one copy of the document.

7. Save your changes, close the document, and exit Word when you are finished.

Exercise 8

Skills Covered:

◆ **Insertion Point Movements** ◆ **Change the View** ◆ **Full Screen View**
◆ **Show/Hide Marks** ◆ **Rulers**

On the Job

Mastering insertion point movements in Word is necessary to enter and edit text anywhere in a document. Changing the view allows you to see your document in different ways in order to select the view most suitable for the current task. You can also display and hide different screen elements to ensure you have the tools you need when you need them.

As the owner of a small gourmet cheese shop, you want to provide your employees with information about a new vacation policy. In this exercise, you will create a document about the policy that you can print and hang in the store.

Terms

Insertion point The flashing vertical line that indicates where the next action will occur.

Web page A document stored on the World Wide Web.

Nonprinting characters Characters, such as paragraph marks and tab symbols, that are not printed in a document but that can be displayed on screen.

Notes

Insertion Point Movements

- The **insertion point** indicates where text will be inserted or deleted.

- You can move the insertion point anywhere in the existing text with keystrokes or mouse clicks.

  ✓ *If Click and Type feature is enabled, you can move the insertion point anywhere in a blank document as well.*

- Using scroll bars to shift the document view does not move the insertion point.

Change the View

- By default, Word starts with documents displayed in Print Layout view.

  • You can change the view at any time.

The View buttons

Normal view ⟶ [buttons] ⟵ Outline view

Web Layout view   Print Layout view

- Normal view is used for most typing, editing, and formatting.
- Print Layout view displays a document on-screen the way it will look when it is printed.
- Web Layout view wraps text to fit the window, the way it would on a **Web page** document.
- Outline view is used to create and edit outlines.

Full Screen View

- In any view, including Print Preview, use Full Screen view to display a document without the title bar, toolbars, ruler, scroll bars, status bar, or taskbar.

- Full Screen view lets you see more of your document on screen at one time.

Full Screen view

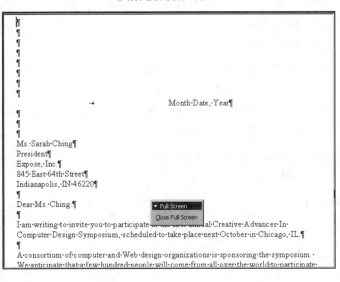

Show/Hide Marks

- When typing, you insert **nonprinting characters** like spaces, tabs, and paragraph marks, along with printing characters like letters and numbers.

- Displaying nonprinting characters is helpful because you see where each paragraph ends and if there are extra spaces or unwanted tab characters.

- On-screen, nonprinting characters are displayed as follows:
  - Space: dot (•)
  - Paragraph: paragraph symbol (¶)
  - Tab: right arrow (→)

Rulers

- The horizontal ruler measures the width of the document page. It displays information such as margins, tabs stops, and indents.

- The vertical ruler measures the height of the document page.
  - ✓ *The vertical ruler is only displayed in Print Layout view and Print Preview.*

Procedures

Insertion Point Movements
With the mouse:

- Click mouse pointer in text where you want to position insertion point.
  - ✓ *If the Click and Type feature is enabled, double-click anywhere in a blank document in Print Layout view to position insertion point.*

With the Keyboard:

To Move	Press
• One character left	←
• One character right	→
• One line up	↑
• One line down	↓
• Previous word	Ctrl + ←
• Next word	Ctrl + →
• Top of screen	Alt + Ctrl + Page Up
• Bottom of screen	Alt + Ctrl + Page Down

- Beginning of document .... Ctrl + Home
- End of document .... Ctrl + End
- Beginning of line .... Home
- End of line .... End

Change View

1. Click **View** .... Alt + V
2. Click **Normal** button ..... N
   OR
   Click **Web Layout** button .... W
   OR
   Click **Print Layout** button .... P
   OR
   Click **Outline** button ..... O

Full Screen View

1. Click **View** .... Alt + V
2. Click **Full Screen** .... U

To display screen elements again:

- Press **Esc** .... Esc
  OR
  Click **Close Full Screen** button Close Full Screen .... Alt + C

Show/Hide Marks

- Click **Show/Hide ¶** button ¶.
  OR
1. Click **Tools** .... Alt + T
2. Click **Options** .... O
3. Click **View** tab............ Ctrl + Tab
4. Select **All** checkbox..... Alt + A
   in Formatting marks section.
5. Click **OK** .... Enter

Show or Hide Ruler

1. Click **View**.................... Alt + V
   - ✓ *Check mark next to ruler indicates ruler is displayed.*
2. Click **Ruler**.......................... R

Exercise Directions

1. Start Word and create a new document.
2. Hide the Office Assistant if it is displayed.
3. Save the new document with the name **WD08**.
4. Display nonprinting characters.
5. Use Click and Type to position the insertion point in the center of the first line and type the heading, as shown in Illustration A.
6. Use Click and Type to position the insertion point flush left, two lines down, then type the first paragraph shown in Illustration A.
   - Notice the paragraph marks that are inserted automatically in the document.
7. Press Enter twice to start a new paragraph and insert a blank line.
8. Type the second paragraph shown in Illustration A.
9. Change to Web Layout view.
10. Change to Normal view.
11. Change to Print Layout view.
12. Hide the rulers.
13. Show the rulers.
14. Hide the Formatting toolbar.
15. Show the Formatting toolbar.
16. Use Print Preview to preview the document.
17. Print one copy of the document.
18. Close the **WD08** document and exit Word, saving all changes.

Illustration A

The Big Cheese Vacation Policy

I would like all employees to be aware of our new vacation policy. As of January 1, vacation time will be directly related to the number of hours worked each month. Specifically, employees will earn 8 hours of vacation time for every 120 hours worked.

The new policy does not affect vacation time you may have already earned. As always, you must clear vacation time with your manager to be sure you are not put on the schedule. Please contact me if you have any questions about this policy.

On Your Own

1. Create a new document in Word.
2. Save the document as **OWD08**.
3. In two or three paragraphs, type some information about yourself. For example, describe your family, where you live, and what you do for fun.
4. Change the view.
5. Display and hide different toolbars.
6. Display and hide the ruler.
7. Close the document and exit Word when you are finished, saving all changes.

Exercise 9

On the Job

Word can automate many tedious tasks involved in creating documents. Word's AutoCorrect feature automatically corrects common spelling errors before you even know you've made them, and AutoText lets you quickly insert words or phrases you type often such as the closing to a letter. In order to perform actions on specific text, you must first select the text. Save changes to a document to keep it up to date and accurate. Saving frequently ensures that you don't lose work in the event of a power failure or computer problem.

Your boss has asked you to create a document for employees of State-of-the-Art Solutions, providing them with the address of Cornerstone Graphics and phone numbers of key personnel.

Terms

AutoCorrect A Word feature that automatically corrects common spelling errors as you type.

Select Identify text on-screen.

Highlight Change the color to make text stand out on-screen.

AutoText A Word feature that lets you automatically insert selections of text or graphics into a document.

Notes

AutoCorrect

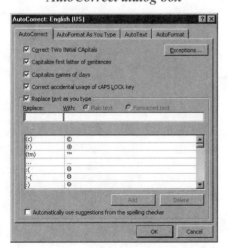

AutoCorrect dialog box

- **AutoCorrect** automatically replaces spelling errors with the correct text as soon as you press the spacebar.

- Word comes with a built-in list of AutoCorrect entries including common typos like *adn* for *and* and *teh* for *the*.

- AutoCorrect can also replace regular characters with symbols, such as the letters T and M with the trademark symbol, ™.

- AutoCorrect also corrects capitalization errors as follows:

  - TWo INitial CApital letters are replaced with one initial capital letter.

  - The first word in a sentence is automatically capitalized.

- The days of the week are automatically capitalized.
- Accidental use of the cAPS lOCK feature is corrected if the Caps Lock key is set to ON.

- You can add words to the AutoCorrect list.
- You can also set Word to use the spelling checker dictionary to determine if a word is misspelled and to correct it automatically.
- If you find AutoCorrect annoying, you can disable it.

Select Text

- You can **select** any amount of text.
- The next action or command affects the selected text.
- Selected text appears **highlighted** on screen as white characters on a black background.

Selected text in a document

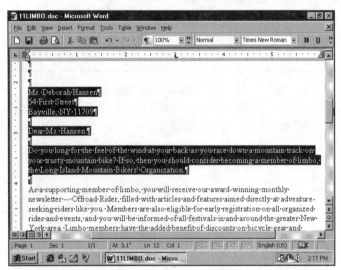

AutoText

- **AutoText** eliminates repetitive typing by automatically inserting saved blocks of text or graphics.
- An unlimited amount of text or graphics may be stored in an AutoText entry.
- Word comes with a built-in list of AutoText entries, including standard letter closings and salutations.
- You can add entries to the AutoText list.

Save Changes

- To keep revisions permanently, you must save the document.
- Saving frequently ensures that no work will be lost if there is a power outage or you experience computer problems.
- Saving replaces the previously saved version of the document with any new changes.

Procedures

Use AutoCorrect

Add words to the AutoCorrect list:

1. Click **Tools**..................`Alt`+`T`
2. Click **AutoCorrect** ....`A`
3. Type misspelled word to add.
4. Click in **With** text box...`Alt`+`W`
5. Type correct word.
6. Click **Add** button

   Add ....`Alt`+`A`
7. Click **OK**..........................`Enter`

AutoCorrect words found in Spelling Checker dictionary:

1. Click **Tools**...................`Alt`+`T`
2. Click **AutoCorrect** ....`A`
3. Select **Automatically use suggestions from the spelling checker** check box...................`Alt`+`G`
4. Click **OK**..........................`Enter`

Disable AutoCorrect:

1. Click **Tools**...................`Alt`+`T`
2. Click **AutoCorrect** ....`A`
3. Deselect **Replace text as you type** checkbox. ....`Alt`+`T`

   ✓ Clicking should remove check mark. If not, click check box again.
4. Click **OK**..........................`Enter`

Select Using the Keyboard

1. Position insertion point to left of first character to select.
2. Use following key combinations:
   - One character right......................`Shift`+`→`
   - One character left ....`Shift`+`←`
   - One line up ....`Shift`+`↑`
   - One line down.....................`Shift`+`↓`
   - To end of line........`Shift`+`End`
   - To beginning of line................`Shift`+`Home`
   - To end of document .....`Shift`+`Ctrl`+`End`
   - To beginning of document ..`Shift`+`Ctrl`+`Home`
   - Entire document.....`Ctrl`+`A`

Select Using the Mouse

1. Position insertion point to the left of first character to select.
2. Hold down left mouse button.
3. Drag to where you want to stop selecting.
4. Release mouse button.

Mouse Selection Shortcuts

One word:
- Double-click word.

One sentence:
1. Press and hold **Ctrl** ....`Ctrl`
2. Click in sentence.

One line:
- Single-click in **selection bar** to the left of the line you want to select.

  ✓ In the selection bar, the mouse pointer changes to an arrow pointing up and to the right.

One paragraph:
- Double-click in **selection bar** to the left of the paragraph you want to select.

Document:
- Triple-click in selection bar.

Cancel a Selection
- Click anywhere in document.

OR

Press any arrow key ....`↓``↑`

✓ Using the arrow keys moves the insertion point to the top or bottom of the selected text. For example, if the entire document is selected, pressing the up arrow will deselect the text and place the insertion point at the top of the document.

Use AutoText

To create an AutoText entry: (Alt+F3)

1. Select text or graphics.
2. Click **Insert**. ....`Alt`+`I`
3. Click **AutoText**....................`A`
4. Click **New** ....`N`
5. Type the entry name.

   ✓ AutoText entry names can have 31 characters including spaces. Use descriptive names.
6. Click **OK** ....`Enter`

To insert an AutoText entry:

1. Type entry name.

   ✓ If entry name is unique, you can type just first three characters. Press Enter to accept AutoText entry when it is displayed.
2. Press **F3** ....`F3`

OR

1. Click **Insert** ....`Alt`+`I`
2. Click **AutoText**....................`A`
3. Click **AutoText**....................`X`
4. Select desired AutoText entry from Enter AutoText entries here text box.
5. Click **Insert** ....`Alt`+`I`

Save Changes (Ctrl+S)
- Click **Save** button.

OR

1. Click **File**....................`Alt`+`F`
2. Click **Save** ....`S`

Exercise Directions

1. Start Word, if necessary.

2. Create a new document and save it as **WD09**.

3. Open the AutoCorrect dialog box.

4. To the AutoCorrect list, add the company name misspelled without hyphens: *State of the Art*; Replace it with the correctly spelled name including hyphens: *State-of-the-Art.*

5. Be sure the Replace text as you type check box is selected, then close the dialog box.

6. Use Click and Type to position the insertion point in the center of the first line of the document, then type the heading.

7. Use Click and Type to position the insertion point flush left, leaving one blank line, then type the first nine lines of text.

   a. Be sure to type the circled errors exactly as shown.

      ✓ *Notice Word automatically corrects the errors.*

   b. Press Enter twice to leave blank lines between paragraphs.

8. Save the changes to the document.

9. Select the three lines that make up Cornerstone Graphics' address.

10. Use the selected text to create an AutoText entry named *cgaddress*.

11. Type the next six lines of text.

12. Insert the *cgaddress* AutoText entry at the end of the document.

13. Save the changes to the document.

14. Preview the document.

15. Print one copy of the document.

16. Close the document and exit Word, saving all changes.

Illustration A

MEMORANDUM

To: All State of the Art Employees
From: Marketing adn Personnel Departments
Regarding: Cornerstone Graphics

First nine lines

As most of you know by now, we hvae reached an agreement with Cornerstone Graphics, whereby we will work jointly on certain Web design projects. COrnerstone, a well-respected graphics design firm, is located at teh following address:

Cornerstone Graphics
920 Marco Place
Venice, CA 90291   *Insert cgaddress AutoText here*

Next six lines

Starting monday, the person you should contact if you need information from Cornerstone is Jake McNeil, Administrative Assistant to the President. His address and phone number are below.

If you have any questions about the agreement, direct them to our Personnel department.

Jake McNeil
(213) 555-1002; extension 113
Cornerstone Graphics
920 Marco Place   *Insert cgaddress AutoText here*
Venice, CA 90291

On Your Own

1. Create a new document in Word.
2. Save the document as **OWD09**.
3. Add your last name to the AutoCorrect list.
4. Type your name and address, deliberately misspelling your last name so that AutoCorrect corrects it.
5. Create an AutoText entry for your address.
6. Draft a paragraph to a friend or relative going on vacation asking him or her to send you a postcard.
7. Use the AutoText entry to insert your address in the note.
8. Save your changes, close the document, and exit Word when you are finished.

Exercise 10

Skills Covered:

◆ **Correct Spelling as You Type** ◆ **Correct Grammar as You Type**
◆ **Check Spelling** ◆ **Check Grammar** ◆ **Use the Thesaurus**

On the Job

A professional document should be free of spelling and grammatical errors. Word can check the spelling and grammar in a document and recommend corrections.

State-of-the-Art Solutions, a consulting firm, and Cornerstone Graphics, a Web page design company, are planning to team up to work with selected clients. In this exercise, your supervisor has asked you to create a press release announcing this agreement.

Terms

Thesaurus A listing of words with synonyms and antonyms.

Synonyms Words with the same meaning.

Antonyms Words with opposite meanings.

Notes

Correct Spelling as You Type

- By default, Word checks spelling as you type and marks misspelled words with a red, wavy underline.

> This·is·an·example·of·a·missspelled·word.¶

- Any word not in the Word dictionary is marked as misspelled, including proper names, words with unique spellings, and many technical terms. Word will also mark double occurrences of words.

- You can ignore the wavy lines and keep typing, correct the spelling, or add the marked word to the dictionary.

- If the wavy underlines distract you from your work, you can turn off the Check spelling as you type feature.

Correct Grammar as You Type

- Word can also check grammar as you type, identifying errors such as punctuation, matching case or tense, sentence fragments, and run-on sentences.

- Word marks grammatical errors with a green, wavy underline.

> This·is·an·example·of·a·grammatical·errors.¶

- Word picks out grammatical errors based on one of five built-in style guides.

- The default grammar style is called Standard. You can select casual, formal, technical, or you can develop a custom style.

- As with the spelling checker, you can ignore the green wavy lines and keep typing, or correct the error.

- If the wavy underlines distract you from your work, you can turn off the Check grammar as you type feature.

Check Spelling

- You can check the spelling in an entire document or in part of a document.

- To check the spelling in part of a document, you must first select the section you want checked.

- The spelling checker identifies any word not in the Word dictionary as misspelled, including proper names, words with unique spellings, and technical terms.

- When Word identifies a misspelled word, you can correct the spelling, ignore the spelling, or add the word to the dictionary.

Correct spelling with Spelling Checker

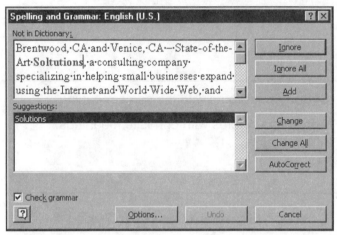

Check Grammar

- By default, Word checks the grammar in a document at the same time that it checks the spelling.

- When Word identifies a grammatical mistake, you can accept the suggestion or ignore it.

Correct grammar with Grammar Checker

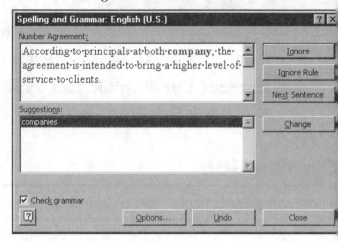

Use the Thesaurus

- Use the **thesaurus** to locate **synonyms**, definitions, and **antonyms** for words typed in a document.

- A thesaurus can improve your writing by helping you eliminate repetitive use of common words and to choose more descriptive words.

Choose synonyms with the Thesaurus

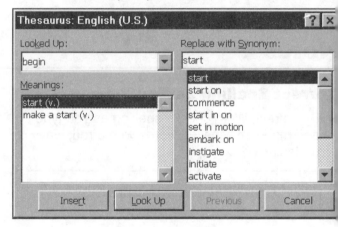

Procedures

Correct Spelling as You Type

1. Right-click red, wavy underline.
2. Click correctly spelled word on context menu.
   OR
   - Click **Ignore All**............. [I]
   - Click **Add** to add word to dictionary...................... [A]

To turn off Automatic Spelling Checker:

1. Click **Tools** .... [Alt]+[T]
2. Click **Options** .... [O]
3. Click the **Spelling & Grammar** tab............. [Ctrl]+[Tab]

4. Deselect **Check spelling as you type** check box.................... [Alt]+[F]
5. Click **OK**.......................... [Enter]

Correct Grammar as You Type

1. Right-click grammatical error marked with green, wavy underline.
2. Click **correct grammar** option on context menu.
   OR
   Click **Ignore** to hide the underline .... `I`

To turn Off Automatic Grammar Checker:

1. Click **Tools**.................... `Alt`+`T`
2. Click **Options**........................ `O`
3. Click the **Spelling & Grammar** tab .... `Ctrl`+`Tab`
4. Deselect **Check grammar** as you type check box ...... `Alt`+`G`
5. Click **OK**...................... `Enter`

Select Grammar Style

1. Click **Tools**.................... `Alt`+`T`
2. Click **Options**........................ `O`
3. Click the **Spelling & Grammar** tab .... `Ctrl`+`Tab`
4. Click **Writing style** drop-down arrow .... `Alt`+`W`
5. Click desired **style** .. `↑↓`, `Enter`
6. Click **OK**.......................... `Enter`

Check Spelling (F7)

1. Position insertion point where you want to start checking.
   ✓ *Word checks document from the insertion point forward.*
   OR
   Select text you want to check.
2. Click **Spelling and Grammar** button `ABC✓`.
   OR
   a. Click **Tools** .... `Alt`+`T`
   b. Click **Spelling & Grammar**........................ `S`

3. Choose from the following options:
   - Click correctly spelled word in **Suggestions** list......................... `Alt`+`N`
   - Change the misspelled word manually in the Not in Dictionary text box.
   - Click **Change**......... `Alt`+`C`
   - Click **Change All** to change the word everywhere in document .... `Alt`+`L`
   - Click **Ignore** to continue without changing word .... `Alt`+`I`
   - Click **Ignore All** to continue without changing word and without highlighting it anywhere else in document .... `Alt`+`G`
   - Click **Add** to add word to dictionary............... `Alt`+`A`
4. Repeat step 3 options for every misspelled word.
5. Click **OK** when Word completes check.............. `Enter`

Check Grammar (F7)

1. Position insertion point where you want to start checking.
   OR
   Select text you want to check.
2. Click **Spelling and Grammar** button `ABC✓`.
   OR
   a. Click **Tools**............. `Alt`+`T`
   b. Click **Spelling & Grammar**...................... `S`
3. Choose from the following options:
   - Click the correct grammar in **Suggestions** list...... `Alt`+`N`
   - Edit the error manually in the Not in Dictionary box.
   - Click **Change**......... `Alt`+`C`
   - Click **Ignore** to continue without changing text .... `Alt`+`I`

   - Click **Ignore Rule** to continue without changing text and without highlighting error if it occurs anywhere else in document .... `Alt`+`G`
   - Click **Next Sentence** to skip highlighted error and continue checking document............... `Alt`+`X`
   - Click **Office Assistant** button `[?]` to display information about grammatical error.
4. Repeat step 3 options for every grammatical error.
5. Click **OK** when Word completes check............. `Enter`

Use Thesaurus (Shift+F7)

1. Click on the word you want to look up.
   ✓ *The insertion point should be positioned within the word.*
2. Click **Tools** .... `Alt`+`T`
3. Click **Language**.................. `L`
4. Click **Thesaurus**................. `T`
5. Choose from the following options:
   - Click **Look up** to display synonyms for word highlighted in Replace with Synonym list. .... `Alt`+`L`
   - Click a word in the **Meanings list** to display synonyms for the word.............. `Alt`+`M`, `↑↓`
   - Click **Antonyms** to display a list of antonyms for selected word.
     ✓ *The Antonyms option is not available for all words in the Thesaurus.*
6. Click the **replacement word** you want in the **Replace with Synonym** list. ..... `Alt`+`S`, `↑↓`
7. Click **Replace**. .... `Alt`+`R`

Exercise Directions

1. Start Word, if necessary.
2. Create a new document and save it as **WD10**.
3. Display paragraph marks.
4. Begin at the top of the screen and type the paragraphs shown in Illustration A, including all the circled errors.

   ✓ *If the Office Assistant offers help of any kind, close it and continue.*

5. Correct the spelling of the word *Solutions*.
6. Correct the grammar for the word *company* in the last sentence of the second paragraph.
7. Check the spelling and grammar starting at the beginning of the document.

   a. Correct the spelling of the word *design*.
   b. Ignore all occurrences of the proper name *Louris*.
   c. Change the semicolon to a period.
   d. Capitalize the word *for* at the beginning of the last sentence.

8. Use the Thesaurus to replace the word *higher* in the last sentence of the first paragraph.

   • If necessary correct the grammar in the modified sentence.

9. Preview the document.
10. Print one copy of the document.
11. Close the document and exit Word, saving all changes.

Illustration A

State-of-the-Art Solutions and Cornerstone Graphics Announce Agreement

Brentwood, CA and Venice, CA – State-of-the-Art Soltutions, a consulting company specializing in helping small businesses expand using the Internet and World Wide Web, and Cornerstone Graphics, a small but successful graphics desing firm, announced that they will begin cooperating on specific accounts. According to principals at both company the agreement is intended to bring a higher level of service to clients.

"Our combined expertise virtually guarantees satisfaction to clients of both companies," claimed Maryanne Costello, Vice President of Marketing at State-of-the-Art. Cornerstone's president Tom Louris agreed;

for more information, contact State-of-the-Art Solutions at 310-555-0821 or Cornerstone Graphics at 213-555-2597.

On Your Own

1. Create a new document.

2. Save the document as **OWD10**.

3. Draft a press release announcing that you are taking a course to learn how to use Microsoft Word 2000. Include information such as your instructor's name, the textbook you are using, and when the course will be completed. You can also include information from your mission statement for the course, which you created in the On Your Own section for Exercise 6.

4. Check and correct the spelling and grammar.

5. Use the Thesaurus to improve the wording of your document.

6. Save your changes, close the document, and exit Word when you are finished.

Exercise 11

◆ **Create a Business Letter** ◆ **Parts of a Business Letter**
◆ **Parts of a Personal Business Letters**
◆ **The Date and Time Feature** ◆ **Shrink to Fit**

On the Job

As a representative of your employer, you write business letters to communicate with other businesses, such as clients or suppliers, or to communicate with individuals, such as prospective employees. For example, you might write a business letter to request a job quote from a supplier, or to inquire about a loan from a bank. You write personal business letters to find a job or communicate with businesses such as your bank or your insurance company. For example, you might write a personal business letter to your insurance company to ask about a claim that needs to be paid. The letter serves as a formal record of your inquiry.

You are the assistant to Greg Julian, president of GJ Computers, a retail computer store interested in building a company Web site. In this exercise, you will create a full-block business letter on behalf of the president of GJ Computers to the president of Cornerstone Graphics, confirming an appointment for the following week.

Terms

Business letter A letter from one business to another business or individual.

Personal business letter A letter from an individual to a business.

Full block A style of letter in which all lines start flush with the left margin.

Modified block A style of letter in which some lines start at the center of the page.

Salutation The line at the start of a letter including the greeting and the recipient's name, such as *Dear Mr. Doe*.

Preprinted letterhead Stationery that already has a company's or individual's name and address printed on it.

Computer clock The clock/calendar built into your computer's main processor to keep track of the current date and time.

Font A set of characters in a particular typeface.

Notes

Create a Business Letter

■ A letter written on behalf of any type of business is considered a **business letter**.

■ A business letter written on behalf of an individual is considered a **personal business letter**.

■ There are two common styles used for business letters:

- In a **full-block** letter, all lines start flush with the left margin.

- In a **modified-block** letter, certain lines start at the center of the page.

  ✓ Modified-block letters are covered in Exercise 24.

Full block

Current Month Date, Year

Ms. Sarah Ching
President
Expose, Inc.
845 East 64th Street
Indianapolis, IN 46220

Dear Ms. Ching:

I am writing to inquire about job opportunities at Expose, Inc. Currently, I am employed at a graphics and desktop publishing company, however Web page design is my true passion.

My qualifications for a job at Expose include a degree in computer graphics design, fluency in HTML, and experience with Java and with Microsoft Corp.'s FrontPage. I have already created Web pages for myself and for friends.

Please take the time to respond to my inquiry, or pass this letter on to someone else at Expose. I look forward to hearing from you.

Sincerely,

Elizabeth O'Meara
622 East 122nd Street
Indianapolis, IN 46220

Modified block

622 East 122nd Street
Indianapolis, IN 46220
Current Month Date, Year

Ms. Sarah Ching
President
Expose, Inc.
845 East 64th Street
Indianapolis, IN 46220

Dear Ms. Ching:

I am writing to inquire about job opportunities at Expose, Inc. Currently, I am employed at a graphics and desktop publishing company, however Web page design is my true passion.

My qualifications for a job at Expose include a degree in computer graphics design, fluency in HTML, and experience with Java and with Microsoft Corp.'s FrontPage. I have already created Web pages for myself and for friends.

Please take the time to respond to my inquiry, or pass this letter on to someone else at Expose. I look forward to hearing from you.

Sincerely,

Elizabeth O'Meara

Parts of a Business Letter

■ The parts of a business letter and the vertical spacing of letter parts are the same regardless of the style.

■ Vertical spacing is achieved by inserting blank lines between letter parts.

■ Word's built-in AutoText list includes many standard letter parts.

■ The parts of a business letter are:
- Date (indented for modified-block style)
- Inside address (to whom and where the letter is going)
- **Salutation**
- Body
- Closing (indented for modified-block style)

- Signature line (indented for modified-block style)
- Title line—the job title of the letter writer (indented for modified-block style)
- Reference initials (the initials of the person who wrote the letter, followed by a slash, followed by the initials of the person who typed the letter)
  - ✓ *Whenever you see "yo" as part of the reference initials in an exercise, type your own initials.*
- Special notations (included only when appropriate):
  - ◆ Mail service notation indicates a special delivery method. It is typed in all uppercase letters two lines below the date. Typical mail service notations include Certified mail, Registered mail, or By Hand.
  - ◆ Subject notation identifies or summarizes the letter topic. The word *Subject* may be typed in all capital letters or with just an initial capital. It is placed two lines below the salutation.
    - ✓ *The abbreviation Re is sometimes used in place of the word Subject.*
  - ◆ Enclosure or attachment notation indicates whether there are other items in the envelope. It is typed two lines below the reference initials in any of the following styles: ENC., Enc., Encl., Enclosure, Attachment.
    - ✓ *If there are multiple items, the number may be typed in parentheses following the notation.*
  - ◆ Copy notation indicates if any other people are receiving copies of the same letter. It is typed two lines below either the enclosure notation or reference initials, whichever is last. It may be typed as Copy to:, c: or pc: (photocopy) with the name(s) of the recipient(s) listed after the colon.

Parts of a Personal Business Letter

- A personal business letter includes the same elements as a business letter minus the title line and reference initials, and includes a return address.
  - ✓ *If the paper has a **preprinted letterhead**, omit the return address.*

- A personal business letter can be full block or modified block.
  - In full block, type the return address following the signature.
  - In modified block, type the return address above the date.

The Date and Time Feature

- Use the Date and Time feature to insert the current date and/or time automatically in a document.
- The inserted date and time are based on your **computer's clock**. A variety of date and time formats are available.

Date and Time dialog box

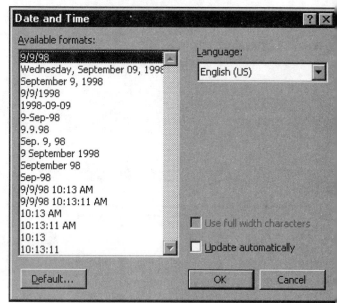

- You can set Word to update the date or time automatically whenever you save or print the document.

Shrink to Fit

- Shrink to Fit automatically reduces the **font** size and spacing in a document just enough to fit the document on one less page.
- Use Shrink to Fit if the last page of a document contains only a small amount of text.
- The Shrink to Fit feature is only available in Print Preview mode.

Procedures

Create Full-Block Business Letter

1. Start 2.5" from the top of the page .... Enter **8x**

   ✓ *Press Enter eight times to leave 2.5" of space.*

2. Insert the date.

3. Leave one blank line and type the mail service notation .... Enter **2x**

4. Leave three blank lines and type the inside address .... Enter **4x**

5. Leave a blank line and type the salutation .... Enter **2x**

6. Leave one blank line and type the subject notation ..... Enter **2x**

7. Leave a blank line and type the letter body .... Enter **2x**

8. Leave a blank line and type the closing .... Enter **2x**

9. Leave three blank lines and type the signature line .... Enter **4x**

10. Type the title line .... Enter

11. Leave a blank line and type the reference initials. ... Enter **2x**

12. Leave a blank line and type the enclosure notation .... Enter **2x**

13. Leave a blank line and type the copy notation .... Enter **2x**

Insert Date and/or Time

1. Position the insertion point.

2. Click **Insert** .... Alt + I

3. Click **Date and Time** .... T

4. Click the desired format

   ✓ *Select **Update automatically** check box if you want date and/or time to update when you save or print document.*

5. Click **OK** .... Enter

Shrink to Fit

1. Click **Print Preview** button 🔍.
   OR
   a. Click **File** .... Alt + F
   b. Click **Print Preview** V

2. Click **Shrink to Fit** button 🖼.

3. Click **Close** button Close.

Exercise Directions

1. Start Word, if necessary.

2. Create a new document and save it as **WD11**.

3. Type the letter shown in Illustration A.

   - Press the Enter key to leave lines between parts of the letter as indicated.

   - Insert the current date so it does not update automatically.

     ✓ *Use the MONTH DAY, YEAR format found third from the top in the Date and Time dialog box.*

   - If the Office Assistant opens and asks if you need help, click Cancel and continue typing.

   - If AutoText balloons are displayed for any letter parts you start to type (for example, CERTIFIED MAIL), press Enter to insert the AutoText.

   - Use the *cgaddress* AutoText entry to complete the inside address. (This AutoText was created in Exercise 9.)

4. Check the spelling and grammar in the document.

   - Accept Word's suggestions to correct errors.
   - Ignore all proper names.

5. Preview the document.

6. If necessary, use the Shrink to Fit option to ensure that the letter fits on a single page.

7. Print one copy of the document.

8. Close the document and exit Word, saving all changes.

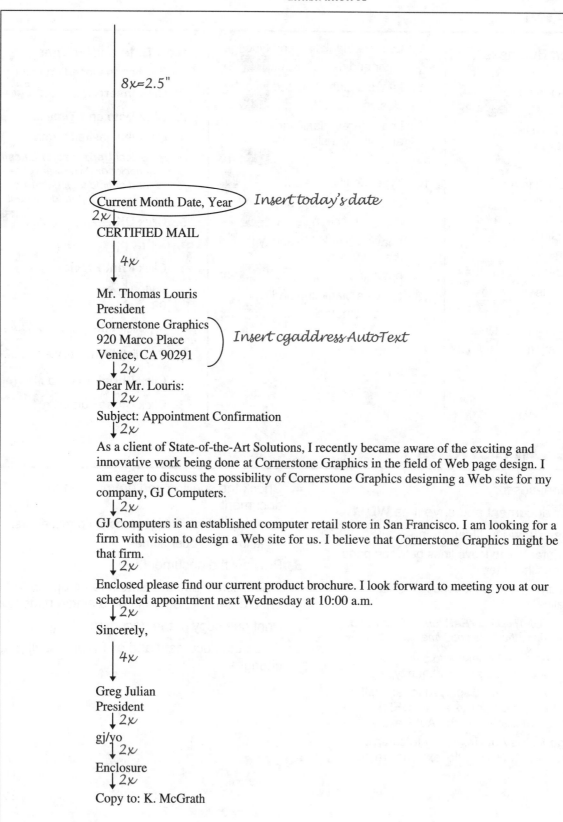

8x=2.5"

Current Month Date, Year   *Insert today's date*

2x

CERTIFIED MAIL

4x

Mr. Thomas Louris
President
Cornerstone Graphics   *Insert cgaddress AutoText*
920 Marco Place
Venice, CA 90291

2x

Dear Mr. Louris:

2x

Subject: Appointment Confirmation

2x

As a client of State-of-the-Art Solutions, I recently became aware of the exciting and innovative work being done at Cornerstone Graphics in the field of Web page design. I am eager to discuss the possibility of Cornerstone Graphics designing a Web site for my company, GJ Computers.

2x

GJ Computers is an established computer retail store in San Francisco. I am looking for a firm with vision to design a Web site for us. I believe that Cornerstone Graphics might be that firm.

2x

Enclosed please find our current product brochure. I look forward to meeting you at our scheduled appointment next Wednesday at 10:00 a.m.

2x

Sincerely,

4x

Greg Julian
President

2x

gj/yo

2x

Enclosure

2x

Copy to: K. McGrath

On Your Own

1. Create a new document in Word.

2. Save the document as **OWD11**.

3. Representing your school or organization, draft a full-block business letter to a local newspaper asking them to include information about upcoming events in a schedule or calendar listing. School events might include athletic contests such as a homecoming football game, club activities, field trips, band and choir concerts, or vacation days.

4. In the letter, indicate that you have attached the necessary information and that you are sending a copy to your instructor.

5. Save your changes, close the document, and exit Word when you are finished.

Exercise 12

On the Job

Handwriting on an envelope looks unprofessional. With Word you can set up and print envelopes to match your letters. You can also create and print mailing labels or return address labels.

You are interested in obtaining a position designing Web pages. In this exercise, you will create a personal business letter asking about job opportunities at Cornerstone Graphics. You will also create an envelope to accompany the document. Finally, you will create return address labels and save them in a separate document.

Terms

Delivery address The recipient's address printed on the outside of an envelope.

Return address The letter-writer's address, typically appearing at the very top of the letter as well as in the upper-left corner of an envelope.

Notes

Envelopes

- Word has a feature that automatically sets up an envelope for printing.

- By default, Word creates standard size 10 envelopes ($4\frac{1}{8}$" by $9\frac{1}{2}$").

- If a letter document is open on-screen, Word picks up the inside address for the envelope's **delivery address**.

- You can print the envelope directly or add it to the beginning of the open document and save it.

The Envelopes page of the Envelopes and Labels dialog box

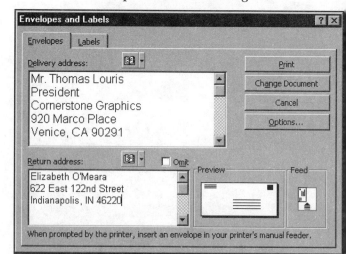

Labels

- Use the Label feature to create mailing labels, **return address** labels, file folder labels, or diskette labels.
- The Label feature automatically sets up a document to print on predefined label types.
- You select the manufacturer and label type loaded in the printer.
- By default, Word creates a full page of labels using the inside address from the current document.
- You can change the default to create labels using the return address or to create a single label.

The Labels page of the Envelopes and Labels dialog box

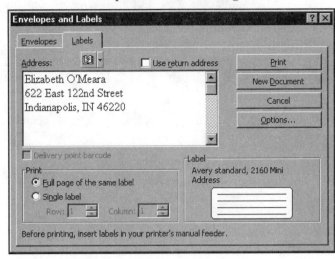

Procedures

Print Envelope

1. Click **Tools**..................`Alt`+`T`
2. Click **Envelopes and Labels**...............................`E`
3. Click **Envelopes** tab ....`Alt`+`E`
4. Type **Delivery address** ....`Alt`+`D`
    - ✓ *If inside address is already entered, skip step 4.*
5. Type **Return address**..`Alt`+`R`
    OR
    Select **Omit** check box ....`Alt`+`M`
    - ✓ *If Omit check box is selected, you cannot type in Return address text box.*
6. Click **Print** button
    `Print`........................`Alt`+`P`
    OR
    Click **Add to Document** ....`Alt`+`A`
    - ✓ *If you enter a new return address, Word will prompt you to save the new address as the default. Select Yes to keep the new return address as the default or select No to retain the previous return address.*

Print Full Page of Labels

1. Click **Tools**.................`Alt`+`T`
2. Click **Envelopes and Labels**...............................`E`
3. Click **Labels** tab ....`Alt`+`L`
4. Click **Options**..............`Alt`+`O`
5. Select **Label products**...`Alt`+`P`, `↕`, `Enter`
6. Select **Product number**..............`Alt`+`U`, `↕`
    - ✓ *Make sure correct printer and tray information are selected.*
7. Click **OK**.........................`Enter`
8. Type **label text in the Address box** ....`Alt`+`A`
    - ✓ *If inside address is already entered, skip step 8.*
9. Make sure labels are loaded in printer.
10. Click **Print** button
    `Print`........................`Alt`+`P`

Print Single Label

1. Click **Tools**.................`Alt`+`T`
2. Click **Envelopes and Labels**................................`E`
3. Click **Labels** tab ....`Alt`+`L`

4. Click **Single label** option button...........................`Alt`+`N`
5. Click **Options**..............`Alt`+`O`
6. Select **Label products** ..`Alt`+`P`, `↕`, `Enter`
7. Select **Product number** ....`Alt`+`U`, `↕`
    - ✓ *Make sure correct printer and tray information are selected.*
8. Click **OK**.........................`Enter`
9. Type **label text in the Address box**...............`Alt`+`A`
    - ✓ *If inside address is already entered, skip step 9.*
10. Make sure labels are loaded in printer.
11. Click **Print** button
    `Print`.........................`Alt`+`P`

Print Return Address Labels

1. Click **Tools**.................`Alt`+`T`
2. Click **Envelopes and Labels**...............................`E`
3. Click **Labels** tab ....`Alt`+`L`
4. Select **Use return address** check box ....`Alt`+`R`
5. Click **Options**..............`Alt`+`O`

6. Select option from
   Label products
   list............ [Alt] + [P] , [↕] , [Enter]

7. Select option from **Product number** list.......... [Alt] + [U] , [↕]

   ✓ *Make sure the correct printer and tray information is selected.*

8. Click **OK** .... [Enter]

9. Make sure labels are loaded in printer.

10. Click **Print** button

    [Print] .... [Alt] + [P]

    ✓ *If you enter a new return address, Word will prompt you to save the new address as the default. Select Yes to keep the new return address as the default or select No to retain the previous return address.*

To save labels to print later:

1. Set up labels following steps above.

   ✓ *Stop before printing labels.*

2. Click **New Document** .... [Alt] + [D]

3. **Save** and name new document [💾] .... [Ctrl] + [S]

Exercise Directions

1. Start Word, if necessary.

2. Create a new document and save it as **WD12-1**.

3. Type the letter shown in Illustration A.

   ✓ *You may type the name and address of the letter writer as shown in the illustration, or use your own name and address.*

4. Check the spelling and grammar.

5. Create an envelope for the letter.

   a. Use the inside address for the president of Cornerstone Graphics.

   b. Enter the return address as it appears in the document you typed – either your own or the one shown in the illustration.

6. Add the envelope to the document.

   • When prompted to save the new return address as the default, choose No.

7. Preview the document.

8. Print the document.

9. Create return address labels for the document.

10. Save the labels in a new document.

    a. Use the return address as it appears in the document.

       ✓ *Do not save the return address as the default*

    b. Create a full page of the same label.

11. Save the new label document with the name **WD12-2**.

12. Preview the new label document. It should look similar to the one in Illustration B depending on the Product # selected.

13. Print the **WD12-2** label document.

14. Close all open documents and exit Word, saving all changes.

Illustration A

Current Month Date, Year

Mr. Thomas Louris
President
Cornerstone Graphics
920 Marco Place
Venice, CA 90291

Dear Mr. Louris:

I am writing to inquire about job opportunities at Cornerstone Graphics. Currently, I am employed at a graphics and desktop publishing company; however, Web page design is my true passion.

My qualifications for a job at Cornerstone include a degree in computer graphics design, fluency in html and experience with Java and with Microsoft Corp.'s FrontPage. I have already created Web pages for myself and for friends.

Please take the time to respond to my inquiry, or pass this letter on to someone else at Cornerstone. I look forward to hearing from you.

Sincerely,

Elizabeth O'Meara
622 East 122nd Street
Indianapolis, IN 46220

Elizabeth O'Meara
622 East 122nd Street
Indianapolis, IN 46220

Elizabeth O'Meara
622 East 122nd Street
Indianapolis, IN 46220

Elizabeth O'Meara
622 East 122nd Street
Indianapolis, IN 46220

Elizabeth O'Meara
622 East 122nd Street
Indianapolis, IN 46220

On Your Own

1. Create a new document in Word.

2. Save the document as **OWD12**.

3. Draft a personal business letter to your employer asking to take a vacation day in the coming month. You can also draft a personal letter to a company with whom you do business asking for a credit on returned merchandise. Record stores, clothing stores, or sporting goods stores are companies you may use.

4. Create an envelope for your letter.

5. Create your own mailing labels using the return address from your letter.

6. Save your changes, close the document, and exit Word when you are finished.

Exercise 13

Skills Covered:

◆ **Internet Basics** ◆ **Access the Internet from Word**
◆ **The Favorites Folder**

On the Job

Log on to the Internet to access information on any subject and to communicate with other people. Use Word's Internet features to make using the Internet easy and familiar.

Your supervisor at State-of-the-Art Solutions is going to Salt Lake City to meet a new client. She has asked you to get information about flights from Los Angeles to Salt Lake. In this exercise, you will access the Internet directly from Word to locate information about flight schedules and fares on Southwest airlines. You will add the site to your Favorites folder before disconnecting.

Terms

Modem A hardware device that controls communication connections between computers.

Internet A worldwide network of computers.

World Wide Web A system for finding information on the Internet through the use of linked documents.

ISP (Internet Service Provider) A company that provides access to the Internet for a fee.

Web browser Software that makes it easy to locate and view information available on the World Wide Web. Common browsers include Internet Explorer and Netscape Navigator.

Web site A set of linked Web pages.

Web page A document stored on the World Wide Web.

Uniform Resource Locator (URL) An address on the Internet.

Hyperlinks or links Text or graphics in a document set up to provide a direct connection with a destination location or document. When you click a hyperlink, the destination displays.

Shareware Software that can be downloaded from the Internet for free or for a nominal fee.

Notes

Internet Basics

■ Anyone with a computer, a **modem**, communications software, and a standard phone line can access the **Internet** and the **World Wide Web**.

■ For a fee, **Internet Service Providers (ISP)** provide you with an e-mail account, **Web Browser** software, and Internet access.

■ To locate a **Web site**, **Web page**, or document, you enter its Internet address, or **Uniform Resource Locator (URL)**.

■ If you don't know the URL of a site, you can search the Web for the site you want.

✓ *Searching the Internet is covered in Exercise 14.*

- Most sites provide **hyperlinks** (also called **links**), to related pages or sites. Text links are usually a different color and underlined to stand out from the surrounding text. Graphics may also be used as links.

- When the mouse pointer rests on a link, the pointer changes to a hand with a pointing finger, and a ScreenTip shows the destination.

Links on a Web page

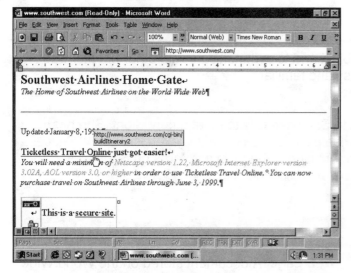

- Some things available via the Internet and World Wide Web include e-mail communication, product information and support, shopping, stock quotes, travel arrangements, real estate information, **shareware,** and games.

Access the Internet from Word

- If you have a connection to the Internet and Web browser software, you can access the Internet directly from Word.

- Word provides access to the Internet through menus and toolbar buttons.

- Word can remain running while you use the Internet, so you can go back and forth from Word to the Internet sites that you have open on your browser.

- You can move back and forth through the Web sites you have visited during the current Internet session.

- Office 2000 comes with the Internet Explorer 5 Web browser, although your computer may be set up to use a different browser.

  ✓ *This exercise assumes you are using Internet Explorer. If your computer is set up to use a different browser, ask your instructor for directions.*

The Favorites Folder

- When you set up Office 2000, it creates a folder called Favorites.

  ✓ *If you are running Windows 95 with IE4 or Windows 98, you will already have a Favorites folder.*

- Use the Favorites folder to store the URLs of Web sites you like to access frequently.

- You can also add locally stored files and folders to your Favorites folder.

- The easiest way to add a URL to the Favorites folder is to use your Web browser.

- Access the Favorites folder from Word, from Windows, or from your Web browser when you want to go directly to one of your favorite sites.

The Favorites Folder list in Word

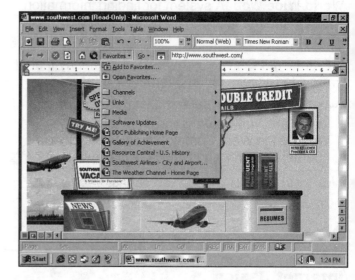

The Web toolbar

Procedures

Access Internet from Word

Display Web toolbar:

1. Click **V**iew .... Alt + V
2. Select **T**oolbars .... T
3. Click **Web**............... ⊞, Enter

   OR

   Right-click on any toolbar and select **Web**.

Go to specific URL:

1. Click **G**o button Go ▾ ... Alt + G
2. Click **O**pen .... O
3. Type the URL.
4. Click **OK**.......................... Enter

   ✓ *Word starts the process for connecting your computer to the Internet. Once connected, it locates and displays the site. You must provide the necessary information to complete the log in.*

Use hyperlink:

1. Move mouse pointer to touch link.
2. Click left mouse button.

Display previously displayed Web page:

- Click **Back** button ⇐ on the Browser's toolbar.

   OR

1. Click **G**o .... Alt + G
2. Click **B**ack........................... B

Display next Web page:

- Click **Forward** button ⇒ on the Browser's toolbar.

   ✓ *If the Back or Forward button is dimmed on the toolbar, there is no page to go to.*

   OR

1. Click **G**o...................... Alt + G
2. Click **F**orward .... F

Disconnect from the Internet from Word (Alt+C):

1. Right-click **connection icon** in Systray.
2. Click **Disconnect from Internet**.

Disconnect from Internet from Word while using your Web browser:

1. Click **Document Close** button X.

   OR

   a. Click **F**ile .... Alt + F
   b. Click **C**lose.................... C

   ✓ *Your browser will ask if you want to disconnect.*

2. Click **Y**es .... Alt + Y

   ✓ *Your browser may prompt you with a different question, such as do you want to hang up?, or do you want to disconnect?. Select the response that is appropriate.*

The Favorites Folder

Use your browser to add a site to your Favorites folder:

1. Open Internet site to add to Favorites.
2. Click **F**avorites .... Alt + A
3. Click **A**dd to Favorites .... A
4. Type site name if necessary .... Alt + N

   ✓ *Your browser automatically enters a site name. You can edit it if you want.*

5. Click **OK** .... Enter

Use Word to add a file to your Favorites folder:

1. Open file to add to Favorites.
2. Click **Favorites** button  on Web toolbar.
3. Click **A**dd to Favorites .... A

   ✓ *The Add to Favorites dialog box is similar to the Save As dialog box.*

4. Type a file name.
5. Click **Add** button .... Enter

Go to a site from your Favorites folder:

1. Click **Favorites** button Favorites ▾ on Web toolbar.
2. Click site name.

   ✓ *If necessary, Word starts your Web browser to connect to the Internet and display the site.*

Exercise Directions

✓ *Use the Internet simulation provided on the CD that accompanies this book to complete this exercise.*

1. Start Word, if necessary.
2. Display the Web toolbar.
3. Open the Internet Simulation:
   a. Click **Go**.
   b. Click **Open**.
   c. In the Address line type the following: D:/Internet/EX13/southwest.htm

      ✓ *If you've copied the Internet simulation files to your hard drive or your CD-ROM drive is a letter other than D:, substitute the correct letter for D.*

   d. Click **OK**.
4. Scroll through the site and read the information provided.
5. Scroll back to the top of the page and click the book labeled *Flight Schedule*.

   ✓ *The book is a graphical hyperlink. The Web page opens in your browser.*

6. Select *Los Angeles* in the Depart *list*.
7. Select *Salt Lake City* in the Arrive *list*.
8. Select the date *August 15*. The Web page should look similar to the one in Illustration A.
9. Click the *Display Schedule* button.
10. Read the flight schedule that is displayed and note the earliest non-stop flight.
11. Click the *Return Schedule* button.
12. Note the last non-stop flight back to L.A.
13. Click the *Back* button on the browser toolbar.
14. Click the *Display Fares* button.
15. Note the best price for a roundtrip ticket.
16. Click the *Back* button on the browser toolbar.
17. Click the *Forward* button on the browser toolbar to check the fares again.
18. Click the *Index link* at the top of the page.
19. Click the *City Information* link.
20. Click *Salt Lake City*.
21. Read the page that is displayed, and note the distance from the airport to the downtown area.
22. Add the page to your Favorites folder.
23. Exit the simulation.
24. Close any open documents and exit Word.

Illustration A

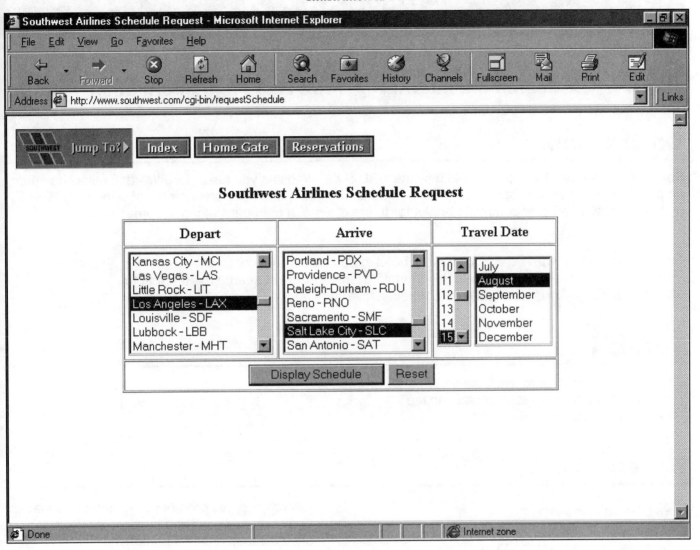

On Your Own

1. If you have access to the Internet, use it to locate a Web site about something that interests you. You can find URLs in newspapers and magazines, in advertisements, and on products. For example, go to a Web site for your hometown newspaper, for a sports team that you follow, or for a product you enjoy.

2. Test out links from the site to other sites on the Internet.

3. When you find a site you like, add it to your Favorites folder.

4. When you are finished, disconnect from the Internet, and exit Word.

Exercise 14

On the Job

Search the Internet when you do not know the URL of the Web site you need. Use Word to select a search engine that can display a list of Web sites that match the information you are looking for. When the Web page is displayed on your computer, print it for future reference or to pass along to someone else.

Your supervisor has asked you to locate a hotel in Salt Lake City in case she needs to spend the night there after her meeting with a new client. In this exercise, you will search the Internet for hotels in Salt Lake City. You will print some of the information that you find.

Terms

Search engine Software available on the Internet that searches for Web sites containing the information you are looking for.

Notes

Search the Internet

- The Internet and World Wide Web contain millions of pages of information.

- If you do not know the URL for a Web site, you can use one of a number of available **search engines** to locate the site.

Select a search engine with Internet Explorer 5

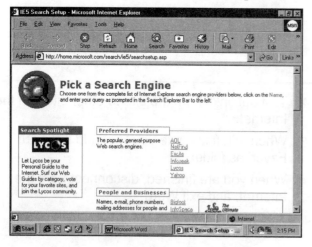

- Search engines prompt you to enter information, and then they display a hyperlinked list of Web sites containing that information.

- The search results vary depending on the information you type and the search engine you use.

- For a successful search, enter specific information, such as a full company name.

Print Web Page Information

- You can print a Web page displayed in Word or displayed in your browser.

- The commands for printing a Web page are the same as for printing a regular Word document.

- Many Web sites contain graphics, such as photographs and artwork. Some printers may not be able to print the graphical content of a Web page.

Procedures

Search Internet

✓ You must have an Internet connection and an account with an ISP in order to Search the Internet or Web. When prompted, you must enter an ID and/or password in order to gain access.

1. Display Web toolbar.
2. Click **Search the Web** button 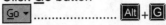.

   OR

a. Click **Go** button

   Go ▾ .... Alt + G

b. Click **Search the Web** ... W

✓ The Search site options will vary depending on ISP. Typical Search sites include Yahoo!, AltaVista, Lycos, Infoseek, and Excite.

3. Click desired search engine.
4. Type search topic in Search text box.
5. Click **Search** button.

   ✓ Button names will vary.

✓ The name on the search button (Find It, Go Get It, etc.) will vary depending on the Search site.

6. Click a hyperlink on the Search Results page to go to that site.

Print Web Page Information
(Ctrl+P)

1. Display the desired Web page.
2. Click **File**..................... Alt + F
3. Click **Print**.......................... P
4. Click **OK** .... Enter

Exercise Directions

✓ Use the Internet simulation provided on the CD that accompanies this book to complete this exercise.

1. Start Word, if necessary.
2. Display the Web toolbar.
3. Open the Internet Simulation:
   a. Click **Go**.
   b. Click **Open**.
   c. In the Address line type the following:
      D:/Internet/E14/altavista.htm

   ✓ If you've copied the Internet simulation files to your hard drive or your CD-ROM drive is a letter other than D:, substitute the correct letter for D.

   d. Click **OK**.
4. In the Search text box type *Salt Lake City Hotels*.

   ✓ The simulation uses the search site AltaVista. If you are using a live Internet connection instead of the simulation, the results of the search will vary depending on the search site used. To use AltaVista, go to the URL http://www.Altavista.com.
5. Click the *Search* button.

6. Click the number 1 link in the search results list, *Motels or Hotels in Salt Lake City Utah*.
7. Click the *Back* button to return to the search results page.
8. Click the number 2 link, *Hotels Lodging Salt Lake City Utah Travelodge City Center Inn Accommodations*.
9. Scroll down the page to read about the hotel.
10. Click the link *Click Here to View map*. The map Web page should look similar to the one in Illustration A.
11. Print the map Web page.
12. Click the *Back* button to go back to the previous page.
13. Add the page to your Favorites folder.
14. Print the page with the information about the *City Center Travelodge*.
15. Exit the simulation.
16. Close all open documents and exit Word.

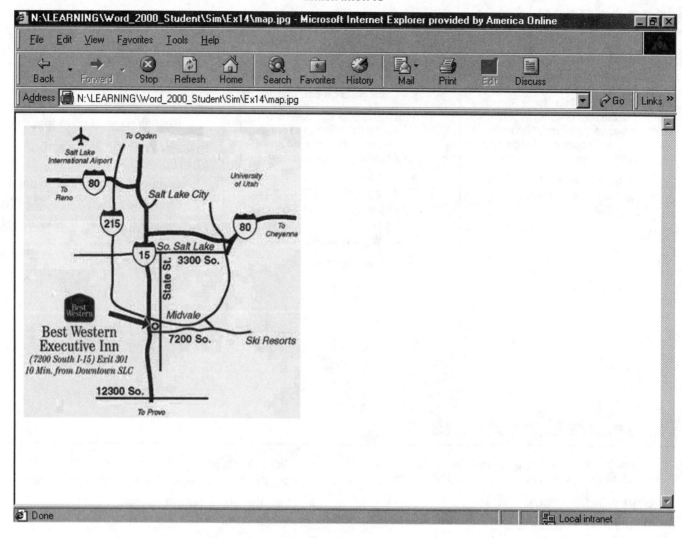

On Your Own

1. If you have access to the Internet, use Word to select a search engine.
2. Search for a Web site about something of interest to you. For example, search for information about a performer, a location, or a subject.
3. Select a few sites from the search results list.
4. Add one that you like to your Favorites folder.
5. Print the Web page.
6. When you are finished, disconnect from the Internet, and exit Word.

Exercise 15

◆ Critical Thinking

State-of-the Art Solutions is planning a seminar on conducting business on the Internet. In this summary exercise, you will use the skills you have learned in Lesson Two to create a letter for your supervisor inquiring about room available at a hotel in Phoenix, AZ. First, you will search the Internet to locate information about a facility. Next, you will create the letter and an envelope. Finally, you will create return address labels.

Exercise Directions

✓ Use the Internet simulation provided on the CD that accompanies this book to complete the first part of this exercise.

1. Start Word, if necessary.

2. Create a new document and save it with the name **WD15-1**.

3. Display the Web toolbar.

4. Open the Internet Simulation:

   a. Click **Go**.

   b. Click **Open**.

   c. In the Address line type the following: D:/Internet/E15/altavista.htm

   ✓ If you've copied the Internet simulation files to your hard drive or your CD-ROM drive is a letter other than D:, substitute the correct letter for D.

   d. Click **OK**.

5. Search for *Hotels in Phoenix Arizona*.

6. Click link 2: *Northwest Lodging, Inc. – Howard Johnson Hotels & Inns*.

7. Scroll down the page and click the *more info* link.

8. Print the informational page that is displayed.

9. Go back to the previous page.

10. Print that page.

11. Exit the simulation.

12. In the **WD15-1** document, display non-printing characters.

13. Make sure AutoCorrect is on.

14. Type the letter in Illustration A exactly as shown, including all circled errors.

15. Insert the current date in the Month Day, Year format.

16. Create an AutoText entry called *sasaddress* for State-of-the-Art's return address.

17. Correct spelling errors.

    • Ignore the writer's last name.

18. Correct grammatical errors.

19. Use the thesaurus to find an appropriate replacement for the word *need*, in the second sentence of the second paragraph.

20. Save the changes you made to the document.

21. Preview the document.

22. Preview the document in Full Screen View.

23. If necessary, use Shrink to Fit to make sure the letter will print on a single page.

24. Create an envelope for the letter and add it to the document. Omit the return address.

25. Print the document.

    Create a full page of return address mailing labels for State-of-the-Art Solutions. Use the sasaddress AutoText entry to enter the address in the Envelopes and Labels dialog box.

26. Save the label document with the name **WD15-2**.

27. Preview the **WD15-2** document and print it.

28. Close all open documents and exit Word, saving all changes.

Month Date, Year *Insert today's date*

Manager
Howard Johnson Inn
3400 N. W. Grand Ave.
Phoenix, AZ 85017

Dear Sir or Madam:

My company, State of the Art Solutions, is sponsoring a seminar on February 9 and February 10 of the coming year. I am writing to inquire about room availability at your hotel for these dates.

The seminar is limited in size, and I believe the Howard Johnson Inn in Phoenix is exceptionally suited for our needs. We would need accommodataions for appromixately 25 attendees. In addition, we would require meeting facilities and catering services for both day I have already visited your Web site and printed selected pages, however, I would also apreciate any additional information you can provide.

Please used the enclosed return address label to respond as soon as possible, or write to the address below. I hope to finalize arrangements for the seminar within the month.

Thank you in advance for your consideration. I look forward to working with you in the future.

Sincerely,

Justin Godere
Seminar COordinator
State of the Art Solutions
P.O. Box 6743211   *Create sasaddress*
Brentwood, CA 90049   *Autotext entry*

JG/yo
enclosure

Lesson 3

Open and Edit Documents

Exercise 16

Skills Covered:

◆ **Open a Recently Saved Document**

◆ **Open a Document Not Recently Saved** ◆ **Save As**

On the Job

When you are ready to revise and improve a document that you've already created and saved, open it again in Word. Use the Save As command to leave the original document unchanged, and save a copy of the document with a new name or in a new location.

The marketing director at State-of-the-Art Solutions has decided to expand the press release about the agreement with Cornerstone Graphics to include information about the planned seminar. In this exercise, you will open the press release document and save it with a new name. You will then add two paragraphs and save the changes. Finally, you will print the document.

Terms

Revise Edit, change, or update a document.

Places bar A strip of buttons on the left side of certain dialog boxes used to open common folders quickly.

Notes

Open a Recently Saved Document

- To **revise** a document that has been saved and closed, open it in Word.
- The four most recently opened documents are listed at the bottom of the File menu.

Recently opened files

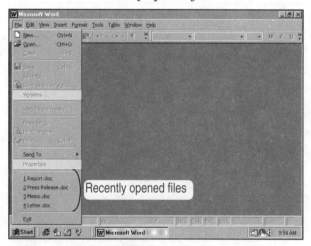

- Click on a document to open it.

Open a Document Not Recently Saved

- Any document stored on disk can be opened from Word, no matter when it was last used.
- Use the Open dialog box to locate and open stored files.

Open dialog box

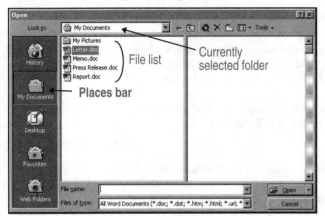

Save As

- The Save As feature lets you save a copy of a document in a different location or with a different file name.
- Use the Save As command to leave the original document unchanged while you edit the new copy.

Save As dialog box

Procedures

Open Recently Saved Document

1. Click **File** .... **Alt**+**F**
2. Click document name at bottom of menu.

Open Document Not Recently Saved *(Ctrl+O)*

1. Click **Open** button 📂.
   OR
   a. Click **File** .... **Alt**+**F**
   b. Click **Open** .... **O**

2. Click **Look in** drop-down arrow .... **Alt**+**I**
3. Select drive or folder.
   ✓ *If necessary double-click folder name.*
   OR
   Click folder in **Places** bar to open it.
4. Double-click document name.
   OR
   Click **Open** .... **O**

Save As

1. Click **File** .... **Alt**+**F**
2. Click **Save As** .... **A**
3. Type new file name.
4. Select new drive and/or folder.
5. Click **Save** button
   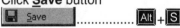 .... **Alt**+**S**

Exercise Directions

1. Start Word, if necessary.
2. Open 💿 **16PRESS**.
   ✓ *If necessary ask your instructor where this file is located.*
3. Save the document as **WD16**.
4. Add the two paragraphs shown in Illustration A to the end of the document.

5. Check the spelling and grammar, correcting all errors.
6. Save the changes.
7. Preview the document.
8. Print the document.
9. Close the document and exit Word, saving all changes.

State-of-the-Art Solutions and Cornerstone Graphics Announce Agreement

Brentwood, CA and Venice, CA – State-of-the-Art Solutions, a consulting company specializing in helping small businesses expand using the Internet and World Wide Web, and Cornerstone Graphics, a small but successful graphics design firm, announced that they will begin cooperating on specific accounts. According to principals at both companies, the agreement is intended to bring a superior level of service to clients.

"Our combined expertise virtually guarantees satisfaction to clients of both companies," claimed Maryanne Costello, Vice President of Marketing at State-of-the-Art. Cornerstone's president Tom Louris agreed.

New paragraphs

To celebrate the new partnership, the two companies are jointly sponsoring a seminar on conducting business on the World Wide Web. Scheduled for next February, the seminar will feature workshops and roundtable discussions aimed at small businesses interested in using the Internet to expand.

For more information, contact State-of-the-Art Solutions at 310-555-0821 or Cornerstone Graphics at 213-555-2597.

On Your Own

1. Open **OWD10**, the document you created in the On Your Own section of Exercise 10, or open ☉ **16NEWS**.

2. Save the document as **OWD16**.

3. Expand the document by adding a paragraph or two to the end. You might add information about using the Internet and World Wide Web, or information about your progress to date.

4. Check the spelling and grammar in the document.

5. Save your changes, close the document, and exit Word when you are finished.

Exercise 17

On the Job

Making changes to existing documents is a key benefit of using Word 2000. Instead of retyping a document to make revisions, you simply open the stored document and add or replace text. You can save the changes to the original document, or use the Save As command to save the changes in a new document.

Many employees of The Big Cheese gourmet food shop have expressed concern over the new vacation policy. You have decided to revise the policy. In this exercise, you will open the vacation policy document and save it with a new name. You will then revise the document and save the changes. Finally, you will print the document so you can post it in the shop.

Terms

Insert mode The method of operation used for inserting new text within existing text in a document. Insert mode is the default.

Overtype mode The method of operation used to replace existing text in a document with new text.

Case The specific use of upper- or lowercase letters.

Proofreaders' marks Symbols written on a printed document to indicate where revisions are required.

Notes

Insert Text

- By default, you insert new text in a document in **Insert mode**. Existing text moves to the right as you type to make room for new text.
- You can insert text anywhere in a document.
- You can also insert nonprinting characters, including paragraph marks to start a new paragraph, tabs, and spaces.

Overtype Mode

- To replace text as you type, use **Overtype mode**.
- In Overtype mode, existing characters do not shift right to make room for new characters. Instead, new characters replace existing characters as you type, deleting existing characters.

- Overtype mode is useful when you have to replace an entire block of text.
- Most editing should be done in Insert mode so you do not accidentally type over text that you need.

Uppercase Mode

- Use Uppercase mode to type all capital letters without pressing the Shift key.
- Uppercase mode affects only letter characters.
- When Uppercase mode is on, the Caps Lock indicator on your keyboard is lit.

Change Case

- You can automatically change the **case** of text in a document.
- There are five case options:
  - Sentence case: First character in sentence is uppercase.
  - lowercase: All characters are lowercase.
  - UPPERCASE: All characters are uppercase.
  - Title Case: First character in each word is uppercase.
  - tOGGLE cASE: Case is reversed for all characters.

Change Case dialog box

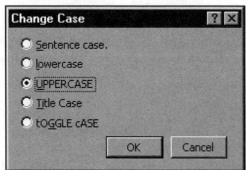

Proofreaders' Marks

- Often you may need to revise a Word document based on a marked-up printed copy of the document. **Proofreaders' marks** on printed documents are written symbols that indicate where to make revisions.
- Following is a list of common proofreaders' marks:
  - ∿∿∿∿ indicates text to be bold.
  - ∧ indicates where new text should be inserted.
  - ⌐ℐ indicates text to be deleted.
  - ¶ indicates where a new paragraph should be inserted.
  - ≡ indicates that a letter should be capitalized.
  - ———— indicates text to be italicized.
  - (highlight) indicates text to highlight.
  -] [indicates text to center.

Procedures

Insert Text

1. Position insertion point to right of character where you want to insert new text.
2. Type new text.

Overtype Mode

1. Position insertion point to left of first character you want to replace.
2. Press **Insert** key.................. Ins

   OR

   Double-click **OVR** indicator OVR on status bar.

   ✓ *OVR indicator appears in bold when active.*
3. Type new text.

Turn Off Overtype Mode

- Press **Insert** key again .... Ins

  OR

- Double-click **OVR** indicator OVR again.

  ✓ *OVR indicator appears dimmed when inactive.*

Uppercase Mode

1. Press **Caps Lock** key .... Caps Lock
2. Type text.

To Turn Off Uppercase mode:

- Press **Caps Lock** key .... Caps Lock

Change Case

1. Select text.

   OR

   Position insertion point where new text will begin.
2. Click **Format**............... Alt + O
3. Click **Change Case** .... E
4. Click the case you want:
   - **Sentence case**............... S
   - **lowercase** L
   - **UPPERCASE** .... U
   - **Title Case**.................... T
   - **tOGGLE cASE**.............. G
5. Click **OK**........................ Enter

Exercise Directions

1. Start Word, if necessary.
2. Open ⊚ **17VACATE**.

   ✓ *If necessary, ask your instructor where this file is located.*

3. Save the document as **WD17**.
4. Make the revisions as indicated in Illustration A.

   a. Insert new text as marked.

   b. Use Overtype mode to replace text as necessary.

   c. Change case as marked.

5. Check the spelling and grammar.
6. Preview the document.
7. Print the document.
8. Close the document and exit Word, saving all changes.

Illustration A

THE BIG CHEESE VACATION POLICY ⟵ *Change to Title case*

I hope that this notice will help clear up any questions you have.
~~I would like all employees to be aware of our new vacation policy~~. As of January 1, vacation time will be <u>directly related to the number of hours worked each month</u>. ⁋Specifically, employees will earn 8 hours of vacation time for every 120 hours worked.

The new policy does not affect vacation time you may have already earned. As always, you must clear vacation time with your manager to be sure you are not put on the schedule. ⁋<u>Please contact me if you have any questions about this policy</u>.

That means that if you regularly work a 40-hour week, you will earn one day of vacation every three weeks. To earn five vacation days, you must work 600 hours, or FIFTEEN WEEKS.

On Your Own

1. Open **OWD12**, the document you created in the On Your Own section of Exercise 12, or open ⊚ **17LETTER** .
2. Save the document as **OWD17**.
3. Make revisions to the document using Insert mode and Overtype mode.

   • If your letter requests a vacation day from your employer, you might revise the letter by requesting an additional vacation day or informing the employer that you need to change the date of the vacation day.

   • If your letter asks for a credit on returned merchandise, you might revise the letter by following up on your first request. State that you have not yet heard anything about the request and that you would like to know when to expect a response.

4. Save your changes, close the document, and exit Word when you are finished.

Exercise 18

Skills Covered:

◆ **Delete Text** ◆ **Use Undo** ◆ **Use Redo**

On the Job

Delete unwanted text from a document. If you don't like the changes you make, you can reverse them using the Undo command. If you decide that you want to keep the changes, you can use the Redo command to reverse an Undo action.

Jonathan Randolph, the chairman of GRONE, a trade organization for gourmet food retailers, has asked you, his assistant, for help on the membership drive. In this exercise, you will open and save a membership letter. Then, you will revise the letter so you can send it to a different prospective member.

Terms

Undo The command for reversing a previous action.

Redo The command for reversing the Undo command.

Acronym A word made up of the first letters of words in a phrase.

Notes

Delete Text

- Use the Delete command to remove text, graphics, or nonprinting characters from anywhere in a document.
- Use the Delete command to correct typing errors and to remove unwanted text from a document.
- You can delete selected text by replacing it with new text or by pressing the Delete key.

Use Undo

- Use the **Undo** command to reverse a single action made in error, such as deleting the wrong word.
- The Undo command also lets you change your mind about an entire series of actions used to edit or format a document.

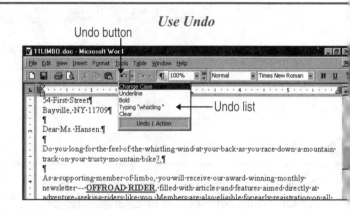

Use Undo

- If the Undo command and the Undo button are dimmed, there are no actions that can be undone

Use Redo

- Use the **Redo** command to reverse actions that you undo.
- When there are no actions to redo, the Repeat command is available from the Edit menu in place of Redo. Use Repeat to repeat the most recent action.

Procedures

Delete Character

1. Position insertion point to left of character or space to delete.
2. Press **Delete** key .... `Del`

OR

1. Place insertion point to right of character or space to delete.
2. Press **Backspace** key .... `Backspace`

Delete Word

1. Place insertion point to right of word to delete.
2. Press and hold **Ctrl** key ...... `Ctrl`
3. Press **Backspace** key .... `Backspace`

OR

1. Place insertion point to left of word to delete.
2. Press and hold **Ctrl** key ...... `Ctrl`
3. Press **Delete** key .... `Del`

Delete Selected Text

1. Select text to delete.
2. Press **Delete** key .... `Del`

OR

1. Select text to delete.
2. Press **Backspace** key .... `Backspace`

Replace Selected Text

1. Select text to replace.
2. Type new text.

Undo Previous Action *(Ctrl+Z)*

- Click **Undo** button � .

OR

1. Click **Edit** .... `Alt`+`E`

   ✓ A description of the last action will be listed on the Edit menu.

2. Click **Undo** .... `U`

Undo Series of Actions *(Ctrl+Z)*

- Click **Undo** button � repeatedly.

OR

1. Click **Undo** drop-down arrow .

   ✓ The most recent action is listed at the top of the Undo drop-down list.

2. Click last action in the series to undo all previous actions.

Redo Previous Action *(Ctrl+Y)*

- Click **Redo** button ↻ .

OR

1. Click **Edit** .... `Alt`+`E`
2. Click **Redo** .... `R`

Redo Series of Actions *(Ctrl+Y)*

- Click **Redo** button ↻ repeatedly.

OR

1. Click **Redo** drop-down arrow ▾ .
2. Click the last action in the series to redo all previous actions.

Repeat Previous Action *(Ctrl+Y or F4)*

1. Click **Edit** .... `Alt`+`E`
2. Click **Repeat** .... `R`

Exercise Directions

1. Start Word, if necessary.
2. Open ✪ **18GRONE**.
3. Save the document as **WD18**.
4. Select and delete the words *Month*, *Date*, *Year*, and insert the current date in their place.
5. Delete then replace the inside address as marked in the illustration.
6. Edit the salutation text as marked.
7. Delete the third paragraph.

   ✓ Don't forget to delete the blank line following it as well.

8. Select the **acronym** *grone* in the third sentence of the first paragraph.
9. Change the selected word to all uppercase.
10. Change all other occurrences of the acronym to uppercase.

   ✓ You can use the Edit, Repeat command.

11. Undo all of the previous change-case actions.
12. Redo the change-case actions.
13. Select the entire document and change it to Toggle Case.
14. Undo the case change.
15. Check the spelling and grammar in the document and make all necessary corrections.
16. Save the changes.
17. Preview the document.
18. Print the document.
19. Close the document and exit Word, saving all changes.

~~Month Date, Year~~ *Today's date*

Ms. Deborah ~~Hansen~~   *Mr. Tyrone Barrows*
54 First Street   *1556 Mass Avenue*
Cambridge, MA 02141   *Boston, MA 02116*

Dear ~~Ms. Hansen~~: *Mr. Barrows*

Are you thrilled by the sight of fine ripe Brie? Do you get goose bumps contemplating a bowl of Ziti al dente with Pesto sauce? If so, then you should consider becoming a member of (grone), Gourmet Retailers of New England.

u.c. (Grone) is an association of discerning shopkeepers such as yourself. Formed in 1985, *u.c.* (grone) was originally started by ten people looking for ways to meet and share information about the gourmet food industry. Now that the organization has grown to more than 150 members, we offer much more than networking opportunities.

Grone sponsors monthly meetings on various topics. In the past we have invited guest speakers, hosted wine tasting evenings, and conducted customer surveys to help our members better meet the needs of their clients.

u.c. Increasing business is just one of the benefits of becoming part of grone. As a member of (grone) you will receive a subscription to our award-winning publication -- Eat Hearty, filled with articles and features aimed directly at quality-savvy marketers like you. Members also receive information about trade events in the area, and are eligible for discounts at many area merchants.

We look forward to seeing you at our next meeting!

Sincerely,

Jonathan Randolph
Chairman

jr/yo

On Your Own

1. Create a new document in Word.

2. Save the file as **OWD18**.

3. Draft a letter that could be sent to more than one person or organization. For example, the letter might ask for contributions to a fund-raising drive for your school club, band, or athletic team. Perhaps you could ask for contributions to help support an upcoming trip your group wants to make.

4. Save the letter.

5. Save the letter with a different name, **OWD18-2**.

6. Revise the letter so you can send it to a different person or organization.

7. Save the changes, close the document, and exit Word.

Exercise 19

Skills Covered:

◆ **Move Text** ◆ **Use Cut and Paste** ◆ **Use Drag-and-Drop Editing**
◆ **Move a Paragraph**

On the Job

Move text to rearrange a document quickly without retyping existing information. You can move any amount of text from a single character to an entire page.

The training director at State-of-the-Art Solutions has asked you to create a memo listing the classes for the coming week. In this exercise, you will create a memo to all employees and type a list of the courses. You will then rearrange the list using cut and paste and drag-and-drop editing.

Terms

Cut To delete a selection from its original location and store it in the Clipboard.

Paste To insert a selection from the Clipboard into a document.

Clipboard A temporary storage area that can hold up to twelve selections at a time.

Drag-and-drop editing The action of using a mouse to drag a selection from its original location and drop it in a new location.

Notes

Move Text

- While editing, you may decide you need to move text that is already typed in a document to a new location.
- Word's move commands can save you from deleting and retyping text.
- Be sure to consider nonprinting characters when you select text to move:
  - Select the space following a word or sentence to move along with text.
  - Select the paragraph mark following a paragraph or line to move paragraph formatting with text.
- Use Undo to reverse a move that you made unintentionally.

Use Cut and Paste

- Use the **Cut** and **Paste** commands to move text in a document.
- The Cut command deletes selected text from its original location and places it in the **Clipboard**, a temporary storage area.
- The Paste command copies the selection from the Clipboard to the insertion point location.
- Up to twelve selections can remain in the Clipboard at one time.
- Use the Clipboard toolbar to access selections for pasting.

Clipboard toolbar

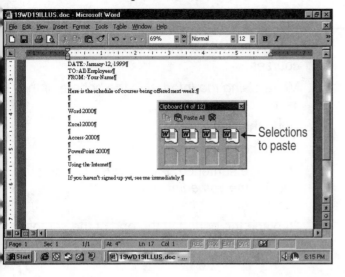

Use Drag-and-Drop Editing

■ Use **drag-and-drop editing** to move text with the mouse.

■ Drag-and-drop editing is convenient when you can see the text to move and the new location on screen at the same time.

Move a Paragraph

■ You can quickly move an entire paragraph up or down in a document.

Procedures

Move Text

1. Select text to move.
2. Press **F2**............................. `F2`
3. Position insertion point at new location.
4. Press **Enter**...................... `Enter`

Use Cut and Paste to Move Text *(Ctrl+X, Cltr+V)*

1. Select text to move.
2. Click **Cut** button `✂`.
   OR
   a. Click **Edit** .... `Alt`+`E`
   b. Click **Cut** .... `T`
3. Position insertion point in new location.
4. Click **Paste** button `📋`.

OR
a. Click **Edit**............... `Alt`+`E`
b. Click **Paste**.................... `P`

Use Clipboard Toolbar

1. Click **View** .... `Alt`+`V`
2. Select **Toolbars** .... `T`
3. Click **Clipboard**.
4. Position insertion point.
5. Click item to paste.
   ✓ Use ScreenTips to identify selections.

Use Drag-and-Drop Editing to Move Text

1. Select text to move.
2. Move mouse pointer anywhere over selected text.
3. Drag selection to new location.

✓ As you drag, mouse pointer changes to a box with a dotted shadow attached to an arrow. Selection does not move until you drop it in step 4.

4. Release mouse button when insertion point is in new location.

Move Paragraph

1. Position insertion point anywhere within paragraph to move.
2. Press .... `Alt`+`Shift`+`↑`
   OR
   Press .... `Alt`+`Shift`+`↓`
3. Repeat step 2 until paragraph is in desired location.

Exercise Directions

1. Start Word, if necessary.
2. Open ⊘**19LIST**.
3. Save the document as **WD19**.
4. Use the following steps to revise the document so it resembles the document shown in Illustration A.
5. Insert a blank line at the beginning of the document.
6. Use Click and Type to enter the word *Memorandum* centered on the first line.
7. Insert eight blank lines at the beginning of the document to move the first line of text down approximately 1.5".
8. Change the word *Memorandum* to all uppercase.
9. Insert four blank lines before the date.
10. Replace the sample date with the correct date.
11. Change the words *Date:, To:, From:,* and *Regarding* to all uppercase.
12. Insert one blank line between each paragraph of text in the remainder of the document.
13. Move *Office 2000* to the top of the list of courses.
14. Move *Using the Internet* to the bottom of the list of courses.
15. Undo the move.
16. Redo the move.
17. Move the sentence: *If you haven't signed up yet see me immediately* to the end of the document.
18. Replace the period at the end of the sentence: *Here is the list of courses being offered next week* with a colon.
19. If you forgot to move blank lines along with the paragraphs, insert the blank lines now.
20. Check the spelling and grammar in the document and correct errors.
21. Preview the document. It should look similar to the one in Illustration A.
22. Print the document.
23. Save the document.
24. Close the document and exit Word.

Illustration A

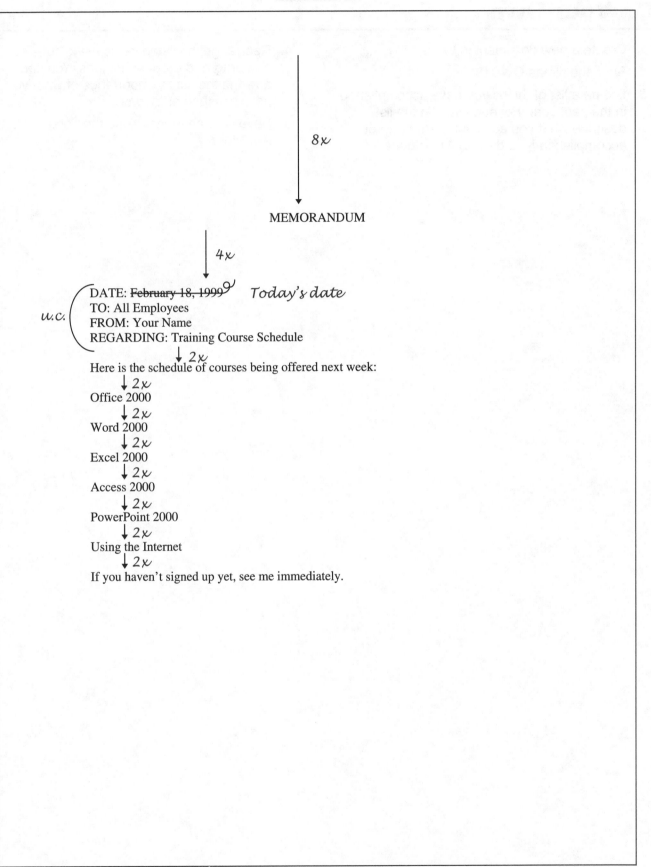

8x

MEMORANDUM

4x

DATE: ~~February 18, 1999~~ *Today's date*

u.c. { TO: All Employees
FROM: Your Name
REGARDING: Training Course Schedule

2x

Here is the schedule of courses being offered next week:

2x

Office 2000

2x

Word 2000

2x

Excel 2000

2x

Access 2000

2x

PowerPoint 2000

2x

Using the Internet

2x

If you haven't signed up yet, see me immediately.

On Your Own

1. Create a new document in Word.

2. Save the file as **OWD19**.

3. Create a list of things you have accomplished in the past year. For each item in the list, describe what you accomplished, how you accomplished it, and when it was done.

4. Rearrange the listed items using cut-and-paste and drag-and-drop techniques. You can arrange the list by importance of what you accomplished or by date.

5. Save your changes, close the document, and exit Word.

Exercise 20

◆ **Use Copy and Paste** ◆ **Use the Drag-and-Drop Feature to Copy**
◆ **Copy Text from a Web Page into a Word Document**

On the Job

Copy or move text from one location to another to speed up your work and avoid repetitive typing. You can copy or move any amount of text from a single character to an entire document. You can even copy information from a Web page into a Word document.

The training director has asked you to emphasize the importance of taking the Microsoft Office 2000 course being offered at State-of-the-Art Solutions. In this exercise, you will revise the memo announcing the courses by inserting and deleting text and blank lines, and by copying existing text. You will also access a Web page with information about the Office 2000 applications and copy some of the information into the memo document.

Terms

Copy To create a duplicate of a selection and store it on the Clipboard.

Formatting Features such as color, fonts, and positioning applied to document text.

Notes

Use Copy and Paste

- Use the Copy and Paste feature to copy existing text from one location in a document and paste it to another location.

- You can also copy and paste information from one document into another document.

- The **Copy** command stores a duplicate of selected text on the Clipboard, leaving the original selection unchanged.

- The Paste command pastes the selection from the Clipboard to the insertion point location.

- You can store up to twelve selections on the Clipboard at one time.

- Use the Clipboard toolbar to choose which selection to paste into the document.

  ✓ *The Clipboard used for moving is also used for copying.*

Use the Drag-and-Drop Feature to Copy

- Use drag-and-drop editing to copy text with the mouse.

- The drag-and-drop feature is convenient when you can see the text to copy and the new location on-screen at the same time.

Copy Text from a Web Page into a Word Document

- Use Copy and Paste to copy text from a Web page into a Word document.

- Text copied from a Web page retains the Web page **formatting** when pasted in a Word document.

- The Copy and Paste commands available in your Web browser are the same as those available in Word.

Procedures

Use Copy and Paste
(Ctrl+C, Ctrl+V)

1. Select **text** to copy.
2. Click **Copy** button 📋 .
   OR
   a. Click **E**dit .... `Alt`+`E`
   b. Click **C**opy .... `C`
3. Position insertion point in new location.
4. Click **Paste** button 📋 .
   OR
   a. Click **E**dit .... `Alt`+`E`
   b. Click **P**aste................... `P`

Use Clipboard Toolbar

1. Click **V**iew .... `Alt`+`V`
2. Select **T**oolbars .... `T`
3. Click **Clipboard**.
4. Select text to copy.
5. Click **Copy** button 📋 on Clipboard toolbar.

6. Position insertion point in new location.
7. Click item to paste.
   - ✓ *Use ScreenTips to identify selections.*
   - ✓ *Click the Copy button to add subsequent selections to the clipboard. (Once the Clipboard toolbar stays open, clicking an item doesn't automatically add it to the clipboard.)*

Use Drag-and-Drop to Copy

1. Select text to copy.
2. Move mouse pointer anywhere over selected text.
3. Press and hold the **Ctrl** key .... `Ctrl`
4. Drag selection to new location .
   - ✓ *As you drag, the mouse pointer changes to a box with a dotted shadow and a plus sign attached to an arrow. The selection does not move until you drop it in step 5.*

5. Release mouse button.
6. Release **Ctrl** key .... `Ctrl`

Copy from a Web Page into a Word Document
(Ctrl+C, Ctrl+V)

1. Display Web page in Word or in your browser.
2. Double-click to position insertion point in Web page text.
3. Select text to copy.
4. Click **E**dit .... `Alt`+`E`
5. Click **C**opy .... `C`
6. Display Word document.
7. Position insertion point in new location.
8. Click **E**dit .... `Alt`+`E`
9. Click **P**aste .... `P`

Exercise Directions

1. Start Word, if necessary.
2. Open the document ⊙**20COURSE** and save it as **WD20**.
3. Revise the document so it looks like the one in the Illustration by using the following steps.
4. Delete three of the blank lines between the title (MEMORANDUM) and the date (leaving only one blank line.
5. Move the insertion point to the end of the document and insert the following text in all uppercase: *THE FOLLOWING COURSES WILL BE OFFERED AGAIN NEXT MONTH:* and then press Enter twice
6. Copy the second and last courses in the list and paste them at the end of the document, leaving a one line space between them.
7. Insert a blank line at the end of the document and type the following text: *Here is the main reason for becoming proficient in Word 2000:,* and then press Enter twice.

8. Display the Web toolbar.
9. Open the Internet Simulation:
   a. Click **Go**.
   b. Click **Open**.
   c. In the Address line type the following: D:/Internet/E20/microsoftoffice.htm
      - ✓ *If you've copied the Internet simulation files to your hard drive or your CD-ROM drive is a letter other than D:, substitute the correct letter for D.*
   d. Click **OK**.
10. Click the *Word 2000 Tour* link.
11. Select the paragraph of text under the heading *The Microsoft Office Word Processor*.
12. Copy the selected text to the Clipboard.
13. Exit the simulation.
14. Display the **WD20** document.
15. Paste the selection on the last line of the document.

16. Check the spelling and grammar in the document.

17. Preview the document. It should look similar to the one in the Illustration.

18. Print the document.

19. Save the document.

20. Close the document and exit Word saving all changes.

Illustration A

MEMORANDUM

DATE: July 21, 1999
TO: All Employees
FROM: Your Name
REGARDING: Training Course Schedule

Here is the schedule of courses being offered next week:

Office 2000

Word 2000

Excel 2000

Access 2000

PowerPoint 2000

Using the Internet

If you haven't signed up yet, see me immediately. THE FOLLOWING COURSES WILL BE OFFERED AGAIN NEXT MONTH:

Word 2000

Using the Internet

Here is the main reason for becoming proficient in Word 2000:

Microsoft Word 2000 gives you the tools to more easily create professional-quality documents and share information—in print, e-mail, and on the Web.

On Your Own

1. Create a new document in Word.

2. Save the file as **OWD20**.

3. Open the document **OWD19**, the list of your personal accomplishments for the past year, which you created in the On Your Own section of Exercise 19, or open **20LIST**.

4. Save the file as **OWD20-2**.

5. Copy each of the items from your list of accomplishments to the new document. Use these accomplishments to help build a letter in which you apply for an officer's position of a group or organization to which you might belong. For example, the group could be a school club or it could a place of employment. The officer's position could be secretary, treasurer, or president.

6. Save your changes, close all open documents, and exit Word.

Exercise 21

Skills Covered:

◆ **Send E-mail from Word**
◆ **Attach a Word Document to an E-mail Message**
◆ **Send a Word Document as E-mail**

On the Job

E-mail is suitable for jotting quick notes such as an appointment confirmation. You can create and format e-mail messages, then send the messages via Outlook or Outlook Express directly from Word. When you need to communicate in more depth, you can attach a Word document to the message, or simply send a document as the message itself. You can exchange e-mail messages via the Internet or an intranet with anyone who has an e-mail account, including coworkers located down the hall, in a different state, or halfway around the world.

You are reporting to your manager about your progress planning the Business on the Web Seminar for State-of-the-Art Solutions. In this exercise, you will create and send a brief e-mail message confirming the dates of the seminar with your boss. You will follow up with a second message to which you will attach a copy of the letter you wrote to the hotel in Phoenix. Finally, you will create a list of prospective participants and send it as e-mail to your manager.

Terms

E-mail (electronic mail) A method of sending information from one computer to another across the Internet or intranet.

HTML (Hypertext Markup Language) A universal file format used for files displayed on the World Wide Web.

Internet A global network of computers.

Intranet A network of computers within a business or organization.

Mail service provider A company that maintains and controls e-mail accounts.

Outlook 2000 A personal management application program that includes e-mail features that comes with the Office 2000 suite.

Outlook Express An e-mail application program.

E-mail address The string of characters that identifies the name and location of an e-mail user.

To: Mail notation that indicates to whom an e-mail message is addressed.

Cc: (carbon copy) Mail notation that indicates to whom you are sending a copy of the message.

Subject The title of an e-mail message.

Message window The area in an e-mail message where the message body is typed.

Online Actively connected to the Internet.

Offline Not connected to the Internet.

Attachment A document attached to an e-mail message and sent in its original file format.

Notes

Send E-mail from Word

- You can create and send **e-mail** messages directly from Word.

- You can edit and format the messages with Word's editing and formatting features, including the spelling and grammar checkers, AutoCorrect, and AutoText.

- Messages created in Word are sent in **.HTML** format so they can be read by almost all e-mail applications.

- To send e-mail messages, you must have the following:
  - A connection to the **Internet** or to an **intranet**.
  - An account with a **mail service provider**.
  - An e-mail application such as **Outlook 2000** or **Outlook Express**.
    - ✓ *To exchange e-mail, the e-mail application must be correctly configured with your e-mail account information.*

- To send an e-mail message you must know the recipient's **e-mail address**.

- E-mail messages have four basic parts:
  - The recipient's address is entered in the **To:** text box.
  - The addresses of other people receiving copies of the message are entered in the **Cc:** text box.
  - A title for the message is entered in the **Subject** text box.
  - The body of the message is typed in the **message window**.

E-mail created and formatted in Word

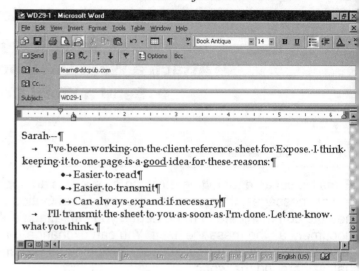

- When you send the message, Word will automatically access the Internet using your Internet connection settings.

- The Internet connection remains **online** in the background until you disconnect, then you are **offline**.

Attach a Word Document to an E-mail Message

- You can attach a Word document to an e-mail message.

- The original document remains stored on your computer, and a copy is transmitted as the **attachment**.

- An attached message is sent in its original file format.

- The message recipient can open the attached Word document on his or her computer in Word, or in another application that is compatible with Word.

Send a Word Document as E-mail

■ You can send an existing Word document as an e-mail message without attaching it to another message.

■ The original document remains stored on your computer, and a copy is transmitted as e-mail.

■ The transmitted document is sent in .HTML format so it retains its original formatting when opened in the recipient's e-mail application.

A Word document ready for transmission

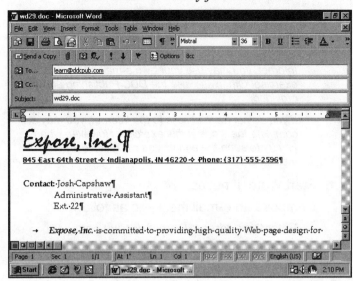

Procedures

Send E-mail Message From Word

1. Click **E-mail** button 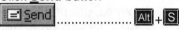.
   OR
   a. Click **File**............... Alt + F
   b. Click **New**..................... N
   c. Click **General** page
      tab....................... Ctrl + Tab
   d. Double-click **E-Mail**
      Message icon .
2. Fill in **To:** information.......... *type* recipient's address
3. Press **Tab**........................... Tab
4. Fill in **CC:** information........ *type* additional recipients' addresses
5. Press **Tab**........................... Tab
6. Fill in **Subject** information.. *type* subject title
7. Press **Tab**........................... Tab
8. Type and format **message text**.
9. Click **Send** button
   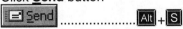.................... Alt + S

   ✓ *Log on to the Internet to transmit message as necessary.*

Attach Word Document to an E-mail Message

1. Compose an e-mail message.

   ✓ *By default, Word enters the document name in the Subject text box. You can edit it if necessary.*

2. Click **Attach File** button .
3. Select file to attach.

   ✓ *Select disk or folder from Look in drop-down list, then double-click folder name to locate file.*

4. Click **Attach** .... A
5. Click **Send** button
   .................... Alt + S

OR

1. Open or create the document to attach.
2. Click **File** .... Alt + F
3. Highlight **Send To** .... D
4. Click **Mail Recipient (as Attachment)** .... A
5. Compose e-mail message.

   ✓ *By default, Word enters the document name in the Subject text box. You can edit it if necessary.*

6. Click **Send** button
   .................... Alt + S

Send a Word Document as E-mail

1. Open document to send
2. Click **E-mail** button .
   OR
   a. Click **File** .... Alt + F
   b. Highlight **Send To** .... D
   c. Click **Mail Recipient** ...... M
3. Fill in **To:** information .... type recipient's address
4. Press **Tab** .... Tab
5. Fill in **CC:** information .... *type* additional recipients' addresses
6. Press **Tab** .... Tab
7. Fill in **Subject information** .... *type subject title*

   ✓ *By default, Word enters the document name in the Subject text box. You can edit it if necessary.*

8. Click **Send a Copy button**
   .... Alt + S

Disconnect from the Internet

• Close your e-mail application.

Exercise Directions

✓ *If you have an e-mail account and access to the Internet, you may use your own e-mail address in this exercise. Otherwise, use the DDC Publishing address provided.*

✓ *If you do not have access to the Internet, you may still complete the steps in this exercise. However, when you try to send the e-mail, you will receive an error message.*

1. Start Word, if necessary.

2. Compose an e-mail message as follows:

   a. Enter the address: *learn@ddcpub.com.*

   b. Enter the subject: *Seminar*

   c. Enter the message: *Just want to confirm that the Seminar is scheduled for February 9 and 10, in Phoenix. Thanks.*

3. Send the message.

   • Enter your user name and password if prompted.

4. In Word, open the document ⊚ **21HOTEL**, save it as **WD21-1**, and then close it.

5. Compose another e-mail message as follows:

   a. Enter the address: *learn@ddcpub.com.*

   b. Enter the subject: *Hotel Letter*

   c. Enter the message: *Boss -- I've attached a copy of the letter I mailed to the hotel in Phoenix. I'll let you know when I hear back. Also, within the hour I'll be sending you the list of companies I think will be interested in participating in the seminar.*

6. Attach the document **WD21-1** to the e-mail message and send it.

7. In Word, create a new document and save it as **WD21-2**.

8. Type the document shown in Illustration A.

   • Use Click and Type to center lines of text and to start lines flush left.

9. Check the spelling and grammar in the document.

10. Save the document.

11. Send the **WD21-2** document as e-mail to *learn@ddcpub.com.*

12. Close all open documents and exit Word, saving all changes.

13. Exit Outlook or Outlook Express, if necessary.

Illustration A

Boss –

As promised, here is the list of clients I believe will be interested in sending someone to the seminar in February. Let me know if you want me to add any other names.

BUSINESS ON THE WEB SEMINAR
POTENTIAL PARTICIPANTS

Forsythe Clothiers, San Francisco, CA

Lewis Brothers Insurance, San Rafael, CA

Beehive Properties, Salt Lake City, UT

First United Cooperative Bank, Provo, UT

Mail Order Gourmet, Santa Barbara, CA

National Flower Zone, Portland, OR

Adams Brothers Computers, Alameda, CA

On Your Own

1. Find out and record e-mail addresses for friends, coworkers, and companies with which you do business. You can find e-mail addresses by asking around, looking on business cards or stationery, or by using the Internet to search for addresses.

2. Send an e-mail message to a friend or co-worker and ask him or her to send one back to you.

3. Create a new document and type a letter to someone else whose e-mail address you have. For example, type a letter to your boss thanking him or her for a promotion, a raise, or for time off, or type a letter to a friend or relative inviting him or her to an event.

4. Save the document as **OWD21**.

5. Close the document.

6. Attach the document to an e-mail message and send it.

Exercise 22

Skills Covered:

- ◆ **Receive E-mail Messages in Outlook or Outlook Express**
- ◆ **Print an E-mail Message** ◆ **Save an E-mail Attachment**

On the Job

To receive e-mail, you use an e-mail application such as Outlook or Outlook Express. You can print an e-mail message using your e-mail application, and save documents attached to e-mail messages to open in Word.

Your manager has suggested you contact Cornerstone Graphics to ask if any of their clients might be interested in attending the Business on the Web Seminar. In this exercise, you will send an e-mail message to Jake McNeil at Cornerstone. He sends a message back with an attached document. You will print the message and save the attachment, which you open in Word.

Terms

Download Retrieve information from the Internet and store it locally on your computer.

Inbox A folder in Outlook and Outlook Express where new e-mail messages are stored.

Notes

Receive E-mail Messages in Outlook or Outlook Express

- To receive electronic mail (e-mail) messages with Microsoft Outlook or Outlook Express you must have a connection to the Internet or to an intranet and an account with a mail service provider.

  ✓ *To exchange e-mail, Outlook or Outlook Express must be correctly configured with your e-mail account information.*

- When you connect to the Internet, the e-mail application **downloads** new messages into a folder called **Inbox**.

- You can read the downloaded messages immediately, while still online, or after you disconnect and are working offline.

- Messages remain in the Inbox until you move them or delete them.

Messages are stored in the Inbox folder

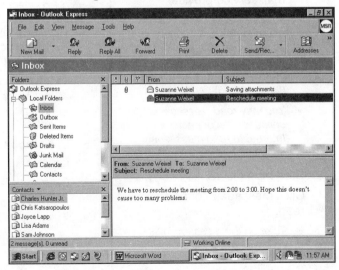

Print an E-mail Message

- You can use Outlook or Outlook Express to print any e-mail message.

- Your computer must be connected to a printer, and the printer must be on and loaded with paper in order to print e-mail message.

Save an E-mail Attachment

- You can save a document attached to an e-mail message so you can open it in another application later.

- An attachment is saved in its original file format. For example, a Word document attached to an e-mail message is saved in Word document format.

- The attachment is saved with its original file name. You select the disk and/or folder where you want to store the file.

Procedures

Receive E-mail Messages in Outlook or Outlook Express

In Outlook:

1. Start **Outlook**.

   ✓ Outlook may automatically connect to your mail service provider and download new messages. Enter account name and password if prompted.

2. Click **Send/Receive** button .... Alt + C
   OR

   a. Click **Tools**............ Alt + T

   b. Click **Send/Receive**....... E
      mail service provider

   ✓ If not already online, Outlook will automatically connect to your mail service provider and download all messages. If prompted, enter your account name and password.

   ✓ You may read messages online, or disconnect from Internet to read messages offline.

3. Click **Inbox** icon... Ctrl + Shift , I

4. Click message to open and read.

   ✓ To open the message in its own window, double-click it.

In Outlook Express:

1. Start **Outlook Express** .

   ✓ Outlook Express may automatically connect to your mail service provider and download new messages. Enter account name and password if prompted.

2. Click **Send and Receive** button Send and Receive .
   OR

   a. Click **Tools**............ Alt + T

   b. Highlight **Send and Receive**................. Alt + S

   c. Click **Send and Receive All** .... Alt + A

   ✓ If not already online, Outlook Express will automatically connect to your mail service provider and download all messages. If prompted, enter your account name and password.

   ✓ You may read messages online, or disconnect from Internet to read messages offline.

3. Click **Inbox** folder .... Ctrl + Y , I , Enter

4. Click message to read.

   ✓ To open the message in its own window, double-click it.

Disconnect Outlook from Internet

1. Click **File** .... Alt + F

2. Click **Work Offline** .... K

3. Click **Yes** .... Y

Disconnect Outlook Express from Internet

1. Click **File**................... Alt + F

2. Click **Work Offline**.............. W

3. Click **Yes**................... Y

Print an E-mail Message

1. Select message.

2. Click **File**................... Alt + F

3. Click **Print**..................... P

4. Click **OK**...................... Enter

Save an E-mail Attachment in Outlook

1. Select message.

2. Click **File**............................ F

3. Click **Save Attachments**..... N

4. Select file name to save.

5. Click the down arrow on the Save In box.

6. Click desired **disk and/or folder**.

7. Click **Save**.................... Alt + S

Save an E-mail Attachment in Outlook Express

1. Select message.

2. Click **File**............................ F

3. Click **Save Attachments**..... V

4. Click desired **disk** and/or **folder**.

5. Click **OK**.......................... Enter

6. Click **Save**................... Alt + S

Exercise Directions

✓ *If you have an e-mail account and access to the Internet, you may use your own e-mail address in this exercise. Otherwise, use the DDC Publishing address provided.*

✓ *If you do not have access to the Internet, you may still complete the steps in this exercise. However, when you try to send the e-mail, you will receive an error message.*

1. Start Word, if necessary.

2. Compose an e-mail message as follows:

   a. Enter the address: *jmcneil@ddcpub.com.*

   b. Enter the subject: *Clients interested in Seminar*

   c. Enter the message: *Hi Jake, I am planning a mailing to invite clients to attend the Business on the Web Seminar. Do you have any names you'd like me to add to the list? Reply by e-mail as soon as possible. Thanks.*

3. Send the message.

   • Enter your user name and password if prompted.

4. Exit Word.

5. Launch Outlook Express.

   ✓ *If you use Outlook, launch Outlook instead.*

6. Download new messages.

   ✓ *The jmcneil@ddcpub.com site is set to automatically return messages to you.*

7. Disconnect from the Internet.

8. Read the new message(s) offline

9. Print the messages.

10. Save the message attachment.

    ✓ *Store the attachment in the same location as the other documents for this exercise.*

11. Exit Outlook Express.

On Your Own

1. Use your e-mail application to download new messages. You should have received replies to messages you sent in Exercises 21 and 22.

2. Print the messages you receive.

3. E-mail someone and ask him or her to send you an e-mail message with a Word document attached to it. If you don't know anyone who can do this, send one to yourself.

4. Download the new message and save the attachment.

5. Open the attachment in Word.

6. When you are finished, close the document, and exit Word.

Exercise 23

◆ Critical Thinking

Now that the seminar is definitely being held in Phoenix, you want to provide participants with information about things they can do in their free time. In this exercise, you will send an e-mail message to your manager telling her about your plan. You will then open a memo about activities in Phoenix and save it with a new name. You will revise the memo using the skills you have learned in this lesson. You will log onto the Internet to locate information about museum tours and copy the information into the memo. You will then send the memo via e-mail. Finally, you will check for e-mail messages you have received.

Exercise Directions

✓ *If you have an e-mail account and access to the Internet, you may use your own e-mail address in this exercise. Otherwise, use the DDC Publishing address provided.*

✓ *If you do not have access to the Internet, you may still complete the steps in this exercise. However, when you try to send the e-mail, you will receive an error message.*

1. Start Word, if necessary.

2. Create an e-mail message as follows:

   To: *learn@ddcpub.com*

   Subject: *Phoenix*

   Message text: *Kate – I'm trying to pull together a list of activities seminar participants can do in their free time. I'll send along what I've got so far so you can take a look. Thanks.*

3. Send the message.

4. In Word, open the document ⊛**23TOUR** and save it as **WD23**.

5. Revise the document to achieve the results shown in Illustration A.

6. Insert eight blank lines at the beginning of the document.

7. Change *Memorandum* to all uppercase.

8. Leave a blank line after *MEMORANDUM*.

9. Change the words *To, From, Regarding*, and *Date* to all uppercase.

10. Replace the sample text with *your name* and *the current date*.

11. Following the Date line, leave blank lines between all paragraphs.

12. Move the paragraph about the art museum down to just above the closing.

13. Insert, delete, and replace other text as marked in Illustration A.

14. Insert three blank lines above the closing so you have room to copy information about the art museum into the document.

15. Save the changes to the document.

16. Display the Web toolbar.

17. Open the Internet Simulation:

   a. Click **Go**.

   b. Click **Open**.

   c. In the Address line type the following: D:/Internet/E23/altavista.htm

      ✓ *If you've copied the Internet simulation files to your hard drive or your CD-ROM drive is a letter other than D:, substitute the correct letter for D.*

   d. Click **OK**.

18. Type *What is the Phoenix Art Museum?* in the Search text box, then click *Search*.

19. Click link 1: *Artcom Museum Tour: Phoenix Art Museum, Phoenix AZ*.

20. Scroll down the page until the section titled *Tours and ArtBreaks* is displayed.

21. Copy the paragraph following the heading *Tours and ArtBreaks* to the Clipboard.

22. Switch back to the **WD23** document.

23. Paste the information from the Clipboard on the middle of the three blank lines above the closing. (Refer to Illustration A.)

24. Check spelling and grammar in the document. Correct errors but ignore proper names.

25. Save the **WD23** document.

26. Preview the document.

27. Print the document.

28. From Word, send a copy of the **WD23** document via e-mail to *learn@ddcpub.com*.

29. Start Outlook Express to check for new messages you may have received.

30. Print any new messages.

31. Exit the simulation.

32. Close any open documents, saving all changes, and exit all open applications.

8x

MEMORANDUM *u. c.*

↓2x

TO: Kate Liu
FROM: ~~Your Name~~ *Your Name*
REGARDING: Activities in Phoenix, AZ
DATE: ~~Today's Date~~ *Today's Date*

u. c.

↓2x

Kate –

↓2x

~~Here's what I've found out about Phoenix so far?~~ *Seems like there's lots to do in Phoenix, Arizona:*

↓2x

There's shopping downtown at Heritage Square.

↓2x

the restored

You can find Native American history at the Pueblo Grand Museum and Culture Park and at the Heard Museum. *both*

↓2x

Outdoor enthusiasts will like the Popago Park Zoo and Botanical Gardens.

↓2x

The Phoenix Art museum reportedly has quite a collection. There are daily tours and other activities. *I got the following information from its Web site:*

* 4x

That's it so far. Talk to you soon.

Copy text from Web page here

104

Lesson 4

Text Formatting

Exercise 24

Skills Covered:

◆ Set Tabs ◆ Horizontal Alignment

On the Job

Align text horizontally to visually improve a document's appearance, to break up the page to make it easier to read, and to call attention to certain lines or paragraphs. You can also use tabs to align text across a line in your document.

Cynthia Harte has hired you to promote her new candy store, The Sweet Tooth. In this exercise, you will create a modified-block business letter telling Ms. Harte what you plan to do. You will also create a document using different alignments to be used as a poster announcing the grand opening sale.

Terms

Tab A location (or measurement) you use to position text anywhere along on a line.

Horizontal alignment The position of text in relation to the left and right page margins.

Flush Lined up evenly along an edge.

Notes

Set tab stops

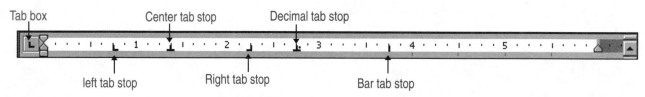

Set Tabs

■ **Tabs** are used to indent a single line of text. For example, in a modified block business letter tabs are used to indent the date, closing, and signature lines to the center of the page.

✓ *Refer to Exercise 11 for more information about business letters.*

■ Each time you press the Tab key, the insertion point advances to the next set tab stop.

■ There are five types of tab stops:

• Left: Text starts flush left with the tab stop.

• Right: Text ends flush right with the tab stop.

• Center: Text is centered on the tab stop.

• Decimal: Decimal points are aligned with the tab stop.

• Bar: A horizontal bar is displayed at the tab stop position. Text starts ¹⁄₁₀" to the right of the bar.

■ By default, left tab stops are set every ½" on the horizontal ruler.

■ You can set any type of tab stop at any point along the ruler.

Tabs dialog box

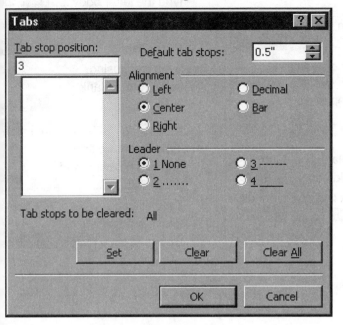

- There are four horizontal alignments:
  - *Left.* Text is **flush** with left margin. The right margin is uneven (or ragged). Left is the default horizontal alignment.
  - *Right.* Text is flush with right margin. The left margin is uneven.
  - *Center.* Text is centered between margins.
  - *Justify.* Text is spaced so both left and right margins are even.
- You can use different alignments in a document.
  - ✓ *You have already used Click and Type to align text horizontally in a document.*

Text aligned

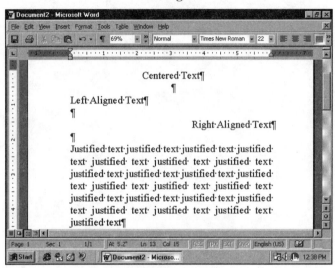

Horizontal Alignment

- **Horizontal alignment** is used to adjust the position of paragraphs in relation to the left and right margins of a page.
  - ✓ *Do not confuse horizontal alignment with tab spacing. Tabs affect text on a single line, whereas horizontal alignment affects an entire paragraph or paragraphs.*

Procedures

Align Horizontally

1. Position insertion point in paragraph to align.
   OR
   Select paragraphs to align.
   OR
   Position insertion point where you intend to type text.
2. Click alignment button:
   - **Center** ≡ ....`Ctrl`+`E`
   - **Right** ≡ ....`Ctrl`+`R`
   - **Justify** ≡ ....`Ctrl`+`J`
   - **Left** ≡ ....`Ctrl`+`L`

Set Tabs

To set a left tab stop:

- Click ruler where you want to set tab stop.

To set a different type of tab stop:

1. Click the **Tab** box `L`.
   - ✓ *Each time you click, tab icon changes. Stop when tab stop you want is displayed.*
2. Click ruler where you want to insert new tab stop.

To set a precise tab stop:

1. Click **Format**..............`Alt`+`O`
2. Click **Tabs** ....`T`
3. Select alignment of tab
   - **Left**......................`Alt`+`L`
   - **Center** ....`Alt`+`C`
   - **Right** ....`Alt`+`R`
   - **Decimal**................`Alt`+`D`
   - **Bar** ....`Alt`+`B`
4. Double-click in the **Tab stop position** ....`Alt`+`T`
5. Type precise position.
6. Click **OK** ....`Enter`

To clear a tab stop:

- Drag tab stop marker off ruler.

OR

1. Click **Format** .... `Alt`+`O`
2. Click **Tabs** .... `T`
3. Select tab stop(s) to clear.
4. Click **Clear** .... `Alt`+`E`
   OR
   Click **Clear All** .... `Alt`+`A`
5. Click **OK** .... `Enter`

Create Modified-Block Business Letter

1. Start 2.5" from top of page .... `Enter` **8x**

   ✓ *Press Enter eight times to leave 2.5" of space.*

2. Set left tab stop at 3".
3. Press **Tab** .... `Tab`
4. Insert date.
5. Leave three blank lines and type inside address .... `Enter` **4x**
6. Leave a blank line and type the salutation .... `Enter` **2x**
7. Leave a blank line and type the letter body ..... `Enter` **2x**
8. Leave a blank line .... `Enter` **2x**
9. Press **Tab** .... `Tab`
10. Type the closing.
11. Leave three blank lines .... `Enter` **4x**
12. Press **Tab** .... `Tab`
13. Type signature line.
14. Move to next line and press **Tab** .... `Enter` , `Tab`
15. Type title line.
16. Leave a blank line and type reference initials .. `Enter` **2x**

Exercise Directions

1. Start Word, if necessary.
2. Create a new document.
3. Save the file as **WD24-1**.
4. Set a left tab at 3" on the horizontal ruler.
5. Type the modified-block business letter as shown in Illustration A.

   ✓ *Press the Tab key to indent the date, closing, and signature lines to the tab stop.*

6. Save the document.
7. Preview the document. It should look similar to the one in Illustration A.
8. Check the spelling and grammar in the document and correct any errors.
9. Print the document.
10. Close the document, saving all changes.
11. Create a new document.
12. Save the new document as **WD24-2**.
13. Type the document shown in Illustration B, using the specified alignments, tab stops, and blank lines between paragraphs.
14. Check and correct the spelling and grammar in the document.
15. Preview the document.
16. Print the document.
17. Close the document and exit Word, saving all changes.

Illustration A

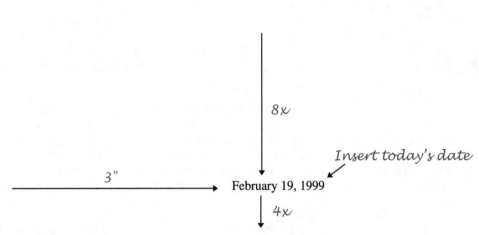

8x

Insert today's date

3″ → February 19, 1999

4x

Ms. Cynthia Harte
The Sweet Tooth
321 Main Street
Hanover, NH 03755
2x
Dear Ms. Harte:
2x
This letter is simply a follow up to our conversation this morning, confirming our agreement regarding the promotion of The Sweet Tooth. I am very excited about this opportunity, and I assure you I have some wonderful ideas!
2x
First of all, I plan to focus a great deal of attention on the grand opening sale. I have already created a document that I think we can use as both an insert in the local newspaper and as a flyer to hand out in the neighborhood. I have enclosed a copy for your approval.
2x
I would also like you to give some thought about ways to get involved in the community. For example, we can find out about fundraisers at the schools and other non-profit organizations and make donations of merchandise or gift certificates. You'd be surprised at the amount of business good will can generate.
2x
Let me know what you think of the enclosed announcement. I will give you a call on Friday.

2x
Sincerely,

4x

Your Name
2x

Enclosure

*Left tab stop
set at 4"*

Flush left   The Sweet Tooth   Ms. Cynthia Harte, Proprietor

] GRAND OPENING [*Centered, all uppercase*

↓ 2x

Justified Announcing the GRAND OPENING of THE SWEET TOOTH, the newest addition to the downtown Main Street shopping area. The Sweet Tooth is chock full of delicious and mouth-watering candy and treats. In addition to our fine selection of CHOCOLATES, FUDGE, and PENNY CANDY, you'll find GIFT ITEMS, NOVELTIES, and our HOMEMADE ICE CREAM!

↓ 2x

] Stop in during our GRAND OPENING celebration to see what the excitement's about! [*Centered*

↓ 2x

FREE SAMPLES

] A Different Item Will Be Available For Tasting Every Day This Week! [*Centered*

↓ 2x

*Left tab stop
set at 1.5"*

Monday	*Left tab stop set at 3.5"*	Vanilla Fudge
Tuesday		Chocolate Bark with Almonds
Wednesday		Peanut Brittle
Thursday		Old Fashioned Peppermint Drops
Friday		Chocolate Fudge
Saturday		Salt Water Taffy
Sunday		Truffles

↓ 2x

] SAMPLE GRAND OPENING SALE PRICES [*Centered*

↓ 2x

Flush left   *Left tab stop at 1.5"*

	Everyday Price	*Left tab stop at 4"*	Grand Opening Price
Fudge	$7.99/pound		$5.59/pound
Truffles	$10.49/pound		$8.99/pound
Small ice cream	$.75		$.50
Large ice cream	$1.25		$.85

Decimal tab stop at 4"   *Decimal tab stop at 4.5"*

↓ 2x

GRAND OPENING RAFFLE

↓ 2x

Justified While you're in the store, take a moment to fill out a raffle entry form. At the end of each day Ms. Harte herself will pick a lucky winner to receive a gift basket worth $50.00! Runners up will receive gift certificates redeemable any time!

↓ 2x

Aligned right

The Sweet Tooth
321 Main Street
Hanover, NH 03755
603-555-9009
www.sweettooth.com

On Your Own

1. Create a new document in Word.

2. Save the file as **OWD24**.

3. Draft an announcement about an upcoming event in your life. For example, the event could be your birthday, graduation, a party, or a vacation trip.

4. Center a title at the top of the announcement.

5. Right-align your name and address below the title.

6. Add two paragraphs that describe the event in detail. Justify these paragraphs.

7. Add other lines giving the time and location of the event as well as directions, if needed. Use left, right, and center alignments to organize and format other lines.

8. Try different vertical alignments until you settle on the one that makes the document look the best.

9. Save the changes, close the document, and exit Word.

Exercise 25

Skills Covered:

◆ **Select Fonts** ◆ **Change Font Size** ◆ **Apply Font Styles**

On the Job

Use fonts, font sizes, and font styles to dress up the appearance of a document. Fonts are a basic means of applying formatting to text and characters. They can set a mood, command attention, and convey a message.

The owner of The Sweet Tooth liked the flyer that you designed, but she wanted it to be more attractive. In this exercise, you will enhance the Grand Opening sale poster using different fonts, font sizes, and font styles.

Terms

Font A particular set of characters in a specific size and style.

Font face The character design of a font set.

Serif A font face that has curved or extended edges.

Sans serif A font face that has straight edges.

Script A font face that looks like handwriting.

Font size The height of an uppercase letter in a font set.

Font style The slant and weight of characters in a font set.

Notes

Select Fonts

■ Each **font** set includes upper- and lowercase letters, numbers, and punctuation marks.

■ There are three basic categories of **font faces**:

  ● **Serif** face fonts have lines, curves, or edges extending from the ends of each character.

    ◆ Serif fonts are easy to read and are often used for document text.

A Serif Font

● **Sans serif** face fonts have straight edges.

    ◆ Sans serif fonts are often used for headings.

A Sans Serif Font

● **Script** face fonts are designed to look like handwriting.

    ◆ Script face fonts are often used to simulate handwriting.
    ◆ Never use script in business documents.

■ The default Word font is Times New Roman, a serif font.

■ The current font name is displayed in the Font box on the Formatting toolbar.

The Font box shows the font name

- Both Word and Windows come with built-in fonts. You can install additional fonts.
- Fonts can be changed before or after you enter text in a document.
- You can set the tone of a document by putting thought into the fonts you select.
  - ✓ *More than three or four font faces makes a document look disjointed and unprofessional.*

Change Font Size

- **Font size** is measured in points. There are 72 points in an inch.
- The default Word font size is 10 points.

- The current font size is displayed in the Font Size box on the Formatting toolbar.

The Font Size box shows the font size

Apply Font Styles

- The most common **font styles** are bold and italic.
- When no style is applied to a font, it is called regular.
- Font styles can be combined for different effects such as bold italic, as in ***style***.

Procedures

Select Font from Font Box

1. Select text.
   OR
   Position insertion point where new text will be typed.
2. Click **Font** drop-down arrow
   .
3. Click **font name** .... ↓, Enter
   - ✓ *The font list is alphabetical. However, the most recently used fonts are listed at the top of the list.*

Select Font from Font Dialog Box

1. Select text.
   OR
   Position insertion point where new text will be typed.
2. Click **Format** .... Alt +O
3. Click **Font** .... F
4. Click font name in **Font** list .... ↓
5. Click **OK** .... Enter

Change Font Size from Font Size Box

1. Select text.
   OR
   Position insertion point where new text will be typed.
2. Click **Font Size** drop-down arrow 10 .
3. Click **font size** .... ↓, Enter

Change Font Size from Font Dialog Box

1. Select text.
   OR
   Position insertion point where new text will be typed.
2. Click **Format** .... Alt +O
3. Click **Font** .... F
4. Click font size in
   Size list .... Alt +S, ↓
5. Click **OK** .... Enter

Apply Font Styles Using Toolbar Buttons

1. Select text.
   OR
   Position insertion point where new text will be typed.
2. Click font style button:
   - **Bold** **B** .... Ctrl +B
   - **Italic** *I* .... Ctrl +I
   - ✓ *To remove font styles repeat steps 1 and 2.*

Select Font Styles from Font Dialog Box

1. Select text.
   OR
   Position insertion point where new text will be typed.
2. Click **Format** .... Alt +O
3. Click **Font** .... F
4. Click font style in **Font style** list .... Alt +Y, ↓
   - ✓ *To remove font styles click Regular.*
5. Click **OK** .... Enter

Exercise Directions

1. Start Word, if necessary.

2. Open ⊘**25POSTER**.

3. Save the document as **WD25**.

4. Apply the fonts, font sizes, and font styles as indicated in Illustration A.

   ✓ *If the specified fonts are not available on your computer, substitute similar fonts. Alternatively, if your instructor gives permission, experiment with different fonts.*

   ✓ *Be careful not to apply formatting to the blank lines between paragraphs. It is recommended that you format the document with paragraph marks displayed.*

5. Change the alignment and set tabs as indicated in Illustration A.

6. Preview the document. It should resemble Illustration A.

   ✓ *If necessary, use Shrink to Fit to reduce the document to a single page.*

7. Save the changes to the document.

8. Revise the document as indicated in Illustration B, including insertions, deletions, and case changes.

   ✓ *To review proofreaders' marks, see Exercise 17.*

9. Check the spelling and grammar.

10. Preview the document.

11. Save the changes to the document.

12. Print the document.

13. Close the document and exit Word, saving all changes.

Illustration A

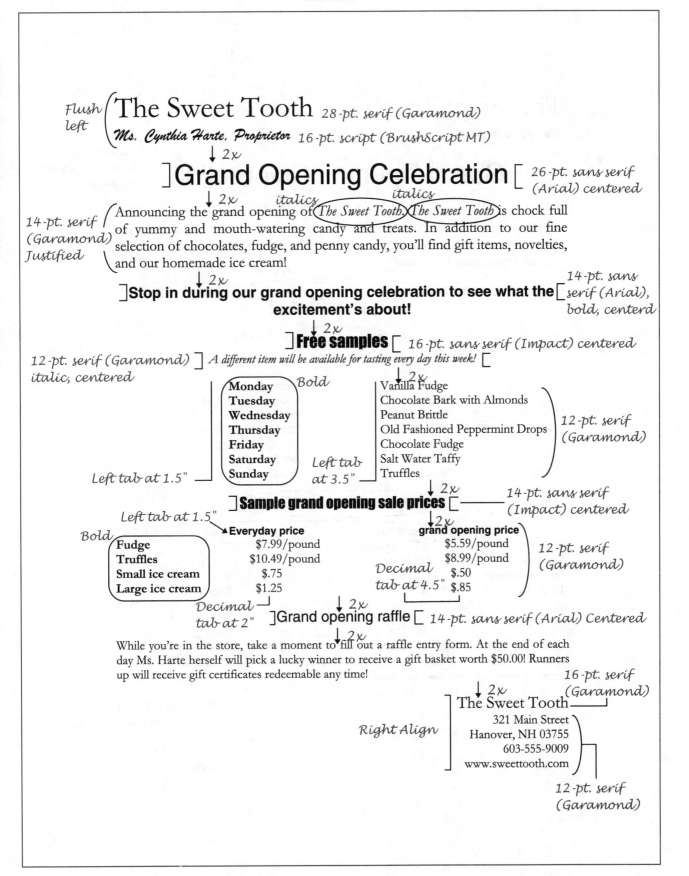

The Sweet Tooth
28-pt. serif (Garamond)

Ms. Cynthia Harte, Proprietor — *16-pt. script (BrushScript MT)*

Flush left

↓ *2x*

Grand Opening Celebration
26-pt. sans serif (Arial) centered

↓ *2x*

14-pt. serif (Garamond) Justified

Announcing the grand opening of *The Sweet Tooth*. *The Sweet Tooth* is chock full of yummy and mouth-watering candy and treats. In addition to our fine selection of chocolates, fudge, and penny candy, you'll find gift items, novelties, and our homemade ice cream!

italics   italics

↓ *2x*

Stop in during our grand opening celebration to see what the excitement's about!
14-pt. sans serif (Arial), bold, centerd

↓ *2x*

Free samples *16-pt. sans serif (Impact) centered*

12-pt. serif (Garamond) italic, centered — *A different item will be available for tasting every day this week!*

↓ *2x*

Monday	*Bold*	Vanilla Fudge
Monday		Vanilla Fudge
Tuesday		Chocolate Bark with Almonds
Wednesday		Peanut Brittle
Thursday		Old Fashioned Peppermint Drops
Friday		Chocolate Fudge
Saturday		Salt Water Taffy
Sunday		Truffles

Left tab at 1.5"   *Left tab at 3.5"*   *12-pt. serif (Garamond)*

↓ *2x*

Sample grand opening sale prices — *14-pt. sans serif (Impact) centered*

↓ *2x*

Left tab at 1.5"

Bold

	Everyday price	**grand opening price**
Fudge	$7.99/pound	$5.59/pound
Truffles	$10.49/pound	$8.99/pound
Small ice cream	$.75	$.50
Large ice cream	$1.25	$.85

12-pt. serif (Garamond)

Decimal tab at 4.5"

Decimal tab at 2"

↓ *2x*

Grand opening raffle *14-pt. sans serif (Arial) Centered*

↓ *2x*

While you're in the store, take a moment to fill out a raffle entry form. At the end of each day Ms. Harte herself will pick a lucky winner to receive a gift basket worth $50.00! Runners up will receive gift certificates redeemable any time!

↓ *2x*

Right Align

The Sweet Tooth — *16-pt. serif (Garamond)*
321 Main Street
Hanover, NH 03755
603-555-9009
www.sweettooth.com

12-pt. serif (Garamond)

115

The Sweet Tooth
Ms. Cynthia Harte, Proprietor

Grand Opening Celebration

, the newest addition to the downtown Main Street shopping area.

Announcing the grand opening of *The Sweet Tooth*. *The Sweet Tooth* is chock full of ~~yummy~~ and mouth-watering candy and treats. In addition to our fine selection of chocolates, fudge, and penny candy, you'll find gift items, novelties, and our homemade ice cream!

delicious

Stop in during our grand opening celebration to see what the excitement's about!

Uppercase

Free samples   *Title case*

A different item will be available for tasting every day this week!

Monday	Vanilla Fudge
Tuesday	~~Chocolate~~ Bark with Almonds
Wednesday	Peanut Brittle
Thursday	Old Fashioned Peppermint Drops
Friday	Chocolate Fudge
Saturday	Salt Water Taffy
Sunday	Truffles

Vanilla

Sample grand opening sale prices   *Uppercase*

	Everyday price	grand opening price
Fudge	$7.99/pound	$5.59/pound
Truffles	$10.49/pound	$8.99/pound
Small ice cream	$.75	$.50
Large ice cream	$1.25	$.85

Title case

Grand opening raffle   *uppercase*

While you're in the store, take a moment to fill out a raffle entry form. At the end of each day Ms. Harte herself will pick a lucky winner to receive a gift basket worth $50.00! Runners up will receive ~~gift certificates redeemable any time!~~

The Sweet Tooth T-Shirts and hats

The Sweet Tooth
321 Main Street
Hanover, NH 03755
603-555-9009
www.sweettooth.com

On Your Own

1. In Word, open the document you created in the On Your Own section for Exercise 16, or open ⊙**25FONTS**.

2. Save the file as **OWD25**.

3. Apply fonts, font styles, and font sizes to the document text. Change the fonts to emphasize various parts of the document. For example, you will probably want to highlight the title by giving it a large, distinctive font.

4. Apply alignments to improve the appearance of the document.

5. Preview the document.

6. Save your changes, close the document, and exit Word.

Exercise 26

◆ **Font Effects** ◆ **Text Effects** ◆ **Underlines** ◆ **Font Color**

On the Job

You can enhance text using font effects, underlines, and colors. These techniques are useful for printed documents or documents you intend to post on the World Wide Web. Some of these formatting features such as text effects, color, shadow, and fancy underline styles are useful for creating exciting documents where text jumps out to capture a reader's attention. Alternatively, some formatting features are useful for adding subtle description to text, such as a single underline or superscript.

The owner of The Sweet Tooth thinks that the promotional poster you have been working on will make a good Web page. In this exercise, you will use font effects, text effects, underlines, and color to enhance and animate the document.

Terms

Font effects Formatting features used to enhance or emphasize text.

Text effects Effects used to animate text on-screen.

Notes

Font Effects

- Word includes numerous **font effects** for enhancing and emphasizing text, including the ones available in the Font dialog box:
  - Strikethrough
  - ~~Double strikethrough~~
  - Superscript
  - Subscript
  - Shadow
  - Outline
  - Emboss
  - Engrave
  - SMALL CAPS
  - ALL CAPS

Text Effects

- Word has six **text effects** you can apply to text for viewing on screen.
- Text effects are animations used in documents designed for the World Wide Web or for PowerPoint presentations.

Underlines

- There are nine types of underlines available in Word:
  - Single (underlines all characters, including nonprinting characters, such as spaces and tabs)
  - Words only
  - Double
  - Dotted

- <u>Thick</u>
- <u>Dash</u>
- <u>Dot dash</u>
- <u>dot dot dash</u>
- <u>Wave</u>

Font Color

- Use color to enhance text in documents that will be printed on a color printer, used in a PowerPoint presentation, or stored as a Web page.

- You can change the color of an underline independently from the color of the font.

Procedures

Apply Font Effects

1. Select text.
   OR
   Position insertion point where new text will be typed.
2. Click **Format**...............
3. Click **Font**...........................
4. Select checkbox for desired effect(s).
   - ✓ Clear check mark to remove effect.
5. Click **OK**...........................Enter
   - ✓ Select text and press Ctrl+Spacebar to remove all character formatting.

Apply Text Effects

1. Select text.
   OR
   Position insertion point where new text will be typed.
2. Click **Format**...............Alt+O
3. Click **Font**...........................F
4. Click **Text Effects** page tab.....................Alt+X
5. Click desired **Animation** .....Alt+A, ↑/↓
   - ✓ View a sample of the effect in the Preview area.
6. Click **OK**...........................Enter

Apply Underlines *(Ctrl+U)*

1. Select text.
   OR
   Position insertion point where new text will be typed.
2. Click **Underline** button .
   - ✓ Repeat steps to remove underline.
   OR
1. Select text.
   OR
   Position insertion point where new text will be typed.
2. Click **Format** ....Alt+O
3. Click **Font**...........................F
4. Click **Underline style** drop-down arrow ....Alt+U
5. Click desired underline type.
   - ✓ Click (None) to remove underline
6. Click **OK** ....Enter

Apply Font Color

1. Select text.
   OR
   Position insertion point where new text will be typed.
2. Click **Format** ....Alt+O
3. Click **Font**...........................F
4. Click **Font color** drop-down arrow ....Alt+C
5. Click desired **color** .., Enter
   - ✓ Click Auto to select default color.
6. Click **OK** ....Enter

OR
1. Select text.
   OR
   Position insertion point where new text will be typed.
2. Click **Font Color** button drop-down arrow **A**▾.
3. Click desired color.

Apply Color to Underlines

1. Select underlined text.
   OR
   Position insertion point where new underlined text will be typed.
2. Click **Format**...............Alt+O
3. Click **Font** ....F
4. Click **Underline color** drop-down arrow..........Alt+I
5. Click desired **color**.
   - ✓ Click Auto to select default color.
6. Click **OK** ....Enter

Exercise Directions

1. Start Word, if necessary.

2. Open ⊘**26POSTER**.

3. Save the document as **WD26**.

4. Revise the document as indicated in Illustration A.

   a. Replace the text *Your Name* with your own name.

   b. Insert the correct date.

   c. Apply font effect, colors, and underlines as indicated.

   d. Apply text effects as indicated

5. Check the spelling and grammar.

6. Preview the document. It should look similar to the one in Illustration A.

   ✓ *The animated effects do not appear in a printed document.*

7. Save the changes.

8. Print the document.

9. Close the document and exit Word, saving all changes.

Illustration A

The Sweet Tooth) *Outline Font effect, Sparkle Text text effect*

Ms. Cynthia Harte, Proprietor) *Engrave effect, Blue font color*

Grand Opening Celebration) *Emboss effect, Blue font color*

Emboss effect, Blue font color

Announcing the grand opening of The Sweet Tooth, the newest addition to the Main Street shopping area. The Sweet Tooth is chock full of delicious and mouth-watering candy and treats. In addition to our fine selection of chocolates, fudge, and penny candy, you'll find gift items, novelties, and our homemade ice cream!

Emboss effect, Blue font color

Stop in during our GRAND OPENING CELEBRATION to see what the excitement's about!

FREE SAMPLES *Emboss, Small Caps font effect, Blue font color*

Double underline in Blue ⟶ <u>A different item will be available for tasting every day this week!</u>

Monday	<u>Vanilla Fudge</u>
Tuesday	<u>Vanilla Bark with Almonds</u>
Wednesday	<u>Peanut Brittle</u>
Thursday	<u>Old Fashioned Peppermint Drops</u>
Friday	<u>Chocolate Fudge</u>
Saturday	<u>Salt Water Taffy</u>
Sunday	<u>Truffles</u>

) *Single underline*

Emboss, Blue, Double wavy underline in blue ⟶ SAMPLE GRAND OPENING SALE PRICES

EVERYDAY PRICE	GRAND OPENING PRICE

Emboss, Small Caps, Blue font

Emboss, Small Caps, Blue font

	EVERYDAY PRICE	GRAND OPENING PRICE
FUDGE	$7.99/pound	$5.59/pound
TRUFFLES	$10.49/pound	$8.99/pound
SMALL ICE CREAM	$.75	$.50
LARGE ICE CREAM	$1.25	$.85

GRAND OPENING RAFFLE) *Las Vegas Lights text effect*

While you're in the store, take a moment to fill out a raffle entry form. At the end of each day Ms. Harte herself will pick a lucky winner to receive a gift basket worth $50.00! Runners up will receive The Sweet Tooth T-shirts and hats!

Emboss, Blue font ⟶ **The Sweet Tooth**
321 Main Street
Hanover, NH 03755
603-555-9009
www.sweettooth.com

<u>Prepared by Your Name, Today's Date</u> ⟵ *Wavy underline, Blue*

On Your Own

1. Open the document **OWD25**, or open
   ⊛ **26FONTS**.

2. Save the document as **OWD26**.

3. Apply font effects to highlight some of the document text.

4. Change the font color for some text.

5. Try some text effects.

6. Try different underline styles.

7. Preview the document.

8. Save your changes, close the document, and exit Word.

Exercise 27

Skills Covered:

◆ Highlight Text ◆ Format Painter

On the Job

You can highlight text to change the color around the text without changing the font color. Highlighting is useful for calling attention to text, and for making text stand out on the page. Use the Format Painter to quickly copy formatting from one location to another. The Format Painter saves you time and makes it easy to duplicate formatting throughout a document.

Your supervisor has asked you to revise a mission statement for Cornerstone Graphics. You want to call attention to specific details and points in the statement, so you will use font effects, underlines, color, and highlights. To save time, you can copy some formatting from one location in the document to another location.

Terms

Highlight formatting Change the color around text in a document.

Notes

Highlight Text

- Highlighting is used to call attention to text in a document.

- Highlighting places a colored rectangle over text in a document.

- Yellow is the default highlight color, but you can change **highlight formatting**.

  ✓ All colors of highlighting are gray when printed on a black and white printer.

Format Painter

- Use the Format Painter to copy formatting from existing formatted text to existing unformatted text.

- The Format Painter saves time because you can copy all the formatting then apply it with one mouse click.

Procedures

Apply Highlights

Highlight existing text:

1. Select text.
2. Click **Highlight** button .
   - ✓ *Repeat steps to remove highlight.*

Change highlight color:

1. Click **Highlight** button drop-down arrow.
2. Click new color.
   - ✓ *Click None to select the automatic background color.*

Copy Formatting

Copy formatting once;

1. Select formatted text.
2. Click **Format Painter** button .
   - ✓ *The mouse pointer looks like an I-beam with a paintbrush.*

   The Format Painter pointer

3. Select text to format.

Copy formatting repeatedly:

1. Select formatted text.
2. Double-click **Format Painter** button.
3. Select text to format.
4. Repeat step 3 until all text is formatted.
5. Click **Format Painter** button to turn off Format Painter.

Exercise Directions

1. Start Word, if necessary.
2. Open ⊘**27GOALS**.
3. Save the document as **WD27**.
4. Revise the document as indicated in Illustration A.
   a. Replace the text *Your Name* with your own name.
   b. Insert the correct date.
   c. Apply font formatting as indicated.
   d. Apply font enhancements as indicated.
5. Check the spelling and grammar.
6. Preview the document. It should look similar to the one in Illustration B.
7. Save the changes.
8. Print the document.
9. Close the document and exit Word, saving all changes.

Illustration A

Cornerstone Graphics *Center, 24-pt. sans serif (Arial)*
Mission Statement *Bold, words only underline*

Prepared by: Your Name *Right align, 12-pt.-serif*
Today's Date *(Times New Roman)*

Small caps, Blue font, bold,
double underline in blue

Cornerstone Graphics is committed to providing quality service to all clients. We strive *Justified 12 pt.-*
for excellence at every level of our organization. We vow to maintain the highest *serif (Times*
standards, pursue state-of-the-art solutions, and guarantee customer satisfaction. *New Roman)*

We respect our employees as well as our clients. We believe that fostering a strong
community within the workplace strengthens our position in the marketplace. We are
confident that our commitment will make us leaders in our industry.
Small Caps, Blue font, Bold, Double underline in blue - *Copy from previous*
At Cornerstone Graphics, we work toward the following three objectives: *company name*

1.   Quality Service ← *Yellow highlight*
2.   Customer Satisfaction ← *Green highlight*
3.   Employee Satisfaction ← *Pink highlight*

Cornerstone Graphics
Mission Statement

Prepared by: Your Name
Today's Date

CORNERSTONE GRAPHICS is committed to providing quality service to all clients. We strive for excellence at every level of our organization. We vow to maintain the highest standards, pursue state-of-the-art solutions, and guarantee customer satisfaction.

We respect our employees as well as our clients. We believe that fostering a strong community within the workplace strengthens our position in the marketplace. We are confident that our commitment will make us leaders in our industry.

At **CORNERSTONE GRAPHICS**, we work toward the following three objectives:

1.   Quality Service
2.   Customer Satisfaction
3.   Employee Satisfaction

On Your Own

1. Open the document **OWD24**, the announcement about an upcoming event in your life, or open ⊙ **27EVENT**.

2. Save the document as **OWD27**.

3. Change the fonts and font sizes used in the document. For example, make important information stand out in a different font and increase the size.

4. Apply underlines where appropriate.

5. Change some font colors to enhance the document.

6. Use the Format Painter to copy existing formatting to unformatted text.

7. Use highlighting to call attention to the items you think are the most important.

8. Preview the document.

9. Save your changes, close the document, and exit Word.

Exercise 28

Skills Covered:

◆ Use Symbols

On the Job

Use symbols to supplement the standard characters available on the keyboard and to add visual interest to documents. For example, you can insert shapes such as hearts and stars into documents as borders or separators.

The owner of The Sweet Tooth has just installed a soda fountain machine. In this exercise, you will design a flyer announcing the new addition to the shop. To complete the flyer you will use font formatting and symbols.

Terms

Symbol A character that is not included on the keyboard.

Notes

Use Symbols

- **Symbols** are characters that cannot be typed from the keyboard, such as hearts, stars, and other shapes as well as foreign alphabet characters.

- Symbols can be inserted and formatted in a document just like regular text characters.

- Several symbol fonts come with Office 2000 and others are available through vendors and shareware.

- Many regular character fonts also include some symbol characters.

- When you insert symbols, the symbol font formatting is applied to the character. You can change the font style and effects just as you can for regular text characters.

Symbol dialog box

Current font

Click here to select a different font

Procedures

Insert Symbols

1. Position insertion point where you want to insert a symbol.
2. Click **Insert**.................. Alt + I
3. Click **Symbol**...................... S
4. Click **Font** drop-down arrow................. Alt + F
5. Select any symbol **font** ....↓, Enter
6. Click desired **symbol**...................... Tab, →
7. Click **Insert**.................. Alt + I
8. Click **Close**........................ Esc

   ✓ You can repeat the steps to insert additional symbols without closing the Symbol dialog box.

Exercise Directions

1. Start Word, if necessary.
2. Open ✐ **28SYMBOL**.
3. Save the document as **WD28**.
4. Format the text as marked in Illustration A.
   a. Use a serif font for the entire document. (Garamond is used in Illustration A.)
   b. Apply font sizes and font styles as shown.
      ✓ Be careful not to change the font size and formatting of the blank lines in the document. They should remain at 12-point Times New Roman.
   c. Apply alignments as shown.
   d. Apply underlines as shown.

5. Use the Wingdings font to insert symbols as marked in Illustration A. Leave a space between symbols and text characters where appropriate.
   ✓ Adjust the font size and formatting of symbol characters the same way you adjust the font size and formatting of text characters.
6. Preview the document.
7. Print the document.
8. Close the document and exit Word, saving the changes.
   ✓ Hint: Use Copy and Paste to copy a symbol from one location to another. Use the Format Painter to copy formatting.

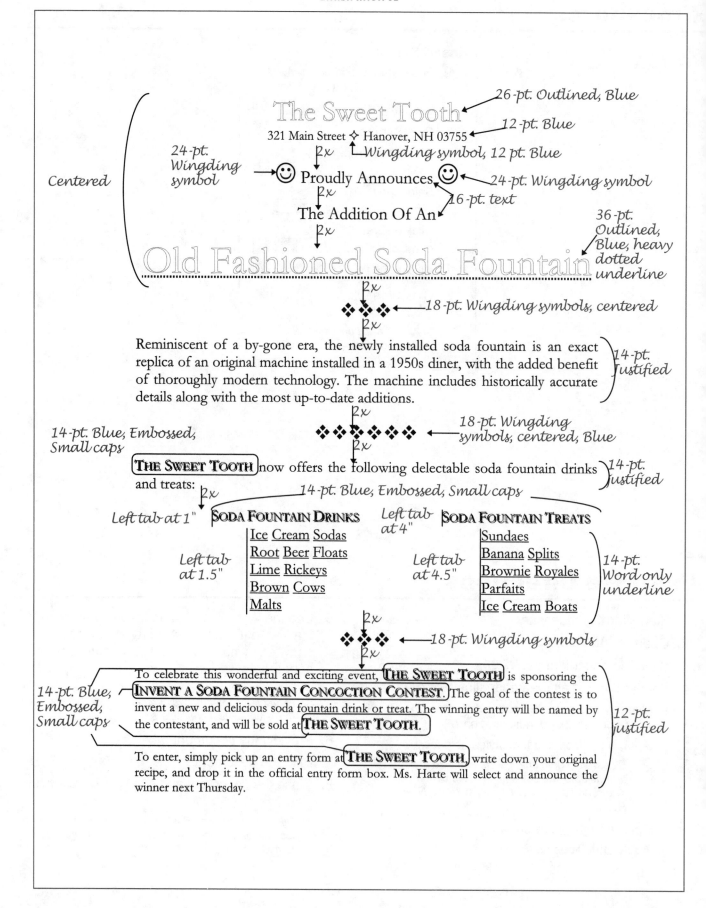

On Your Own

1. Open the document **OWD27**, the announcement document, or open ⊘ **28EVENT**.

2. Save the document as **OWD28**.

3. Use symbols to enhance the announcement. For example, use symbols as separators between words or paragraphs, or use them to decorate or emphasize the document.

4. Try different symbol fonts.

5. Try changing the font size for a symbol inserted in a document.

6. Try repeating a symbol to create a line across the page.

7. Save your changes, close the document, and exit Word.

Exercise 29

Skills Covered:
◆ Bulleted Lists ◆ Numbered Lists ◆ Sort

On the Job

Lists are an effective way to present items of information. Use a bulleted list when the items do not have to be in any particular order, like a grocery list or a list of objectives. Use a numbered list when the order of the items is important, such as directions or instructions. Use Sort to organize a list into alphabetical or numerical order.

The owner of The Sweet Tooth has asked you to create a handout announcing the rules for a contest she's running in the store. The flyer will include a bulleted list and a numbered list. You will sort the bulleted list in alphabetical order.

Terms

Bullet A dot or symbol that marks an important line of information or designates items in a list.

Sort To organize items into a specified order.

Notes

Bulleted Lists

- Use **bullets** to mark lists when the order of items does not matter.
- Word has seven built-in bullet symbols, but uses a simple black dot by default.
- A variety of bullet styles are available in the Bullets and Numbering dialog box, or you can create a customized bullet using a symbol.
- Word automatically carries bullet formatting forward to new paragraphs in a list.

Select a bullet style in the Bullets and Numbering dialog box

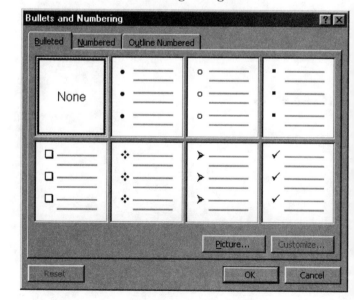

Numbered Lists

- Use numbers to mark lists when the order of items matters, such as with directions or how-to steps.

- Word automatically renumbers a list when you add or delete items.

- Word comes with seven numbering styles, but the default numbering style is an arabic numeral followed by a period.

- You can select a different number style in the Bullets and Numbering dialog box.

- Word automatically carries number formatting forward to new paragraphs in a list.

Select a number style in the Bullets and Numbering dialog box

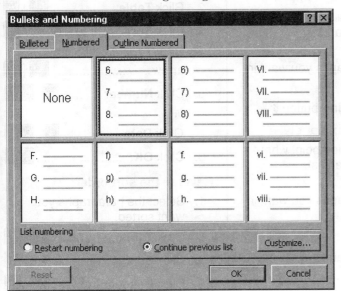

Sort

- Word can automatically **sort** items into alphabetical, numerical, or chronological order.

- A sort can be ascending (A to Z or 0 to 9) or descending (Z to A or 9 to 0).

- The default sort order is alphabetical ascending.

- Although the Sort command is on the Table menu, sorting is useful for arranging lists, paragraphs, or rows in a table.

Options for a default sort

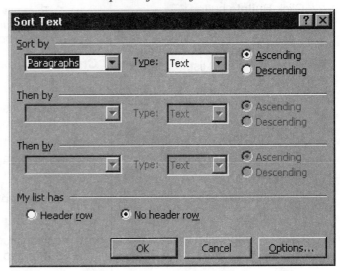

Procedures

Create Bulleted List

Use the default bullet:

1. Position insertion point where you want to start list.
   OR
   Select paragraphs you want in the list.
2. Click **Bullets** button .

Select a different bullet:

1. Position insertion point where you want to start list.
   OR
   Select paragraphs you want in the list.
2. Click **Format** .... `Alt`+`O`
3. Click **Bullets and Numbering** .... `N`
4. Click **Bulleted** page tab .... `Alt`+`B`
5. Click desired Bullet style .... `↕↔`
6. Click **OK** .... `Enter`

Customize bullet:

1. Position insertion point where you want to start list.
   OR
   Select paragraphs you want in list.
2. Click **Format** .... `Alt`+`O`
3. Click **Bullets and Numbering** .... `N`
4. Click **Bulleted** page tab .... `Alt`+`B`
5. Click desired **Bullet style** .... `↓``↑``→``←`
6. Click **Customize** .... `Alt`+`T`
7. Click desired **Bullet** character .... `Alt`+`U`, `→``←`
   OR
   a. Click **Bullet** button
      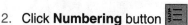 .... `Alt`+`B`
   b. Select desired **Font** .... `Alt`+`F`, `↑↓`, `Enter`

---

c. Click desired **symbol** ....`Tab`, `↕↔`
d. Click **OK** .... `Enter`
8. Click **OK** .... `Enter`

Turn off bullets:

- Click **Bullets** button .
  ✓ *To remove existing bullets, select bulleted list then click Bullets button.*

Create Numbered List

Use default number style:

1. Position insertion point where you want to start list.
   OR
   Select paragraphs you want in list.
2. Click **Numbering** button.

Select different number style:

1. Position insertion point where you want to start list.
   OR
   Select paragraphs you want in list.
2. Click **Format**............... `Alt`+`O`
3. Click **Bullets and Numbering** .... `N`
4. Click **Numbered** page tab .... `Alt`+`N`
5. Click **Number style** .... `↕↔`
6. Click **OK** .... `Enter`

Turn off numbering:

- Click **Numbering** button.
  ✓ *To remove numbers, select numbered list, then click Numbering button.*

Sort a List

Use default sort order:

1. Select the paragraphs you want sorted.
2. Click **Table**.................. `Alt`+`A`
3. Click **Sort**............................ `S`
4. Click **OK**.......................... `Enter`

Use a numerical or chronological sort:

1. Select the paragraphs you want sorted.
2. Click **Table**.................. `Alt`+`A`
3. Click **Sort**............................ `S`
4. Click **Type** drop-down arrow .... `Alt`+`Y`
5. Click **Number** .... `↓`, `Enter`
   OR
   Click **Date** .... `↓`, `Enter`
6. Click **OK**.......................... `Enter`

Reverse the sort order:

1. Select the paragraphs you want sorted.
2. Click **Table**.................. `Alt`+`A`
3. Click **Sort**............................ `S`
4. Click **Descending**........ `Alt`+`D`
5. Click **OK**.......................... `Enter`

Exercise Directions

1. Start Word, if necessary.

2. Open ⊘**29LISTS**.

3. Save the document as **WD29**.

4. Format the document shown in Illustration A.

   ✓ *Use the Format Painter to copy formatting from one location to another.*

   a. Use a 48-point serif font for the headline, in all uppercase.

   b. Center the headline, apply a thick underline and a shadow, and change the font color to blue.

   c. Use a serif font for remaining text in the sizes and styles specified in Illustration A.

   d. Use alignments specified in Illustration A.

   e. Insert symbols as specified.

   f. Make sure blank lines between paragraphs are set to 10 points.

      ✓ *Change font size before pressing Enter or go back and format paragraph marks on blank lines.*

5. Create a bulleted list using the five prizes.

6. Create a numbered list using the three entry steps.

7. Change the bullet.

8. Check the spelling and grammar.

9. Preview the document. It should look like the one in the Illustration A.

10. Sort the bulleted list into ascending alphabetical order.

11. Print the document.

12. Close the document and exit Word, saving all changes.

48-pt. serif, all caps bold, thick underline shadow effect, centered

INVENT A SODA FOUNTAIN CONCOCTION CONTEST

↓2x

The Sweet Tooth Candy Shop and Soda Fountain is sponsoring a Soda Fountain Concoction Contest. Over $1,000 worth of prizes will be awarded.

16-pt. serif justified

↓2x

☞ Prizes include: 18-pt. serif

↓2x

26-pt. Wingdings symbol

➢ Caps
➢ Chocolates
➢ Gift Certificates
➢ Soda Drinks
➢ T-shirts

16-pt. serif bulleted list

↓3x   18-pt. serif   Blue font, double underline

☞ Entering is as easy as 1-2-3:

↓2x

1) Pick up an entry form at The Sweet Tooth, 321 Main Street, Hanover, NH.
2) List the required ingredients, and steps for creating the concoction.
3) Return the entry form to The Sweet Tooth by December 31.

16-pt. serif, Numbered list

↓2x

Be sure to pick up your entry form and enter today! 16-pt. serif

↓2x

No purchase necessary. Employees of The Sweet Tooth are not eligible. 10-pt. serif, centered

On Your Own

1. Create a new document in Word.

2. Save the file as **OWD29**.

3. Type a bulleted list of five things you'd like to accomplish in the next year. These can be goals for school, work, or personal development. Examples might include earning a better grade in math, completing a project on the job, or getting in better shape by exercising and eating right.

4. Sort the list in alphabetical order.

5. Type a numbered list that includes at least five steps describing how you expect to accomplish one of the items in the bulleted list.

6. Change the sort order of the bulleted list to descending order.

7. Save your changes, close the document, and exit Word.

Exercise 30

Once again, the training director at State-of-the-Art Solutions has asked you to create a document. In this exercise, you will type and format a list of upcoming course offerings. You will use the skills you have learned in Lesson 4 to organize the information using alignments, tabs, and lists. You will also improve the appearance of the document by applying font formatting and effects.

Exercise Directions

1. Start Word, if necessary.

2. Open ⊘**30COURSE**.

3. Save the document as **WD30**.

4. Follow steps 5 through 15 to edit and format the document to achieve the result shown in Illustration A.

5. Format the first line in an 18-point sans serif font in all caps, blue, with an outline effect.

6. Format the second line in a 16-point sans serif font in all caps.

7. Format the third line in a 16-point sans serif font.

8. Center the first three lines.

9. Format the fourth line in the same 16-point sans serif font with an underline in Title Case. Use a tab to align the text *Training Schedule* at the right end of the line.

10. Format the three heading lines in the same 16-point sans serif font in Title Case, using a tab to align the course names at the right.

11. Format the course descriptions using a 12-point serif font, justified.

12. Format the lists with a 14-point serif font.

13. Sort the numbered list alphabetically.

14. Highlight the item about obtaining approval from your supervisor.

15. Customize the bullet using a symbol from the Wingdings font.

16. Preview the document. It should look similar to the document in Illustration A.

17. Print the document.

18. Save the document and close it.

19. Exit Word.

Illustration A

STATE-OF-THE-ART SOLUTIONS
TRAINING DEPARTMENT
Presents

↓ *2x*

January - March   **Training Schedule** ← *Right tab*

↓ *2x*

January   **Microsoft Word 1** ← *Right tab*

This introductory course will cover the basics of using Microsoft Word 2000 to create common business documents. By the end of the course you will know how to: create and print text-based documents such as letters and envelopes, and apply formatting.   *12-pt. serif, justified*

↓ *2x*

February   **Microsoft Word 2** ← *Right tab*

A continuation of the Word I course, this introductory level class will delve into some of the more intriguing features of Microsoft Word 2000. By the end of the course you will know how to conduct a mail merge, set up a document in columns, include headers and footers, and insert pictures into documents.   *12-pt. serif, justified*

↓ *2x*

March   **Microsoft Word 3** ← *Right tab*

This final course in the Microsoft Word series covers the advanced features. By the end of this course you will know how to work with tables, create and modify outlines, use e-mail and Internet features in Word, and share documents with other users.   *12-pt. serif, justified*

↓ *2x*

The Microsoft Word 3 course in March takes the bulk of three days. To enroll you must do the following:

↓ *2x*

Numbered list sorted alphabetically

A. Clear your schedule for three days
B. Complete Microsoft Word 1
C. Complete Microsoft Word 2
D. Obtain written approval from your supervisor ← *Highlight*

↓ *2x*

Future offerings include:

↓ *2x*

Bullet list using Wingding symbol as bullet

🖥 An Overview of Microsoft Excel
🖥 Databases Made Easy with Microsoft Access
🖥 Presenting…PowerPoint
🖥 Microsoft Office 2000
🖥 Accessing the Internet

14-pt. serif

↓ *2x*

For more information, contact Greg in Training, ext. 432. e-mail: gwalsh@sas.com.   *12-pt. serif, centered*

16-pt. sans serif, title case

139

Lesson 5

Document Formatting

Exercise 31

On the Job

Align text vertically to make the best use of white space and to improve readability.

The owner of The Sweet Tooth Candy Shop has asked you to create a flyer announcing the winner of the contest. In this exercise, you will type a document using font formatting and horizontal alignments, and then you will vertically align the document on the page.

Terms

Vertical alignment The position of text in relation to the top and bottom page margins.

Notes

Vertical Alignment

- **Vertical alignment** is used to adjust the position of all text on a page in relation to the top and bottom margins.

- There are four vertical alignments:
  - *Top:* Text begins below the top margin. Top is the default vertical alignment.
  - *Center:* Text is centered between the top and bottom margins.
  - *Justified:* Paragraphs are spaced to fill the page between the top and bottom margins.
  - *Bottom:* The last line of text begins just above the bottom margin.

- Centering vertically improves the appearance of some short documents, such as letters and memos.

- Vertical justification improves the appearance of documents that contain nearly full pages of text.

Procedures

Align Vertically

1. Click **File** .... `Alt`+`F`
2. Click **Page Setup** .... `U`
3. Click **Layout**
   page tab .... `Alt`+`L`
4. Click
   Vertical alignment ..... `Alt`+`V`
5. Select **Vertical alignment**
   option:
   - **Top**
   - **Center**
   - **Justified**
   - **Bottom**
6. Click **OK** .... `Enter`

Exercise Directions

1. Start Word, if necessary.
2. Create a new document.
3. Save the file as **WD31**.
4. In a serif font, type the document as shown in Illustration A, using the specified alignments, formatting, and blank lines between paragraphs.
5. Preview the document.
6. Center the document vertically.
7. Preview the document again.
8. Align the document vertically with the bottom of the page.
9. Preview the document again.
10. Justify the document vertically.
11. Preview the document one more time.
12. Print the document.
13. Close the document and exit Word, saving all changes.

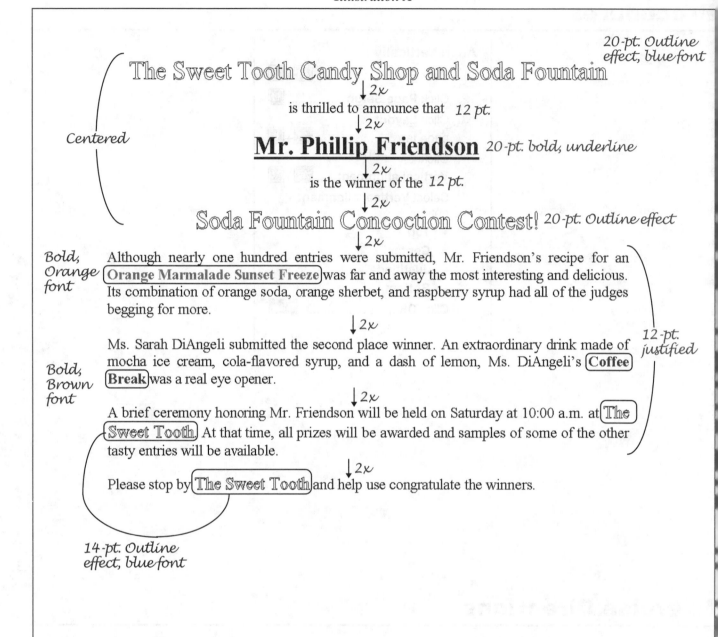

20-pt. Outline effect, blue font

The Sweet Tooth Candy Shop and Soda Fountain

↓2x

is thrilled to announce that *12 pt.*

↓2x

Mr. Phillip Friendson *20-pt. bold, underline*

↓2x

is the winner of the *12 pt.*

↓2x

Soda Fountain Concoction Contest! *20-pt. Outline effect*

↓2x

Centered

Bold, Orange font

Although nearly one hundred entries were submitted, Mr. Friendson's recipe for an Orange Marmalade Sunset Freeze was far and away the most interesting and delicious. Its combination of orange soda, orange sherbet, and raspberry syrup had all of the judges begging for more.

↓2x

Ms. Sarah DiAngeli submitted the second place winner. An extraordinary drink made of mocha ice cream, cola-flavored syrup, and a dash of lemon, Ms. DiAngeli's Coffee Break was a real eye opener.

↓2x

Bold, Brown font

A brief ceremony honoring Mr. Friendson will be held on Saturday at 10:00 a.m. at The Sweet Tooth. At that time, all prizes will be awarded and samples of some of the other tasty entries will be available.

↓2x

Please stop by The Sweet Tooth and help use congratulate the winners.

12-pt. justified

14-pt. Outline effect, blue font

On Your Own

1. In Word, open the document **OWD28**, the announcement you created in the On Your Own Section of Exercise 28, or open ⊛**31Event**.

2. Save the file as **OWD31**.

3. Try different vertical alignments until you settle on the one that makes the document look the best.

4. Save the changes, close the document, and exit Word.

Exercise 32

Skills Covered:

◆ **Line Spacing** ◆ **Paragraph Spacing** ◆ **Indent Text**

On the Job

Format documents using the right amount of space between lines, paragraphs, and words to make the pages look better and the text easier to read. Use indents to call attention to a paragraph, to achieve a particular visual effect, or to leave white space along the margins for notes or illustrations.

You want to improve the appearance of the training course list you created for State-of-the-Art Solutions. In this exercise, you will use line spacing, paragraph spacing, and indents to format the course list.

Terms

Line spacing The amount of white space between lines of text in a paragraph.

Leading Line spacing measured in points.

Paragraph spacing The amount of white space between paragraphs.

Indent A temporary left and/or right margin for lines or paragraphs.

Notes

Line Spacing

- **Line spacing** sets the amount of vertical space between lines. By default line spacing in Word is set to single space. Line spacing can be measured in either lines (single, double, etc.) or in points.

- When line spacing is measured in points, it is sometimes called **leading** (pronounced *ledding*).

> By default, Word uses leading that is 120% of the current font size. For a 10-point font, that means 12-point leading. This paragraph is formatted with the default leading for a 12-point font (14.4 pts.).

> Increase leading to make text easier to read. In this paragraph, the font is still 12 points, but the leading has been increased to exactly 16 points.

> Decrease leading to fit more lines on a page. In this paragraph, the leading has been set to exactly 10 points, while the font size is still 12 points. Keep in mind that decreasing leading makes text harder to read.

- Line spacing measured in lines can be set to single spaced, 1.5 spaced, or double spaced.

Paragraph Spacing

- **Paragraph spacing** can affect space before or after paragraphs.

- Amount of space can be specified in lines or in points. The default is points.

- Use increased paragraph spacing in place of extra returns or blank lines.

Indent Text

- There are five types of **indents**:
  - *Left* indents text from the left margin.
  - *Right* indents text from the right margin.
  - *Double* indents text from both the left and right margins.
  - *First line* indents just the first line of a paragraph from the left margin.
  - *Hanging* indents all lines but the first line from the left margin.
- Indent markers on the horizontal ruler show where current indents are set.

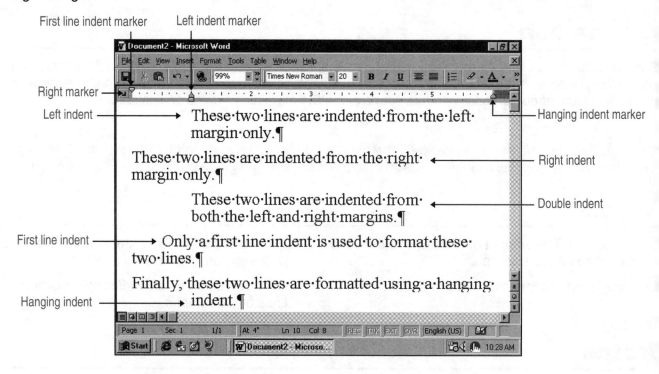

First line indent marker   Left indent marker

Right marker →

Left indent →   These two lines are indented from the left margin only.¶

These two lines are indented from the right margin only.¶   ← Right indent

These two lines are indented from both the left and right margins.¶   ← Double indent

First line indent →   Only a first line indent is used to format these two lines.¶

Hanging indent →   Finally, these two lines are formatted using a hanging indent.¶

Hanging indent marker

Procedures

Set Line Spacing
(Ctrl+1, Ctrl+2, Ctrl+5)

1. Position insertion point where text will be typed.
   OR
   Position insertion point in paragraph to change.
   OR
   Select paragraphs to change.
2. Click **F**o**rmat** .... `Alt`+`O`
3. Click **P**aragraph .... `P`
4. Click **I**ndents and Spacing page tab .... `Alt`+`I`
5. Click **Li**ne spacing ..... `Alt`+`N`
6. Select a **line spacing option:** .... `↓`, `Enter`
   - Single
   - 1.5 lines

   - Double
   OR
   a. Select **leading option:** .... `↓`, `Enter`
      - **At least** to set a minimum leading.
      - **Exactly** to set an exact leading.
      - **Multiple** to specify a percentage by which to increase leading.
   b. Click **A**t box .... `Alt`+`A`
   c. Type value in points.
7. Click **OK** .... `Enter`

Set Paragraph Spacing

1. Position insertion point where text will be typed.
   OR
   Position insertion point in paragraph to change.
   OR
   Select paragraphs to change.
2. Click **F**o**rmat** .... `Alt`+`O`
3. Click **P**aragraph .... `P`
   ✓ *To open the Paragraph dialog box quickly, right-click paragraph to format, then click Paragraph.*
4. Click **I**ndents and Spacing page tab .... `Alt`+`I`
5. Click **B**efore text box ... `Alt`+`B`
   OR
   Click **Af**ter text box ...... `Alt`+`E`

6. Type amount of space to leave.

   ✓ Type li *after value to specify lines.*

7. Click **OK** .... Enter

Indent Text

Indent from the left:

1. Position insertion point where text will be typed.

   OR

   Position insertion point in paragraph to change.

   OR

   Select paragraphs to change.

2. Click **Increase Indent**

   button .

   OR

   Click **Decrease Indent**

   button .

   OR

   Drag **Left-indent** marker on ruler.

Indent from the left and/or right:

1. Position insertion point where text will be typed.

   OR

   Position insertion point in paragraph to change.

   OR

   Select paragraphs to change.

2. Drag **Left-indent** marker on ruler.

3. Drag **Right-indent** marker on ruler.

   OR

   a. Click **Format** .... Alt+O

   b. Click **Paragraph** .... P

   c. Click **Indents and Spacing** page tab .... Alt+I

   d. Click **Left** text box .. Alt+L

   e. Type distance from left margin.

   f. Click **Right** text box .... Alt+R

   g. Type distance from right margin.

   h. Click **OK** .... Enter

Indent first line only *(Tab)*:

1. Position insertion point where text will be typed.

   OR

   Position insertion point in paragraph to change.

   OR

   Select paragraphs to change.

2. Drag **First Line indent** marker .

   OR

   a. Click **Format** .... Alt+O

   b. Click **Paragraph** .... P

   c. Click **Indents and Spacing** page tab .... Alt+I

   d. Click **Special** drop-down arrow .... Alt+S

   e. Click **First line** ..... ↓, Enter

   f. Click **By** text box ..... Alt+Y

   g. Type amount to indent.

   h. Click **OK** .... Enter

Hanging indent *(Ctrl+T)*:

1. Position insertion point where text will be typed.

   OR

   Position insertion point in paragraph to change.

   OR

   Select paragraphs to change.

2. Drag **Hanging indent** marker .

   OR

   a. Click **Format** .... Alt+O

   b. Click **Paragraph** .... P

   c. Click **Indents and Spacing** page tab .... Alt+I

   d. Click **Special** drop-down arrow .... Alt+S

   e. Click **Hanging** ..... ↓, Enter

   f. Click **By** text box ..... Alt+Y

   g. Type amount to indent.

3. Click **OK** .... Enter

Exercise Directions

1. Start Word, if necessary.

2. Open 💿 **32COURSE**.

3. Save the document as **WD32**.

4. Follow steps 5 through 8 to achieve the results shown in Illustration A.

5. Apply font formatting as shown in Illustration A.

   ✓ *Unless otherwise specified, all text is 12-point sans serif. (Arial is used in Illustration A.)*

6. Change case as marked in Illustration A.

7. Set alignments and tabs as marked in Illustration A.

8. Set line spacing, paragraph spacing, and indents as shown in Illustration A.

9. Check spelling and grammar.

10. Preview the document.

11. Print the document.

12. Close the document and exit Word, saving all changes.

STATE-OF-THE-ART SOLUTIONS ← *18-pt. Outline effect, blue font, all caps 6 pts. Of space after*

Centered

TRAINING DEPARTMENT ← *16-pt. all caps*

Presents ← *16-pt., 6-pts of space after*

January - March   Training Schedule ← *Right tab, 16-pt. - Underline 12-pts. of space after*

3 pts. before 3 pts. after

January   Microsoft Word 1 ← *Right tab*

Indent .5" from right and left

This introductory course will cover the basics of using Microsoft Word 2000 to create common business documents. By the end of the course you will know how to: create and print text-based documents such as letters and envelopes, and apply formatting. — *Single space, justified, 3 pt of space before, and 6-pts after*

3 pts. before 3 pts. after

February   Microsoft Word 2 ← *Right tab*

Indent .5" from right and left

A continuation of the Word I course, this introductory level class will delve into some of the more intriguing features of Microsoft Word 2000. By the end of the course you will know how to conduct a mail merge, set up a document in columns, include headers and footers, and insert pictures. — *Single space, justified, 3 pt of space before, and 6-pts after*

3 pts. before 3 pts. after

March   Microsoft Word 3 ← *Right tab*

Indent .5" from right and left

This final course in the Microsoft Word series covers the advanced features. By the end of this course you will know how to work with tables, create and modify outlines, use e-mail and Internet features in Word, and share documents with other users. — *Single space, justified, 3 pt of space before, and 6 pts after*

We have hired highly qualified instructors to teach these classes.

Following is a brief description of each of the instructors. — *Double-spaced 1st line indent .5"*

Word 1. The instructor for the introductory Word class is Cathy Bennet. Ms. Bennet has ten years experience in computer training.

14-pt. Bold, underline, blue

Word 2. Joseph Castaldy is the instructor for the intermediate Word class. Mr. Castaldy has been involved in computer training for eight years.

Word 3. Mary Rose Jarvis will be teaching the advanced Word class. Ms. Jarvis is one of the most highly regarded corporate trainers in California. She has more than twelve years of corporate training experience.

1½ lines spacing left align 0 pts. Before, 6 pts. After Hanging indent by .75"

For more information, contact Greg in Training, ext. 432. e-mail: gwalsh@sas.com. ← *10-pt. centered*

On Your Own

1. Create a new document in Word.

2. Save the file as **OWD23**.

3. Think of some documents that could benefit from line spacing, paragraph spacing, and indent formatting. For example, many instructors require reports and papers to be double spaced. First drafts of documents that will be read by others should be double spaced so reviewers can jot notes or make corrections. A resume can be set up neatly using spacing and indent features, as can a reference list.

4. Create a resume describing your school experience, outside activities such as clubs or athletic teams, and any work experience.

5. Use spacing and indent features to format the resume.

6. Use alignments and font formatting to enhance the text and to call attention to important items.

7. Use lists and symbols if appropriate.

8. Save your changes, close the document, and exit Word.

Exercise 33

Skills Covered:

◆ **Format a One-Page Report** ◆ **Set Margins** ◆ **Set Page Orientation**

On the Job

Format a one-page report so that when you print it it looks good on the page. Set margins to meet expected requirements and to improve the document's appearance and readability. For example, leave a wider margin in a report if you expect a reader to make notes or comments; leave a narrower margin to fit more text on a page.

New clients may want to know the history of a company. In this exercise, you'll create a one-page report providing background information about Cornerstone Graphics, Inc. The report will be used as part of a corporate information package sent to prospective clients.

Terms

Gutter Space added to the margin to leave room for binding.

Margins The amount of white space between the text and the edge of the page on all four sides.

Section In Word, a segment of a document defined by a section break. A section may have different page formatting from the rest of the document.

Portrait orientation The default position for displaying and printing text horizontally across the shorter side of a page.

Landscape orientation Rotating document text so it displays and prints horizontally across the longer side of a page.

Notes

Format a One-Page Report

- Traditionally, a one-page report is set up as follows:
  - Text starts 2" from the top of the page.
  - Text is justified.
  - Lines are double spaced.
  - First-line indents are .5" or 1".
  - The report title is centered and all uppercase.
  - Spacing following the title ranges from ¾" to 1" (approximately four lines).
  - Unbound reports have left and right margins of 1".

- A **gutter** on bound reports makes the left margin wider than right margin.
  - ✓ *Use the Mirror margins option to set gutter width on inside margin of each page.*

Set Margins

- **Margins** are measured in inches.
- Default margins are 1.25" on the left and right and 1" on the top and bottom.
- Margin settings affect an entire document, or the current **section**.
  - ✓ *To set margins for a paragraph, use indents as described in Exercise 32.*

150

- On the rulers, areas outside the margins are shaded gray, while areas inside the margins are white.

  ✓ *To see both vertical and horizontal rules, use Print Layout view.*

- Light gray bars mark the margins on the rulers.

Set Page Orientation

- There are two page orientations available:
  - **Portrait**
  - **Landscape**

- Portrait is the default orientation, and is used for most documents, including letters, memos, and reports.

- Use landscape orientation to display a document across the wider length of the page. For example, if a document contains a table that is wider than the standard 8.5" page, Word will split it across two pages. When you change to landscape orientation, the table will fit on the 11" page.

Procedures

Set Margins in Print Layout View

1. Move the mouse pointer over the margin marker on the ruler.

   ✓ *The mouse pointer changes to a double-headed arrow, and the ScreenTip identifies the margin.*

2. Drag the margin marker to new location.

   ✓ *Press and hold the Alt key while you drag to see the margin measure units.*

Set Margins in Any View

1. Click **File** .... `Alt`+`F`
2. Click **Page Setup** .... `U`
3. Click **Margins** tab........ `Alt`+`M`
4. Click **Top** text box .... `Alt`+`T`
5. Type top margin width.
6. Click **Bottom** text box.............................. `Alt`+`B`
7. Type bottom margin width.
8. Click **Left** text box .... `Alt`+`F`
9. Type left margin width.
10. Click **Right** text box.............................. `Alt`+`H`
11. Type right margin width.
12. Click the **Apply to** drop-down arrow .... `Alt`+`Y`
13. Select **This point forward**.
    OR
    Select **Whole document**.
14. Click **OK** .... `Enter`

Set Page Orientation

1. Click **File**..................... `Alt`+`F`
2. Click **Page Setup** .... `U`
3. Click **Paper Size** text box .... `Alt`+`S`
4. Click **Portrait** .... `I`
   OR
   Click **Landscape** .... `C`
5. Click **OK** .... `Enter`

Exercise Directions

1. Start Word, if necessary.

2. Create a new document and save it as **WD33**.

3. Set 1" margins on the left and right and .75" margins on the top and bottom.

4. Set a left tab stop at 1".

   ✓ *Refer to Exercise 24 for more information on setting tabs.*

5. Type the report as shown in Illustration A.

6. Title formatting:
   - Use a 26-point sans serif font for the title, in all uppercase.
   - Center it and leave 54-points of space after it.

7. Heading formatting:
   - Use a 14-point bold, sans serif font for the headings in title case. Left align the headings and leave 6 points of space before each one and after each one.

8. Body text formatting:
   - Use a 12-point serif font for the body text. Justify and double-space all body text paragraphs.
   - Leave 6 points of space before each paragraph and after each one. Indent the first line of each body text paragraph by 1".

9. Credential list formatting:
   - Use a 12-point serif font, justified and single spaced. Indent all three paragraphs 1" from left and 1" from right.
   - Insert a Wingdings symbol at the beginning of each paragraph sized to 28-points. Then apply a .5" hanging indent to each paragraph.
   - Set line spacing to exactly 11-points and set paragraph spacing to 6 points before and 6-points after.

10. If the document extends onto a second page, change the top and bottom margins to .5".

11. Check the spelling and grammar.

12. Change the page orientation to Landscape.

13. Preview the document.

14. Change the page orientation back to Portrait.

15. Preview the document.

16. Print the document.

17. Close the document and exit Word, saving all changes.

Illustration A

Title → # CORNERSTONE GRAPHICS

Cornerstone Graphics is a small but successful graphics design firm based in Venice, California. Tom Louris, a recent graduate of U.C.L.A., started the firm on a shoestring in 1992. His keen eye for detail and his talent for graphics design have paid off. The company has steadily and consistently increased its client base and gross income. Currently, Cornerstone employs over 25 people.

Growth and Expansion ← *Heading*

In 1998, Louris recognized the growing importance of The World Wide Web, and expanded the scope of Cornerstone's business to include Web page design. The designers at Cornerstone have the technical skills and the artistic ability needed to create effective and appealing Web pages.

Cornerstone has recently reached an agreement with State-of-the-Art Solutions, a consulting company specializing in helping clients expand business on the Web. The alliance will enable Cornerstone to tap the resources and expertise of State-of-the-Art to bring expanded opportunities to all types of clients.

Cornerstone's Credentials ← *Heading*

 Cornerstone has recruited and maintained a talented and technically savvy staff of Web page designers.

 Cornerstone is committed to working closely with each client and to providing a personalized service not readily available at other, larger firms.

 Cornerstone places client satisfaction above all other goals and guarantees all work.

Credential list

On Your Own

1. Create a new document in Word.
2. Save the file as **OWD33**.
3. In the third person, draft a one-page report about yourself. For example, draft a document that you could include in a directory for an organization of which you are a member. Think of the *About the Author* paragraphs found in books and magazines, or the *About the Performers* paragraphs found in a theater program.
4. Double space the report.
5. Use correct document formatting for a one-page report.
6. Use other formatting effects, including fonts, lists, and symbols.
7. Save your changes, close the document, and exit Word.

Exercise 34

On the Job

Create a hyperlink to connect related documents to each other, to connect a Word document to a Web site, or to connect one location in a document to another location in the same document. For example, create hyperlinks from a table of contents in a report to each chapter heading or from a report topic to an Internet site where more information can be found. Hyperlinks let you expand the boundaries among documents and among computers because, in effect, you can link to information stored anywhere on the Internet.

You are in charge of creating a document welcoming participants to the Business on the Web Seminar. First you will create a hyperlink from one part of a document welcoming participants to the Business on the Web Seminar to another part of the same document. Next, you will create a hyperlink from the notice to an invitation to meet the people speaking at the seminar. You will then edit the first link and remove it. Finally, you will link the first notice to a Web site about things to do in Phoenix.

Terms

Hyperlink Text or graphics linked to a destination file or location. Click the link to jump to the destination.

HTML The file format used to stored documents on the World Wide Web.

Hyperlink destination The location displayed when the hyperlink is clicked.

Hyperlink source The document where the hyperlink is inserted.

Bookmark A nonprinting character that you insert and name so that you can quickly find a particular location in a document.

Hypertext Text formatted as a hyperlink.

Notes

Create Hyperlinks

- **Hyperlinks** can be used to link locations within a single document or to link two documents.

- Hyperlinks can be created in any Word document including Word documents saved as **HTML** files.

- You can change existing text to a hyperlink or type new text to create a hyperlink.

- A **hyperlink destination** does not have to be in the same file format as the **hyperlink source** document. For example, you can link a Word document file to an HTML file or to an Excel file, etc.

- The hyperlink destination can be a file stored on your computer, on your company intranet, or a site on the Internet.

- You can create a hyperlink within a document for moving to the top of the document, to a specific heading, or to a **bookmark**.

  ✓ *Bookmarks are covered in Exercise 63.*

- Word uses its AutoFormat feature to format URLs typed in a document as hyperlinks.
- By default, Word formats **hypertext** in blue with a continuous underline.
- By default, once hypertext has been used, it changes to violet.

Edit Hyperlinks

- You can edit hyperlink text.
- You can change a hyperlink destination.
- You can remove a hyperlink completely.
- You can change hyperlink formatting.

Procedures

Create Hyperlinks *(Ctrl+K)*

Create hyperlink within a document:

1. Position insertion point where you want to insert hyperlink.
   OR
   Select text to change to a hyperlink.
2. Click **Insert Hyperlink** button 🌐.
   OR
   a. Click **Insert** .... `Alt`+`I`
   b. Click **Hyperlink**............. `I`
3. Click **Place in this document** in Places bar .... `Alt`+`A`
4. In the **Select a place in this document list**, click hyperlink destination........... `Alt`+`C`, `↓`

   ✓ If necessary click the expand symbol **+** to expand the list to show additional headings and/or bookmarks.

5. Click **OK**.......................... `Enter`

   ✓ If existing text is not selected, Word uses the destination name as the hyperlink text.

Create hyperlink to a different document:

1. Position insertion point where you want to insert hyperlink.
   OR
   Select text to change to a hyperlink.
2. Click **Insert Hyperlink** button 🌐.
   OR

   a. Click **Insert**............ `Alt`+`I`
   b. Click **Hyperlink** .... `I`
3. Click **Existing File or Web Page** in the Places bar.......... `Alt`+`X`
4. In the **Type the file or Web page name** text box, type the hyperlink destination file name .... `Alt`+`E`
   OR

   a. Click **Recent Files** . `Alt`+`C` to display a list of recently used files.
   b. Click the file name in the list of files.
   OR

   a. Click **File** .... `Alt`+`F`
   b. Locate and click file name.
   c. Click **OK** .... `Enter`

5. Edit **Text to display** .... `Alt`+`T`

   ✓ Word automatically completes the file name as you type based on recently used file names; stop typing to accept the entry or keep typing to enter the name you want.

   ✓ Word displays this text as the hyperlink in the document.

6. Click **OK** .... `Enter`

Create hyperlink to a Web page:

1. Position insertion point where you want to insert the hyperlink.
   OR
   Select text to change to a hyperlink.

2. Click **Insert Hyperlink** button 🌐.
   OR

   a. Click **Insert** ....`Alt`+`I`
   b. Click **Hyperlink**.............. `I`
3. Click **Existing File or Web Page** in Places bar ......`Alt`+`X`
4. Type the **destination URL** in the **Type the file or Web page name** box... `Alt`+`E`

   ✓ Word automatically completes the URL as you type based on other URLs you have typed in the past. Stop typing to accept the entry, or keep typing to enter the URL you want.

   OR

   a. Click **Browsed Pages** .... `Alt`+`B` to display a list of Web pages you have recently accessed.
   b. Click the URL or site name you want in the list of files.
5. Edit **Text to display** .... `Alt`+`T`

   ✓ Type the text you want displayed for the hyperlink.

6. Click **OK**.......................... `Enter`

Edit Hyperlinks

Remove hyperlink:

1. Right-click hyperlink text.
2. Select **Hyperlink** .... `H`
3. Click **Remove Hyperlink**..... `R`

   ✓ This removes the hyperlink, but not the text.

Edit hyperlink text:
1. Right-click hyperlink text.
2. Select **Hyperlink**.................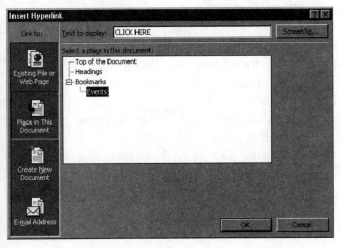
3. Click **Select Hyperlink** ....
4. Type new hyperlink text.
   ✓ Only the first word you type will be formatted as a hyperlink.

Change hyperlink destination:
1. Right-click hyperlink text.
2. Select **Hyperlink**.................
3. Click **Edit Hyperlink** ....
4. Select new destination.
5. Click **OK** ....Enter

Change hyperlink formatting:
1. Right-click hyperlink text.
2. Select **Hyperlink** ....
3. Click **Select Hyperlink**........
4. Select new formatting using standard formatting techniques.

Exercise Directions

1. Start Word, if necessary.
2. Open 34LIST.
3. Save the document as **WD34-1**, and then close it.
4. Open 34LINKS.
5. Save the document as **WD34-2**, and keep it open.
   ✓ Refer to Illustration A to see what hyperlinks should be inserted.
6. Press Ctrl+End to go to the end of the document.
7. Select the text CLICK HERE in the last line of the document.
8. Insert a hyperlink to the top of the document.

9. Click the hyperlink text to see if the hyperlink works correctly.
   ✓ The Web toolbar is displayed.
10. Select the text *CLICK HERE* at the end of the paragraph beginning *We have assembled....*

11. Insert a hyperlink to the document **WD34-1**.
12. Click the hyperlink text to see if the hyperlink works correctly.
13. Click the Back button on the Web toolbar to return to the **WD34-2** document.
14. Format the text of both hyperlinks to all lower case.
    ✓ Remember to select the hyperlink before applying the formatting.
15. Remove the hyperlink to the top of the document.
16. Select the text *CLICK HERE* at the end of the paragraph beginning *Also, Phoenix....*
17. Insert a hyperlink to the Arizona home page: D:/Internet/E34/main.htm
    ✓ If you've copied the Internet simulation files to your hard drive or your CD-ROM drive is a letter other than D:, substitute the correct letter for D.
18. Click the link.
    ✓ You may be prompted to sign on to your ISP.
19. Click the *Back* button on your browser's toolbar to return to the **WD34-2** document.
20. Click the *Forward* button on Word's Web toolbar to go to the Arizona home page.
21. Click the link *az living*.
22. Scroll down the page until you see the red buttons listing city names, then click the link *Phoenix's Point of Pride*.
23. Print the Phoenix Web page.
24. Exit the simulation.
25. Exit Word, saving all changes.

BUSINESS ON THE WEB

Phoenix, AZ   February 9 and 10

Welcome to the ***Business on the Web Seminar,*** sponsored by State-of-the-Art Solutions.

The agenda is chock full of forums, lectures, and roundtables which you are sure to find exciting and informative. Whether you are just beginning to explore the opportunities available on the World Wide Web, or whether you have established your business on the Web, we believe that this seminar will provide you with new tools for growth and success.

We have assembled some of the most successful Web entrepreneurs to conduct this seminar. The speakers will be present at a cocktail hour hosted by State-of-the-Art Solutions every evening in the hotel lobby. Please stop by for some refreshments, to meet the speakers, or just to socialize. For a list of speakers, CLICK HERE.

Create hyperlink to WD34-1.

Also, Phoenix is a wonderful city to visit. If you have free time while you are here, we invite you to participate in the many events and activities taking place throughout the area. To connect to a Web site for more information about things to do in Phoenix, CLICK HERE.

Create hyperlink to Arizona home page

If you have any questions about the seminar, the speakers, or extracurricular activities please contact Justin Godere, Seminar Coordinator.

CLICK HERE to Return to the Top of the Document
Create hyperlink to top of document

On Your Own

1. Open the document **OWD33**, the one-page report about yourself that you created in the On Your Own section of Exercise 33, or open ⊙ **34REPORT**.

2. Save the file as **OWD34**.

3. Open the document **OWD32**, the resume you created in the On Your Own section of Exercise 32, or open ⊙ **34RESUME**

4. Save the file as **OWD34-2**, and then close it.

5. Create a hyperlink from the **OWD34** report document to the **OWD34-2** resume document.

6. Create a link back to the report from resume.

7. If you have access to the Internet, try linking the report to a Web site that you like.

8. Test the links.

9. Save the changes to all documents, close the documents, and exit Word.

Exercise 35

◆ **Critical Thinking**

The owner of The Sweet Tooth has asked you to create a one-page report providing information about ways you think you could increase business. In this exercise, you will create the report, as well as a sample advertisement. You will then link the two documents together.

Exercise Directions

1. Start Word, if necessary.
2. Open ☉**35SWEET**.
3. Save the document as **WD35-1**.
4. Follow steps 5 through 19 to edit and format the document to achieve the result shown in Illustration A.
5. Change the top and bottom margins to .75" and the left and right margins to 1".
6. Leave 2" (144 pts.) of space above the title.
7. Format the title in a 26-point serif font in blue with an outline effect and center it.
   - ✓ *If the title does not fit on a single line, select a different font or use a font size.*
8. Leave 54 points of space following the title.
9. Format all body text paragraphs as follows:
   - 12-point sans serif font
   - Justified
   - Double-spaced
   - First line indented by .5"
   - Leave 3 points of space after.
10. Format the two headings as follows:
    - 14-point bold sans serif font, all uppercase
    - Left-aligned, no indent
    - Double-spaced
    - Leave 3 points of space after
11. Format the three ad outlets as follows:
    - Numbered list
    - Single spaced
    - No space between items
    - Leave 12 points of space following the third item

12. Format the four benefits of using the Web as follows:
    - Bulleted list
    - Single spaced
    - No space between.
    - Double-indent 1" from the left and the right margins
13. Center the document vertically on the page.
14. Preview the document. It should look similar to the document in Illustration A.
15. Print the document.
16. Save the document and close it.
17. Create a new document in Word and save it as **WD35-2.doc**.
18. Type and format the document shown in Illustration B.
19. Create a hyperlink from the text CLICK HERE on the last line of the **WD35-2** to the **WD35-1** document.
20. Test the hyperlink.
21. Create a hyperlink from the first item in the numbered list on the **WD35-2** to the **WD35-2** document.
22. Test the hyperlink.
23. Save and close all open documents and exit Word.

Illustration A

The Sweet Tooth Business Improvement Plan

In today's highly competitive marketplace, there are many steps a small business can take to increase profits. The following report outlines two actions that the owner The Sweet Tooth Candy Shop can take to quickly improve business.

ADVERTISING

The fastest method of increasing visibility is to increase the store's advertising in the local arena. The Sweet Shop should consider the following ad outlets:

1. Print ads in all local newspapers
2. Radio spots
3. T.V. spots on local cable

WEB SITE DEVELOPMENT

The second method recommended for increasing both visibility and business is to develop a presence on the World Wide Web. A web site could provide the following benefits:

- ✓ Provide information to virtually everyone with access to the Internet
- ✓ Provide communication with customers via e-mail
- ✓ Advertise special events and sales
- ✓ Provide a retail outlet

The Sweet Tooth ← *26-pt. serif, outline effect, blue, centered*

321 Main Street ✧ Hanover, NH 03755 ← *12-pt. serif, centered*

Wingding symbol ⟶ ↓ *3x*

Spring Sale ← *48-pt. serif, outline effect, blue, centered*

↓ *2x*

Save from 10% to 50% at our first ever Spring Sale! *20-pt. serif, bold, centered*

↓ *2x*

Sale items include:

Bullet list, customized with Wingding symbol

- ☺ **Truffles**
- ☺ **Fudge**
- ☺ **Penny Candy**
- ☺ **Boxed Candy**
- ☺ **Dipped Fruits**
- ☺ **And More!**

18-pt. bold, serif, left aligned

↓ *2x*

Bring In This Ad And We'll Give You An Additional 5% Off Your Entire Purchase! *18-pt. bold, serif, justified, indent .75" from left and right.*

2" (144 pts.)

CLICK HERE to return to the Business Improvement Plan *16-pt. serif, centered*

Created hyperlink to WD35-1

162

Lesson 6

Manage Documents

Exercise 36

◆ **Open a Document as Read-only** ◆ **Open a Document from Windows**

On the Job

Open a document as read-only when you do not want revisions to affect the original file. For example, if you want to proofread a finished document, or if you want to review an existing document to see if it can be revised for a different purpose, you would open it as read-only. Open a document from Windows to save time.

The training director at State-of-the-Art Solutions has asked you to review the course list to see if it needs to be updated. In this exercise, you will open the document as read-only so you can read it without worrying about changing it accidentally. You will then save it with a different file name so that you can go ahead and change the dates.

Terms

Read-only A mode of operation in which revisions cannot be saved in the original document.

Notes

Open a Document as Read-only

- Opening a document as **read-only** is a safeguard against accidentally making changes.

- Word prompts you to use the Save As feature to save revisions made to a document opened as read-only in a new document with a different file name.

- The words *Read-Only* appear in the title bar of a document opened as read-only.

Read-only appears in the title bar

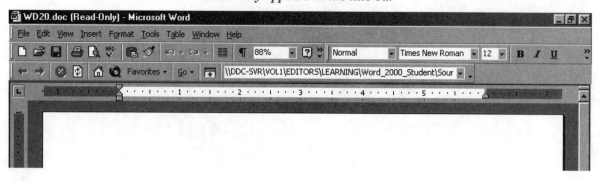

Open a Document from Windows

- Use the Windows Start Menu to open a document and start Word at the same time.
  - You can open any Office 2000 document using the Open Office Document dialog box accessed directly from the Windows Start menu.
    - ✓ *The Open Office Document dialog box is similar to Word's Open dialog box.*

Open Office Document dialog box

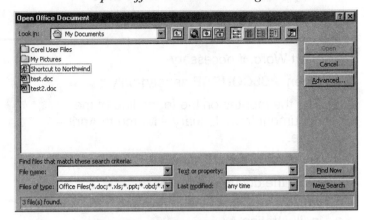

- Click the Documents menu to open one of 15 most-recently used files.
- Locate and open any document using Windows Explorer.

Procedures

Open a Document as Read-only *(Ctrl+O)*

1. Click **Open** button 📂.
   OR
   a. Click **File**.................**Alt**+**F**
   b. Click **Open**.....................**O**
2. Right-click document name.
   - ✓ *Point mouse at file name you want to open, then click right mouse button.*
   OR
   a. Click document name.
   b. Click **Open** drop-down arrow .
3. Click **Open Read-Only**........**R**

Open a Word Document with Office Shortcut Bar

1. Click **Open Office Document** button 📂 on Office shortcut bar.
   OR
   a. Click **Start** button
      Start...............**Ctrl**+**Esc**
   b. Click **Open Office Document** button 📂.
2. Click **Look in** drop-down arrow.................**Alt**+**I**
3. Click drive or folder.
   - ✓ *If necessary, double-click folder name.*
4. Double-click document name.
   OR
   Click **Open**.................**Alt**+**O**

Open a Word Document from the Documents Menu

1. Click **Start** button
   Start.....................**Ctrl**+**Esc**
2. Select **Documents**.............**D**
3. Click document name.

Open a Word Document From Windows Explorer

1. Right-click **Start** button
   Start.
2. Click **Explore**.....................**E**
3. Select drive where folder/file is located.
4. Open folder.
5. Double-click document name that you want to open.

Exercise Directions

1. Start Word, if necessary.
2. Open ⊘**36COURSE** as read-only.
3. Edit the months on the fourth line of the document from January – March to April – June.
4. Try to save the changes.
5. Save the document as **WD36**.
6. Change the dates in the document as indicated in Illustration A.
7. Preview the document.
8. Print the document.
9. Close the document and exit Word, saving all changes.

Illustration A

STATE-OF-THE-ART SOLUTIONS

TRAINING DEPARTMENT
Presents

April   *June*

~~January~~ - ~~March~~   **Training Schedule**

January   *April*

~~January~~   **Microsoft Word 1**

This introductory course will cover the basics of using Microsoft Word 2000 to create common business documents. By the end of the course you will know how to: create and print text-based documents such as letters and envelopes, and apply formatting.

May

~~February~~   **Microsoft Word 2**

A continuation of the Word I course, this introductory level class will delve into some of the more intriguing features of Microsoft Word 2000. By the end of the course you will know how to conduct a mail merge, set up a document in columns, include headers and footers, and insert pictures.

June

~~March~~   **Microsoft Word 3**

This final course in the Microsoft Word series covers the advanced features. By the end of this course you will know how to work with tables, create and modify outlines, use e-mail and Internet features in Word, and share documents with other users.

We have hired highly quailed instructors to teach these classes. Following is a brief description of each of the instructors.

Word 1. The instructor for the introductory Word class is Cathy Bennet. Ms. Bennet has ten years experience in computer training.

Word 2. Joseph Castaldy is the instructor for the intermediate Word class. Mr. Castaldy has been involved in computer training for eight years.

Word 3. Mary Rose Jarvis will be teaching the advanced Word class. Ms. Jarvis is one of the most highly regarded corporate trainers in California. She has more than twelve years of corporate training experience.

For more information, contact Greg in Training, ext. 432. e-mail: gwalsh@sas.com.

On Your Own

1. Open **OWD31**, the event announcement document you created in the On Your Own section of Exercise 31, as read-only, or open ⊙ **36EVENT** as read-only.

2. Change the vertical alignment of the document.

3. Change the date of the event.

4. Change some of the formatting in the document.

5. Change the symbols you used in the document.

6. Try saving the changes.

7. Save the document as **OWD36**.

8. Close the document and exit Word.

Exercise 37

On the Job

Preview a document before opening it or printing it to make sure it is the correct file. Print files without opening them to save time.

By now you've created several documents for The Sweet Tooth. To save time, you want to preview some of the documents and print them without opening them.

Notes

Preview a File Before Opening It

- You can preview a document before opening it in the Open dialog box.

- Previewing is useful for checking a document you want to print without opening it.

- Once you select to preview files in the Open dialog box, the preview is displayed until you change the view.

Preview a document in the Open dialog box

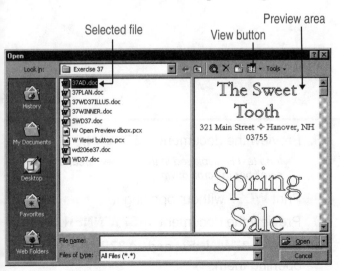

Print a Document without Opening It

- To save time, you can print a document from the Open dialog box without opening it.

- Print without opening when you are certain the document is ready for printing.

  ✓ *You can also print a document without opening it from the Open Office dialog box or from Windows Explorer.*

Print Multiple Files

- You can select more than one file at a time for printing in the Open dialog box.

- Selecting multiple files for printing sends them all to the printer, where they will be printed one after the other.

- All selected files must be in the same folder.

Procedures

Preview a Document

1. Click **File** .... `Alt`+`F`
2. Click **Open** .... `O`
3. Click **Views** button drop-down arrow `⊞ ▾`.
4. Click **Preview** .... `V`
5. Click document name to preview.
   - ✓ *If necessary, select drive and/or folder to locate document.*

Turn Preview Off

1. Click **File** .... `Alt`+`F`
2. Click **Open** .... `O`
3. Click **Views** button drop-down arrow `⊞ ▾`.

---

4. Select another view:
   - Click **List** `▤` .... `L`
   - Click **Details** `▦` .... `D`
   - Click **Properties** `▤` .... `R`

- ✓ *Or click the Views button repeatedly to cycle through the Views options.*

Print a File without Opening It

1. Click **File** .... `Alt`+`F`
2. Click **Open** .... `O`
3. Right-click document name.
   - ✓ *If necessary, select drive and/or folder to locate document.*

   OR

   Click **Tools** button

   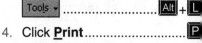 .... `Alt`+`L`
4. Click **Print** .... `P`

Print Multiple Files

1. Click **File** .... `Alt`+`F`
2. Click **Open** .... `O`
3. Click the first document name.
4. Press and hold **Ctrl** .... `Ctrl`
5. Click each additional document name.
6. Click the right-mouse button.

   OR

   Click **Tools** button

   `Tools ▾` .... `Alt`+`L`
7. Click **Print** .... `P`

Exercise Directions

1. Start Word, if necessary.
2. Open ✪ **37AD**.
3. Save the document as **WD37**.
4. Make the formatting changes to achieve the results shown in Illustration A.
5. Check the spelling and grammar.
6. Save the changes.
7. Close the document.

8. Preview the document ✪ **37PLAN**.
   - ✓ *If no text is displayed in the preview area, use the scroll bar to scroll down.*
9. Print **WD37** without opening it.
10. Preview the document ✪ **37WINNER**.
11. Print ✪ **37WINNER** and ✪ **37PLAN** without opening them.
12. Exit Word.

Illustration A

The Sweet Tooth *30 pts.*

321 Main Street ✧ Hanover, NH 03755

Spring Sale *48-pt. bold, Shadow effect*

Underline

Save from <u>10% to 50%</u> at our first ever Spring Sale!

Sale items include:

- ☺ <u>Truffles</u>
- ☺ <u>Fudge</u>
- ☺ <u>Penny Candy</u>
- ☺ <u>Boxed Candy</u>
- ☺ <u>Dipped Fruits</u>
- ☺ <u>And More!</u>

20 pts., Double underline in blue

Underline

BRING IN <u>THIS AD</u> AND WE'LL GIVE YOU <u>AN ADDITIONAL 10%</u> OFF YOUR ENTIRE PURCHASE!

20 pts., all uppercase

Underline

On Your Own

1. Start Word.

2. Preview some of the documents you have created in the On Your Own sections of previous exercises, or preview ⊙ **37EVENT**, ⊙ **37RESUME**, and ⊙ **37REPORT**.

3. Hide the preview.

4. Display the preview again.

5. Print several of the documents without opening them.

6. When you are finished, exit Word.

Exercise 38

Skills Covered:

◆ **Document Properties**

On the Job

Use document properties to identify important information about a file, such as the name of the author and the main topic.

Cornerstone Graphics has hired you to do some promotional work similar to the work you have done for The Sweet Tooth. You need to write a letter to the company president confirming your agreement. In this exercise, you will open the confirmation letter you wrote to The Sweet Tooth as read-only, save it with a new name, and then modify it to send to Cornerstone Graphics. You will enter document properties to help differentiate the letter to Cornerstone from the letter to The Sweet Tooth.

Terms

Document Properties Categories of information about a document.

Keywords Important words found in a document. Keywords can be used to classify a document.

Notes

Document Properties

- With the **Document Properties** feature you can save information that is unique to a particular document.

- Document Properties lets you enter information in five categories.

- Three of the more useful categories are:
  - *General properties.* Include the type of document, its size, its location, when it was created, last accessed, and last modified.
    - Use General properties to check file storage and access information.
  - *Summary properties.* Include a document title, subject, author, **keywords**, and comments.
    - Use Summary properties to save summary information with a document.
  - *Statistical properties.* Include the number of pages, paragraphs, lines, words, characters, and bytes in the document.

- Use Statistical properties to create documents of a specific length or word count.

- You can set Word to display the Properties dialog box automatically each time you save a document.

The Summary page of the Properties dialog box

Procedures

Use Document Properties

1. Click **File**..................... `Alt`+`F`
2. Click **Properties**................. `I`
3. Select desired tab....... `Ctrl`+`Tab`
   For example:
   - Click **Summary** tab and type summary information.
   - Click **Statistics** tab to see statistical information.
   - Click **General** tab to see file storage and access information.
4. Click **OK** .... `Enter`

Automatically Display Properties Dialog Box

1. Click **Tools** .... `Alt`+`T`
2. Click **Options** .... `O`
3. Click **Save** tab .... `Ctrl`+`Tab`
4. Select **Prompt for document properties** check box............................. `Alt`+`I`
5. Click **OK** .... `Enter`

Exercise Directions

1. Start Word, if necessary.
2. Open ⊙ **38LETTER** as read-only.
3. Save the document as **WD38**.
4. Make the revisions indicated in Illustration A.
5. Check the number of words in the document.
6. Enter the following summary information:
   - Title: Cornerstone Promotions
   - Subject: Confirm Agreement
   - Author: Your name
   - Manager: N/A
   - Company: Cornerstone Graphics
   - Category: Promotions
   - Keywords: Cornerstone Graphics, Promotions, Confirmation, Tom Louris, Advertising
   - Comments: Follow up to verbal agreement.
7. Print the document.
8. Close the document and exit Word, saving all changes.

Illustration A

May 17, 1999 *(Insert current date)*

~~Ms. Cynthia Harte~~ *Mr. Thomas Louris*
~~The Sweet Tooth~~ *Cornerstone Graphics*
~~321 Main Street~~ *920 Marco Place*
~~Hanover, NH 03755~~ *Venice, CA 90291*

~~Dear Ms. Harte~~: *Mr. Louris*

This letter is simply a follow up to our conversation this morning, confirming our agreement regarding the promotion of ~~The Sweet Tooth~~ *Cornerstone Graphics*. I am very excited about this opportunity, and I assure you I have some wonderful ideas!

First of all, I plan to focus a great deal of attention on the ~~grand opening sale~~ *Business on the Web seminar at which you are a featured speaker.* I have already created a document that I think we can use as ~~both an insert in the local~~ *a direct mail piece.* ~~newspaper and as a flyer to hand out in the neighborhood.~~ I have enclosed a copy for your approval.

I would also like you to give some thought about ways to get involved in the community. For example, we can ~~find out about fundraisers at the schools and other non-profit~~ ~~organizations and make donations of merchandise or gift certificates.~~ *have employees volunteer at the local schools to teach Web design.* You'd be surprised at the amount of business good will can generate.

Let me know what you think of the enclosed announcement. I will give you a call on Friday.

Sincerely,

Your Name

Enclosure

On Your Own

1. Open **OWD36**, the document you created in the On Your Own section of Exercise 36, as read-only, or open ⊘ **38EVENT** as read-only.

2. Check the number of words in the document.

3. Note the file size, date created, and date last modified.

4. Enter document properties, including Title, Subject, Manager, Company, Category, Keywords, and Comments.

5. Try saving the document.

6. Save the document as **OWD38**.

7. Close the document and exit Word.

Exercise 39

On the Job

Use Word 2000 to locate, save, and open documents saved in different file types. You can display all types of files in the Open dialog box, and you can open compatible files in Word. Once open, you can use the Save As command to save the documents as standard Word document files. Find a file with Word when you don't know where it is stored or what it is named. The Find files feature is useful if you forget the file information or if someone else created the file you need to use.

The assistant to the president at Cornerstone Graphics has e-mailed you a text file containing copy for a press release. Your assistant has downloaded the file and stored it somewhere on your computer. In this exercise, you will use Word to locate and open the text file. You will also save the text file as a Word document file. Finally, you will edit and format the file so you can submit it to newspapers.

Terms

File type The format in which the file is stored. Usually, the file type corresponds to the application used to create the file.

File extension A dot followed by three or four characters attached to a file name, used to indicate the file type. For example, a .doc file extension indicates a Word document file.

File icon The icon used to represent a file in a file list, such as Windows Explorer or Word's Open dialog box.

Compatible file type A file type that Word can open even though it was created and saved using a different application.

Property A unique aspect of a file.

Condition A comparison such as *equal to*, *greater than*, or *including*.

Value Text or numbers that you specify.

Notes

File Types

- Files are saved in different **file types**, depending on the application used to create, save, and open the file.

- In Windows and Windows applications, file types can be identified by the **file extension** and by the **file icon**.

- Word can open documents saved in **compatible file types**. For example, Word 2000 can open text files, Web page files, and files created with other versions of Word.

- You can save a compatible file in its original file type or as a Word document file.

- Some common file types include the following:
  - Word document files .doc
  - Word template files .dot
  - Text files .txt
  - Web pages .htm
  - Excel workbooks .xls
  - Access databases .mdb
  - PowerPoint presentations .ppt

Find Files

- Word can help you find a file even if you can't remember the file name.

- Word can search for files by looking for a unique aspect called a **property**. You can search based on more than one property.

- Word has a long list of properties it can search for, including the Document Properties you learned about in Exercise 38.

- To narrow down a search, select the property and a **condition**, then enter a **value**. For example, you can select the property *Author*, the condition *includes words*, then enter a first name or last name. Word will locate files with the specified words in the Author text box of the Document Properties dialog box.

Find dialog box

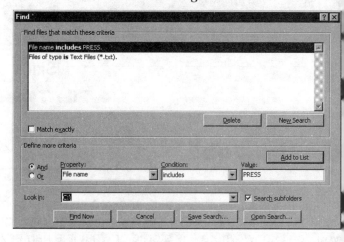

- Word searches in the current folder, but you can also search subfolders.

- Once the search is complete, Word displays a list of files with the matching value in the Open dialog box.

Procedures

Open a Compatible File Type (Ctrl+O)

1. Click **File** .... `Alt`+`F`
2. Click **Open** .... `O`
3. Click the **Look in** drop-down arrow .... `Alt`+`I`
4. Select the disk or folder.
   - ✓ *Alternatively, click the folder you want to open in the Places bar.*
5. Click the **Files of type** drop-down arrow .... `Alt`+`T`
6. Click the file type.
7. Click the desired file name.
8. Click **Open** .... `Alt`+`O`
   - ✓ *If the File Conversion dialog box is displayed, click OK.*

Save a Compatible File (Ctrl+S)

1. Open the compatible file.
2. Click **File** .... `Alt`+`F`
3. Click **Save** .... `S`

4. Click **Yes** .... `Y`
   to save the file in its original format.
   OR
   Click **No** .... `N`
   to save the file as a Word document.

Save a Compatible File As a New File in Word Format

1. Open the compatible file
2. Click **File** .... `Alt`+`F`
3. Click **Save As** .... `A`
4. Click the **Files of type** drop-down arrow .... `Alt`+`T`
5. Click the **Word document (*.doc)**.
6. Click the **File name** text box .... `Alt`+`N`
7. Type the new file name.
8. Click **Save** .... `Alt`+`S`

Find Files

1. Click **File** .... `Alt`+`F`
2. Click **Open** .... `O`

3. Click the **Look in** drop-down arrow .... `Alt`+`I`
4. Select the disk or folder.
   - ✓ *Alternatively, click the folder you want to open in the Places bar.*
5. Click **Tools** drop-down arrow `Tools ▾` .... `Alt`+`L`
6. Click **Find** .... `F`
7. Click **Property** drop-down arrow .... `Alt`+`P`
8. Select property.
   - ✓ *Word automatically enters a condition.*
9. Click **Value** text box ..... `Alt`+`U`
10. Type value.
11. Click **Add to List** button
    `Add to List` .... `Alt`+`A`
12. Click **Find Now** .... `Alt`+`F`

To search subfolders:

- Click the **Search Subfolders** check box in the Find dialog box .... `Alt`+`H`

178

Exercise Directions

1. Start Word, if necessary.
2. Find the file ☉ **39PRESS.txt**.
   a. Select the Property Files of type, and select Text files in the Condition drop down box.
   b. Select the Property File Name, and type PRESS in the Value text box.
3. Open the text file.
   ✓ *If Word asks you what converter to use, click OK to select the default option.*
4. Save the file as **WD39.doc**.

5. Edit and format the document to achieve the results shown in Illustration A.
   a. In a 14-point sans serif font, centered, insert the headline: *Louris to Speak at Business on the Web Seminar*.
   b. Leave an inch of space following the headline.
   c. Change all existing text to 12 points, justified.
   d. Apply boldface to the name of the city and state at the beginning of the release.
6. Preview the document.
7. Print the document.
8. Save the document and close it.
9. Exit Word.

Louris to Speak at Business on the Web Seminar

Venice, CA - Thomas Louris, President of Cornerstone Graphics, has been invited to appear as the keynote speaker at the Business on the Web Seminar in February. The seminar is being sponsored by State-of-the-Art Solutions, a consulting company based in Brentwood.

Mr. Louris founded Cornerstone Graphics in 1992. The firm provides all types of graphics design, but has recently begun specializing in Web site development.

According to Mr. Louris, the seminar will offer forums, lectures, and roundtable discussions on many aspects of conducting business on the World Wide Web. Attendees will come from around the country and will have a variety of business experience.

"Some attendees are just starting out, while others have successful companies. The one uniting factor is curiosity about how to exploit Internet technology to improve the bottom line," said Mr. Louris in a recent interview.

For more information about Cornerstone Graphics or about the Business on the Web seminar, contact Jake McNeil, 213-555-1002.

On Your Own

1. Start Word.
2. Find and open the file ⊘ **39THANKS.txt**. This is a thank you note for gifts received.
3. Save the document as **OWD39**.
4. Apply formatting to the document to improve its appearance.
5. Save the document, close, it, and exit Word.

Exercise 40

Skills Covered:

◆ **Save as Web Page** ◆ **Web Layout View** ◆ **Web Page Preview**
◆ **Open an HTML Document** ◆ **Save a Web Page Locally**

On the Job

Documents on the World Wide Web must be in HTML format. With Word, you can easily prepare documents for storage on the Web. You can save existing documents in HTML format, and you can use all of Word's features and tools to edit and format HTML documents. When you complete a document in HTML format, you can store it on a Web server so everyone with access to the Web can access the document. You can also save a Web page stored on the Internet as an HTML file on your own computer.

Cynthia Harte, the owner of The Sweet Tooth, has asked you to create a document that can serve as a Web page for the store's new Web site. In this exercise, you will create a new Word document and save it as a Web page. You will also use the Internet to locate a Web page, and then save it locally on your computer in HTML format. Finally, you will open the HTML document in Word and link it to the Web page you created.

Terms

HTM An extension given to files saved in HTML format.

Web server A computer connected to the Internet used to store Web page documents.

HTML (Hypertext Markup Language) It is the file format used for files accessed on the World Wide Web.

Notes

Save as Web Page

- You can save an existing Word document in HTML format. Word preserves the formatting in the new document.

- You can return the document to its original Word format at any time.

- When you save a document as a Web page, Word abbreviates the file extension to **HTM**.

- Word automatically creates a folder to store graphics files associated with the Web page.

  ✓ *Use caution when moving or renaming the graphics file or the folder they are stored in. The graphics files are linked to the HTML document. If they are not available, the page will display without graphics elements.*

The Save As Web page dialog box

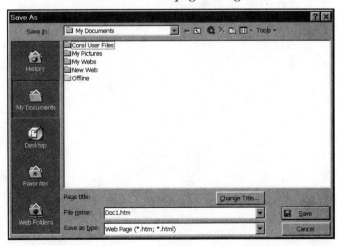

Web Layout View

- Web Layout view displays documents in Word as they will look on the Web.

- Web Layout view lets you edit a document for viewing on screen, instead of for printing on a page.

- Features of Web Layout view include:
  - Word wrapping to fit the window, not a page.
  - Graphics positioned as they would be in a Web browser.
  - Backgrounds (if there are any) displayed as they would be in a browser.

- Use Web Layout view to edit Word documents for use as Web pages.

- The Word documents can be in regular Word format (.doc extension) or in HTML format (.htm extension) for editing in Web Layout view. However, to store a document on a **Web server** for access on the Web, it must be in HTML format.

Web Page Preview

- Use Web Page Preview to see how a Word document will look in a Web browser.

- You can display regular Word documents or HTML documents in Web Page Preview.

- When you preview a Web page document, Word opens the document in your default browser.

- You cannot edit a document in Web Page Preview.

A document in Web Page Preview

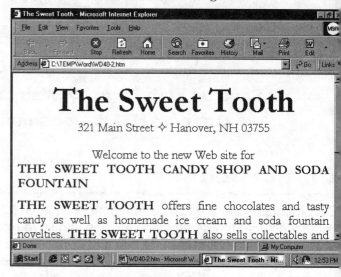

Open an HTML Document

- You open an **HTML** document in Word the same way you open a regular Word document.

- The document displays in Web Layout view.

- When you save the document, it remains in HTML format.

  ✓ *If you try to open an HTML document from Windows, the document displays it in your Web browser, not in Word.*

Save a Web Page Locally

- You use your browser's Save command to save a Web page as an HTML document on your computer.

- You can save a complete Web page, including graphics, or you can save the page without graphics; placeholders will be displayed instead.

Procedures

Save as HTML

1. Open the document.
2. Click **File** .... `Alt`+`F`
3. Click **Save as Web Page** ..... `G`
4. Type file name.
   - ✓ *If necessary, open the folder, disk, or server where the file will be stored.*
5. Click **Save** .... `Alt`+`S`

Return to Word Format

1. Open the document.
2. Click **File** .... `Alt`+`F`
3. Click **Save As** .... `A`
4. Click Save as type drop-down arrow .... `T`
5. Click Word document (*.doc).
   - ✓ *If necessary, open the folder, disk, or server where the file will be stored.*
6. Click **Save** .... `Alt`+`S`

Use Web Layout View

1. Open the document.
2. Click **Web Layout view** button ▣.
   OR
   a. Click **View** .... `Alt`+`V`
   b. Click **Web Layout** .... `W`

Use Web Page Preview

1. Click **File** .... `Alt`+`F`
2. Click **Web Page Preview** .... `B`

Close Web Page Preview

1. Click **File** .... `Alt`+`F`
2. Click **Close** .... `C`

Open HTML Document

1. Click **File** .... `Alt`+`F`
2. Click **Open** .... `O`

3. Click file name.
   - ✓ *If necessary, open the folder or disk where the file is stored.*
4. Click **Open** .... `Alt`+`O`

Save Web Page Locally

1. Display the Web page in your browser.
2. Click **File** .... `Alt`+`F`
3. Click **Save As** .... `A`
4. Click **Save as type** drop-down arrow .... `Alt`+`T`
5. Click Web page, HTML only (*.htm, *.html).
6. Click **File name** text box .... `Alt`+`N`
7. Type file name.
   - ✓ *If necessary, select folder and/or disk where you want to store the file.*
8. Click **Save** .... `Alt`+`S`

Exercise Directions

1. Start Word, if necessary, and create a new document.
2. Save the document as **WD40-1**.
3. Type and format the document shown in Illustration A.
4. Save the document as a Web page with the name **WD40-2.htm**.
5. Display it in Web Page Preview.
6. Close Web Page Preview.
7. Close the **WD40-2.htm** document.
8. Display the Web toolbar or start.
9. Open the Internet Simulation:
   a. Click **Go**.
   b. Click **Open**.
   c. In the Address line type the following: D:/Internet/E40/candyusa.htm
      - ✓ *If you've copied the Internet simulation files to your hard drive or your CD-ROM drive is a letter other than D:, substitute the correct letter for D.*
   d. Click **OK**.

10. Click the *Candy Trivia* link.
11. Click the *Chocolate! Erasing the Myths* link.
12. Save the displayed Web page as **WD40-3.htm**.
13. Exit the simulation.
14. Open the file **WD40-2.htm**.
15. Create a hyperlink from the text Chocolate Myths, at the bottom of the document, to the **WD40-3.htm** file.
16. Test the link.
17. Click the Back button on the Web browser to return to the **WD40-2.htm** document.
18. Save the document in its original Word format, with the name **WD40-4.doc**.
19. Close all open files and exit Word, saving all changes.
20. Close all open files and exit Word, saving all changes.

Illustration A

The Sweet Tooth ← *48-pt. serif Bold, Blue, centered*

321 Main Street ✧ Hanover, NH 03755 ← *18-pt. serif, blue, centered*

↑— *Wingdings symbol*

Welcome to the new Web site for ← *18-pt. serif centered, 18 pts. before*

THE SWEET TOOTH CANDY SHOP AND SODA FOUNTAIN

THE SWEET TOOTH offers fine chocolates and tasty candy as well as homemade ice cream and soda fountain novelties. **THE SWEET TOOTH** also sells collectables and gift items. Please stop by our convenient Main Street Location to see for yourself.

Small caps, bold, blue

Check this page daily for information about

What's Going on at **THE SWEET TOOTH**

Daily Specials

Sale Items in our Gift Shop

18-pt. serif, justified

Here are some links to other interesting Web pages:

Chocolate Myths ← *18-pt. serif, centered*

On Your Own

1. Create a new document in Word.

2. Save the file as **OWD40**.

3. Use this document to create your own personal Web page. Think about what you want to include on your Web page. You should include your name and other information about yourself—what you like to do, who are your favorite musicians and sports teams, where you go to school or where you work.

4. Add some other information you think will be interesting: favorite sayings, upcoming events in your life, or fun things your family or friends plan to do.

5. Apply formatting to make the document look good.

6. Save the document as a Web page in HTML format.

7. View the document in Web Layout view.

8. Use Web Page Preview to look at your new Web page in your browser software.

9. Close Web Page Preview.

10. Close the document and exit Word.

Exercise 41

On the Job

The title of a Web page is displayed at the top of the screen in your Web browser. You can enter any title you want. You can enhance and edit HTML documents by adding elements such as a background, and by applying a theme.

The owner of The Sweet Tooth wants you to improve the appearance of the Web page you already designed. In this exercise, you change the page title and apply a theme. You also apply a background to another Web page, link the pages together, and test them in your browser.

Terms

Graphics object A picture, chart, shape, or other element that can be inserted into a Word document.

Clip art Picture files that can be inserted into a document.

Background The color, pattern, or fill displayed on the page behind data in a document.

Fill effect A texture, shading, picture, or pattern used as a background.

Theme A collection of formatting settings applied to a document.

Web bullets Graphics files inserted as bullet markers.

Graphics lines Graphics files inserted as horizontal lines or dividers.

Notes

Web Page Titles

- Web page titles are displayed in the Web Browser title bar.
- By default, Word uses the first line of text in a document as the Web page title.
- You can set or change the page title name from the Save As dialog box.

Set Page Title dialog box

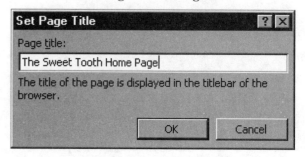

Web Page Graphics

- In order for HTML documents to display correctly on all Web browsers, many visual elements must be inserted as **graphics objects**.

- For example, horizontal lines, bullets, and even background textures are inserted as graphics objects in HTML documents.

- All associated graphics files are stored in the same location as the HTML document so that the HTML document can be displayed correctly.

  ✓ *If the graphics files are moved or deleted, the document will not be displayed correctly. For example, bullets and lines may not appear.*

- Graphics inserted in an HTML document must be in .gif or .jpeg (.jpg) file format.

- In general, .gif is used for drawings and **clip art**, including bullets and lines, and .jpeg is used for photographs and background textures.

  ✓ *Graphics objects can be used as hyperlinks. Simply select the object, then insert the hyperlink as instructed in Exercise 34.*

- Word comes with .gif and .jpeg formatted graphics files for use in regular documents and HTML documents.

  ✓ *For more information on working with graphics, see Lesson 11.*

Fill Effects dialog box

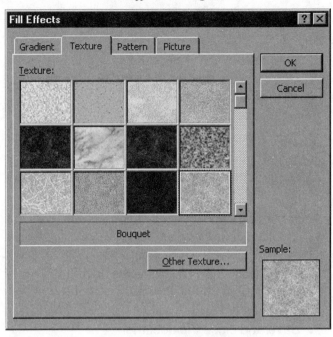

Backgrounds

- By default, Word documents—including HTML documents—have a plain white **background**.

- Add visual interest or create an effect by applying a color or pattern, or a **fill effect** to a document background.

- You should coordinate backgrounds for pages in a Web site to establish continuity.

Themes

- Word comes with built-in **themes** you can use to format any Word document.

- Each theme includes a background, font formatting, and graphics elements such as **Web Bullets** and horizontal **graphics lines**.

- You can select a theme to apply consistent formatting to a document.

- Themes can be used with any Word document, but they are particularly useful for formatting Web pages.

Procedures

Set a Web Page Title

1. Click **File** .... Alt + F
2. Click **Save As** .... A
3. Click **Change Title** button
   Change Title... .... Alt + C
4. Type new title.
5. Click **OK**.
6. Click **Save** button
   Save .... Alt + S

Backgrounds

1. Open file to format.
2. Click **Format** .... Alt + O
3. Click **Background** .... K
4. Click desired color.
   OR
   a. Click **Fill Effects** .... F
   b. Click desired
      page tab .... Ctrl + Tab
   c. Select desired effect.

d. Click **OK** .... Enter

Themes

1. Open file to format.
2. Click **Format** .... Alt + O
3. Click **Theme** .... H
4. Select desired
   Theme .... Alt + T , ↑ , ↓
5. Click **OK** .... Enter

Exercise Directions

1. Start Word, if necessary.

2. Open the document ⊘ **41HOME.htm** and save it as **WD41-1.htm**.

3. Change the Web Page Title to *The Sweet Tooth Home Page*.

4. Change the three items *What's Going on...*, *Daily Specials*, and *Sale Items* into a bulleted list, using the default bullet style.

5. Apply the Sweets theme.

   ✓ *If the Sweets theme is not available, select a different theme.*

6. Use Web Page Preview to preview the document. It should look similar to the one in Illustration A.

7. Save and close the document.

8. In Word, open the document ⊘ **41CHOC.htm** and save it as **WD41-2.htm**.

9. Change the Web Page Title to *The Sweet Tooth Web Site*.

10. Delete the names of the contacts at the top of the document.

11. Apply the Water Droplets background texture to the page.

12. Use Web Page Preview to preview the page.

13. Close Web Page Preview and apply the Bouquet background texture to the page.

14. Preview the page again.

15. Close Web Page Preview.

16. Save the document and close it.

17. Open the **WD41-1** document.

18. Insert a hyperlink from the text *Chocolate Myths* at the bottom of the page to the **WD41-2** document.

19. Change to Web Page Preview.

20. Test the link.

21. Use your browser's Back button to return to the **WD41-1** page.

22. Close your browser.

23. Close all open documents and exit Word, saving all changes.

Illustration A

The Sweet Tooth

321 Main Street ✧ Hanover, NH 03755

Welcome to the new Web site for

THE SWEET TOOTH CANDY SHOP AND SODA FOUNTAIN

THE SWEET TOOTH offers fine chocolates and tasty candy as well as homemade ice cream and soda fountain novelties. **THE SWEET TOOTH** also sells collectables and gift items. Please stop by our convenient Main Street Location to see for yourself.

Check this page daily for information about

● What's Going on at **THE SWEET TOOTH**

On Your Own

1. Start Word and open **OWD40.htm**, the Web page you created in the On Your Own section of Exercise 40, or open ⊙ **41MYPAGE.htm**.

2. Save the document as **OWD41.htm**.

3. Change the Web Page title to *Your Name's Web Page* (substitute your own name for the text My Personal.)

4. If there is not already a bulleted list on your Web page, create one.

5. Apply a theme.

6. Try a different theme.

7. Keep trying themes until you find one you like.

8. Try changing just the background on the page.

9. If you don't like the background you apply, use Undo to remove it.

10. Use Web Page Preview to preview the document.

11. Save the document, close it, and exit Word.

Exercise 42

◆ Critical Thinking

You are a Web designer and have been hired to create a Web site for the Business on the Web Seminar.

Exercise Directions

1. Start Word, if necessary.
2. Display the Web toolbar.
3. Open the Internet Simulation:
   a. Click **Go**.
   b. Click **Open**.
   c. In the Address line type the following: D:/Internet/E42/www.carizona.htm
      - ✔ *If you've copied the Internet simulation files to your hard drive or your CD-ROM drive is a letter other than D:, substitute the correct letter for D.*
   d. Click **OK**.
4. Click the *Phoenix* link.
5. Click the *Dining* link.
6. Scroll down and click the *Fine* link.
7. Save the page listing fine dining restaurants as a Web page only in HTML format with the name **WD42-1**.
8. Click *Back* to return to the Dining page.
9. Click the *Western* link.
10. Save the page listing Western style restaurants as a Web page only in HTML format with the name **WD42-2**.
11. Exit the simulation.
12. In Word, open the **WD42-1.htm** document.
    - ✔ *If your ISP prompts you to log on to the Internet, click Cancel to work offline.*
13. Apply the Blue Tissue Paper background texture to the page.
    - ✔ *To hide the gray lines, click Table, Hide Gridlines. You learn more about tables in Exercise 43–51.*
14. Save the page and close it.
15. Open the **WD42-2.htm** document.
    - ✔ *If your ISP prompts you to log on to the Internet, click Cancel to work offline.*

16. Apply the Blue Tissue Paper background texture to the page.
    - ✔ *To hide the gray lines, click Table, Hide Gridlines. You learn more about tables in exercise 43 – 51.*
17. Save the page and close it.
18. Locate the document ☉ **42LOURIS.txt** and open it as read only.
19. Save the document as **WD42-3.doc**, and then close it.
20. Locate the document ☉ **42SPEAKS.doc** and open it.
21. Save the document as a Web page with the name **WD42-4.htm**, and the title Seminar Speakers.
22. Apply the Blueprint theme to the page.
23. Insert a hyperlink from the text Tom Louris in the first bulleted item, to the **WD42-3.doc** document.
24. Save the document and close it.
25. Locate the document ☉ **42HOME.doc** and open it.
26. Save the document as a Web page with the name **WD42-5.htm**, and the title, Business on the Web Home Page.
27. Apply the Clearday theme to the page.
28. Create a hyperlink from the text click here at the end of the third paragraph to the **WD42-4.htm** page.
29. Create a hyperlink from first bulleted item to the **WD42-1.htm** page.
30. Create a hyperlink from the second bulleted item to the **WD42-2.htm** page. The page should look similar to the one shown in Illustration A.
31. Display the **WD42-5** document in Web Page Preview.

32. Test the links, using the Back button on your browser to return to the **WD42-5** page.

33. Close Web Page preview.

34. Save and close all open documents.

35. Exit Word.

Illustration A

BUSINESS ON THE WEB

Phoenix, AZ   February 9 and 10

Welcome to the *Business on the Web Seminar,* sponsored by State-of-the-Art Solutions.

The agenda is chock full of forums, lectures, and roundtables which you are sure to find exciting and informative. Whether you are just beginning to explore the opportunities available on the World Wide Web, or whether you have established your business on the Web, we believe that this seminar will provide you with new tools for growth and success.

We have assembled some of the most successful Web entrepreneurs to conduct this seminar. The speakers will be present at a cocktail hour hosted by State-of-the-Art Solutions every evening in the hotel lobby. Please stop by for some refreshments, to meet the speakers, or just to socialize. For a list of speakers, click here.

Also, Phoenix is a wonderful city to visit. If you have free time while you are here, we invite you to participate in the many events and activities taking place throughout the area. In particular, dining out offers some exciting opportunities. Use these links to find out more about dining in Phoenix:

▪ Fine Dining
▪ Western Dining

If you have any questions about the seminar, the speakers, or extracurricular activities please contact Justin Godere, Seminar Coordinator.

Lesson 7

Tables

Exercise 43

◆ **Create a Table** ◆ **Move the Insertion Point in a Table**
◆ **Enter Data in a Table** ◆ **Format a Table**

On the Job

Create tables to organize data into columns and rows. Any information that needs to be presented in side-by-side columns can be set up in a table. For example, a price list, an invoice, a resume, and a script are all types of documents for which you should use a table. The table format lets you align information side by side and across the page so the information is easy to read.

State-of-the-Art Solutions has expanded its training course schedule. In this exercise, you will create a list being offered. You will set up the course list in a table.

Terms

Table A grid comprised of horizontal rows and vertical columns into which you can enter data.

Column A vertical series of cells in a table.

Row A horizontal series of cells in a table.

Column markers Markers on the horizontal ruler that indicate column borders.

Border line A line drawn around the edges of an element, such as a table or a table cell. Borders can also be drawn around paragraphs and pages. (Learn more about borders in Exercise 49.)

Gridline A nonprinting line that indicates the boundaries of cells in a table.

End of row/cell marks Nonprinting characters used to mark the end of a cell or a row in a table.

Cell The rectangular area at the intersection of a column and a row in a table, into which you enter data.

Notes

Create a Table

- **Tables** are easier to use than tabbed columns when setting up and organizing data in **columns** and **rows**.

- You can create a table in any Word document.

- You select the number of columns and rows you want in the table.

- Word creates the table at the insertion point location.

- By default, Word sizes the columns equally across the width of the page.

- **Column markers** on the horizontal ruler show the location of the right border of each column.

- By default, Word places a ½-pt. **border line** around all cells in a table.

A table with four columns and four rows

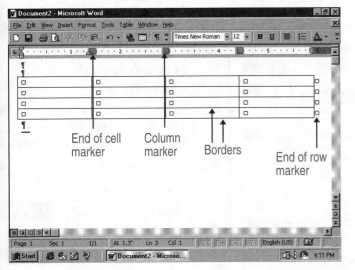

- Tables have three unique nonprinting elements:
  - **Gridlines**
  - **End of cell markers**
  - **End of row markers**

Move the Insertion Point in a Table

- You must position the insertion point in a table where you want characters to be entered.

- You can move the insertion point with the keyboard or mouse.

Enter Data in a Table

- You enter data in the **cells** of a table.

- Row height increases automatically to accommodate as many lines of data as you type.

- Column width does not change automatically. Text wraps at the right margin of a cell the same way it wraps at the right margin of a page.

- When you press Enter in a cell, Word starts a new paragraph within the cell.

- You can edit and format text within a cell the same way you do outside a table.

Format a Table

- You can format text within a table using standard Word formatting techniques. For example, use font formatting, alignments, spacing, and indents to enhance text in a table.

- You can apply formatting to selected text, or to selected cells, columns, or rows.

  ✓ *You select text in a cell using the same techniques you use to select text outside a table. Learn about selecting table components such as cells, rows, and columns in Exercise 44.*

- Use Table AutoFormat to quickly apply formatting effects to an existing table.

- AutoFormat styles include border lines, shading, color, fonts, and other formatting.

The Table AutoFormat dialog box

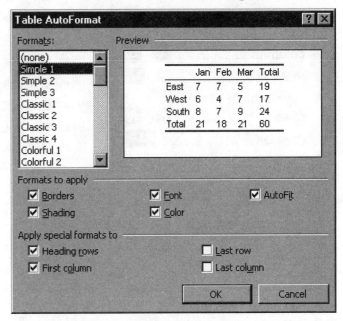

- AutoFormat overrides existing formatting. Therefore, you should apply AutoFormat first, then apply additional formatting as needed.

Procedures

Create a Table

Use the Toolbar button:
1. Position insertion point.
2. Click **Insert Table** button 🔲.
3. Drag the mouse pointer across the grid to select desired number of columns and rows.
4. Release the mouse button.

Use Menu commands:
1. Position the insertion point.
2. Click **Table** .... `Alt`+`A`
3. Select **Insert** .... `I`
4. Click **Table** .... `T`
5. Type **number of columns** .... `Alt`+`C`
6. Press **Tab** .... `Tab`
7. Type **number of rows** .... `Alt`+`R`
8. Click **OK** .... `Enter`

Show/Hide gridlines:
1. Click **Table** .... `Alt`+`A`
2. Click **Show Gridlines** .... `G`
   OR
   Click **Hide Gridlines** .... `G`

Move the Insertion Point in a Table

With the Mouse:
- Click mouse pointer where you want to position insertion point.

With the Keyboard:
   To Move
- One cell left .... `Shift`+`Tab` or `←`
- One cell right .... `Tab` or `→`
- One cell up .... `↑`
- One cell down............... `↓`
- First cell in table .... `Ctrl`+`Home`

Enter Data in a Table
1. Click in desired cell.
2. Type data.
3. Press Tab.
4. Type data in next cell.
5. Repeat until all data is entered.

Format a Table

Apply AutoFormat:
1. Click **Table** .... `Alt`+`A`
2. Click **Table AutoFormat** ...... `F`
3. Select format .... `Alt`+`T`, `↓`
4. Click **OK** .... `Enter`

Format text in a table:
1. Select text to format.
2. Apply formatting as with regular document text.

Exercise Directions

1. Start Word, if necessary.
2. Create a new document and save it as **WD43**.
3. Using a sans serif font, type the text shown in Illustration A using the specified formatting.
4. Create the table shown in Illustration A.
   a. Insert a table with three columns and five rows.
   b. Enter the data as shown.
5. Apply the Grid 8 AutoFormat to the table.
6. Apply bold to all of the course names.
   - Select the text then apply the formatting.
7. Preview the document. It should look similar to Illustration B.
8. Save the changes and print the document
9. Close the document and exit Word.

Illustration A

STATE-OF-THE-ART SOLUTIONS

18-pt. outline effect, all uppercase, blue, 6 pts. After

TRAINING DEPARTMENT

16 pts., all uppercase, 72 pts. After

Centered

MEMORANDUM

16 pts., all uppercase 72 pts. after

Left tab at 1"

12 pts.

To: → All Employees
From: → Your Name
Re: → Class Schedule
↓ 2x

Here is the schedule of courses being offered next week. If you haven't signed up yet, see me immediately.

↓ 3x

Course Name	Location	Time
Word 1	Conference Room A	8:30 – 11:45
Word 2	Conference Room A	1:30 – 3:30
Excel 3	Conference Room B	8:30 – 11:45
Intro to the Internet	Media Lab	1:30 – 3:30

STATE-OF-THE-ART SOLUTIONS
TRAINING DEPARTMENT

MEMORANDUM

To: All Employees
From: Your Name
Re: Class Schedule

Here is the schedule of courses being offered next week. If you haven't signed up yet, see me immediately.

Course Name	Location	Time
Word 1	Conference Room A	8:30 – 11:45
Word 2	Conference Room A	1:30 – 3:30
Excel 3	Conference Room B	8:30 – 11:45
Intro to the Internet	Media Lab	1:30 – 3:30

On Your Own

1. Think of documents that would benefit from table formatting. Some examples include a weekly schedule, meeting agenda, travel itinerary, sales report, telephone/address list, and roster.

2. Create a new document in Word.

3. Save the file as **OWD43**.

4. Use a table to set up the document as a telephone list. The list could include friends, family members, or members of a club or organization to which you belong.

5. Use at least two columns—one for the name and one for the telephone number. You may use more columns if you want to include mailing addresses, e-mail addresses, cell phone numbers, or other information.

6. Include at least five names in the list.

7. Apply an AutoFormat to the table. If you are not satisfied with the results, try a different AutoFormat.

8. Save the changes, close the document, and exit Word.

Exercise 44

◆ **Select in a Table** ◆ **Insert Columns, Rows, or Cells**
◆ **Delete Columns, Rows, or Cells**

On the Job

You can change the structure of a table to add or delete columns, rows, or cells. You can even delete the entire table. In order to make changes affecting the table structure, you must first select the elements you want to change.

State-of-the-Art Solutions wants you to change the training course schedule. In this exercise, you add a column to the schedule table and add and delete rows.

Terms

Table components Parts of a table, including columns, rows, and cells.

Notes

Select in a Table

- As with other Word features, you must select **table components** before you can affect them with commands.
- You select text within a cell using the standard selection commands.
  - ✓ *Selecting text is covered in Exercise 9.*
- You can select one or more columns, one or more rows, one or more cells, or the entire table.
- Selected table components appear highlighted.

Insert Columns, Rows, or Cells

- You can insert columns, rows, or cells anywhere in a table.
- If necessary, you specify where to insert the new component—above, below, to the left, or to the right of the current component.

Delete Columns, Rows, or Cells

- You can delete any column, row, or cell.
- If necessary, you specify how to shift remaining components to fill in the area left by the deletion.
- You can delete an entire table.
- Data entered in a deleted column, row, or cell is deleted as well.

Procedures

Select in a Table

1. Position insertion point within table component to select.

   ✓ *For example, click in cell if selecting cell; click anywhere in row if selecting row, etc.*

2. Click **Table** .... Alt + A
3. Click **Select** C
4. Click one of the following:
   - **Table** .... T
   - **Column** C
   - **Row** .... R
   - **Cell** .... E

Select with the mouse:

Column

1. Position mouse pointer at top of column until pointer resembles a down-pointing arrow ↓ .
2. Click.

Row

1. Position mouse pointer to left of row until pointer resembles a right-pointing arrow ⇗ .
2. Click.

Cell

1. Position mouse pointer to right of left cell border until pointer resembles a right-pointing arrow ➚ .
2. Click.

Select adjacent components:

1. Select first components.
2. Press and hold Shift .... Shift
3. Click in last component to select.

   ✓ *This method enables you to select adjacent columns, adjacent rows, or adjacent cells.*

Insert Columns, Rows, or Cells

1. Position insertion point within table.

   ✓ *To insert more than one component, select as many as you want to insert. For example, to insert two columns, select two columns.*

2. Click **Table** .... Alt + A
3. Click **Insert** I
4. Click one of the following:
   - **Columns to the Left** L
   - **Columns to the Right** ... R
   - **Rows Above** .... A
   - **Rows Below** .... B
   - **Cells** .... E

   ✓ *Select option for shifting existing cells to make room for new cells, then click OK.*

Delete Columns, Rows, or Cells

1. Select cells, or click in the row or column to delete.
2. Click **Table** .... Alt + A
3. Click **Delete** .... D
4. Click one of the following:
   - **Columns** C
   - **Rows** .... R
   - **Cells** .... E

   ✓ *Select option for shifting existing cells to fill in deleted cell area, then click OK.*

Delete Entire Table

1. Click anywhere in table.
2. Click **Table** .... Alt + A
3. Click **Delete** .... D
4. Click **Table** .... T

Exercise Directions

1. Start Word, if necessary.
2. Open ☺ **44COURSE**.
3. Save the document as **WD44**.
4. Select the last two rows in the table.
5. Insert two new rows above the selected rows.
6. Enter the following data in the new rows:

Word 3	Conference Room A	8:30–11:45
Excel 2	Conference Room B	3:00–4:30

7. Insert another new row between the Word 3 and Excel 2 rows, and enter the following data:

Excel 1	Conference Room B	1:30–3:30

8. Insert a new column between the Location column and the Time Column.
9. Enter the following data in the new column:

   Days
   Monday, Wednesday
   Monday, Wednesday
   Tuesday, Thursday
   Tuesday, Thursday
   Tuesday, Thursday
   Monday, Wednesday
   Friday

10. Delete the row for the Word 1 course.
11. Apply the Columns 5 AutoFormat to the table.
12. Preview the document. It should look similar to the one in Illustration A.
13. Save the changes and print the document
14. Close the document and exit Word.

Illustration A

STATE-OF-THE-ART SOLUTIONS
TRAINING DEPARTMENT

MEMORANDUM

To: All Employees
From: Your Name
Re: Class Schedule

Here is the schedule of courses being offered next week. If you haven't signed up yet, see me immediately.

Course Name	Location	Days	Time
Word 2	Conference Room A	Monday, Wednesday	1:30 – 3:30
Word 3	Conference Room A	Tuesday, Thursday	8:30 – 11:45
Excel 1	Conference Room B	Tuesday, Thursday	1:30 – 3:30
Excel 2	Conference Room B	Tuesday, Thursday	3:00 – 4:30
Excel 3	Conference Room B	Monday, Wednesday	8:30 – 11:45
Intro to the Internet	Media Lab	Friday	1:30 – 3:30

On Your Own

1. Open **OWD43**, the document you created in the On Your Own section of Exercise 43, or open ⊙ **44TABLE**.

2. Save the document as **OWD44**.

3. Add two new rows to the table.

4. Add a new column

5. Fill in the data for the new rows and column.

6. Delete one row.

7. Apply a different AutoFormat to the table.

8. Save the document, close it, and exit Word.

Exercise 45

◆ **Set Alignments within Table Cells** ◆ **Align Table on the Page**
◆ **Column Width and Row Height**

On the Job

Use alignment options and tabs to make tables easy to read. Numbers are usually aligned flush right in a cell, while text can be flush left, centered, or justified. You can vertically align data in a cell as well. Decimal tabs are especially useful in tables for aligning dollar values. Other ways to improve the appearance of a table include aligning the table horizontally on the page, and adjusting column width and row height.

Cynthia Harte at The Sweet Tooth has asked you to create a flyer announcing sale prices on chocolates. In this exercise, you will create a document listing sale price information. You will use different alignment options to set up the data in the table. You will also set **row heights** and **column widths**, and you will align the table horizontally on the page.

Terms

Row height The height of a row in a table, measured in inches.

Column width The width of a column in a table, measured in inches.

Notes

Set Alignments within Table Cells

- You can set horizontal alignment within a cell the same way you set alignment in a document.

- In a table, numbers are usually right-aligned, and text is either left-aligned or centered.

- All tab stops can be used within a table cell, but the most useful is the decimal tab stop.

- Decimal tab stops let you align numbers such as dollar values within a cell, or in a row.

- You can vertically align data at the top of the cell, centered in the cell, or at the bottom of the cell. The default is at the top.

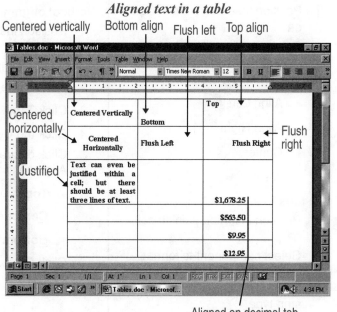

Aligned text in a table

Aligned on decimal tab

205

Align Table on the Page

- You can left-align, right-align, or center a table on the page.

Column Width and Row Height

- By default, Word creates columns of equal width, sized so the table is the same width as the page.

- Rows are sized according to the font size on the line where the table is inserted.

- Row height automatically increases to accommodate lines of text typed in a cell.

- You can drag column borders to increase or decrease column width.

- In Print Layout view, you can drag row borders to increase or decrease row height.

  ✓ *You cannot drag row borders In Normal view.*

- You can set precise measurements for columns, rows, cells, and entire tables in the Table Properties dialog box.

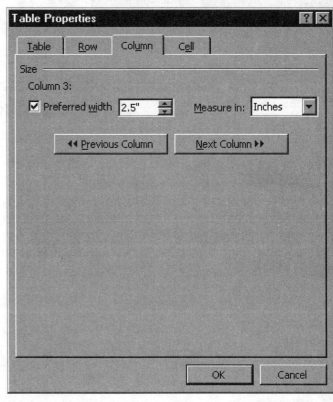

The Column page of the Table Properties Dialog Box

Procedures

Set Alignments within Table Cells

Horizontal alignment:

1. Position insertion point in cell.
   OR
   Select component to format.
2. Click desired alignment button on Formatting toolbar:
   - Align Left ▤
   - Align Right ▤
   - Center ▤
   - Justify ▤

Set tabs in a cell:

1. Position insertion point in cell.
   OR
   Select component to format.
2. Click Tab box at left end of horizontal ruler to select tab stop type.
3. Click desired position on horizontal ruler.

Advance insertion point one tab stop:

- Press .... `Ctrl`+`Tab`

Vertical alignment:

1. Position insertion point in cell.
   OR
   Select component to format.
2. Click **Ta̲ble** .... `Alt`+`A`
3. Click **Table P̲roperties** .... `R`
4. Click the **Ce̲ll** tab .... `Alt`+`E`
5. Click desired Vertical Alignment option:
   - **To̲p** ☐
   - **C̲enter** ▤
   - **B̲ottom** ▤
6. Click **OK** .... `Enter`

Align Table in Document

1. Select table.
2. Click desired alignment button on Formatting toolbar
   - **Center** ▤
   - **Align Right** ▤
   - **Align Left** ▤

OR

1. Click anywhere in table.
2. Click **Ta̲ble** .... `Alt`+`A`
3. Click **Table P̲roperties** .... `R`
4. Click the **T̲able** tab .... `Alt`+`T`
5. Click desired Alignment option:
   - **L̲eft** ▦
   - **C̲enter** ▦
   - **Rig̲ht** ▦
6. Click **OK** .... `Enter`

Change Column Width

1. Position mouse pointer on column border.

   ✓ *Pointer changes to a double-vertical line with arrows pointing left and right.*

2. Drag border left or right.
   OR
   a. Click in column.
   b. Click **Table**.............. Alt + A
   c. Click **Table Properties** ... R
   d. Click **Column** page tab........................... Alt + U
   e. Select **Preferred Width** check box..... Alt + W
   f. Press **Tab** .... Tab
   g. Type column width
   h. Click **OK**..................... Enter

Change Row Height

1. Click **Print Layout View** button ▣ .

2. Position mouse pointer on row border.

   ✓ *Pointer changes to a double-vertical line with arrows pointing up and down.*

3. Drag border up or down.
   OR
   a. Click in column
   b. Click **Table**............. Alt + A
   c. Click **Table Properties** .. R
   d. Click **Row** page tab .... Alt + R

   e. Select **Specify Height** check box .... Alt + S
   f. Press **Tab** .... Tab
   g. Type row height in inches.

      ✓ *Select Exactly in Row height is box to fix row height at specified size.*

4. Click **OK** .... Enter

Exercise Directions

1. Start Word, if necessary.
2. Create a new document and save it as **WD45**.
3. Create the document shown in Illustration A.
4. Format the heading as follows:
   a. Type the first line in a 28-point serif font, with an outline font effect, in blue, centered.
   b. Type the second line in a 14-point serif font in blue, also centered. Use a Wingding symbol to separate the street address from the city.
5. Set the heading, Valentine's Day Sale, to a 22-pt. serif font, underlined.
6. Set alignment in the table as follows:
   a. Center the data in the first row vertically and horizontally.
   b. Vertically align all other rows with the bottom of the cells.
   c. Right-align the data in the Size column.

   d. Right-align the prices in the Regular Price column.
   e. Use a decimal tab to align the prices in the Sale Price column.
7. Set column 1 to be 1.5" wide.
8. Set the other columns to be 1" wide.
9. Set row 1 to be at least .75" high.
10. Set all remaining rows to be exactly .5" high.
11. Make the text in the first row bold.
12. Center the entire table on the page.
13. Preview the document. It should look similar to Illustration A.
14. Print the document.
15. Save the document.
16. Close the document and exit Word.

The Sweet Tooth
321 Main Street ✧ Hanover, NH 03755

VALENTINE'S DAY SALE

Candy	Size	Regular Price	Sale Price
Raspberry Creams	10 ounces	$12.99	$9.99
Raspberry Creams	16 ounces	$16.99	$12.99
Caramels	10 ounces	$11.99	$8.99
Caramels	16 ounces	$15.99	$11.99
Cashew Turtles	16 ounces	$18.99	$12.99
Assorted Truffles	16 ounces	$21.99	$15.99
White Chocolate Assortment	32 ounces	$48.99	$35.00
Milk Chocolate Assortment	32 ounces	$45.99	$29.99

On Your Own

1. Open **OWD44**, the document you created in the On Your Own section of Exercise 44, or open ⊙ **45TABLE**.

2. Save the document as **OWD45**.

3. Adjust the column widths and row heights by dragging the table borders.

4. Set precise column widths and row heights.

5. Use different alignments in the table.

6. Center the table on the page.

7. Save the changes, close the document, and exit Word.

Exercise 46

Skills Covered:

◆ **Tables and Borders Toolbar** ◆ **Draw a Table** ◆ **Merge and Split Cells**

On the Job

Word's Draw Table tool gives you great flexibility to organize tables the way you want them, not necessarily in rigid columns and rows. You can lay out the table cells exactly as you want them in order to organize text and data. You can then merge and split cells, if necessary.

Your supervisor at State-of-the-Art Solutions has asked you to suggest sites for the next seminar. In this exercise, you will create a memo to your supervisor, and include a table in which you can enter information about possible locations. To complete the table you will use the Draw table tool, and you will merge and split cells. You will also use different alignments and formatting to improve the appearance of the table.

Terms

Merge Combine multiple adjacent cells together to create one large cell.

Split Divide one cell into multiple cells, either vertically to create columns or horizontally to create rows.

Notes

Tables and Borders toolbar

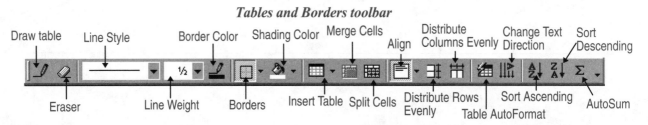

Tables and Borders Toolbar

- Use the Tables and Borders toolbar to create and format tables.
  - ✓ *If the toolbar is in your way while working, move it or dock it across the top of the document window.*

Draw a Table

- Word's Draw Table feature lets you create tables with uneven or irregular columns and rows.

A table drawn with uneven columns and rows

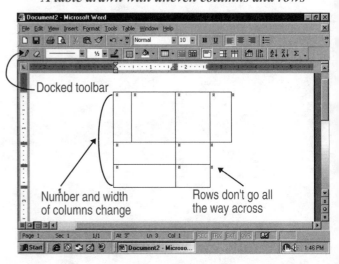

Docked toolbar

Number and width of columns change

Rows don't go all the way across

■ When you draw a table, the mouse pointer functions as a pencil.

■ You drag the pointer to draw lines vertically or horizontally to create cell borders.

   ✓ *Word creates straight lines at 90 degree angles to existing table borders, even if you do not drag in a straight line.*

■ You can draw a diagonal line across a cell as a visual element or border, not to split the cell diagonally.

■ New cells can be drawn anywhere. Rows and columns do not have to extend across the entire table.

■ You must use Print Layout view to draw a table.

■ You can combine the Insert Table command with the Draw Table command to customize any table.

Merge and Split Cells

■ **Merge** adjacent cells together to create one larger cell.

■ You can merge horizontally adjacent cells or vertically adjacent cells.

■ Merging is useful for creating a heading row across a table.

■ **Split** a cell to make multiple cells where there is currently only one.

■ You can use the eraser tool to erase borders between cells.

Procedures

Display Tables and Borders Toolbar

- Click **Tables and Borders** button.
OR
1. Click **View** .... Alt + V
2. Click **Toolbars** .... T
3. Click **Tables and Borders**
OR
1. Right-click any toolbar
2. Click **Tables and Borders**

Draw a Table

1. Click **Table** .... Alt + A
2. Click **Dra̲w Table** .... W
   OR
   Click **Draw Table** button on Tables and Borders toolbar.
   ✓ *The mouse pointer resembles a pencil.*
3. Click where you want to position upper-left corner of the table.

4. Drag diagonally down and to the right.
5. Release mouse button where you want to position lower-right corner of the table.
   ✓ *This draws one cell.*
6. Drag mouse pointer to draw horizontal borders and vertical borders.
   ✓ *As you drag, Word displays a dotted line where the border will be. Once you drag far enough, Word completes the line.*
7. Click **Esc** .... Esc
   to turn off Draw Table
   OR
   Click **Draw Table** button .

Merge Cells

1. Select cells to merge.
2. Click **Merge Cells** button.
   OR
   a. Click **Table** .... Alt + A
   b. Click **Merge Cells** .... M

Erase Table Borders

1. Click **Eraser** button on Tables and Borders toolbar.
2. Drag over borders to erase.
3. Click **Esc** .... Esc
   to turn off Eraser
   OR
   Click **Eraser** button.

Split Cells

1. Select cell to split.
2. Click **Split Cells** button.
   OR
   a. Click **Table** .... Alt + A
   b. Click **Sp̲lit Cells** .... P
3. Enter **Number of ro̲ws** to create..... 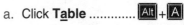 Alt + R, type number
4. Enter **Number of co̲lumns** to create.....  Alt + C, type number
5. Click **OK** .... Enter

Exercise Directions

1. Start Word, if necessary.
2. Open ⊙ **46MEMO**.
3. Save the document as **WD46**.
4. Move the insertion point to the last line of the document.
5. Use the Draw Table tool to draw a cell approximately 4" wide and 4" high.

   ✓ *Use the rulers as guides to measure the height and width of cells as you draw, but don't worry if the table components are not sized exactly.*

6. Divide the cell into two columns by drawing a vertical line through the cell. Try to size the columns as follows:

   > Column 1 – 1.5" wide
   > Column 2 – 2.5" wide

7. Divide the table into four rows, about 1" high each.
8. Merge the cells in the top row to create one cell the width of the table.
9. Leaving the top row intact, use the Split Cells tool to divide each of the cells in the right hand column into two rows (refer to Illustration A to see the desired result).

   ✓ *Split each cell into one column and two rows.*

10. Enter the text shown in Illustration A, using the following formatting and alignments to achieve the desired result:

    a. Row 1 (Table title): 18-point sans serif, bold. Centered both horizontally and vertically.

    b. City names: 14-point serif, bold, aligned left and centered vertically.

    c. Attractions: 14-point serif, centered horizontally and aligned vertically with the cell bottom.

11. Select table and center horizontally on the page.
12. Preview the document. It should look similar to the one in the Illustration A.
13. Print the document.
14. Save the changes to the document.
15. Close the document and exit Word.

Illustration A

STATE-OF-THE-ART SOLUTIONS
TRAINING DEPARTMENT
MEMORANDUM

To: Justin Godere
From: Your Name
Re: Seminar Sites

Dear Justin:

As you requested, I have put together a list of possible sites for the next seminar:
Internet Commerce in the 21st Century. My personal favorite is San Diego.
Check out the Sea World Web site! Let me know if you need more details about
any of the locations.

Potential Sites for Internet Commerce in the 21st Century Seminar	
San Diego, CA	Great Climate!
	Sea World
Cleveland, OH	Rock and Roll Hall of Fame
	Jacob's Field
Orlando, FL	Disney
	Universal Studios

On Your Own

1. Create a new document and save it as **OWD46**.

2. Create a weekly schedule for yourself by drawing a table. For example, the first column may be time periods, and the first row may be the days of the week.

3. Fill in the schedule using uneven columns and rows.

4. If necessary, merge and split cells to create the schedule correctly.

5. Use different alignments in the table.

6. Center the table on the page.

7. Save the document, close it, and exit Word.

Exercise 47

◆ Move and Resize Tables ◆ Rotate Text ◆ Wrap Text

On the Job

You can position and format a table in a text document so it complements the document text. Once a table is in place in a document, you can easily move it and resize it. You can set Word to wrap document text around the table, and you can rotate text in table cells to achieve the exact effect you need.

You want to convince your supervisor at State-of-the-Art Solutions to trust your judgment on the site selection for the next seminar. To make sure he notices your suggestions, you want to improve the appearance of the table. In this exercise, you will add a column to the table and change the size of the table. You will also move the table on the page and set the document text to wrap around the table. As part of the table you will include a hyperlink to the Web site for Sea World, so your supervisor can see the types of extracurricular activities that would be available in San Diego.

Terms

Rotate text Shift the position of text so it runs top to bottom or bottom to top, instead of left to right.

Wrap Control the way text flows around an object such as a table.

Notes

Move and Resize Tables

- You can drag the table anchor to move the table anywhere on the page.
- You can drag the sizing handle to change the table size.

Move and resize tables

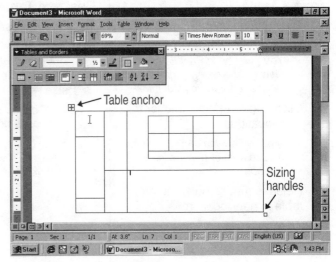

Rotate Text

- **Rotate text** direction within a cell so text runs from left to right, from top to bottom, or from bottom to top.

Rotate text

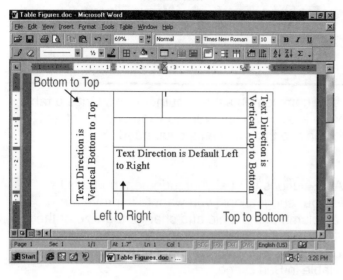

Wrap Text

- By default, tables are inserted on a blank line above or below existing text.

- You can set Word to **wrap** text around the table.

- Wrapping text around a table integrates the table object into the text so text appears above, below, and on either side of the table.

Wrap text around a table

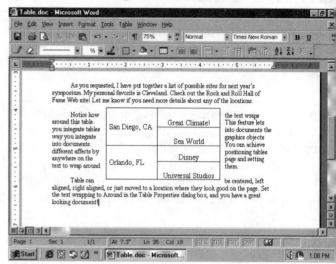

Procedures

Move a Table

1. Rest mouse pointer on table so handles are displayed.

   ✓ *You must be in Print Layout view for the sizing handle and table anchor to be available.*

2. Click and drag table anchor to new location.

   ✓ *A dotted outline moves with the mouse pointer to show new location.*

3. Release mouse button to drop table in new location.

Resize a Table

1. Rest mouse pointer on table so handles are displayed.

2. Click and drag sizing handle to increase or decrease table size.

   ✓ *A dotted outline moves with the mouse pointer to show new size.*

3. Release mouse button to resize table.

Rotate Text

1. Click in cell to format.
   OR
   Select components to format.

2. Click **Change Text Direction** button ![icon].

   ✓ *Click the button to toggle through the three available directions.*

Wrap Text

1. Click in table.

2. Click **T\u0332able**.................`Alt`+`A`

3. Click **Table P\u0332roperties**........`R`

4. Click **T\u0332able** tab....................`T`

5. Click **A\u0332round**.......................`A`

6. Click **OK**...........................`Enter`

216

Exercise Directions

1. Start Word, if necessary.

2. Open ⊚ **47MEMO**.

3. Save the document as **WD47**.

4. Use the Draw Table tool to draw a new cell on the left side of the table. Size the new cell to the full height of the table and approximately 1" wide.

5. In the new cell, set the text to run vertically bottom to top.

6. Type the company name: *State-of-the-Art Solutions* in a bold, blue, 20-point sans serif font.

7. Center the company name horizontally and vertically.

8. Select the entire table and align it on the right side of the page.

9. Set text to wrap around the table.

10. Move the table up so the text wraps around it.

    ✓ *Position the table so the top row begins at about 3" on the vertical ruler.*

11. Resize the table to increase its width to about 5.5".

12. In the table, use the text *Sea World* to create a hyperlink to the Web site: D:/Internet/E47/seaworld.htm

13. Test the hyperlink.

    ✓ *If you've copied the Internet simulation files to your hard drive or your CD-ROM drive is a letter other than D:, substitute the correct letter for D.*

14. Click the *California* link to go to the site for the San Diego facility.

15. Click the *Park Information* link to find out when the park is open and how much it costs to get in.

16. Close the simulation.

17. In Word, preview the **WD47** document. It should look similar to the one in Illustration A.

18. Print the document.

19. Save the changes to the document.

20. Close the document and exit Word.

STATE-OF-THE-ART SOLUTIONS
TRAINING DEPARTMENT
MEMORANDUM

To: Justin Godere
From: Your Name
Re: Seminar Sites

Dear Justin:

As you requested, I have put together a list of possible sites for the next seminar:
Internet Commerce in the 21st Century. My personal favorite is San Diego. Check out the Sea World Web site! Let me know if you need more details about any of the locations.

State-of-the-Art Solutions	Potential Sites for Internet Commerce in the 21st Century Seminar	
	San Diego, CA	Great Climate!
		Sea World
	Cleveland, OH	Rock and Roll Hall of Fame
		Jacob's Field
	Orlando, FL	Disney
		Universal Studios

On Your Own

1. Create a new document in Word.

2. Save the file as **OWD47**.

3. Type a personal business letter to an employer or to your parents explaining why you need a raise. Write at least two paragraphs about why you deserve the raise and what you plan to do with the additional funds. Include information about how you spend the money you receive now.

4. To illustrate your point, draw a table in the letter and list items that you have purchased in the past two weeks. For example, include CDs, books, meals, movie tickets, and other expenses. The table should have at least three columns—the date, the item, and the cost. List at least four items.

5. Merge a row across the top of the table and type in a title.

6. Try rotating text in some of the cells.

7. Use different alignments in the table cells.

8. Set the text in the letter to wrap around the table.

9. Try moving and resizing the table to improve the appearance of the letter.

10. When you are satisfied with the appearance of the table and the letter, save the changes, close the document, and exit Word.

Exercise 48

Skills Covered:

◆ Calculate in a Table ◆ Number Formats ◆ Sort Rows

On the Job

Perform basic calculations in tables to total values in a column or row. If the values change, you can update the result without redoing the math! At the same time, you can format the calculation results with one of Word's built in number formats. Sorting rows, like sorting paragraphs or lists, helps you keep your tables in order.

The owner of The Sweet Tooth Candy Shop wants you to enhance the flyer advertising the Valentine's Day sale. In this exercise, you will first sort the rows. Then, you will insert a row where you can calculate the cost of a special Valentine's Gift Basket. Finally, you will resize the table and make sure it is positioned correctly on the page.

Terms

Spreadsheet An application used for setting up mathematical calculations, such as Microsoft's Excel.

Function A built-in **formula** for performing calculations, such as addition in a table

Formula A mathematical equation.

Field A placeholder used to insert information that changes, such as the date, the time, a page number, or the results of a calculation.

Notes

Calculate in a Table

- Word tables include basic **spreadsheet functions** so you can perform calculations on data entered in tables.

- By default, Word assumes you want to add the values entered in the column above the current cell, or in the row beside the current cell.

- Word enters the calculation result in a **field** so it can be updated if the values in the table change.

- For anything other than basic calculations use an Excel worksheet, not a Word table.

The Formula dialog box for totaling a row

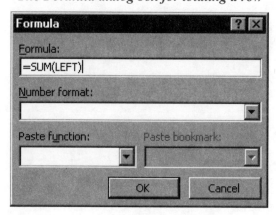

Number Formats

- When you set up a calculation in a table you can select a number format to use for the result.
- Number formats include features such as dollar signs, commas, percent signs, and decimal points.

Formula dialog box

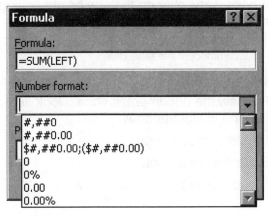

Sort Rows

- Sort rows in a table the same way you sort lists or paragraphs.
  - ✓ *See Exercise 29.*
- Rows can be sorted according to the data in any column.
- For example, in a table of names and addresses, rows can be sorted alphabetically by name or by city, or numerically by ZIP Code.
- Word rearranges the rows in the table but does not rearrange the columns.

Procedures

Total Values in a Column or Row

1. Click in cell where you want the total to be displayed.
2. Click **Table** .... Alt + A
3. Click **Formula** .... O
   - ✓ *By default, Word enters the formula for totaling the values in the cells in the column above or the row to the left.*
4. Click **Number format** .... Alt + N
5. Click desired format ...... ↑, ↓
6. Click **OK** .... Enter

Update the Total

1. Select the cell where the total is displayed.
2. Press **F9** F9

Sort Rows

1. Display Tables and Borders toolbar.
2. Select the data in the column by which you want to sort.
3. Click Sort **Ascending** button [A/Z↓] on Tables and Borders toolbar to sort from A to Z or from 0 to 9.
   OR
   Sort **Descending** button [Z/A↓] on Tables and Borders toolbar to sort from Z to A or from 9 to 0.
   - ✓ *If the sort does not include the first row, click Table, Sort and select the No header row option button, then click OK.*

Exercise Directions

1. Start Word, if necessary.

2. Open ⊘ **48SALE**.

3. Save the document as **WD48**.

4. Sort the table rows in descending order based on the data in the Sale Price column.

   ✓ *Remember not to sort the header row.*

5. Insert a new row at the bottom of the table.

6. In the Candy column of the new row, enter Super Gift Basket.

7. In the Size column of the new row, enter 20 pounds.

8. In the Regular Price column of the new row, calculate the total of the items already entered in the table.

9. In the Sale Price column of the new row, enter $115.00.

10. Delete the row for the Cashew Turtles.

11. Update the calculation result in the table.

12. Resize the table so it is approximately 5 ½ inches wide and 4 inches high.

13. If necessary, change the row height setting for all rows from Exactly to At least.

   ✓ *This will allow the row height to increase to accommodate the table data.*

14. Center the table horizontally on the page.

15. Preview the document. It should look similar to the one in Illustration A.

16. Print the document.

17. Save the document.

18. Close the document and exit Word.

Illustration A

The Sweet Tooth
321 Main Street ✧ Hanover, NH 03755

VALENTINE'S DAY SALE

Candy	Size	Regular Price	Sale Price
White Chocolate Assortment	32 ounces	$48.99	$35.00
Milk Chocolate Assortment	32 ounces	$45.99	$29.99
Assorted Truffles	16 ounces	$21.99	$15.99
Raspberry Creams	16 ounces	$16.99	$12.99
Caramels	16 ounces	$15.99	$11.99
Raspberry Creams	10 ounces	$12.99	$9.99
Caramels	10 ounces	$11.99	$8.99
Super Gift Basket	20 pounds	$174.93	$115.00

On Your Own

1. Open the document **OWD47**, the letter asking for a raise that you wrote in the On Your Own section of exercise 47, or open ☉**48RAISE**.
2. Save the file as **OWD48**.
3. Sort the rows in the table into descending numerical order, according to the amount of the expenses.
4. Add a row to the bottom of the table.
5. Label the row Total.
6. Calculate the total amount of expenses in the table. Make sure the result is displayed in dollar format.
7. Change one or more of the values in the table.
8. Update the calculation.
9. Apply an AutoFormat to the table.
10. Save the changes, close the document, and exit Word.

Exercise 49

Skills Covered:

◆ Cell Borders and Shading

On the Job

Cell borders and shading let you dress up your tables to make them look good, as well as to highlight important information.

The owner of The Sweet Tooth likes the flyer you have created advertising the Valentine's Day sale, but wants you to add some visual enhancements. In this exercise, you will use cell borders and shading to format the table.

Terms

Line style The appearance of a line.

Line weight The thickness of a line.

Shading A color or pattern used to fill the background of a cell.

Notes

Cell Borders and Shading

- By default, Word applies a ½-pt. black solid line border around all table cells.

- Use the Tables and Borders toolbar button to change the borders and shading of table cells.

- You can select borders and shading before you draw new cells, or apply them to selected cells.

  - Select a different **line style**.

  - Select a different **line weight**.

  - Change the border color.

  - Erase or add border lines.

  - Add color or **shading**.

- Selected border and shading formatting remains in effect until new formatting is selected.

  - ✓ When table borders are removed, you can see table cells on-screen by displaying gridlines.

Procedures

Apply Cell Borders

1. Select cell(s) to format.
2. Click **Borders** drop-down arrow ▦ ▾.
3. Click Border style.

   ✓ *Border buttons are toggles— click to display border, click again to hide border.*

Select Line Style

1. Click **Line Style** drop-down arrow [———— ▾].
2. Click desired line style.

   ✓ *Click No Border to remove border lines.*

3. Apply newly selected line style to cell(s) as desired.

Select Line Weight

1. Click **Line Weight** drop-down arrow [¼ ▾].
2. Click desired line weight
3. Apply newly selected line weight to cell(s) as desired.

Select Line Color

1. Click **Border Color** button ▨.
2. Click desired color
3. Apply newly selected line color to cell(s) as desired.

Select Cell Shading

1. Click **Shading Color** drop down arrow ▨ ▾.
2. Click desired color
3. Click **No Fill** to remove shading or color.

Exercise Directions

1. Start Word, if necessary.
2. Open ⊙ **49SALE**.
3. Save the document as **WD49**.
4. Sort the rows in ascending order according to the values in the Sale Price column.

   ✓ *Remember not to sort the header row.*

5. Apply a dark blue double-line ¾-inch border around the outside of the table.
6. Apply the same border across the bottom of all cells in the first row.
7. Remove the border lines between the cells in the first row.

   ✓ *Do not merge the cells; simply remove the border lines.*

8. Apply a 20% gray shade fill to all of the cells in the first row.
9. Change the color of the font in the first row to dark blue.
10. Apply a 12.5% gray shading to all of the cells in the bottom row.
11. Change the text in the bottom row to boldface.
12. Preview the document.

13. Print the document.
14. Save the document.
15. Close the document and exit Word.

Illustration A

The Sweet Tooth
321 Main Street ✧ Hanover, NH 03755

VALENTINE'S DAY SALE

Candy	Size	Regular Price	Sale Price
White Chocolate Assortment	32 ounces	$48.99	$35.00
Milk Chocolate Assortment	32 ounces	$45.99	$29.99
Assorted Truffles	16 ounces	$21.99	$15.99
Raspberry Creams	16 ounces	$16.99	$12.99
Caramels	16 ounces	$15.99	$11.99
Raspberry Creams	10 ounces	$12.99	$9.99
Caramels	10 ounces	$11.99	$8.99
Super Gift Basket	**20 pounds**	**$ 174.93**	**$115.00**

On Your Own

1. Open **OWD46**, the document you created in the On Your Own section of Exercise 46, or open ⊙ **49TABLE**.

2. Save the document as **OWD49**.

3. Apply cell borders to cells in the table.

4. Apply cell shading to cells in the table.

5. Preview the document.

6. Save the document, close it, and exit Word.

On the Job

Use tables in an HTML document to organize and align data on a Web page. Tables let you define different areas on a page because you can format each cell differently. Use Web Page templates to create new Web Page documents. The templates include formatting such as fonts, styles, and bullet lists as well as tables. All you have to do is fill in the content and set up any necessary hyperlinks.

The owner of The Sweet Tooth has asked you to design two new Web pages to link to the company Web site. In this exercise, you will design a Web page advertising gift items that are for sale and a Web page listing monthly events. You will create the first page using a table in a Word document and saving it in HTML format. You will create the second page using a Web Page template.

Terms

Template A Word document on which new documents are based. Templates include formatting settings, text, and graphics used to create the new document.

Notes

Use Tables in HTML Documents

- Some standard Word features are not available when editing HTML documents in Word, and some Word formatting techniques are not displayed in HTML documents. For example, you cannot use Word tabs to align data in an HTML document.

- Creating tables in HTML documents lets you overcome some of the formatting limitations because you can align data in columns and rows and vary the formatting from cell to cell.

- Steps for creating, modifying, and formatting tables in HTML documents are the same as in regular Word documents.

- You can insert more than one table on a Web page.

A table is used to define areas on a Web page

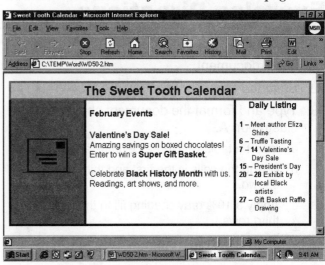

Use Web Page Templates

- Word comes with built-in **templates** for creating Web page documents.
- Select a template to create a document in HTML format and save as a Web page.

Select a Web page template in the New dialog box

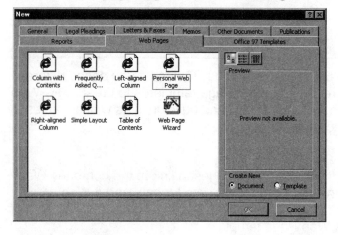

- Most Web page templates use tables to align text and graphics.
- Web page templates usually include text already formatted as hyperlinks.
- Web page templates may include sample text and graphics.
- To complete the document, you replace the sample text and graphics and edit or insert hyperlinks.

Procedures

Create a Web Page Using a Template

1. Click **File** .... Alt + F
2. Click **New** .... N
3. Click **Web Pages** tab .... Ctrl + Tab
4. Click desired template icon.

5. Click **OK** .... Enter
   - ✓ *If the document contains elements such as decorative borders that are not supported by the default Browser, Word displays a warning message. Click Continue to create the page.*
6. Replace directional text and graphics.

7. Apply formatting as needed.
8. Create hyperlinks as needed.
9. **Save** and name the document .... Ctrl + S
   - ✓ *Word saves the document in HTML format.*

Exercise Directions

1. Start Word, if necessary, and create a new blank document.
2. Save the document as **WD50-1**.
3. Type and format the document shown in Illustration A.
   a. Insert a table with three columns and four rows.
   b. Merge the cells in the first and third rows as shown.
   c. Apply a 10% gray shading fill to the first and third rows.

   d. Size the row heights as follows:
      - Row 1, approximately 1"
      - Row 2, approximately 1.5"
      - Row 3, approximately 3.5"
      - Row 4, approximately .5"
   e. Type the text in the table in a serif font, using the specified sizes, styles, and alignments.
   f. Insert the symbols shown from the Webdings font, sized at 72 points.
   g. Apply a 3-point black single line border to the top and bottom of each row. Leave the default border on the left and right sides of all cells.

4. Save the changes, and then save the document as a Web page with the name **WD50-2.htm**, and the Web Page title, *Sweet Tooth On-Line Store*.

5. Preview the document using Web Page Preview.

6. Close the document.

7. Create a new document based on the Simple Layout Web Page Template.

8. Save the document as **WD50-3.htm**, with the Web Page title *Sweet Tooth Calendar*.

9. Type and format the document shown in Illustration B:

   a. Create a new row across the top of the table for the Main Heading.

   b. Merge the new row into one cell, and set it to At Least .33" high.

   c. In place of the sample text Main Heading, type the text *The Sweet Tooth Calendar*, in 18-point sans serif, bold, centered horizontally and vertically.

   d. In the second row left-hand cell, insert the Webding symbol of an envelope as shown, sized at 72 points, and centered horizontally and vertically.

   e. Below the symbol, type *Click Here to Send Us E-Mail* in 12-point sans serif, bold.

   f. In the second row middle cell, replace the sample text with the text shown.

      • Use a 12-point sans serif font.

      • Apply bold face to the text: *February Events, Valentine's Day Sale!, Super Gift Basket*, and *Black History Month*.

      • Change the font color of the text Valentine's Day Sale to red.

      • Center the text in the cell vertically and left align it horizontally.

   g. In the second row right-hand cell, type the text shown.

      • Type the heading in 12-point bold sans serif, centered.

      • Type the remaining text in 10-point sans serif.

      • Apply bold face to the dates.

      • Use a hanging indent to align the text as shown.

   h. Size the second row to At Least 2.25" high.

   i. Insert a third row along the bottom of the table, sized to At Least .5" high.

   j. In the bottom row, type the text shown in the left and right cells, in 12-point sans serif bold, centered horizontally and aligned on the bottom, vertically. Leave the middle cell in the bottom row blank.

   k. Apply a 10% gray shading fill to the cell in the first row, and a turquoise 3-point single line outside border.

   l. Apply a 40% gray shading fill to the left cell in the middle row.

   m. Apply a black 3-point single line border on all sides of the cells in the second row except the top, and on the bottom, left and right of the bottom row.

10. Use Web Page Preview to preview the document. It should look similar to the one in Illustration B.

11. Close Web Page Preview.

12. Create a hyperlink from the text in the lower right cell to the **WD50-2** Web page.

13. Test the hyperlink.

14. Create a hyperlink from the text in the lower right cell of the **WD50-2** Web page to the **WD50-3** Web page.

15. Save the document and close it.

16. Use Web Page Preview to preview the **WD50-3** page again.

17. While in Web Page Preview test the hyperlinks between the two documents.

18. Close Web Page Preview.

19. Close all open documents and exit Word.

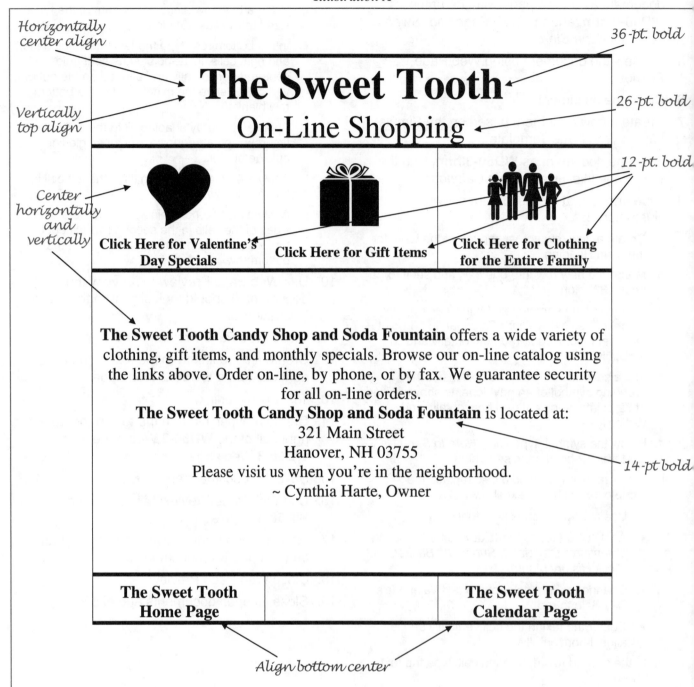

Horizontally center align

36-pt. bold

The Sweet Tooth
On-Line Shopping

Vertically top align

26-pt. bold

12-pt. bold

Center horizontally and vertically

Click Here for Valentine's Day Specials

Click Here for Gift Items

Click Here for Clothing for the Entire Family

The Sweet Tooth Candy Shop and Soda Fountain offers a wide variety of clothing, gift items, and monthly specials. Browse our on-line catalog using the links above. Order on-line, by phone, or by fax. We guarantee security for all on-line orders.
The Sweet Tooth Candy Shop and Soda Fountain is located at:
321 Main Street
Hanover, NH 03755
Please visit us when you're in the neighborhood.
~ Cynthia Harte, Owner

14-pt bold

The Sweet Tooth Home Page

The Sweet Tooth Calendar Page

Align bottom center

Illustration B

The Sweet Tooth Calendar		
Click Here To Send Us E-Mail	**February Events** **Valentine's Day Sale!** Amazing savings on boxed chocolates! Enter to win a **Super Gift Basket**. Celebrate **Black History Month** with us. Readings, art shows, and more.	**Daily Listing** **1** – Meet author Eliza Shine **6** – Truffle Tasting **7 – 14** Valentine's Day Sale **15** – President's Day **20 – 28** Exhibit by local Black artists **27** – Gift Basket Raffle Drawing
The Sweet Tooth Home Page		**The Sweet Tooth On-Line Store**

On Your Own

1. Start Word and create a new HTML document using one of the Web Page templates that includes a table.

2. Save the document with the name **OWD50**.

3. Type text to provide information about some part of your life. For example, make a page about your family, or about a club or organization to which you belong.

4. Open the document **OWD41**, the personal home page you created in the on Your Own Section of Exercise 41, or open 💿 **50WEB**.

5. Save the document as **OWD50-2**.

6. Create hyperlinks between the **OWD50** page you just created and the **OWD50-2** home page.

7. Test the links.

8. Save all changes, close all open documents, and exit Word.

Exercise 51

Your boss at Cornerstone Graphics has asked you to design an invoice to send to The Sweet Tooth. You've decided that this is a great opportunity to use your table skills.

Exercise Directions

1. Start Word and create a new blank document.

2. Save the document as **WD51**.

3. Using either the Draw Table tool or the Insert Table command, create the table shown in Illustration A.

   - Size the cells as closely as possible to the sizes indicated on Illustration A.

   ✓ *If you use the Insert Table command, you will have to merge and split cells to achieve the desired results.*

4. Remove all borderlines from the table.

5. Display gridlines, if necessary, so you can see the cells on-screen.

6. Center the table horizontally on the page.

7. Enter the text shown in Illustration B, using the specified formatting and alignment.

8. In the right cell of the row labeled Total, use a formula to calculate the total cost amount owed. Format the result using the dollar number format.

9. Apply borderlines as shown in Illustration B.

10. Preview the document. It should look similar to the one in Illustration B.

11. Print the document.

12. Save the document.

13. Close the document and exit Word.

Illustration A

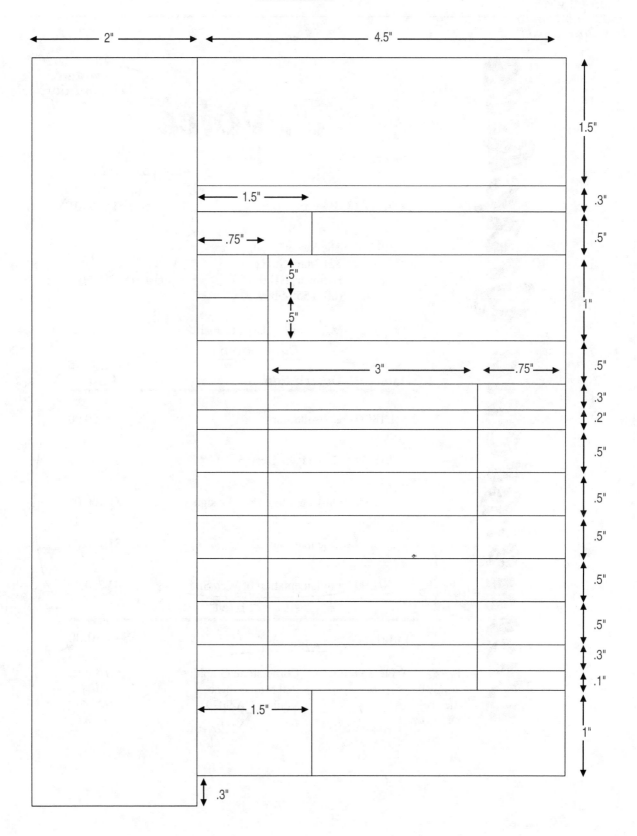

65-pt. serif, rotate bottom to top align top left

Cornerstone Graphics

48-pt. serif, centered horizontally and vertically

Invoice

Align top right

February 18, 1999

Invoice #TST9901

Align top left

12-pt. serif

Bill To: The Sweet Tooth
321 Main Street
Hanover, NH 03755
(603) 555-9009

Att.: Ms. Cynthia Harte, Owner

Align bottom left

Date	Description	Cost
1/18/99	Consultation	$500.00
2/18/99	Home Page Design	$1,200.00
3/7/99	On-Line Store Page Design	$1,100.00
3/21/99	Calendar Page Design	$1,100.00
4/1/99	Implementation of Web Site	$750.00

14-pt. Bold, serif, align bottom center

12-pt. serif

Align top right

Align top left

Align top right

Total $4,650.00

12 pt. Serif

14-pt. bold, serif, Align bottom left

Please remit to: Cornerstone Graphics
920 Marco Place
Venice, CA 90291

Align top right

Align top left

14-pt., Align bottom right

Sum formula

Lesson 8

Merge

Exercise 52

On the Job

Use Mail Merge to customize documents such as letters or standard reports. For example, with Mail Merge you can store a document with standard text, such as a form letter, and then insert personalized names and addresses on each copy that you generate or print. Mail Merge can help you generate mass mailings, prepare monthly reports, or update catalogs or lists quickly and easily.

The event coordinator for State-of-the-Art Solutions has asked you to send out confirmation letters to people participating in the Business on the Web seminar, as well as to people participating in a different seminar—Internet Commerce. In this exercise, you will use Mail Merge to create a form letter that will be personalized with each participant's name and address and customized according to the seminar.

Terms

Mail merge A process that inserts variable data into a standardized document to produce a personalized or customized document.

Main document The document containing the standardized text that will be printed on all documents.

Data source The document containing the variable data that will be inserted during the merge.

Merge document The customized document resulting from a merge.

Merge field A placeholder in the main document that marks where and what will be inserted from the data source document.

Header row The first row in a table. In a data source document, the header row contains the merge field names.

Field One item of variable data, such as a first name, a last name, or a ZIP Code.

Record A collection of variable data, about one person or thing. In a form letter merge for example, each record contains variable data for each person receiving the letter: first name, last name, address, city, state, and ZIP Code.

Data form A dialog box used to enter merge field data.

Notes

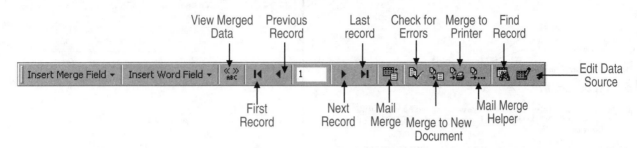

Mail Merge toolbar

Mail Merge

- Use **Mail merge** to customize boilerplate documents such as form letters, lists, standardized reports, envelopes, or invitations.
- Mail Merge is a three-step process:
  - Create a **main document**.
  - Create a **data source** document.
  - Merge the two to generate the customized **merge documents**.

Main document

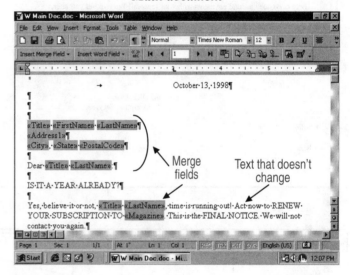

Main document

Variable data entered in columns and rows

Text that doesn't change

October 13, 1998

«Title» «FirstName» «LastName»
«Address1»
«City», «State» «PostalCode»

Merge fields

Dear «Title» «LastName»:

IS IT A YEAR ALREADY?

Yes, believe it or not, «Title» «LastName», time is running out! Act now to RENEW YOUR SUBSCRIPTION TO «Magazine». This is the FINAL NOTICE. We will not contact you again.

Please use the enclosed customer card to ENSURE THAT YOUR SUBSCRIPTION IS RENEWED.

Just check off the one, two, or three-year subscription offer. The longer the term, the lower the per issue cost! Or call 1-800-555-2200 to renew OVER THE PHONE.

There is no need to send payments with your renewal! We will bill you later.

Remember, this is your FINAL NOTICE. Call 1-800-555-2200! That's 1-800-555-2200. Act now to avoid missing a single issue of «Magazine»!

Sincerely,

Al Dickenson
Subscription Services

Ad/yo

Enc.

Data source document

Title	FirstName	LastName	Address1	City	State	PostalCode	Magazine
Mr.	Jeffrey	Levine	2902 Karen Rd.	Seaford	NY	11786	Offroad Rider Magazine
Ms.	Liz	Mahoney	7865 Stuart Dr.	Leavitttown	NY	11756	Offroad Rider Magazine
Ms.	Melanie	Jackson	89 Beaumont Ave.	Brooklyn	NY	11235	Offroad Rider Magazine
Mr.	Alex	Daniels	592 Roosevelt Parkway	W. Hempstead	NY	11552	Long Island Monthly

Results of the merge

Variable data replaces merge fields

October 13, 1998

Mr. Jeffrey Levine
2902 Karen Rd.
Seaford, NY 11786

Dear Mr. Levine:

IS IT A YEAR ALREADY?

Yes, believe it or not, Mr. Levine, time... SUBSCRIPTION TO Offroad Rider M... contact you again.

Please use the enclosed customer card... RENEWED.

Just check off the one, two, or three-ye... lower the per issue cost! Or call 1-800-...

There is no need to send payments with...

Remember, this is your FINAL NOTIC... Act now to avoid missing a single issu...

Ad/yo

Enc.

October 13, 1998

Ms. Liz Mahoney
7865 Stuart Dr.
Leavitttown, NY 11756

Dear Ms. Mahoney:

IS IT A YEAR ALREADY?

Yes, believe it or not, Ms. Mahoney, time is running out! A... SUBSCRIPTION TO Offroad Rider Magazine. This is the... contact you again.

Please use the enclosed customer card to ENSURE THAT... RENEWED.

Just check off the one, two, or three-year subscription offe... lower the per issue cost! Or call 1-800-555-2200 to renew...

There is no need to send payments with your renewal! We...

Remember, this is your FINAL NOTICE. Call 1-800-555-... Act now to avoid missing a single issue of Offroad Rider M...

Sincerely,

Al Dickenson
Subscription ...

Ad/yo

Enc.

October 13, 1998

Ms. Melanie Jackson
89 Beaumont Ave.
Brooklyn, NY 11235

Dear Ms. Jackson:

IS IT A YEAR ALREADY?

Yes, believe it or not, Ms. Jackson, time is running out! ... SUBSCRIPTION TO Offroad Rider Magazine. This is t... contact you again.

Please use the enclosed customer card to ENSURE THA... RENEWED.

Just check off the one, two, or three-year subscription of... lower the per issue cost! Or call 1-800-555-2200 to rene...

There is no need to send payments with your renewal! W...

Remember, this is your FINAL NOTICE. Call 1-800-55... Act now to avoid missing a single issue of Offroad Ride...

Sincerely,

Al Dickens...
Subscriptio...

Ad/yo

Enc.

October 13, 1998

Mr. Alex Daniels
592 Roosevelt Parkway
W. Hempstead, NY 11552

Dear Mr. Daniels:

IS IT A YEAR ALREADY?

Yes, believe it or not, Mr. Daniels, time is running out! Act now to RENEW YOUR SUBSCRIPTION TO Long Island Monthly. This is the FINAL NOTICE. We will not contact you again.

Please use the enclosed customer card to ENSURE THAT YOUR SUBSCRIPTION IS RENEWED.

Just check off the one, two, or three-year subscription offer. The longer the term, the lower the per issue cost! Or call 1-800-555-2200 to renew OVER THE PHONE.

There is no need to send payments with your renewal! We will bill you later.

Remember, this is your FINAL NOTICE. Call 1-800-555-2200! That's 1-800-555-2200. Act now to avoid missing a single issue of Long Island Monthly!

Sincerely,

Al Dickenson
Subscription Services

Ad/yo

Enc.

Mail Merge Helper dialog box

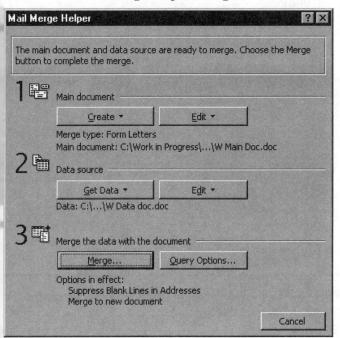

- The Mail Merge toolbar has buttons for accessing Mail Merge features and command.

Create a Main Document

- Create a main document that contains data that will remain the same on every merged document.

- Include all text, spacing, punctuation, and formatting.

- Insert **Merge fields** in the main document where variable data will appear.

Merge fields in a document

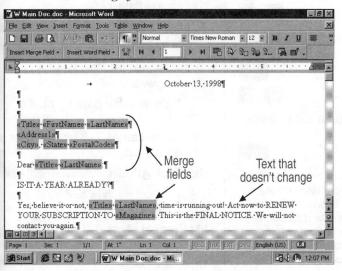

- Four types of main documents are available:
  - *Form letter*   used for letters or other regular Word documents such as reports, flyers, or memos.
  - *Catalog*   used for lists such as rosters, inventories, or directories.
  - *Envelopes*   used to create personalized envelopes.
  - *Labels*   used to created personalized labels.

Create a Data Source Document

- Create a data source document that contains the variable data that will be inserted in place of the merge fields during the merge. For example, you can store names and addresses for a form letter, envelopes or labels, store product information for an inventory, or store sales figures for a monthly report.

- Data in a data source document is stored in a table format.

- The **header row** contains the merge field names.

- Each column in the table contains data for one **field**; each row contains data for one **record**.

Data source document

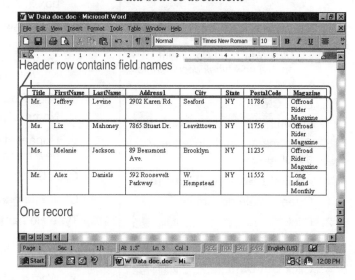

- Word makes it easy to enter data into a data source document using a **data form**.

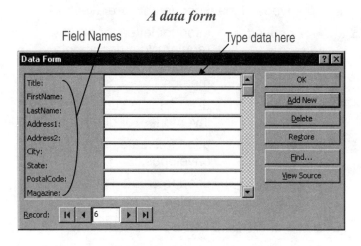

A data form

Field Names — Type data here

- Fields in a data source document may be left blank.
- A data source document may be used many times with different main documents.

Procedures

Create Form Letter Main Document

1. Create a document containing the data and formatting that will not change.
2. Click **Tools**.................. `Alt`+`T`
3. Click **Mail Merge**................. `R`
4. Click **Create** button

   `Create ▼` .... `Alt`+`C`
5. Click **Form Letter** .... `L`
6. Click **Active Window** button

   `Active Window` .. `Alt`+`A`

   ✓ *Click New Main Document to open a new blank document to use.*

7. Click **Close**
   button `Close` .... `Esc`
8. Save, name, and close the document.

Create Data Source Document

1. Open a main document.
2. Click **Tools**.................. `Alt`+`T`
3. Click **Mail Merge**................. `R`
4. Click **Get Data**............. `Alt`+`G`
5. Click **Create Data Source** .. `C`
6. Click **Field Names in Header Row** .... `Alt`+`N`

   to display a list of built-in merge field names.
7. Do one of the following:

Remove unwanted merge fields:

a. Select merge field to delete .... `↑`, `↓`
b. Click **Remove Field Name** .... `Alt`+`R`
c. Repeat steps a and b for each merge field to remove.

Create new merge fields:

a. Click **Field name** box.......................... `Alt`+`F`
b. Type new merge field name.

   ✓ *Do not include spaces in field names.*

c. Click **Add Field Name**...................... `Alt`+`A`
d. Repeat steps a–c for each new merge field to add.

8. Click **OK** .... `Enter`
9. Click **File name** .... `Alt`+`N`
10. Type file name for data source document.
11. Click **Save** .... `Enter`

   ✓ *Word displays the Mail Merge Helper. If Word displays a message telling you there are no records in the data source, click Edit Data Source to begin entering records using the following procedure, starting with step 6.*

Enter Data Source Records

1. Open the main document.
2. Click **Tools** .... `Alt`+`T`
3. Click **Mail Merge** .... `R`
4. Click the **Data Source Edit** drop-down list arrow .... `Alt`+`D`
5. Click name of data source document in drop-down list.

   ✓ *Word displays first blank data form.*

   OR

a. Open the main document.
b. Click **Edit Data Source** button `✎▾`.

6. Type variable data for first merge field.
7. Press **Enter** .... `Enter`
   or **Tab** .... `Tab`

   ✓ *Press Shift+Tab to move to previous field.*

8. Type variable data for next merge field.
9. Repeat steps 7–8 until all data is entered.
10. Click **Add New**............. `Alt`+`A`

   ✓ *Word displays next blank data form.*

11. Repeat steps 6–10 until data for all records is complete.
12. Click **OK**............................ `Esc`

   ✓ *Word displays the main document.*

13. Close and save the file.

   ✓ *Word prompts you to save the data source document.*

14. Save and close the data source document.

Insert Merge Fields in a Main Document

1. Open the main document.
2. Position insertion point where first merge field goes.
3. Click the **Insert Merge Field** button | Insert Merge Field ▾ | on Mail Merge toolbar.
4. Click desired field.........⬆, ⬇
5. Insert spacing, paragraphs, and/or punctuation as necessary.

   ✓ *For example, press the spacebar between FirstName and LastName fields and type a comma followed by a space after the City field.*

6. Repeat steps 2–5 until all merge fields are in place.
7. Save the document.

Preview Merged Documents main level

1. Open the main document.
2. Click the **View Merged Data** button 🔲 on Mail Merge toolbar.
3. Click the **Next Record** button ▶.

   OR

   Click the **Previous Record** button ◀.
4. Click the **View Merged Data** button again to display merge fields 🔲.

Merge Documents

1. Open the main document.
2. Click the **Merge to New Document** button 🔲 to create a new document containing all form letters.

   ✓ *You can save the document to use again.*

   OR

   Click the **Merge to Printer** button 🔲 to print the form letters.

Exercise Directions

1. Start Word, if necessary.
2. Create a new document and save it as **WD52-1**.
3. Using a 12-point serif font, type the letter shown in Illustration A. Type the letter exactly as shown, including text, formatting, and punctuation that won't change, but leaving out all variable data.

   ✓ *Variable data is shown in all uppercase letters in the Illustration.*

4. Use the Mail Merge Helper to make **WD52-1** a form letter main document.
5. Create a new data source document named **WD52-2**.

6. Remove the following fields:
   - Country
   - HomePhone
   - WorkPhone
7. Add a new field named *Seminar*.
8. Enter the records from the table on page 245 into the data source document.
9. Insert the merge fields into the main document (**WD52-1**) as shown in Illustration B.
10. Preview the merged documents.
11. Merge the documents to a new document.
12. Save the new document as **WD52-3**.
13. Print the merge documents.
14. Close all open documents, saving changes as necessary, then exit Word.

State-of-the-Art Solutions

P.O. Box 6743211, Brentwood, California 90049

Today's Date

TITLE FIRSTNAME LASTNAME
JOBTITLE
COMPANY
ADDRESS1
ADDRESS2
CITY, STATE POSTALCODE

Dear TITLE LASTNAME:

This letter is to confirm receipt of your registration for the SEMINAR seminar scheduled for February, in Phoenix, AZ. The event promises to be chock full of interesting and innovative information. We hope you are as excited about the event as we are!

Please note the updated schedule included on the following page. We will continue to notify you if additional changes are made; however, we believe this schedule will remain intact.

I look forward to seeing you in February, TITLE LASTNAME.

Sincerely,

Steven Godere
Event coordinator

SG/yo

Illustration B

Title	FirstName	LastName	JobTitle	Company	Address1	Address2	City	State	Postal Code	Seminar
Mr.	Jeffrey	Levine	Manager	Forsythe Clothiers	2902 Karen Rd.	Suite 61 East	San Francisco	CA	94109	Business on the Web
Ms.	Liz	Mohoney	Director	Beehive Properties	7865 Stuart Dr.		Salt Lake City	UT	84122	Internet Commerce
Ms.	Melanie	Jackson	Assistant Manager	Brooklyn Design	89 Beaumont Ave.		Brooklyn	NY	11235	Business on the Web
Mr.	Alex	Daniels	Manager	Long Island Gardens	592 Roosevelt Parkway	Suite 21A	W. Hempstead	NY	11552	Business on the Web
Mr.	Suhail	Nakahmi	Manager	Applewood Bookstore	73 Applewood Lane		Cambridge	MA	02129	Internet Commerce

On Your Own

1. Think of ways Mail Merge would be useful to you. For example, are you involved in any clubs or organizations that send out mass mailings? Do you send out "Holiday Letters" every year? Do you invite the same people to parties for different occasions? Are you responsible for regular reports that contain variable data, such as sales reports or forecasts?

2. Open the document **OWD18**, the letter you created in the On Your Own section of Exercise 18 asking for donations, or open ⊙ **52LETTER**.

3. Save the file as **OWD52**.

4. Delete all variable information from the letter, including the inside address, and the name on the salutation line.

5. Use Mail Merge to make **OWD52** a Main Document.

6. Create a Data Source document that includes at least five records. Make sure you have all the fields you will need to set up the main document, such as first and last names, salutation, and address fields.

7. Save the Data Source document as **OWD52-2**.

8. In the **OWD52** Main Document, insert the merge fields necessary to customize the document, such as the inside address and the salutation line.

9. Merge the documents into a new file.

10. Save the merge document file as **OWD52-3**.

11. Save all open documents, close all open documents, and exit Word.

Exercise 53

Skills Covered:

◆ Use an Existing Data Source ◆ Modify an Existing Data Source

On the Job

If you have an existing data source document, you can merge it with any main document to create new merge documents. This saves you time because you don't have to retype repetitive data. You can also add records to an existing data source or make changes to keep it up-to-date.

The event coordinator at State-of-the-Art Solutions has asked you to contact seminar attendees to ask their preference for smoking or non-smoking accommodations. In this exercise, you will modify an existing data source document. You will add records for two last-minute registrants for the Business on the Web seminar, delete the record for one cancellation, and edit the records for one attendee who has a new job title and one who has moved to a new office. Finally, you will create a new form letter main document and merge it with the modified data source document.

Terms

Data source table A table created automatically by Word in a data source document to store data source records.

Notes

Use an Existing Data Source

- Once you create and save a data source document, you can use it with different main documents.

- Using an existing data source saves you the time and trouble of retyping existing data.

Modify an Existing Data Source

- You can modify an existing data source in two ways:
  - You can modify the data source document table.
  - You can modify data in a data form.

A data source document table

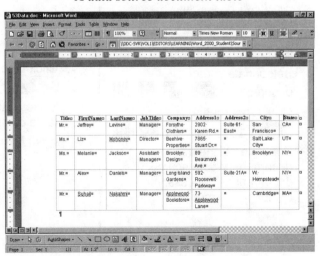

- Use the **data source table** when you want to work with the entire data source document at one time.

- Use the data form when you want to work with one record at a time.
- You can edit the data source document using the same techniques you use to edit any table.

Procedures

Use an Existing Data Source Document

1. Open a main document.
2. Click **Tools**................. Alt+T
3. Click **Mail Merge**................ R
4. Click **Get Data** button
   [Get Data ▾] .... Alt+G
5. Click **Open Data Source** .... O
6. Select data source document ..... Shift+Tab, ↑, ↓
7. Click **Open** button
   [Open] .... Alt+O
8. Continue editing main document or data source document as necessary to complete the merge.

Modify an Existing Data Source Document

Modify a data source using a table:

1. Click **File** .... Alt+F
2. Click **Open** .... O
3. Select data source document file.
4. Click **Open** button
   [Open] .... Alt+O
5. Make changes using standard table commands.
6. Save the changes.

Modify a data source using a data form:

1. Open **main document**.
2. Click **Edit Data Source** button 📇.
3. Click **Next Record** button ▶ until record to edit is displayed.
   OR
   - Click **Add New** to add new record
   - Click **Delete** to delete displayed record
4. Edit record.
   ✓ *Click Restore button to undo changes.*
5. Repeat steps 3 through 4 until all changes are complete.
6. Click **OK**................ [OK]
   ✓ *Click View Source button to display data source document table.*

Exercise Directions

1. Start Word, if necessary.

2. Open ⊙ **53DATA**.

3. Save the document as **WD53-1**.

   ✓ *This will be used as the data source document.*

4. Add the following record to the table:
   Ms.
   Julie
   Jarvis
   Manager
   Northeast Pet Supply Co.
   49 Webster St.
   Etna
   NH
   03750
   Business on the Web

5. Change the title for Melanie Jackson from Assistant Manager to Manager.

6. Save the document and close it.

7. Create a new document in Word and save it as **WD53-2**.

   ✓ *This will be used as the main document.*

8. Use the Mail Merge helper to make **WD53-2** a form letter main document.

9. Use the **WD53-1** document as the data source.

10. Type the main document (**WD53-2**) as shown in Illustration A.

    a. Type the document text using a 12-point serif font and standard block letter styling.

    b. Insert the merge fields as shown.

11. Preview the merge documents.

12. Edit the data source document as follows:

    a. Display the data form.

    b. Display the record for Alex Daniels.

    c. Change the address from 592 Roosevelt Parkway Suite 21A to 1031 Roosevelt Parkway Suite 52D.

    d. Add the following record to the data source
       Ms.
       Cynthia
       Harte
       Owner
       The Sweet Tooth
       321 Main St.
       Hanover
       NH
       03755
       Business on the Web

13. Delete the record for Jeffrey Levine.

14. Close the data form.

15. Preview the merge documents.

16. Merge to a new document.

17. Print the merge documents.

18. Save the merge document form letters file as **WD53-3**.

19. Save and close all open files and exit Word.

Insert today's date

February 19, 1999

«Title»«FirstName» «LastName»
«JobTitle»
«Company»
«Address1»
«Address2»
«City», «State» «PostalCode»

Dear «Title» «LastName»,

I am in the process of securing accommodations for all participants in the «Seminar» seminar in February. To better meet your individual needs, I would like to know if you prefer a smoking room or a non-smoking room.

Please notify me of your preference as soon as possible. I can be reached by phone at 310-555-0821, or via e-mail at jgodere@mail.canet.com.

I look forward to seeing you in February.

Sincerely,

Justin Godere
Seminar Coordinator

JG/yo

On Your Own

1. Open **OWD52-2**, the data source document you created in the On Your Own section of Exercise 52, or open ⊘ **53SOURCE**.

2. Save the file as **OWD53**, and close it.

3. Create a new document and save it as **OWD53-2**.

4. Make **OWD53-2** a form letter main document that uses the **OWD53** data source.

5. Edit the main document by typing a form letter thanking the people who responded to the letter you wrote asking for contributions. Don't forget to include the appropriate merge fields.

6. Make some changes to the data source. For example, edit a record, delete a record, or add a new record.

7. Preview the merge documents.

8. Merge to a new document and save it as **OWD53-3**.

9. Save and close all open documents, and exit Word.

Exercise 54

On the Job

Sort a data source before a merge in order to generate merged documents in a particular order. For example, you can sort the records alphabetically by last name or numerically by ZIP Code. Merge selected records when you don't need a merge document for every record. For example, you can generate a letter for people in one city, but not for people in a different city.

Due to lack of enrollment, the Internet Commerce seminar sponsored by State-of-the-Art Solutions has been canceled. In this exercise, you will create a form letter to send to people who have already registered for the seminar. Before merging the selected records, you will sort them into alphabetical order.

Terms

Sort Arrange records into a alphabetical or numerical order.

Conditions A set of criteria that must be matched in order for a record to be included in a merge.

Criteria A set of specific data which defines the conditions.

Field One column in a data source table.

Comparison operator A relational operator, such as equal to or greater than, that defines the way conditions are determined

Comparison data The specific information which must be entered in a record in order for the record to be included in a merge.

Notes

Sort a Data Source

- **Sorting** records in a data source is similar to sorting rows in any table.

- Sorting a data source is useful for organizing merge documents into a particular order. For example, the post office may require letters sorted by ZIP Code, or you may find it easier to keep track of records sorted alphabetically.

- You can sort a data source alphabetically, numerically, or by date in ascending or descending order.

- Records can be sorted based on data entered in any column in the data source table.

Merge Selected Records

- You can merge selected records instead of all the records in the data source document.

- You can specify records to merge by record number. For example, you can merge records 1 through 5.

- You can also define **conditions** that must be met in order for a record to be included in a merge.

- Each condition includes a set of **criteria**.

- To specify criteria, you select a **field**, a **comparison operator**, and **comparison data**.

- When you merge the records, Word compares each record to the specified criteria. If the record matches the criteria, it is included. If the record does not match the criteria, it is excluded. For example, you can specify that only records with a ZIP Code equal to 01752 should be merged.

- You can specify up to six conditions for each merge in the Query Options dialog box.

- You must clear the conditions used for a previous merge in order to set new conditions.

The Query Options dialog box

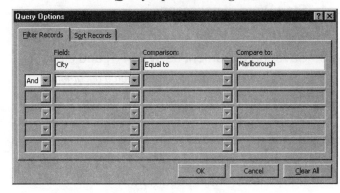

Procedures

Sort Data Source

1. Open main document.
2. Click **Edit Data Source** button .
3. Click **View Source** button
   View Source .... Alt + V
4. Click in **field** to sort by.
5. Click either:
   - **Sort Ascending** button
   - **Sort Descending** button
6. Click **Mail Merge Main Document** button.
7. Merge records to new document or to printer as desired.
   OR
   a. Open main document.
   b. Click **Edit Data Source** button.

c. Click **View Source** button
   View Source .... Alt + V
d. Click **Table**............. Alt + A
e. Click **Sort** .... S
f. Click **Sort by** drop-down arrow
g. Click field to sort by
h. Click **Type** drop-down arrow .... Alt + Y
i. Click type of sort.
j. Click either:
   - **Ascending** option .... Alt + A
   - **Descending** option............... Alt + D
k. Click **OK** .... Enter
l. Click **Mail Merge Main Document** button.
m. Merge records to new document or to printer as desired.

Merge Selected Records

1. Open main document
2. Click **Mail Merge Helper** button.
3. Click **Query Options** button
   Query Options... .... Alt + Q
4. Click **Clear All** button
   Clear All to clear previous conditions...... Alt + C
5. Click **Field** drop-down arrow
6. Click **field to compare**.
7. Click **Comparison** drop-down arrow.
8. Select **comparison operator**.
9. Click **Compare to** text box . Tab
10. Type **comparison data**.
11. Click **OK** .... Enter
12. Click **Close** button 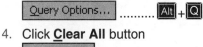.
13. Merge records to new document or to printer as desired

253

Exercise Directions

1. Start Word, if necessary.
2. Open ⊘ **54DATA**.
3. Save the document as **WD54-1**, and close it.
   - ✓ *This will be used as the data source document.*
4. Create a new document in Word and save it as **WD54-2**.
   - ✓ *This will be used as the main document.*
5. Use the Mail Merge helper to make **WD54-2** a form letter main document.
6. Use the **WD54-1** document as the data source.
7. Edit the main document (**WD54-2**) as shown in Illustration A.
   a. Type the document text using a 12-point serif font and standard block letter styling.
   b. Insert the merge fields as shown.
8. View the data source.
9. Sort the records in alphabetical order, ascending, by last name.
10. Close the data source and preview the merge documents.
11. Specify a merge to include only the records for people signed up for the Internet Commerce seminar.
12. Preview the merge documents.
13. Merge to a new document.
14. Print the merge documents.
15. Save the merge document form letters file as **WD54-3**.
16. Save and close all open files, and exit Word.

Illustration A

Insert today's date

February 19, 1999

«Title»«FirstName» «LastName»
«JobTitle»
«Company»
«Address1»
«Address2»
«City», «State» «PostalCode»

Dear «Title» «LastName»,

I am sorry to inform you that due to lack of interest, we have had to cancel the «Seminar» seminar scheduled for February. We will be sending you a full refund of your registration fee under separate cover.

There are still a few spots left at our Business on the Web seminar, also scheduled for February. If you are interested, please contact my office immediately.

We regret any inconvenience this may have caused.

Sincerely,

Justin Godere
Seminar Coordinator

JG/yo

On Your Own

1. Open **OWD53**, the data source document you created in the On Your Own section of Exercise 53, or open ⊘ **54SOURCE**.

2. Save the file as **OWD54**, and close it.

3. Create a new document and save it as **OWD54-2**.

4. Make **OWD54-2** a form letter main document that uses the **OWD54** data source.

5. Edit the main document by typing a form letter telling the people who responded to the letter you wrote asking for contributions that you will be in the neighborhood and will stop by to say thank you in person. Don't forget to include the appropriate merge fields.

6. Sort the data source into alphabetical order.

7. Set conditions to select only some records for the merge. For example, select only those records for a particular city.

8. Preview the merge documents.

9. Merge to a new document and save it as **OWD54-3**.

10. Save and close all open documents, and exit Word.

Exercise 55

Skills Covered:

◆ Merge Envelopes or Labels

On the Job

You can create envelopes and labels using Mail Merge. Using an existing data source makes it easy to create envelopes and labels to accompany a form letter merge that you created previously.

Your boss has asked you to send out a mailing for State-of-the-Art Solutions. Since you already have a mailing list together, you can save time creating envelopes and labels with a mail merge.

Notes

Merge Envelopes or Labels

- To create envelopes using Mail Merge, create an Envelopes main document.

- To create labels using Mail Merge, create a Mailing Labels main document.

- You can create a new data source document as covered in Exercise 52, or use an existing data source document as covered in Exercise 53.

- On an envelopes or mailing labels main document, you only need to insert the merge fields necessary for setting up a mailing address.

- You can merge the envelopes or labels to a printer or to a new document to save and/or print at a later time.

- To set up mail merge envelopes, you must know the size of the envelopes to print.

- To set up mail merge mailing labels, you must know the size and type of the labels to print.

Merge fields on envelope

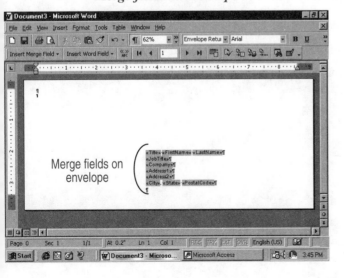

257

Procedures

Merge Envelopes

1. Open a new document.
2. Click **Tools** .... `Alt`+`T`
3. Click **Mail Merge** .... `R`
4. Click **Create** button
   `Create ▾` .... `Alt`+`C`
5. Click **Envelopes** .... `E`
6. Click **Active Window** button
   `Active Window` .. `Alt`+`A`
7. Create or open a data source document.
   ✓ *Word displays a message asking you to set up the Main Document.*
8. Click **Set Up Main Document** .... `Alt`+`S`
9. Click **Envelope Size** ... `Alt`+`S`
10. Click desired size ....`↑`, `↓`, `Enter`
11. Click **OK** .... `Enter`
12. Insert Merge Fields to set up address as it should appear on the envelope as follows:
    a. Position insertion point where first merge field goes.
    b. Click the **Insert Merge Field** button
       `Insert Merge Field ▾` ...... `Alt`+`S`
    c. Click field to insert ....`↑`, `↓`, `Enter`

---

d. Insert spacing, paragraphs, and/or punctuation as necessary.
e. Repeat steps b-d until all merge fields are in place as they should appear on the envelope.
13. Click **OK** .... `Tab`+`Enter`
    ✓ *Word displays the Mail Merge Helper.*
14. Click **Merge** .... `Alt`+`M`
    ✓ *Word displays the Merge dialog box.*
15. Click **Merge** .... `Alt`+`M`
    ✓ *The default options merge the envelopes to a new document that you can save and/or print.*

Merge Labels

1. Open a new document.
2. Click **Tools** .... `Alt`+`T`
3. Click **Mail Merge** .... `R`
4. Click **Create** button
   `Create ▾` .... `Alt`+`C`
5. Click **Mailing Labels** .... `M`
6. Click **Active Window** button
   `Active Window` .. `Alt`+`A`
7. Create or open a data source document.
   ✓ *Word displays a message asking you to set up the Main Document.*

---

8. Click **Set Up Main Document** .... `Alt`+`S`
9. Select Label Options as necessary.
10. Click **OK** .... `Enter`
11. Insert Merge Fields to set up address as follows:
    a. Position insertion point where first merge field goes.
    b. Click **Insert Merge Field** button
       `Insert Merge Field ▾` .... `Alt`+`S`
    c. Click field to insert ....`↑`, `↓`
    d. Insert spacing, paragraphs, and/or punctuation as necessary.
    e. Repeat steps b-d until all merge fields are in place.
12. Click **OK** .... `Tab`+`Enter`
    ✓ *Word displays the Mail Merge Helper.*
13. Click **Merge** .... `Alt`+`M`
    ✓ *Word display the Merge dialog box.*
14. Click **Merge** .... `Alt`+`M`
    ✓ *The default options merge the labels to a new document that you can save and/or print.*

Exercise Directions

1. Start Word, if necessary.
2. Open ⊙ **55DATA**.
3. Save the document as **WD55-1**, then close it.
   ✓ *This will be used as the data source document.*
4. Create a new blank document that you can use to create an envelopes main document.
5. Save the document as **WD55-2**.
6. Use the Mail Merge Helper to make **WD55-2** an envelopes main document.
7. Use **WD55-1** as the data source.
8. Insert the necessary merge fields to set up the envelopes main document the way you want the addresses to appear.
9. Preview the merge document. The first envelope should look similar to the one in Illustration A.
10. Merge the envelopes to a new document and save it as **WD55-3**.
11. Print the merge documents.
12. Save and close **WD55-2**, the envelope main document.
13. Create a new blank document that you can use to create a labels main document.
14. Save the document as **WD55-4**.
15. Use the Mail Merge Helper to make **WD55-4** a labels main document.
16. Use **WD55-1** as the data source.
17. Insert the necessary merge fields to set up the labels main document the way you want the addresses to appear.
18. Preview the merge document. The first page of labels should look similar to the one in Illustration B, depending on the label options you selected.
19. Merge the labels to a new document and save it as **WD55-5**.
20. Print the merge documents.
21. Save and close all open files, and exit Word

Illustration A

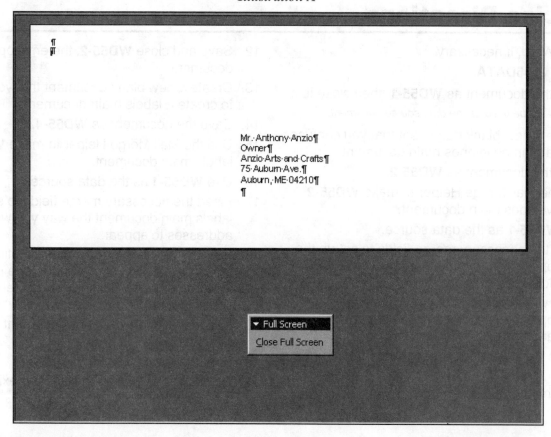

Illustration B

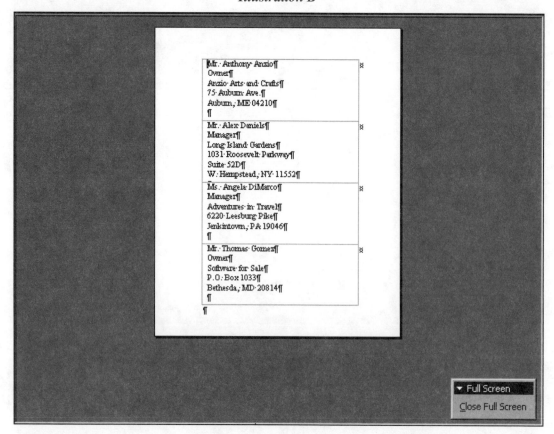

On Your Own

1. Open the document **OWD54**, the data source document you created in the On Your Own section of the Exercise 54, or open ⊙ **55SOURCE**.

2. Save the document as **OWD55**, then close it.

3. Create a new document and save it as **OWD55-2**.

4. Make **OWD55-2** a main document for either envelopes or mailing labels.

5. Use **OWD55** as the data source.

6. Change the sort order of the records in the data source.

7. Merge the envelopes or labels to a new a document, and save it as **OWD55-3**.

8. Save and close all open documents, and exit Word.

Exercise 56

◆ **Critical Thinking**

The event coordinator for State-of-the-Art Solutions has asked you to create a mailing about next year's seminar. In this exercise, you will create a form letter to let people know the location and dates of the seminar. You will include information about the location that you copy from a Web site. You will use an existing data source to generate the form letters, but you will select to merge the records for people who attended the Business on the Web seminar only, because you want to send a different letter to people who attended different seminars. Finally, you will generate envelopes to accompany the form letters.

Exercise Directions

1. Start Word, if necessary.

2. Open the document ⊚ **56DATA**, and save it as **WD56-1**.

   ✓ *This document will be your data source.*

3. Close **WD56-1**.

4. Create a new document and save it as **WD56-2**.

   ✓ *This document will be your form letter main document.*

5. Use Mail Merge Helper to make **WD56-2** a form letter main document.

6. Use **WD56-1** as the data source.

7. Type the letter shown in Illustration A.

   a. Use a 12-point serif font.

   b. Set margins to 1" on all sides.

   c. Include merge fields as shown.

   d. Omit the paragraph marked Insert from Web site.

8. Display the Web toolbar.

9. Open the Internet Simulation:

   a. Click **Go**.

   b. Click **Open**.

   c. In the Address line type the following: D:/Internet/E56/sandiegodirect.htm

   ✓ *If you've copied the Internet simulation files to your hard drive or your CD-ROM drive is a letter other than D:, substitute the correct letter for D.*

   d. Click **OK**.

10. Click the link *Museums*.

11. When you have finished browsing the page, click the *Back* button.

12. Click the link *Beaches*.

13. When you have finished browsing the page, click the *Back* button

14. Click the link *Hotel Del Coronado*.

15. Copy the first full paragraph of text describing the hotel to the Clipboard.

16. Paste the data into the **WD56-2** form letter main document as marked on Illustration A.

   ✓ *Adjust paragraph spacing and formatting so the document looks like the one in Illustration A. If necessary, use Shrink to Fit to insure that the document fits on a single page.*

17. Exit the simulation.

18. Save the **WD56-2** document.

19. Add the following records to the data source (**WD56-1**):

   Mr. Gary Dubin
   Designer
   Active Designs, Inc.
   2121 West 55th St.
   Chicago, IL 60606
   Seminar: Business on the Web

   Ms. Elizabeth Doone
   Graphic Artist
   Sunrise Designs
   465 Sunrise Blvd.
   Suite 224
   Ft. Lauderdale, FL 33329
   Seminar: Internet Commerce

Ms. Janice Loring
Designer
Expose, Inc.
922 East 64th St.
Indianapolis, IN 46220
Seminar: Business on the Web

Mr. Antonio DiBuono
Designer
Delaware Designs
6322 E. Main St.
Wilmington, DE 19886
Seminar: Business on the Web

Ms. Katharine Peterson
Systems Manager
Community Hospital
220 Clinical Dr.
Mail Stop 22E
East Lansing, MI 48824
Seminar: Internet Commerce

20. Sort the data source numerically by Postal Code.

21. Set conditions so that only the people who attended the Business on the Web seminar will receive the letter.

22. Preview the merge documents.

23. Merge to a new document.

24. Save the document as **WD56-3**.

25. Print the merge documents.

26. Save and close all open documents.

27. Create a new blank document and save it as **WD56-4**.

28. Make the new document an envelopes main document with **WD56-1** as the data source.

29. In the envelopes main document, insert the necessary merge fields to set up an address on the envelopes.

30. Set conditions so that envelopes will be printed for the people who attended the Business on the Web seminar only.

31. Preview the envelope merge documents.

32. Merge the documents to a new document.

33. Save the envelope merge document as **WD56-5**.

34. Print the merge documents.

35. Save and close all open documents.

36. Exit Word.

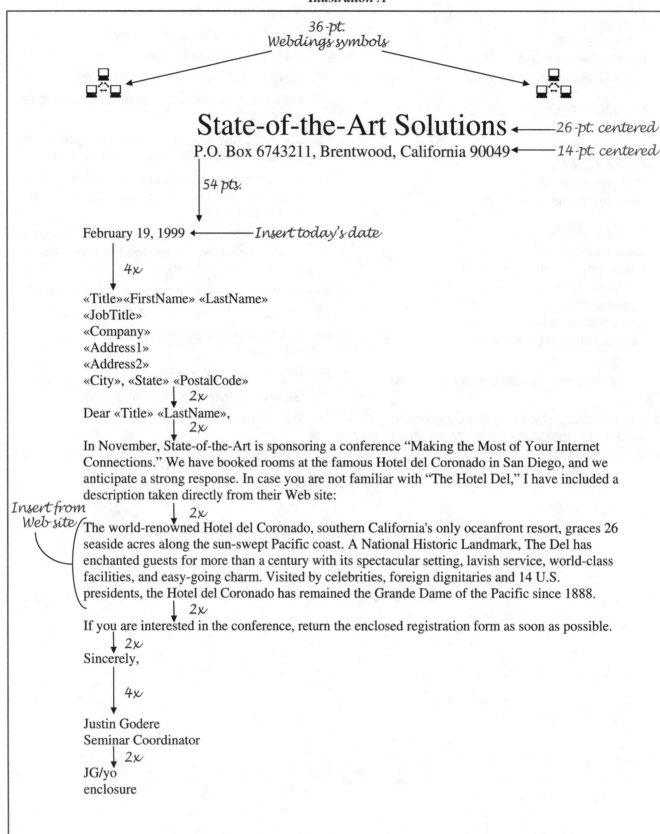

36-pt.
Webdings symbols

State-of-the-Art Solutions ← *26-pt. centered*
P.O. Box 6743211, Brentwood, California 90049 ← *14-pt. centered*

54 pts.

February 19, 1999 ← *Insert today's date*

4x

«Title»«FirstName» «LastName»
«JobTitle»
«Company»
«Address1»
«Address2»
«City», «State» «PostalCode»

2x

Dear «Title» «LastName»,

2x

In November, State-of-the-Art is sponsoring a conference "Making the Most of Your Internet Connections." We have booked rooms at the famous Hotel del Coronado in San Diego, and we anticipate a strong response. In case you are not familiar with "The Hotel Del," I have included a description taken directly from their Web site:

2x

Insert from Web site

The world-renowned Hotel del Coronado, southern California's only oceanfront resort, graces 26 seaside acres along the sun-swept Pacific coast. A National Historic Landmark, The Del has enchanted guests for more than a century with its spectacular setting, lavish service, world-class facilities, and easy-going charm. Visited by celebrities, foreign dignitaries and 14 U.S. presidents, the Hotel del Coronado has remained the Grande Dame of the Pacific since 1888.

2x

If you are interested in the conference, return the enclosed registration form as soon as possible.

2x

Sincerely,

4x

Justin Godere
Seminar Coordinator

2x

JG/yo
enclosure

Lesson 9

Multiple-Page Documents

Exercise 57

◆ **Create an Outline** ◆ **Edit an Outline**
◆ **Collapse and Expand Outlines** ◆ **Number an Outline**

On the Job

Create an outline to organize ideas for any document that covers more than one topic, such as an article, a report, a presentation, or a speech. For example, you might create an outline to list the chapters or headings in a report or to arrange main subjects for a presentation. The outline serves as a map you can use to follow as you complete the entire document.

As head of marketing for Cornerstone Graphics, you are always trying to appeal to new customers. In this exercise, you will create an outline for a marketing document. The outline will include five levels of topics about why clients should use Web pages.

Terms

Outline A document that lists levels of topics.

Style A set of formatting features that can be applied all at once.

Promote To move up one level in an outline.

Demote To move down one level in an outline.

Collapse To hide subtopics in an outline.

Expand To show subtopics in an outline.

Notes

Outline toolbar

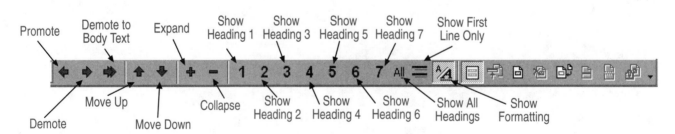

Create an Outline

- Use Outline view to create and edit **outlines**.
- Outline topics are set up in levels, which are called headings: Heading 1 is a main topic, Heading 2 is a subtopic, Heading 3 is a sub-subtopic, and so on up to 9 heading levels.
- Word automatically applies different **styles** to different levels in an outline.
- Headings that have subheadings under them are preceded by an Expand Outline symbol ⊞.

■ Headings that do not have subheadings or all the subheadings are expanded are preceded by a Collapse Outline symbol ▭.

■ Regular document text is called Body Text.

A document in Outline view

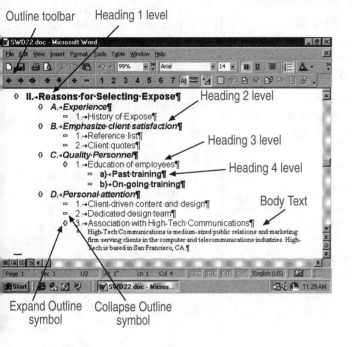

Edit an Outline

■ You can edit an outline using the same techniques you use to edit regular document text. For example, you can insert and delete text at any location.

■ To reorganize an outline, you can **promote** or **demote** headings levels. For example, you can demote a Heading 1 level paragraph to a Heading 2 level paragraph.

■ You can also move headings and subheadings up or down the outline to reorganize the outline.

Collapse and Expand Outlines

■ When you want to work with only some heading levels at a time you can **collapse** the outline.

■ Collapsing an outline hides some heading levels.

■ You **expand** the outline to see hidden, or collapsed, levels.

Number an Outline

■ Traditional outlines are numbered with different number and letter styles used to represent different levels.

■ Word comes with seven built-in outline numbering styles.

■ You can select a numbering style before or after typing the outline.

Select an outline numbering style in the Bullets and Numbering dialog box

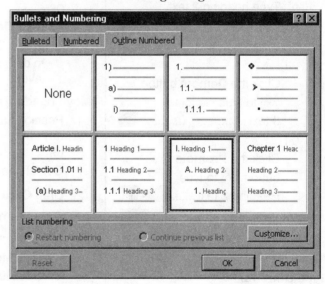

Procedures

Create an Outline

1. Click the **Outline View** button 🔲.
   OR
   a. Click **View** .... `Alt`+`V`
   b. Click **Outline** .... `O`
2. Type Heading 1 text.
3. Press **Enter** .... `Enter`
   ✓ *Heading level is carried forward to the new paragraph.*
4. Type more Heading 1 text.
   OR
   a. Click the **Demote** button ➡ .... `Tab`
   b. Type heading 2 text.
5. Press **Enter** .... `Enter`
6. Type Heading text.
   OR
   • Click the **Demote** button ➡ to type Heading 3 text .... `Tab`
   OR
   • Click the **Promote** button ⬅ to type Heading 2 text .... `Shift`+`Tab`
7. Press **Enter** .... `Enter`
8. Continue until outline is complete.

Type Body Text

1. Position insertion point where you want to type Body Text.
2. Click **Demote to Body Text** button ➡ .... `Ctrl`+`Shift`+`N`
3. Type text.

Edit an Outline

Select headings:
1. Click outline symbol preceding the heading ➕ or ➖.
   ✓ *The heading and all subheadings are selected.*
2. Make desired changes.

Change heading levels:
1. Position insertion point anywhere on heading line.
   OR
   Select heading.
2. Click **Promote** button ⬅ .... `Shift`+`Tab`
   to promote heading one level.
   OR
   • Click **Demote** button ➡ .... `Tab`
   to demote heading one level.

Move headings:
1. Position insertion point anywhere on the heading line.
   OR
   Select heading to move.
2. Drag **Outline symbol** (➕ or ➖) to a new location.
   OR
   • Click **Move Up** ⬆ to move heading up one line.
   • Click **Move Down** ⬇ to move heading down one line.

Collapse and Expand an Outline

• Click **Show Heading** button corresponding to level of heading(s) you want displayed.
OR
• Double-click **Outline symbol** ➕ or ➖ preceding heading.

Show entire outline:
• Click **All** button `All` .... `Alt`+`L`

Number an Outline

1. Position the insertion point where the outline will begin.
   OR
   Select headings to number.
2. Click **Format** .... `Alt`+`O`
3. Click **Bullets and Numbering** .... `N`
4. Click **Outline Numbered** page tab .... `Alt`+`U`
5. Select numbering style.
   ✓ *Select None to remove numbering.*
6. Click **OK** .... `Enter`

Exercise Directions

1. Start Word, if necessary.

2. Create a new document.

3. Save it as **WD57**.

4. Change to Outline view.

5. Select the Numbering style used in Illustration A.

6. Type the outline shown in the illustration.

   a. Press Tab or click Demote to demote a heading.

   b. Press Shift+Tab, or click Promote to promote a heading.

   c. Press Ctrl+Shift+N or click Demote to Body Text to type regular text.

7. Collapse all but headings 1, 2, and 3.

8. Display all headings.

9. Move the heading *User-driven* up above the heading *Multimedia*.

10. Demote *User-driven* two levels.

11. Promote *Emphasize client satisfaction* and all of its subheadings one level.

12. Promote *Quality Personnel* one level.

13. Enter summary information in the Document Properties dialog box as follows:

    • Title: *Why Use the Web?*

    • Subject: *Reasons for developing a Web Site*

    • Author: *Your name*

    • Manager: *Your instructor or supervisor*

    • Company: *Cornerstoner Graphics*

    • Category: *Marketing*

    • Keywords: *Web, on-line, links, design*

    • Comments: *Use this outline to develop a marketing document.*

14. Check the spelling in the document.

15. Print the document.

    ✓ *The document will print on two pages.*

16. Close the document and exit Word, saving all changes.

Heading 2

I. Reasons for Developing a Web Site ← *Heading 1*

  A. Exposure

    1. Millions use the Web ← *Heading 3*

Heading 4

      a) Millions are already on-line
      b) Millions more getting on-line

    2. International audience
      a) Maintain international contacts
      b) Expand business overseas
    3. 24-hour access

  B. Flexibility
    1. Customization
      a) Links to other pages
      b) Links to other sites
    2. Interactive
      a) Collect customer information ← *Heading 5*
        (1) Customize product to suit
        (2) High response rate
      b) Multimedia

Move up and demote

    3. User-driven

  C. Cost
    1. Compares favorably to other marketing tools
      a) Compare to advertising
        (1) Print
        (2) Radio
        (3) TV
    2. Delivers a lot

II. Reasons for Selecting Cornerstone Graphics
  A. Experience
    1. History of Cornerstone
    2. Emphasize client satisfaction
      a) Reference list
      b) Client quotes

Promote

    3. Quality Personnel
    4. Education of employees
      a) Past training
      b) On-going training

  B. Personal attention
    1. Client-driven content and design
    2. Dedicated design team
    3. Association with State-of-the-Art Solutions
      State-of-the-Art Solutions is medium-sized consulting firm serving clients interested in expanded business on the World Wide Web. State-of-the-Art is based in Brentwood, CA.

On Your Own

1. Create a new document in Word.

2. Save the file as **OWD57**.

3. Draft an outline for a speech or presentation you'd like to give. Include at least three levels. For example, draft an outline for a presentation you have to give to a class, to an organization, or for a speech to a family member about a household issue that has been on your mind.

4. Examine the outline and make sure all headings are at the correct level. Change the levels if necessary.

5. Try rearranging the headings to see if you can improve the organization of the speech.

6. Save your changes, close the document, and exit Word.

Exercise 58

On the Job

Make a long document easier to read and work in by inserting page breaks, section breaks, and page numbers. Page breaks let you control where a new page should start, avoiding page layout problems such as headings at the bottom of a page. Section breaks let you change page formatting in the middle of a document.

The head of marketing at Cornerstone Graphics has given you the first two pages of a report about why businesses should use Web sites. In this exercise, you will format the document using page breaks and section breaks. You will also insert page numbers.

Terms

Soft page break The place where Word automatically starts a new page when the current page is filled with text.

Hard page break A nonprinting character that tells Word to start a new page, even if the current page is not filled with text.

Section A portion of a document.

Section break A nonprinting character that tells Word to start a new section within a document.

Widow line The last line of a paragraph printed alone at the top of a page.

Orphan line The first line of a paragraph printed alone at the bottom of a page.

Notes

Insert Hard Page Breaks

- A standard 8.5" by 11" sheet of paper with 1" top and bottom margins has 9" of vertical space for entering text.
  - ✓ *The number of lines depends on the font size and line spacing settings.*
- Word inserts a **soft page break** to start a new page when the current page is full.
- Soft page breaks adjust automatically if text is inserted or deleted, so a break always occurs when the current page is full.

- Insert a **hard page break** to start a new page before the current page is full. For example, insert a hard page break before a heading that falls at the bottom of a page; the break forces the heading to the top of the next page.
- Breaks move like characters when you insert and delete text. Therefore, you should insert hard page breaks after all editing is complete to avoid having a break occur at an awkward position on the page.
- In Normal view, a soft page break is marked by a dotted line across the page.
- In Normal view, a hard page break is marked by a dotted line with the words Page Break centered in it.

Page breaks in a document

Hard page break   Soft page break

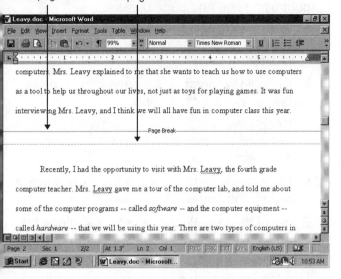

■ In Print Layout view, all page breaks look like the space between sheets of paper.

Page breaks in Print Layout view

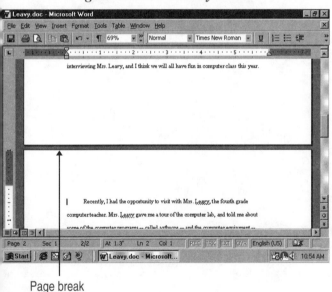

Page break

Insert Section Breaks

■ A default Word document contains one **section**.

■ You can divide a document into multiple sections to apply different formatting to each section. For example, you can set different margins, headers, or footers for each section.

■ There are four types of **section breaks**:

- *Next page* inserts a section break and a page break so that the new section will start on the next page.

- *Continuous* inserts a section break so that the new section will start at the insertion point.

- *Even page* inserts a section break and page breaks so the new section will start on the next even-numbered page.

- *Odd page* inserts a section break and page breaks so the new section will start on the next odd-numbered page.

Break dialog box

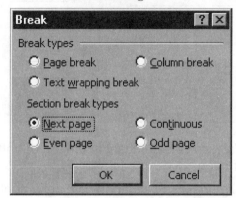

■ In Normal view, section breaks are displayed as dotted double lines across the width of the page with the words Section Break in the middle, followed by the type of break in parentheses.

✓ In Print Layout view section breaks are displayed only if nonprinting characters are displayed.

Section breaks in a document

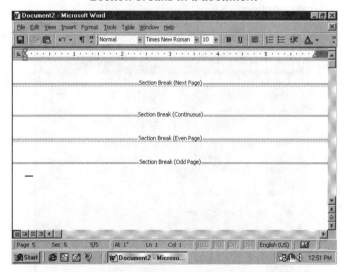

Insert Page Numbers

- Use Word's page number feature to insert page numbers in documents.

- By default, page numbers print on the bottom right of each page.

- Set options to control page number placement:

Page Numbers dialog box

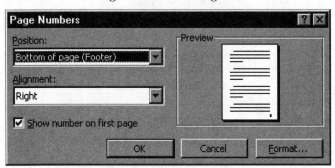

- *Position* sets numbers at the top or bottom of page.

- *Alignment* sets numbers left, right, centered, inside (along binding), or outside (along outer edge) of the page.

- *Show number on first page* shows or suppresses the page number on the first page.

- You can change the page number format to select a different number style, to include chapter numbers, or to restart numbering in a new section.

Page Number Format dialog box

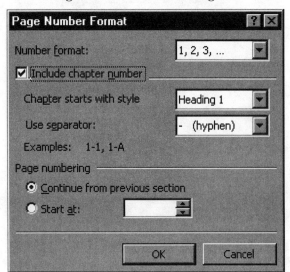

Control Text Flow

- Word includes the following options for controlling line and page breaks:
  - **Widow/Orphan** control, for preventing either the first or last line of a paragraph printing on a different page.
  - Keep lines together, for preventing a page break within a paragraph.
  - Keep with next, for preventing a page break between the current paragraph and the following paragraph.
  - Page break before, for forcing a page break before the current paragraph.

- Some of these options are default settings for Word's built-in heading styles that you use to create outlines.

- Use the Paragraph dialog box to access these options.

Procedures

Insert a Hard Page Break (Ctrl+Enter)

1. Click **Insert** .... `Alt`+`I`
2. Click **Break** .... `B`
3. Click **Page break** .... `Alt`+`P`
4. Click **OK** .... `Enter`

Delete a Hard Page Break

1. In Normal view, position insertion point on hard page break.
2. Press **Delete** key .... `Del`

Insert a Section Break

1. Click **Insert** .... `Alt`+`I`
2. Click **Break** .... `B`
3. Click the option button for desired break:
   - **Next page** .... `Alt`+`N`
   - **Continuous** .... `Alt`+`T`
   - **Even page** .... `Alt`+`E`
   - **Odd page** .... `Alt`+`O`
4. Click **OK** .... `Enter`

Delete a Section Break

1. In Normal view, position insertion point on section break.
2. Press **Delete** key .... `Del`

Insert Page Numbers

1. Click **Insert** .... `Alt`+`I`
2. Click **Page Numbers** .... `U`
3. Click the **Position** drop-down arrow .... `Alt`+`P`
4. Select **Bottom of page (Footer)** .... `Enter`
   OR
   Top of page (Header) .... `↑`, `Enter`
5. Click the **Alignment** drop-down arrow .... `Alt`+`A`
6. Select alignment option: .... `↑`, `Enter`
   - **Right**
   - **Left**
   - **Center**
   - **Inside**
   - **Outside**
7. Select **Show number on first page** if desired .... `Alt`+`S`
8. Click **OK** .... `Enter`

Change Page Number Formatting

1. Click **Insert** .... `Alt`+`I`
2. Click **Page Numbers** .... `U`
3. Click **Format** .... `Alt`+`F`
4. Click the **Number format** drop-down arrow .... `Alt`+`F`
5. Select **format** .... `↓`, `Enter`
   - **Arabic numerals** .... 1,2,3,4,5,etc.
   - **Lowercase letters** .... a,b,c,d,e,f,etc.
   - **Uppercase letters** ...... A,B,C,D,E,F, etc.
   - **Lowercase Roman numerals** ....i,ii,iii,iv,v, etc.
   - **Uppercase Roman numerals** ..... I,II,III,IV,V, etc.
6. Click **OK** .... `Enter` to close Page Number Format dialog box.
7. Click **OK** .... `Enter` to close Page Number's dialog box.

Control Text Flow

1. Click **Format** .... `Alt`+`O`
2. Click **Paragraph** .... `F`
3. Click **Line and Page Breaks** tab .... `Alt`+`P`
4. Select or deselect desired option(s):
   - **Widow/Orphan control** .... `Alt`+`W`
   - **Keep lines together** .... `Alt`+`K`
   - **Keep with next** ...... `Alt`+`X`
   - **Page break before** .... `Alt`+`B`
5. Click **OK** .... `Enter`

Exercise Directions

1. Start Word, if necessary.
2. Open 58REPORT.
3. Save the document as **WD58**.
4. Insert a page number flush right on the top of both pages in the document.
5. Preview the document. Notice that there is a page break in the middle of the paragraph under the heading 2, *Expand Customer Base* (at the bottom of page 1).
6. Close Print preview.
7. Click in the paragraph at the bottom of page 1.
8. Use the Keep lines together option to set Word so that it won't insert a page break in the paragraph. Notice that Word moves the heading and paragraph to the top of page two.
9. Undo the paragraph formatting.
10. Click in the Heading 2, *Expand Customer Base*, then display the Line and Page Breaks page of the Paragraph dialog box. Notice that the Keep with next option is selected. It is part of the heading 2 style.
11. Close the dialog box without making any changes.
12. Insert a continuous section break at the beginning of the heading *Reasons for Developing a Web Site*.
13. Change the margins in section 1 to 1.5" on the left and right.
14. Insert a page break at the beginning of the heading *Expand Customer Base*.
15. Insert a continuous section break at the beginning of the heading *Flexibility*.
16. Change the margins in section 3 to 1" on the left and right.
17. Check the spelling and grammar in the document.
18. Save the document.
19. Preview the document. It should look similar to the one in Illustration A.
20. Print one copy of the document.
21. Close the document and exit Word.

Illustration A (Page 1 of 2)

Page Number ——→ 1

Cornerstone Graphics

920 Marco Place ✧ Venice, CA 90291 ✧ Phone: (213) 555-1002
www.cornerstone.com ✧ email@cornerstone.com

What is Web Page Design?

Section 1 margins 1.5" left and right

The World Wide Web is comprised of interconnected documents stored on the global network of computers known as the Internet. The documents are called Web pages. Linked pages are called Web sites. Web sites are uniquely formatted to provide information, collect information, and to capture the attention of consumers.

In today's global marketplace, a presence on the World Wide Web is vital to business success. Creating effective and appealing Web pages is both a skill and an art form that takes technical knowledge, creative abilities, and practice.

Continuous section break

Reasons for Developing a Web Site

Studies show that millions of people have access to the Internet at home and/or at work. Forecasts predict that in the near future, Internet access will be as ubiquitous as television and telephones, and those left off the Web will be left behind in competition.

Due to the vast numbers of Internet users around the world, it is simple and cost effective to contact customers, suppliers, and others on-line. The cost of maintaining a Web site is minimal, especially in comparison to other types of marketing. Savings are made throughout the organization, including travel and entertainment costs.

Hard page break

Page Number ———→2

Expand Customer Base

These same contacts will lead to business expansion opportunities, with a minimum of actual travel. Another benefit is that a huge amount of information about businesses, markets, regulations, etc. is available on-line. Research can be successfully accomplished from a home office, without requiring costly travel and time spent abroad.

Continuous section break

Flexibility

Work can be accomplished regardless of time zone differences and work habits. Not only can your staff use the Web to communicate with others, but also people around the world can contact you even in the middle of the night. Information is available 24 hours a day, seven days a week.

Section 3
margins 1" Web sites can be created to suit the customers' needs. Information, design, links, and
left and right
other features can be developed per customer specifications. Sites can include as many or as few pages as the customer requires. Pages may include order forms, product catalogues, general information, contact names, and so on. Sites can link to existing sites, or other newly developed sites.

Web sites can dispense information and collect information. As customers access the site, demographic information can be collected. Products can be targeted to specific customers. Customers can quickly find the information and/or products they need, and respond immediately, in real time. Customer response can dictate the future development of the site.

Web sites can include graphics, video, and sound in addition to text-based information. For example, sites can be enhanced by the inclusion of video clips of sales presentations or photographs of products.

On Your Own

1. Start Word.

2. Draft and format a multiple page document, or open ⊙**58GUIDES**. The document might be a letter, a report, a short story, an outline, or an autobiography. Try to include at least three pages. If necessary, double-space the document and increase the width of the margins.

3. Save the file as **OWD58**.

4. Insert page breaks if necessary so that headings or paragraphs start at the top of a page instead of at the bottom of one.

5. Insert at least one section break. Change the margins for section 2.

6. Print the document.

7. Save the document, close it, and exit Word.

Exercise 59

Skills Covered:

♦ **Create Headers/Footers** ♦ **Different First Page Headers/Footers**
♦ **Different Odd/Even Headers/Footers**
♦ **Different Section Headers/Footers**

On the Job

Use headers and footers when you need to print information on the top or bottom of every page. You can customize documents by creating different headers and footers on the first page, on odd and even pages, and for different sections. Using different headers and footers helps readers understand which section of a document they are currently in.

The head of marketing at State-of-the-Art Solutions has sent you the entire marketing document for final formatting. In this exercise, you will insert page breaks to make the document look good, and you will insert section breaks in order to create section-appropriate headers and footers. Once the breaks are in place, you will create the headers and footers.

Terms

Header Repetitive text or graphics printed at the top of pages in a document.

Footer Repetitive text or graphics printed at the bottom of pages in a document.

Notes

Create Headers/Footers

- Create a **header** and/or **footer** to print repetitive information such as page numbers, dates, author, or subject on every page of a document.

- Headers and footers are not displayed in Normal view. Use Print preview or Print Layout view to see them on the screen.

- By default, headers print .5" from the top of page, and footers print .5" from the bottom of page.

- You can apply headers and footers to the entire document or to the current section.

- Use Header/Footer toolbar buttons to customize headers and footers.

Different First Page Headers/Footers

- Set Word to print a different header/footer on the first page of a document or section.

- Leave the first page header/footer blank to omit the header/footer from the first page.

Different Odd/Even Headers/Footers

- Print different headers on odd and even pages.

- Using different headers/footers on odd and even pages gives you an opportunity to include more information, and to customize the appearance of a document.

Header and Footer toolbar

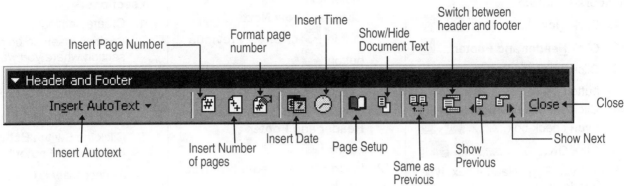

Different Section Headers/Footers

- By default, new sections have the same header/footer as the previous section.
- You can change the header/footer for every section in a document.

Procedures

Create Headers/Footers

Create a header on every page:

1. Click **View**.................... Alt+V
2. Click **Header and Footer** .... H
3. In the Header box, type header text.
   - ✓ Use formatting options as desired, including fonts, font effects, alignment, tabs, and spacing.
4. Click **Close** button Close .... Alt+C on the Header/Footer toolbar.

Create a footer on every page:

1. Click **View**.................... Alt+V
2. Click **Header and Footer** .... H
3. Click the **Switch Between Header and Footer** button .
4. In the Footer box, type footer text.
   - ✓ Use formatting options as desired, including fonts, font effects, alignment, and tabs.
5. Click **Close** button Close .... Alt+C on the Header/Footer toolbar.

Insert page numbers, date, and/or time in a header/footer:

1. Click **View** .... Alt+V
2. Click **Header and Footer**.... H
3. Click the **Switch Between Header and Footer** button as needed.
4. Click desired toolbar button(s):
   - **Insert Page Number** #
   - **Insert Date**
   - **Insert Time**
5. Click **Close** button Close .... Alt+C on the Header/Footer toolbar.
   - ✓ Combine text and page numbers, date, or time to achieve different effects. For example, type Page, *press the spacebar once to leave a space, then insert page number.*

Create first page header/footer:

1. Click **View**.................... Alt+V
2. Click **Header and Footer** .... H
3. Click the **Page Setup** button .
4. Select the **Different first page** check box .... Alt+F
5. Click **OK** .... Enter
6. In **First Page Header box**, type header text.
   - ✓ Leave blank to suppress header on first page.
7. Click **Switch Between Header and Footer** button .
8. In **First Page Footer** box, type footer text.
   - ✓ Leave blank to suppress footer on first page.
9. Click **Close** button Close .... Alt+C on Header/Footer toolbar.

Create different odd and even headers/footers:

1. Click **View** .... `Alt`+`V`
2. Click **Header and Footer**.... `H`
3. Click the **Page Setup** button `[icon]`.
4. Click the **Different odd and even** check box.......... `Alt`+`O`
5. Click **OK**.......................... `Enter`
6. In Even Page Header box, type header text.

   ✓ *If Odd Page Header box displays first, click Show Next button to display Even Page Header.*

7. Click the **Switch Between Header and Footer** button `[icon]`.

8. In **Even Page Footer** box, type footer text.
9. Click the **Show Next** button `[icon]` or **Show Previous** button `[icon]`.
10. In **Odd Page Footer box**, type footer text.
11. Click the **Switch Between Header and Footer** button `[icon]`.
12. In **Odd Page Header** box, type header text.
13. Click **Close** button `Close` .... `Alt`+`C` on Header/Footer toolbar.

Create different headers/footers in sections:

1. Create sections.
2. Position insertion point in section where you want header/footer.
3. Click **View**.................... `Alt`+`V`
4. Click **Header and Footer** .... `H`
5. Click the **Switch Between Header and Footer** button as necessary `[icon]`.
6. Click **Same as Previous** button `[icon]`.

   ✓ *By default, Same as Previous button is toggled on. Click it to toggle it off. If button is already toggled off, skip step 6.*

7. Enter header/footer information.
8. Click **Close** button `Close` .... `Alt`+`C` on Header/Footer toolbar.

Exercise Directions

1. Start Word, if necessary.
2. Open ⊙ **59REPORT**.
3. Save the file as **WD59**.
4. Make sure the document is displayed in Print Layout view and that Show/Hide Paragraph marks is turned on, so you can see where page breaks occur.
5. Insert a next page section break at the beginning of heading III: *Reasons for Developing a Web Site*.
6. Insert a hard page break at the beginning of the heading B. *Flexibility*.
7. Insert a next page section break at the beginning of the heading IV. *Reasons for Selecting Cornerstone*.
8. Create a footer for the entire document that includes the page number, centered. Precede the page number with the word Page.

9. Create headers as follows:
   - Section 1 – no header
   - Section 2 even pages: the company name flush left (Cornerstone Graphics) and your name flush right.
   - Section 2 odd pages: the section name flush left (Reasons for Developing a Web Site) and the date flush right.
   - Section 3 even pages: same as section 2 even pages.
   - Section 3 odd pages: the section name flush left (Reasons for Selecting Cornerstone) and the date flush right.
10. Save the document.
11. Preview the document. The Illustration shows the way the headers and footers on pages 2 and 3 should look.
12. Print one copy of the document.
13. Close the document and exit Word.

Illustration A (Page 1 of 2)

*Section 2
even page
header* ——→ Cornerstone Graphics   Your Name

III. Reasons for Developing a Web Site

A. Exposure

1. Millions use the Web

Studies show that literally millions of people have access to the Internet at home and/or at work and that new connections are being made by the thousands. Forecasts predict that in the near future, Internet access will be as ubiquitous as television and telephones, and those left off the Web will be left behind in competition.

2. International audience

Due to the vast numbers of Internet users around the world, it is simple and cost effective to contact customers, suppliers, and others on-line. Personal relationships can be established and maintained using computers, instead of scheduling expensive travel.

These same contacts will lead to business expansion opportunities, with a minimum of actual travel. Another benefit is that a huge amount of information about businesses, markets, regulations, etc. is available on-line. Research can be successfully accomplished from a home office, without requiring costly travel and time spent abroad.

Page 2

283

Section 2 → Reasons for Developing a Web Site   Today's date
odd page
header

B. Flexibility

1. Customization

Web sites can be created to suit the customers' needs. Information, design, links, and other features can be developed per customer specifications. Sites can include as many or as few pages as the customer requires. Pages may include order forms, product catalogues, general information, contact names, and so on. Sites can link to existing sites, or other newly developed sites.

2. Interactive Capabilities

Web sites can dispense information and collect information. As customers access the site, demographic information can be collected. Products can be targeted to specific customers. Customers can quickly find the information and/or products they need, and respond immediately, in real time. Customer response can dictate the future development of the site.

Web sites can include graphics, video, and sound in addition to text-based information. For example, sites can be enhanced by the inclusion of video clips of sales presentations or photographs of products.

3. 24-hour access

Work can be accomplished regardless of time zone differences and work habits. Not only can your staff use the Web to communicate with others, but also people around

Page 3

284

On Your Own

1. Open **OWD58**, the document you created in the On Your Own section of Exercise 58, or Open ⊚ **59GUIDES**.

2. Save the document as **OWD59**.

3. Create headers and footers for the document.

4. Use different Odd and Even or different section headers and footers so that you can include more information. For example, include the page numbers and the date on even pages and your name and the title of the document on odd pages

5. Preview the document.

6. Save the document, close it, and exit Word.

Exercise 60

On the Job

Include footnotes or endnotes in documents to provide information about the source of quoted material, or to supplement the main text. Insert comments in a document when you want to include a private note to the author, another reader, or to yourself, in much the same way you might attach a slip of paper to a hard copy print out.

As the head of marketing for a magazine about candy making, you've been conducting a readership survey. In this exercise, you will insert footnotes and comments into a multi-page document that provides the results of the survey. You will also format the document, add a header, and insert a section break.

Terms

Footnote An explanation or reference to other material printed at the bottom of a page.

Endnote An explanation or reference to other material printed at the end of a document.

Citation A reference to the source of quoted material.

Note mark A field code inserted in the document to reference footnote or endnote text.

Note text The text of the footnote or endnote citation.

Comment A hidden note attached to a document for reference.

Comment pane A window where comment text is typed, edited, and displayed.

Comment mark A hidden field code used to identify comments.

Notes

Footnotes and Endnotes

- **Footnotes** or **endnotes** are required elements of documents that include quoted material, such as in research papers.

- Standard footnotes and endnotes include the **citation** for the quoted material, including the name of the author, publication name, publication date, and page number where material is located.

- Footnotes or endnotes can also provide explanations or supplement text. For example, an asterisk footnote might provide information about where to purchase a product mentioned in the text.

- Word automatically sets up footnotes as follows: inserts a **note mark** in text, inserts a separator line following the last line of text on the page, and inserts the note number corresponding to the note mark below the separator line. You then type and format the **note text**.

Footnotes in a document

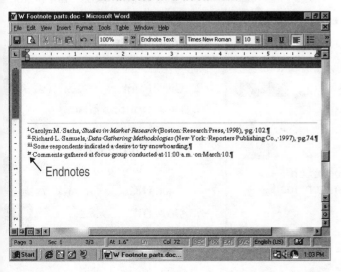

- Endnotes include the same parts as footnotes but are printed at the end of a document.

- Footnotes and endnotes are not displayed in Normal view; to see them, use Print Preview or Print Layout view.

- The text of footnotes and endnotes can be displayed in a ScreenTip by resting the mouse pointer on the note mark.

- It is easiest to insert footnotes or endnotes in Print Layout view.

- Word uses Arabic numerals for footnote marks. If endnotes are used in the same document, the marks are Roman numerals.

Endnotes in a document

- You can select a different number format or a symbol for the note mark.

- Word automatically updates numbering if you add or delete footnotes or endnotes, or rearrange the document text.

Footnote and Endnote dialog box

Comments

- Insert **comments** to annotate text, communicate with readers, or to attach reminders or questions.

- You type and edit comments in the **comment pane**.

- Word automatically highlights the word closest to the insertion point with yellow to indicate that a comment is there.

- Word also inserts a **comment mark** as hidden text. Comment marks include a number and the author's initials in brackets.

- Comments can be displayed in a ScreenTip by resting the mouse pointer on the comment mark.

- Comments can be printed with a document.

- The Reviewing toolbar includes buttons for inserting and editing comments.

Reviewing toolbar

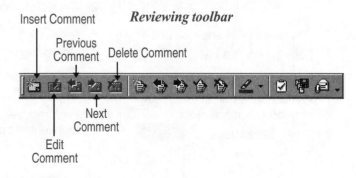

Procedures

Footnotes and Endnotes

Insert footnotes in Print Layout view:

1. Position insertion point after text to note.
2. Click **Insert**..................... `Alt`+`I`
3. Click **Foot_note**.................... `N`
4. Click **Footnote**........... `Alt`+`F`
5. Click **OK**.......................... `Enter`
6. Type note text.
7. Click anywhere in document window ...... `Shift`+`F5`

Insert endnotes in Print Layout view:

1. Position insertion point after text to note.
2. Click **Insert**.................. `Alt`+`I`
3. Click **Foot_note**.................... `N`
4. Click **Endnote**............ `Alt`+`E`
5. Click **OK**.......................... `Enter`
6. Type note text.
7. Click in document text .... `Shift`+`F5`

Display note text:

1. Click **Tools**.................. `Alt`+`T`
2. Click **Options**..................... `O`
3. Click **View tab**............ `Ctrl`+`Tab`
4. Select **Screentips** check box .... `Alt`+`R`
5. Click **OK**.......................... `Enter`
6. Rest mouse pointer on note mark in text.

Edit footnote or endnote:

1. Double-click reference mark in text.
2. Edit footnote or endnote text.
3. Click in document text... `Shift`+`F5`

Delete footnote or endnote:

1. Position insertion point to right of reference mark in text.
2. Press **Backspace** ...... `Backspace`
   ✓ Mark is selected.

---

3. Press **Backspace** ...... `Backspace`
   ✓ Note is deleted.

Change footnote or endnote mark in print layout view:

1. Position insertion point after text to note.
2. Click **Insert**.................. `Alt`+`I`
3. Click **Foot_note** .... `N`
4. Click **Footnote** .... `Alt`+`F`
   or **Endnote** .... `Alt`+`E`
5. Click **Custom Mark** ..... `Alt`+`C`
6. Type character in text box.
   OR
   a. Click **Symbol**.......... `Alt`+`S`
   b. Select desired font ... `Alt`+`F`, `↓`,`↑`, `Enter`
   c. Click symbol to use.
   d. Click **OK** .... `Enter`
7. Click **OK** .... `Enter`
8. Type note text.
9. Click in **document text** .... `Shift`+`F5`

Comments

Insert a comment:

1. Position insertion point where you want to insert comment.
2. Click **Insert**.................. `Alt`+`I`
3. Click **Comment** .... `M`
4. Type comment text.
5. Click **Close** button
    .... `Shift`+`Alt`+`C`

Display comment text:

1. Click **Tools** .... `Alt`+`T`
2. Click **Options** .... `O`
3. Click **View tab** .... `Ctrl`+`Tab`
4. Select **Screentips** check box .... `Alt`+`R`
5. Click **OK** .... `Enter`
6. Rest mouse pointer on highlighted comment mark.

✓ If there is no highlighting in text, click _Tools_, _Options_ and select Screentips on View check box on View tab, then click OK.

Display comment marks:

1. Click **Tools** .... `Alt`+`T`
2. Click **Options** .... `O`
3. Click the **View** page tab .... `Ctrl`+`Tab`
4. Click the **Hidden text** check box.................... `Alt`+`I`
5. Click **OK**.......................... `Enter`

Edit a comment:

1. Display comment marks.
2. Double-click comment mark.
   OR
   a. Right-click highlighted text.
   b. Click **Edit Comment** ...... `E`
   OR
   a. Display **Reviewing** toolbar... `Alt`+`V`,`T`, `↓`,`↑`
   b. Click **Edit Comment** button 📖 on the Reviewing toolbar.
3. Edit comment text.
4. Click **Close** button
    .... `Shift`+`Alt`+`C`

Delete a comment:

1. Right-click highlighted text.
2. Click **Delete Comment**........ `M`
   OR
   Click **Delete Comment** button 📖 on the Reviewing toolbar.

Print comments with a document:

1. Click **File**..................... `Alt`+`F`
2. Click **Print**............................ `P`
3. Click **Options** button
    .... `Alt`+`O`
4. Select **Comments** check box.................... `Alt`+`C`
5. Click **OK**......................... `Enter`
6. Click **OK**......................... `Enter`

Exercise Directions

1. Start Word, if necessary.

2. Open ⊘ **60SURVEY**.

3. Save the document as **WD60**.

4. Insert footnotes (five in total) as shown in Illustration A.

5. Insert comments (three in total) as marked on Illustration A.

6. Display comment marks if they are not already visible.

7. Change the formatting in the document as follows:

   a. Change the first line title to 26 points.

   b. Increase paragraph spacing after the second line to 24 points.

   c. Increase paragraph spacing after all other paragraphs in the document to 6 points.

   d. Increase the font size of the underlined heading *Highlights of The Candy Kitchen Magazine Subscriber Survey* to 16 points, center it, and increase the paragraph spacing after it to 24 points.

   e. Increase the font size of the three bold subheadings to 14 points.

8. Insert a next page section break before the heading *Highlights of The Candy Kitchen Magazine Subscriber Survey*.

9. Create a header for the second section only. On the first line, include the document title, *Readership Survey*, flush left, and the date flush right. On the second line, include your name flush left and the page number flush right.

10. Change the top and bottom margins for the second section to 1.25", and the left and right margins to 2".

11. Delete the second comment.

12. Preview the document.

13. Print the document with the comments.

14. Close the document and exit Word, saving all changes.

The Candy Kitchen Magazine
P.O. Box 765 ♦ Falmouth, MA 02536 ♦ (508) 555-2200

Last January, in response to a slip in subscription sales[1], The Candy Kitchen Magazine commissioned a full-scale readership survey. The intent was to determine demographics of our current market as well as identify ways to target new consumers. According to industry research, surveys can prompt changes leading to significant increases in circulation. [2]

The survey was conducted by Market Information Resources, a market research and analysis company based in New York City. The research was conducted from January through March. Data gathering was primarily via telephone, reader response cards, and direct mail solicitation. As a final step, focus groups were assembled and monitored. These methodologies are noted for producing accurate data. [3]

Insert comment:
375 Madison Ave.
10016
212-555-6100

The preliminary results of the survey have been compiled and are now available for analysis. This report includes only highlights of the survey; the complete report will be available in two weeks. Shortly thereafter, Candy Publishing, Inc., our parent company, will formulate a business plan based on the findings.

Insert comment: S. Tournier has results

Please direct all questions and comments to Mr. Steven Tournier, Director of Research at Market Information Resources.

Highlights of The Candy Kitchen Magazine Subscriber Survey
Subscriber Profile

Current The Candy Kitchen Magazine subscribers are typically women with children. They consider themselves to be educated consumers, and are active in their communities.

Readers listed cooking[4], spending time with family, and volunteerism as activities that they most enjoy.

Subscriber Demographics

Current subscribers fall into the following basic categories:

Age	35-55
Female	88%
Income	$25K-$55K

Insert comment: Most obvious point-need to target men!

Reader Comments

Following is a sampling of comments made by current subscribers in a focus group setting[5]:

"Many recipes are too time-consuming."
"Always the same writers. It gets kind of boring after a while."
"Seem to cover the same things issue after issue."
"I like the articles about family activities."

---

[1] 1999 Annual Circulation Analysis, Candy Publishing, Inc.
[2] Carolyn M. Sachs, *Studies in Market Research* (Boston: Research Press, 1998), pg. 102.
[3] Richard L. Samuels, *Data Gathering Methodologies* (New York: Reporters Publishing Co., 1997), pg.74.
[4] Some respondents indicated a desire to cook professionally.
[5] Comments gathered at focus group conducted at 11:00 a.m. on March 10.

On Your Own

1. Open the document **OWD59** that you used in the On Your Own section of Exercise 59, or open ◈ **60GUIDES**.

2. Save the document as **OWD60**.

3. Insert at least three footnotes to provide citations or to supplement text with additional information.

4. Insert at least three endnotes.

5. Insert at least two comments as reminders to yourself or to someone else who might read the document.

6. Print the document, including comments.

7. Save the document, close it, and exit Word.

Exercise 61

Skills Covered:

◆ **Use Document Map** ◆ **Copy or Move Text from One Page to Another**

On the Job

The Document Map helps you quickly locate sections of a long document without spending time scrolling through pages. Use cut, copy, and paste to copy or move data from one page in a document to another.

The head of marketing has asked you to make some changes to the marketing document about Web page design. In this exercise, you will use the Document Map to navigate through the document to locate text you need to rearrange. You will also copy and move text within the document.

Terms

Document Map A vertical pane that opens on the left side of the document window to show the major headings and sections in a document; click a topic in the pane to go to it.

Heading A paragraph formatted in one of Word's built-in Heading styles or a paragraph formatted like a heading. For example, a paragraph formatted in a larger font size than normal text and/or with bold or italic font styles.

Notes

Use Document Map

- **Document Map** is useful for navigating through long documents.

- Word displays the Document Map in a pane on the left side of the document window.

- The Document Map shows **headings** and major topics in an outline format.

  ✓ *Outlines are covered in Exercise 57.*

- If there are no headings or major topics, the Document Map is empty.

- You can expand and collapse the Document Map as you would an outline to show the headings you need.

The Document Map

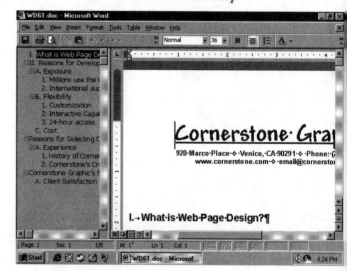

Copy or Move Text from One Page to Another

■ Use standard copy and move techniques to copy or move text from one page in a document to another page.

✓ *Moving text is covered in Word, Exercise 19; Copying text is covered in Word, Exercise 20.*

■ Use Cut and Paste to move text.

■ Use Copy and Paste to copy text.

■ Copying and/or moving text may affect hard page breaks already inserted in a document.

Procedures

Use Document Map

Display Document Map:

1. Click **View** .... Alt + V
2. Click **Document Map** .... D
   OR
   Click **Document Map**
   button .

Hide Document Map:

1. Click **View** .... Alt + V
2. Click **Document Map** .... D
   OR
   Click **Document Map**
   button .

Jump to a heading:

● Click desired heading in Document Map.

Expand/collapse heading:

1. Right-click anywhere in Document Map.
2. Click level of heading to Expand/Collapse.
   OR
   Click **Expand** ➕ or **Collapse**
   ➖ button next to headings in Document Map.

Copy or Move Text from One Page to Another

Use Copy and Paste:
(Ctrl+C, Ctrl+V)

1. Select the text to copy.
2. Click **Copy** button .
   OR
   a. Click **Edit** .... Alt + E
   b. Click **Copy** C
3. Display other page and position insertion point in new location.
4. Click **Paste** button .
   OR
   a. Click **Edit** .... Alt + E
   b. Click **Paste** .... P

Move text from one page to another:

1. Select text to move.
2. Press **F2** F2
3. Display other page and position insertion point at new location.
4. Press **Enter** .... Enter

Use Cut and Paste to Move Text:
(Ctrl+X, Cltr+V)

1. Select text to move.
2. Click **Cut** button .
   OR
   a. Click **Edit** .... Alt + E
   b. Click **Cut** .... T
3. Display other page and position insertion point at new location.
4. Click **Paste** button .
   OR
   a. Click **Edit** .... Alt + E
   b. Click **Paste** .... P

Exercise Directions

1. Start Word.
2. Open ⊘ **61REPORT**.
3. Save the document as **WD61**.
4. Display the Document Map.
5. Cut the Heading I. *Cornerstone Graphic's Mission Statement* and the paragraph following it to the Clipboard.
6. Using the Document Map move the insertion point to the beginning of the Heading B. *Client Satisfaction* near the end of the document.
7. Paste the mission statement information into the document before the Heading B. *Client Satisfaction*.
8. Use the Document Map to move the insertion point to the beginning of the heading III: *Reasons for Selecting Cornerstone*.
9. Insert a hard page break.
10. Use the Document Map to move the insertion point to the beginning of the Heading IV. *Cornerstone Graphic's Mission Statement*.
11. Insert a hard page break.
12. Move the insertion point to the beginning of the Heading A. *Client Satisfaction*.
13. Copy the first sentence under the Heading A. *Client Satisfaction to the Clipboard*.
14. Move the insertion point to the beginning of the Heading A. *Experience*.
15. Paste the sentence from the Clipboard to the end of the paragraph under the Heading A. *Experience*.
16. Hide the Document Map.
17. Create a header for all pages but the first. Include the report title, *Web Pages*, flush left and the current date flush right.
18. Create a centered footer for all pages with the word *Page*, followed by the page number.
19. Preview the document. It should look similar to the document shown in Illustration A.
20. Save the document.
21. Close the document and exit Word.

Cornerstone Graphics

920 Marco Place ✧ Venice, CA 90291 ✧ Phone: (213) 555-1002
www.cornerstone.com ✧ email@cornerstone.com

I. What is Web Page Design?

The World Wide Web is comprised of interconnected documents stored on the global network of computers known as the Internet. The documents are called Web pages. Linked pages are called Web sites. Web sites are uniquely formatted to provide information, collect information, and to capture the attention of consumers around the world.

In today's global marketplace, a presence on the World Wide Web is vital to business success. Creating effective and appealing Web pages is both a skill and an art form that takes technical knowledge, creative abilities, and practice.

II. Reasons for Developing a Web Site

A. Exposure

1. Millions use the Web

Studies show that literally millions of people have access to the Internet at home and/or at work and that new connections are being made by the thousands. Forecasts predict that in the near future, Internet access will be as ubiquitous as television and telephones, and those left off the Web will be left behind in competition.

Page 1

2. International audience

Due to the vast numbers of Internet users around the world, it is simple and cost effective to contact customers, suppliers, and others on-line. Personal relationships can be established and maintained using computers, instead of scheduling expensive travel.

These same contacts will lead to business expansion opportunities, with a minimum of actual travel. Another benefit is that a huge amount of information about businesses, markets, regulations, etc. is available on-line. Research can be successfully accomplished from a home office, without requiring costly travel and time spent abroad.

B. Flexibility

1. Customization

Web sites can be created to suit the customers' needs. Information, design, links, and other features can be developed per customer specifications. Sites can include as many or as few pages as the customer requires. Pages may include order forms, product catalogues, general information, contact names, and so on. Sites can link to existing sites, or other newly developed sites.

2. Interactive Capabilities

Web sites can dispense information and collect information. As customers access the site, demographic information can be collected. Products can be targeted to specific customers. Customers can quickly find the information and/or products they need, and

Web Pages   4/29/99

respond immediately, in real time. Customer response can dictate the future development

of the site.

Web sites can include graphics, video, and sound in addition to text-based

information. For example, sites can be enhanced by the inclusion of video clips of sales

presentations or photographs of products.

3. 24-hour access

Work can be accomplished regardless of time zone differences and work habits.

Not only can your staff use the Web to communicate with others, but also people around

the world can contact you even in the middle of the night. Information is available 24

hours a day, seven days a week.

C. Cost

The cost of maintaining a Web site is minimal, especially in comparison to other

types of marketing. Savings are made throughout the organization, including travel and

entertainment costs.

Page 3

III. Reasons for Selecting Cornerstone

A. *Experience*

Cornerstone is one of the first businesses devoted exclusively to Web site design. With no side businesses or other interests, the firm can devote 100% of its attention to quality Web site design and customer satisfaction. At Cornerstone, nothing comes before client satisfaction.

1. History of Cornerstone

Cornerstone Graphics is a graphics design company based in Venice, CA. Tom Louris started Cornerstone in 1992. The company has steadily and consistently increased its client base and gross income. Currently, Cornerstone employs over 25 people.

This year, Cornerstone reached an agreement with State-of-the-Art Solutions, a medium-sized public relations and marketing firm serving clients in the computer and telecommunications industries. The alliance will enable Cornerstone to tap the resources and expertise of State-of-the-Art Solutions and bring expanded opportunities to all types of clients.

2. Cornerstone's Credentials

- Cornerstone has recruited and maintained a talented and technically savvy staff of Web page designers.
- Cornerstone is committed to working closely with each client and to providing a personalized service not readily available at other, larger firms.
- Cornerstone places client satisfaction above all other goals and guarantees all work.

Illustration A (Page 5 of 5)

Web Pages   4/29/99

IV. Cornerstone Graphic's Mission Statement

Cornerstone Graphics is committed to providing high-quality Web page design for all types of businesses and individuals. We pride ourselves on our customer satisfaction rate.

A. Client Satisfaction

At Cornerstone, nothing comes before client satisfaction. Cornerstone Graphics is committed to providing high-quality Web page design for all types of businesses and individuals. We pride ourselves on our customer satisfaction rate.

Page 5

On Your Own

1. Open the document OWD60 that you used in the On Your Own section of Exercise 60, or open ⊚61GUIDES.

2. Save the document as OWD61.

3. Use the Document Map to navigate through the document.

4. Move text from one page in the document to another. (You can always use Undo to revert back, if necessary.)

5. Copy text from one page in the document to another.

6. If necessary, adjust page breaks.

7. Save the document, close it, and exit Word.

Exercise 62

◆ Preview Multiple Pages ◆ Drag and Drop Text from One Page to Another ◆ Print Specific Pages

On the Job

Preview multiple pages to see how an entire multi-page document will look when it is printed. For example, when you preview more than one page at a time you can see headers and footers on every page and determine whether the text flow from one page to the next looks professional. Printing specific pages or selected text is an option that can save paper and time if you find that you only need hard copies of parts of a document.

The head of marketing for Cornerstone Graphics has asked you to prepare a sample of a lengthy document to show to the company president. In this exercise, you will preview the entire document to determine which sections you need to include in the sample. You will then print selected pages.

Terms

Magnifier The mouse pointer used to zoom in or out on a page in Print Preview.

Notes

Preview Multiple Pages

- By default, Print preview displays one page at a time.
- You can change the Print preview display to show multiple pages at one time.
- When you preview multiple pages, Word displays two rows of three pages at one time. Decrease the zoom setting in Print preview to show more pages at once.
- The more pages displayed, the smaller the pages appear on the screen, so the harder it is to read the text.
- Use the **Magnifier** tool 🔍 to zoom in on a page to get a better look.
- Preview multiple pages to get an overall view of the document, not to edit or format text.
  - ✓ You can edit in Print preview, but it is difficult if the pages are small.

A six-page document in Print preview

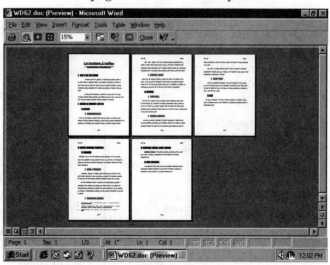

Drag and Drop Text from One Page to Another

- If you can see both locations on the screen at the same time, you can use the drag-and-drop methods for copying or moving text.

Print Specific Pages

- Select Print options to print a specific page, several pages, selected text, or the current page.
- In the Print dialog box, you can specify consecutive pages or nonconsecutive pages. You can also specify pages to print by page number.

Set print options in the Print dialog box

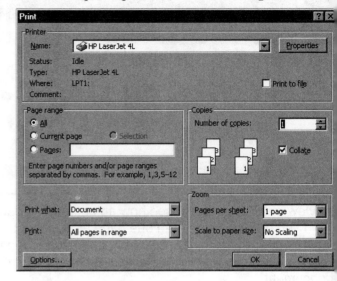

Procedures

Preview Multiple Pages

1. Click **Print Preview** button 🔍.
   OR
   a. Click **File** .... `Alt`+`F`
   b. Click **Print Preview** .... `V`
2. Click **Multiple Pages** button ⊞.
3. Drag across number of rows and pages to display.
4. Release mouse button.

Zoom In in Print Preview

1. If necessary, click in document to position the insertion point.
2. Position the magnifier mouse pointer over the area to enlarge ⊕.
   - ✓ *The magnifier is selected by default. If magnifier pointer is not displayed, click Magnifier button on Print Preview toolbar.*
3. Click mouse once.
4. Click again to zoom out ⊖.

Change Back to One Page Preview

- Click **One Page** button ▣.

Use Drag-and-Drop Editing to Copy Text

1. Display multiple pages in Print preview.
   - ✓ *If necessary, click magnifier button to turn off zoom feature.*
2. Select text to copy.
3. Move mouse pointer anywhere over selected text.
4. Press and hold **Ctrl** .... `Ctrl`
5. Drag selection to new location 🖑.
6. Release mouse button.
7. Release **Ctrl** .... `Ctrl`

Use Drag-and-Drop Editing to Move Text

1. Display multiple pages in Print preview.
2. Select text to move.
   - ✓ *If necessary, click magnifier button to turn off zoom feature.*
3. Move mouse pointer anywhere over selected text.
4. Drag selection to new location.
5. Release mouse button when the insertion point is in new location.

Print Specified Pages *(Ctrl+P)*

Print single page:
1. Click **File** .... `Alt`+`F`
2. Click **Print** .... `P`
3. Click **Pages** .... `Alt`+`G`
4. Type page number.
5. Click **OK** .... `Enter`

Print consecutive pages:
1. Click **File** .... `Alt`+`F`
2. Click **Print** .... `P`
3. Click **Pages** .... `Alt`+`G`
4. Type page range as follows: first page number, hyphen, last page number. For example: 3-5
   - ✓ *Do not type spaces.*
5. Click **OK** .... `Enter`

Print nonconsecutive pages:
1. Click **File** .... `Alt`+`F`
2. Click **Print** .... `P`
3. Click **Pages** .... `Alt`+`G`
4. Type each page number separated by commas. For example: 3,5,7
   - ✓ *Do not type spaces.*
5. Click **OK** .... `Enter`
   - ✓ *You can combine consecutive and nonconsecutive pages. For example, 2-5,7,10.*

Print current page:

1. Click **File** .... `Alt`+`F`
2. Click **Print** .... `P`
3. Click **Current Page** ...... `Alt`+`E`
4. Click **OK** .... `Enter`

Print selected text:

1. Select text to print.
2. Click **File** .... `Alt`+`F`
3. Click **Print** .... `P`
4. Click **Selection** .... `Alt`+`S`
5. Click **OK** .... `Enter`

Exercise Directions

1. Start Word, if necessary.
2. Open ⊙ **62REPORT**.
3. Save the document **WD62**.
4. Use Print preview to preview the first two pages of the document.
5. Zoom in on the top of page 2.
6. Zoom back out.
7. Use drag-and-drop to move the heading 2. *International Audience* and the paragraph below it (from the top of page 2), to just before the heading 1. *Millions use the Web* (near the bottom of page 1). After the move, the pages should look similar to those shown in Illustration A.

8. Preview all pages of the document at once.
9. Zoom in on the bottom of page 4.
10. Close Print Preview
11. Display the Document Map.
12. Use the Document Map to go to the heading III. *Reasons for Selecting Cornerstone*.
13. Print the current page.
14. Select the paragraph of text under the heading IV. *Cornerstone's Mission Statement* and print it.
15. Save the document.
16. Print pages 1 and 3.
17. Close the document and exit Word.

Cornerstone Graphics

920 Marco Place ✧ Venice, CA 90291 ✧ Phone: (213) 555-1002
www.cornerstone.com ✧ email@cornerstone.com

I. What is Web Page Design?

The World Wide Web is comprised of interconnected documents stored on the global network of computers known as the Internet. The documents are called Web pages. Linked pages are called Web sites. Web sites are uniquely formatted to provide information, collect information, and to capture the attention of consumers around the world.

In today's global marketplace, a presence on the World Wide Web is vital to business success. Creating effective and appealing Web pages is both a skill and an art form that takes technical knowledge, creative abilities, and practice.

II. Reasons for Developing a Web Site

A. Exposure

1. International audience

Due to the vast numbers of Internet users around the world, it is simple and cost effective to contact customers, suppliers, and others on-line. Personal relationships can be established and maintained using computers, instead of scheduling expensive travel.

Web Pages   4/30/99

These same contacts will lead to business expansion opportunities, with a minimum of actual travel. Another benefit is that a huge amount of information about businesses, markets, regulations, etc. is available on-line. Research can be successfully accomplished from a home office, without requiring costly travel and time spent abroad.

2. Millions use the Web

Studies show that literally millions of people have access to the Internet at home and/or at work and that new connections are being made by the thousands. Forecasts predict that in the near future, Internet access will be as ubiquitous as television and telephones, and those left off the Web will be left behind in competition.

B. Flexibility

1. Customization

Web sites can be created to suit the customers' needs. Information, design, links, and other features can be developed per customer specifications. Sites can include as many or as few pages as the customer requires. Pages may include order forms, product catalogues, general information, contact names, and so on. Sites can link to existing sites, or other newly developed sites.

2. Interactive Capabilities

Web sites can dispense information and collect information. As customers access the site, demographic information can be collected. Products can be targeted to specific customers. Customers can quickly find the information and/or products they need, and

Page 2

On Your Own

1. Open the document **OWD61** the document you used in the On Your Own section of Exercise 61 or open ⊛**62GUIDES**.

2. Save the document as **OWD62**.

3. Preview multiple pages of the document at one time.

4. Use drag-and-drop editing to copy or move text from one page in the document to another.

5. Print the last page of the document.

6. Print the first paragraph of the document.

7. Save and close the document, and exit Word.

Exercise 63

Skills Covered:

◆ **Find and Replace** ◆ **Create Bookmarks** ◆ **Select Browse Object**

On the Job

Use the Find, Bookmark, and Browse object features to locate specific parts of a document, including text, graphics, paragraph marks, etc. Use the Find and Replace feature when you want to automatically replace existing text with new text.

The training director at State-of-the-Art Solutions has asked for your help completing a document listing all of the training courses offered next year. In this exercise, you will use Find to locate parts of the document where you need to insert bookmarks. You will use Find and Replace to correct the spelling of an instructor's name and to remove unnecessary paragraph marks. Finally, you will use Browse by Object to locate parts of the document where you need to make changes.

Terms

Bookmark A nonprinting character that you insert and name so that you can quickly find a particular location in a document.

Browse object A specified element that Word locates and displays when you scroll through a document.

Notes

Find and Replace

■ Use Word's Find command to locate specific text, nonprinting characters, formatting, graphics, objects, and other items in a document.

Find page of the Find and Replace dialog box

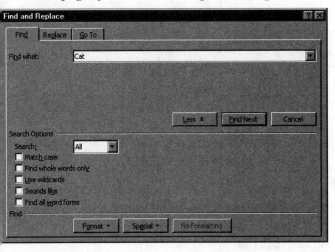

■ Combine Find with Replace to replace items.

■ The Find and Replace commands are useful for correcting errors that occur several times in a document, such as a misspelled name.

■ You can find and replace formatting, symbols, and special characters such as paragraph marks.

Replace page of the Find and Replace dialog box

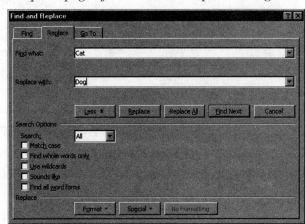

Create Bookmarks

- Use a **bookmark** to mark a specific location in a document such as where you stopped working, or where you need to insert information.
- You can use many bookmarks in one document.
- Use descriptive bookmark names to make it easier to find the bookmark location that you want.
- Use the Go To feature to go directly to a bookmark.

Go To page of Find and Replace dialog box

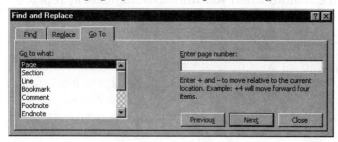

Select Browse Object

- Use **browse object** to scroll to specific points in a document.
- There are twelve browse objects from which to choose.
- When you choose the Go To browse object, you must specify the object to go to.
- When you choose the Find browse object, you must enter text to Find and/or Replace.

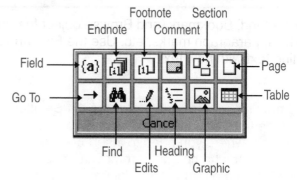

Procedures

Find Text *(Ctrl+F)*

1. Click **Edit** .... `Alt`+`E`
2. Click **Find** .... `F`
3. Click **Fi̱nd what** .... `Alt`+`N`
4. Type text to find.
5. Click **More** (if necessary) .... `Alt`+`M`
6. Select options:
   - **Match case** .... `Alt`+`H` to find only words in same case as text to find.
   - **Find whole words only** .... `Alt`+`Y` to find text as a whole word, not as part of a longer word.
   - **Use wildcards** ...... `Alt`+`U` to find words specified with wildcard characters.
   - **Sounds like** .... `Alt`+`K` to find homonyms.
   - **Find all word forms** .... `Alt`+`W` to find all grammatical forms of text.
7. Click **Find Next** .... `Alt`+`F`

8. Repeat step 7 until finished.
   ✓ *Click Cancel at any time to close the dialog box.*
9. Click **OK** .... `Enter`
10. Click **Cancel** .... `Esc`

Replace Text *(Ctrl+H)*

1. Click **Edit** .... `Alt`+`E`
2. Click **Replace** .... `E`
3. Click **Find what** .... `Alt`+`N`
4. Type text to find.
5. Press **Tab** .... `Tab`
   OR
   Click **Replace with** ..... `Alt`+`I`
   ✓ *To replace with nothing (delete), leave the Replace with text box blank.*
6. Type replacement text.
7. Click **More** (if necessary) .... `Alt`+`M`
8. Select options.
9. Click **Find** Next........... `Alt`+`F`
10. Click **Replace** .... `Alt`+`R`
    OR
    Click **Replace All** .... `Alt`+`A`

11. Repeat steps 9–10 until done.
    ✓ *Click Cancel at any time to close the dialog box.*
12. Click **OK**........................... `Enter`
13. Click **Cancel** .... `Esc`

Find and Replace Special Characters *(Ctrl +H)*

1. Click **Edit** .... `Alt`+`E`
2. Click **Replace** .... `E`
3. Click **Find what** .... `Alt`+`N`
4. Click **Special** .... `Alt`+`E`
5. Select special character.
6. Press **Tab** .... `Tab`
   OR
   Click **Replace with** ...... `Alt`+`I`
   ✓ *To replace with nothing (delete), leave Replace with text box blank.*
7. Click **More** .... `Alt`+`M`
8. Click **Special** .... `Alt`+`E`
9. Select special character.
10. Click **Find Next**........... `Alt`+`F`

11. Click **Replace** .... Alt+R
    OR
    Click **Replace All** .... Alt+A
12. Repeat steps 10–11 until done.
    ✓ *Click Cancel at any time to close the dialog box.*
13. Click **OK** .... Enter
14. Click **Cancel** .... Esc

Create a Bookmark

1. Position the insertion point where you want the bookmark.
2. Click **Insert** .... Alt+I
3. Click **Bookmark** .... K
4. Click in the **Bookmark name** text box .... Alt+B
5. Type bookmark name.
6. Click **Add** button
    Add .... Alt+A

Go To Bookmark (*Ctrl+G*)

1. Press **F5** F5
    OR
    a. Click **Edit** .... Alt+E
    b. Click **Go To** .... G
2. Click Bookmark in the **Go to what** list .... Alt+O
    ✓ *Select any object in the Go to what list to browse directly to that object.*
3. Click **Enter bookmark name** .... Alt+E
4. Type bookmark name.
    OR
    Select bookmark name from drop-down list.
5. Click **Go To** .... Alt+T
6. Click **Close** button Close .... Esc

Browse by Object

1. Click the **Select Browse Object** button ⊙.
2. Click the desired browse object.
    ✓ *If you select Find or Go To, the Find and Replace dialog box is displayed.*
3. Click the **Previous** button ▲ to scroll up to the previous browse object.
    OR
    Click the **Next** button ▼ to scroll down to the next browse object.

Exercise Directions

1. Start Word, if necessary.
2. Open ☉**63COURSE**.
3. Save the document as **WD63**.
4. Use the Find command to locate the first reference to *Access 2000*.
5. Create a bookmark named *Access*.
6. Use the Find command to locate the first reference to *Greg Moliver*.
7. Create a bookmark named *GregM*.
8. Use the Find and Replace command to locate and replace all occurrences of the name *Mary Rose Jarvis* with the correct name *Maryanne Jarvis*.
9. Display nonprinting characters, if they are not already displayed.
10. Use the Find and Replace feature to locate all occurrences of two consecutive paragraph marks and replace them with a single paragraph mark.
    a. Enter the special character for paragraph marks twice times in the Find what text box.
    b. Enter the special character for paragraph marks once in the Replace with text box.
11. Go to the *GregM* bookmark.
12. Replace the text *in the training department* following the bookmark with the text *assistant to the training director*.
13. Select the Heading Browse object.
14. Browse to the Previous Heading until the insertion point is on the heading Instructors.
15. Insert the word *Class* in front of the word Instructors.
16. Create a footer on all pages that has the title *Training Schedule* flush left and the page number preceded by the word *Page* flush right.
17. Check the spelling and grammar in the document.
18. Preview the document. It should look similar to the one in Illustration A.
19. Print the document.
20. Close the document and exit Word, saving all changes.

STATE-OF-THE-ART SOLUTIONS
Annual Training Schedule

Schedule

January   Introduction to Word 2000

This introductory course will cover the basics of using Microsoft Word 2000 to create common business documents. By the end of the course you will know how to create and print text-based documents such as letters and envelopes, and apply formatting.

February   Intermediate Word 2000

A continuation of the Introductory Word course, this intermediate level class will delve into some of the more intriguing features of Microsoft Word 2000. By the end of the course you will know how to conduct a mail merge, set up a document in columns, include headers and footers, and insert pictures.

March   Advanced Word 2000

This final course in the Microsoft Word series covers the advanced features. By the end of this course you will know how to work with tables, create and modify outlines, use e-mail and Internet features in Word, and share documents with other users.

April   Beginning Excel 2000

This introductory course will cover the basics of using Microsoft Excel 2000 to create business documents. By the end of the course you will know how to create and print simple spreadsheets, create and use formulas and functions, and apply formatting.

May   Intermediate Excel 2000

A continuation of the beginning Excel course, this class will delve into some of the more intriguing features of Microsoft Excel 2000. By the end of the course you will know how to nest functions, perform what-if analysis, and use multi-sheet workbooks.

June   Advanced Excel 2000

This course covers the advanced features of Excel. By the end of this course you will know how to work with pivot tables, create and modify charts and maps, and generate reports.

July   Introduction to Access 2000

This introductory course will cover the basics of using Microsoft
Access 2000 to create databases. By the end of the course you will
know how to create a database, enter data in forms and tables, and
print database reports.

August   Advanced Access 2000

A continuation of the introductory Access course, the Advanced
level class will cover the more intriguing features of Microsoft
Access 2000. By the end of the course you will know how to create
and modify custom forms and reports, generate queries, calculate
in a database, and set up relationships between tables.

September   PowerPoint 2000

The comprehensive class covers the entire scope of creating slide
presentations with PowerPoint 2000. By the end of the course you
will know how to create and edit a slide show, change slide layout,
insert objects on slides, incorporate sound and video in a slide
show, and run a slide show.

October   Introduction to Office 2000

This overview will introduce you to each of the Office 2000
applications. By the end of this class you will know how to use the
Office 2000 applications to create business documents such as
letters, memos, spreadsheets, and reports.

November   Integration with Office 2000

This results-oriented course will cover the basics of using all of the
Microsoft Office 2000 applications together to complete projects. By
the end of the course you will know how to integrate an excel chart
in a Word document, create a PowerPoint presentation from a
Word outline, print PowerPoint handouts using Word, export
Access data into an Excel worksheet, and link an Excel worksheet
with an Access database.

December   Introduction to the Internet

In this class, you will learn how to log on and access information
using the Internet and the World Wide Web. You will learn how to
enter URLs, use a Search engine, and store Web sites in your
Favorites folder.

Class Instructors

As always, we have hired highly qualified instructors to teach all of out training classes. Following is a brief bio for of each of the instructors.

Word. The instructor for the Word classes is Cathy Bennet. Ms. Bennet has ten years experience in computer training.

Excel. Joseph Castaldy is the instructor for the Excel classes. Mr. Castaldy has been involved in computer training for eight years.

Access. Maryanne Jarvis will be teaching the Access classes. Ms. Jarvis is one of the most highly regarded corporate trainers in California. She has more than twelve years of corporate training experience.

PowerPoint. Karen Blanchard will be teaching the PowerPoint class. Ms. Blanchard has her own presentation design firm, and has used PowerPoint for many years.

Office. Maryanne Jarvis will be teaching the Office classes. Ms. Jarvis is one of the most highly regarded corporate trainers in California. She has more than twelve years of corporate training experience.

Internet. Joseph Castaldy is the instructor for the Internet classes. Mr. Castaldy has been involved in computer training for eight years.

Registration Information

To register for any of the above classes you must first obtain permission from your supervisor. Then, fill out the following information and return this page to Greg Moliver, assistant to the training director.

Name: _____

Department: _____

Phone Extension: _____

Class: _____

Month: _____

Reasons for taking the class: _____

_____

_____

_____

_____

_____

For more information, contact Greg in Training, ext. 432. e-mail: gwalsh@sas.com.

On Your Own

1. Open **OWD62**, the document you created in the On Your Own section of Exercise 62, or open ⊘ **63GUIDES**.

2. Save the file as **OWD63**.

3. Insert at least two bookmarks in the document. For example, you can use bookmarks to mark an important topic or a topic where you need to insert more information.

4. Use Find and Replace to replace a name that appears frequently in the document.

5. Try using Find and Replace to replace formatting in the document. For example, replace bold text with italics, or one font with a different font.

6. Use the Browse by Object feature to go to each of the bookmarks in the document.

7. Use Browse by Object to go to the comments in the document.

8. Save the changes, close the document, and exit Word.

Exercise 64

Skills Covered:

◆ **Track Changes** ◆ **Accept/Reject Changes**
◆ **Customize Revision Marks**

On the Job

Track changes made to a document to monitor when and how edits are made. Tracking changes lets you consider revisions before incorporating them into a document. If you agree with the change, you can accept it, but if you disagree with the change you can reject it. You can track changes made by one person, or by many people, which is useful when you are collaborating on a document with others.

Your coworker in the marketing department of The Candy Kitchen Magazine has asked for your input on the introduction to the readership survey report. In this exercise, you will use revision tracking to edit the readership survey document.

Terms

Revision marks Formatting applied to text in a document to identify where insertions, deletions, and formatting changes have been made.

Notes

Track Changes

- Turn on Word's Track Changes feature to apply **revision marks** to all insertions, deletions, and formatting changes in a document.

- When Track Changes is active, the TRK button on the status bar is bold and Word applies revision marks as you edit a document.

- By default Word displays inserted text in color with an underline and deleted text in color with a strikethrough.

- While tracking changes, deleted text is marked but not erased from the document until the change is accepted.

- Word also inserts a vertical line to the left of any changed line to indicate where revision marks occur in the document.

Changes in a document

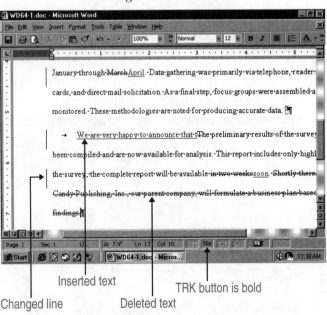

Inserted text

TRK button is bold

Changed line

Deleted text

315

- By default, Word applies different colors to revision marks for up to eight different users working on the same document.
- Word marks changes on screen and in printed documents by default.

Accept/Reject Changes

- Revision marks remain stored as part of a document until the changes are either accepted or rejected.
- To incorporate edits into a document file, accept the changes.
- To cancel the edits and erase them from the file, reject the changes.
- Word provides three methods for reviewing, accepting, and deleting changes:
  - The Accept or Reject Changes dialog box.
  - The Reviewing toolbar.
  - Context menus.

Name of editor and type of change are displayed in the Accept or Reject dialog box

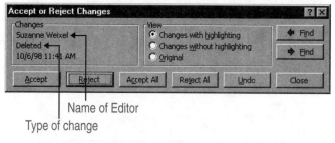

Name of Editor
Type of change

The Reviewing toolbar

Track Changes Next Change
Reject Change

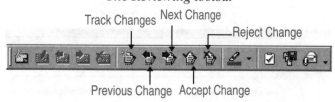

Previous Change Accept Change

Context menu for tracking changes

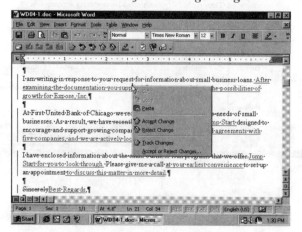

- Use the Accept or Reject Changes dialog box to read a description of a change before you accept or reject it.
- Use the Reviewing toolbar buttons to locate changes, then accept or reject them.
- Use the context menu to accept or reject a change quickly.

Customize Revision Marks

- You can change the way Word displays revision marks.
  - You can change the color and/or formatting used to mark insertions.
  - You can change the color and/or formatting used to mark deletions.
  - You can select the color and/or formatting to mark formatting changes.
  - You can change the color and/or formatting used to mark changed lines.
- You can set Word to display marks on the screen but not in printed documents, or in the printed document but not on the screen.

Track Changes dialog box

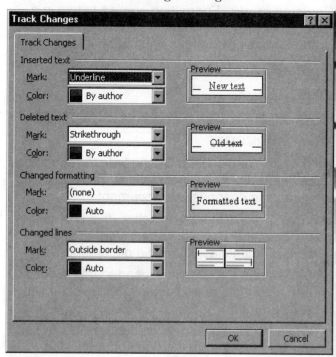

Procedures

Turn Track Changes On or Off

- Double-click button **TRK** indicator `TRK` on status bar to toggle feature on and off.

OR

1. Click **T**ools .... `Alt`+`T`
2. Click **T**rack Changes .... `T`
3. Click **H**ighlight Changes .... `H`
4. Click **T**rack changes while editing .... `Alt`+`T`
5. Click **OK** .... `Enter`

   ✓ *Deselect Track changes while editing check box to turn off Track Changes feature.*

OR

1. Click **V**iew .... `Alt`+`V`
2. Select **T**oolbars .... `T`
3. Click **Reviewing**.
4. Click **Track Changes** button to toggle feature on and off.

   ✓ *If Track Changes is active, right-click revision mark in document and click Track Changes to toggle feature off.*

Use Context Menu

1. Right-click a revision mark.
2. Click **Acc**ept Change .... `E`

   OR

   Click **R**eject Change .... `R`

Use Reviewing Toolbar

1. Click **Next Change** button to browse forward from insertion point.

   OR

   Click **Previous Change** button to browse back from insertion point.
2. Click **Accept Change** button to incorporate change into document.

   OR

   Click **Reject Change** button to delete change from document.

Open Accept or Reject Changes Dialog Box

1. Right-click the **TRK** indicator `TRK`.
2. Click **A**ccept or Reject Changes .... `A`

OR

1. Click **T**ools .... `Alt`+`T`
2. Select **T**rack Changes .... `T`
3. Click **A**ccept or Reject Changes .... `A`

OR

1. Right-click a revision mark.
2. Click **A**ccept or Reject Changes .... `A`

Use Accept or Reject Changes Dialog Box

1. Click **F**ind button `➡ Find` to browse forward from insertion point.

   OR

   Click **F**ind button `⬅ Find` to browse back from insertion point.
2. Click one of the following:

   - **A**ccept .... `Alt`+`A` to incorporate change into document.
   - **R**eject .... `Alt`+`R` to delete change from document.
   - **A**ccept All .... `Alt`+`C` to incorporate all changes into document.
   - Re**j**ect All .... `Alt`+`J` to delete all changes from document.
   - **U**ndo .... `Alt`+`U` to reverse most recent accept or reject action.
3. Click **Close** button `Close` .... `Esc`

Customize Revision Marks

1. Right-click **TRK** indicator `TRK`.
2. Click **O**ptions .... `O`

OR

   a. Click **T**ools .... `Alt`+`T`
   b. Select **T**rack Changes... `T`
   c. Click **H**ighlight Changes . `H`
   d. Click **O**ptions .... `Alt`+`O`

3. Use drop-down lists to select desired Mark and/or Color options for the following:

   ✓ *Select By Author as Color option to use different colors for up to eight users.*

   - **Inserted Text**
     ◆ Select **M**ark and/or C**o**lor options.
   - **Deleted Text**
     ◆ Select **M**ark and/or C**o**lor options.
   - **Changed Formatting**
     ◆ Select **M**ark and/or C**o**lor options.
   - **Changed Lines**
     ◆ Select **M**ark and/or C**o**lor options.

4. Click **OK** .... `Enter`

Select When Revision Marks are Displayed

1. Click **T**ools .... `Alt`+`T`
2. Select **T**rack Changes .... `T`

   OR

   Right-click **TRK** indicator `TRK`.
3. Click **H**ighlight Changes .... `H`
4. Click **Highlight changes on screen** .... `Alt`+`S` to show revision marks while editing.
5. Click **Highlight changes in printed document** ...... `Alt`+`P` to show revision marks in printed document.
6. Click **OK** .... `Enter`

Exercise Directions

1. Start Word, if necessary.

2. Open 64SURVEY.

3. Save the document as WD64-1.

4. Turn on the Track Changes feature.
   - Make sure options are set to display changes on the screen *and* in printed documents.

5. Make the insertions and deletions shown in Illustration A.

6. Change the color of inserted text to green and deleted text to violet.
   - ✓ *If these colors are already in use on your computer system, select different colors.*

7. Save the document and then print it.

8. Save the document as WD64-2.

9. Starting at the top of the document, accept the first four revisions.

10. Reject the next four revisions.

11. Accept any remaining revisions.

12. Turn off the Track Changes feature.

13. Save the document.

14. Print the document.

15. Close the document and exit Word.

Illustration A

The Candy Kitchen Magazine

P.O. Box 765 ◆ Falmouth, MA 02536 ◆ (508) 555-2200

Last January, in response to a slip in subscription sales[1], The Candy Kitchen
minor

Magazine commissioned a full-scale readership survey. The intent was to determine
of the survey   *the*

demographics of our current market as well as identify ways to target new consumers.
to

According to industry research, surveys can prompt changes leading to significant

increases in circulation. [2]

The survey was conducted by Market Information Resources, a market research

and analysis company based in New York City. The research was conducted from
April

January through ~~March.~~ Data gathering was primarily via telephone, reader response

cards, and direct mail solicitation. As a final step, focus groups were assembled and

monitored. These methodologies are noted for producing accurate data. [3]

The preliminary results of the survey have been compiled and are now available

for analysis. This report includes only highlights of the survey; the complete report will
soon

be available ~~in two weeks.~~ Shortly thereafter, Candy Publishing, Inc., our parent

company, will formulate a business plan based on the findings.

Please direct all questions ~~and comments~~ to Mr. Steven Tournier, Director of

Research at Market Information Resources.

---

[1] 1999 Annual Circulation Analysis, Candy Publishing, Inc.
[2] Carolyn M. Sachs, *Studies in Market Research* (Boston: Research Press, 1998), pg. 102.
[3] Richard L. Samuels, *Data Gathering Methodologies* (New York: Reporters Publishing Co., 1997), pg.74.

On Your Own

1. Open **OWD38**, the invitation to an event that you used in the On Your Own section of Exercise 38, or open ⊘ **64EVENT**.

2. Save the document as **OWD64**.

3. Turn on the Track Changes feature.

4. Customize revision marks.

5. Make changes to the document.

6. Print the document with revision marks.

7. Review the changes, accepting some and rejecting others.

8. If the document is more than one page, add a footer to the second page, including your name, a document title, and the page number.

9. Save the document, close it, and exit Word.

Exercise 65

Skills Covered:

◆ **Open Multiple Documents** ◆ **Arrange Documents on Screen**
◆ **Copy/Move Text from One Document to Another**
◆ **Compare Documents**

On the Job

Open multiple documents when you need to work with more than one document at a time. For example, if you are planning a meeting, you may need to work with an agenda and a list of attendees at the same time. You can easily copy or move text from one document to another. You can view one open document at a time, or you can arrange the documents so they are all visible on screen. Compare documents to track the differences between them. Comparing documents is useful if you make changes to a document without using revision marks.

The Introduction to the readership survey report for The Candy Kitchen Magazine has undergone many revisions. In this exercise, you will put the finishing touches on the final version. First, you will open the survey report document and a document containing information you need to copy into the survey. Next, you will copy the information from one open document to the other. Finally, you will compare the final version of the survey to an earlier version to make sure you approve of all of the changes.

Terms

Active document The document in which the insertion point is currently located. Commands and actions occur in the active document.

Tile Arrange windows so they do not overlap on-screen.

Notes

Open Multiple Documents

- You can open multiple Word documents at the same time.

- Each open document is represented by a button on the Windows taskbar.

- By default, the **active document** is displayed on-screen, while other open documents are hidden.

- Only one document can be active at a time. You can identify the active document window by the following:

  - The active document window contains the insertion point.

- The active document window has a brighter title bar than other open document windows.

- The active document window is represented by the "pressed in" taskbar button.

Arrange Documents on Screen

- You can arrange all open documents on-screen at the same time.

- Word **tiles** open documents horizontally one above the other.

- The more open documents there are, the smaller each document window is on-screen. Therefore, editing with more then two documents arranged on screen is difficult.

- Even when multiple documents are displayed on-screen, only one document is active.

Multiple open documents

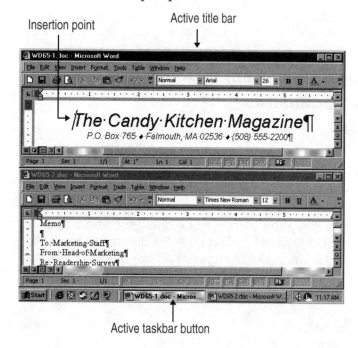

Insertion point

Active title bar

Active taskbar button

Copy/Move Text from One Open Document to Another

- Use standard Cut, Copy, and Paste commands to copy and/or move text from one open document to another.
- If you can see both documents on-screen, use drag-and-drop-editing to copy/move text from one location to another.

  ✓ *Moving and copying are covered in Exercises 19 and 20.*

Compare Documents

- Compare two documents when you want to highlight differences between them.
- When you compare documents, Word inserts revision marks to show the differences.
  - Text included in the active document but not in the document to compare is marked as inserted.
  - Text included in the document to compare but not in the active document is marked as deleted.
- You can review the revision marks to accept or reject the changes.

  ✓ *Revision marks are covered in Exercise 64.*

Procedures

Open Multiple Documents (Ctrl+O)

1. Open first document.
2. Open second document.
3. Continue opening documents as desired.

Open multiple documents stored in same folder:

1. Click **File** .... `Alt`+`F`
2. Click **Open** .... `O`
3. Click first file name.
4. Press and hold **Ctrl**.
5. Click additional file names.
6. Click **Open** .... `Enter`

Arrange documents on screen:

1. Open all documents.
2. Click **Window** .... `Alt`+`W`
3. Click **Arrange All** .... `A`

Display active document only:

- Click active document's **Maximize** button `□`.

Switch among open documents:

- Click in desired document.

OR

- Press `Ctrl`+`F6` until desired document is active.

OR

1. Click **Window**.
2. Click desired document name.

Copy or Move Text From One Document to Another

Use Copy and Paste (Ctrl+C, Ctrl+V):

1. Select the text to copy.
2. Click **Copy** button `📋`.

OR

   a. Click **Edit** .... `Alt`+`E`
   b. Click **Copy** .... `C`

3. Display other document and position insertion point in new location.

4. Click **Paste** button `📋`.

OR

   a. Click **Edit** .... `Alt`+`E`
   b. Click **Paste** .... `P`

Move text:

1. Select text to move.
2. Press **F2**.............................. F2
3. Display other document and position insertion point at new location.
4. Press **Enter**...................... Enter

Use cut and paste (Ctrl+X, Cltr+V):

1. Select text to move.
2. Click **Cut** button ✂.
   OR
   a. Click **E**dit .... Alt + E
   b. Click **Cu**t .... T
3. Display other document and position insertion point at new location.
4. Click **Paste** button 📋.
   OR
   a. Click **E**dit .... Alt + E
   b. Click **P**aste .... P

Use drag-and-drop editing to copy text:

1. Arrange documents on screen.
2. Select text to copy.
3. Move mouse pointer anywhere over selected text.
4. Press and hold **Ctrl** .... Ctrl
5. Drag selection to new location 🔖.
6. Release mouse button.
7. Release **Ctrl** .... Ctrl

Use drag-and-drop editing to move text:

1. Arrange Documents on Screen
2. Select text to move.
3. Move mouse pointer anywhere over selected text.
4. Drag selection to new location.
5. Release mouse button when the insertion point is in new location.

Compare Documents

1. Open one document.
2. Click **T**ools .... Alt + T
3. Highlight **T**rack Changes.... T
4. Click **C**ompare Documents C
5. Select document to compare
6. Click **O**pen...................... Enter

Exercise Directions

1. Start Word, if necessary.
2. Open 💿 **65SURVEY**.
3. Save the document as **WD65-1**.
4. Open 💿 **65MEMO**.
5. Save the document as **WD65-2**.
6. Arrange the documents so both are visible on-screen.
7. Copy the address and phone number from the end of the memo (**WD65-2**) to the end of the survey introduction (**WD65-1**).
8. Maximize the survey introduction (**WD65-1**).
9. Delete the last sentence in the first paragraph, including the footnote.
10. Save the changes.
11. Make the memo (**WD65-2**) the active document.
12. Save and close the memo (**WD65-2**).
13. Compare **WD65-1** to 💿 **65SURVEY**.
14. Preview **WD65-1**. It should look similar to the document in Illustration A.
15. Review the changes marked by comparing the two documents.
16. Accept all changes.
17. Save the document.
18. Print the document.
19. Close the document and exit Word.

The Candy Kitchen Magazine
P.O. Box 765 ♦ Falmouth, MA 02536 ♦ (508) 555-2200

Last January, in response to a minor slip in subscription sales[1], The Candy Kitchen Magazine commissioned a full-scale readership survey. The intent of the survey was to determine the demographics of our current market as well as to identify ways to target new ~~consumers. According to industry research, surveys can~~ consumers. ~~prompt changes leading to significant increases in circulation.~~[2]

The survey was conducted by Market Information Resources, a market research and analysis company based in New York City. The research was conducted from January through March. Data gathering was primarily via telephone, reader response cards, and direct mail solicitation. As a final step, focus groups were assembled and monitored. These methodologies are noted for producing accurate data. [3]

The preliminary results of the survey have been compiled and are now available for analysis. This report includes only highlights of the survey; the complete report will be available in two weeks. Shortly thereafter, Candy Publishing, Inc., our parent company, will formulate a business plan based on the findings.

Please direct all questions to Mr. Steven Tournier, Director of Research at Market Information Resources. 375 Madison Avenue, New York, NY 10016, 212-555-6100.

---

[1] 1999 Annual Circulation Analysis, Candy Publishing, Inc.
~~Carolyn M. Sachs, *Studies in Market Research* (Boston: Research Press, 1998), pg. 102.~~
[3] Richard L. Samuels, *Data Gathering Methodologies* (New York: Reporters Publishing Co., 1997), pg.74.

On Your Own

1. Open **OWD64**, the invitation to an event that you used in the On Your Own section of Exercise 64, or open ⊚ **65EVENT**.

2. Save the document as **OWD65**.

3. If there are revision marks in the document, accept them all.

4. If track changes is active, turn it off.

5. Create a new document and save it as **OWD65-2**.

6. Arrange the two open documents on screen.

7. Copy the entire contents of **OWD65** to **OWD65-2**.

8. Save and close **OWD65-2**.

9. Make changes to **OWD65**. For example, change the date of the event, or the location of the event, or rearrange some of the content.

10. Save the changes.

11. Compare **OWD65** to **OWD65-2**.

12. Review the revisions, accepting the ones you want to keep and rejecting all others.

13. Save the document, close it, and exit Word.

Exercise 66

◆ Critical Thinking

Your supervisor at Northern New England Credit Union has asked you to edit and format a multi-page document. The document, which outlines a new small business loan program called Smart Loans, is provided without formatting. It is up to you to edit the document, apply formatting, set spacing and margins, insert footnotes and comments, insert breaks where necessary, and add a header and footer. You will also copy information from a Web page into the document.

Exercise Directions

1. Start Word, if necessary.
2. Open ⊚ 66LOAN.
3. Save the document as **WD66-1**.
4. Find and replace all occurrences of the text *Program Name* with the actual program name: *Smart Loans*.
5. Insert a bookmark with the name *Intro* on the ninth line at the beginning of the text Introduction.
6. Insert footnotes and comments as shown on Illustration A.
7. Apply formatting as follows:
   a. Center the first two lines.
   b. Apply 26-point sans serif to line 1.
   c. Set paragraph spacing after line 2 to 54 points.
   d. Set remaining text to 12-point serif.
   e. Set a left tab stop at 2.5" on the horizontal ruler for lines 4, 5, 6, 7, and 8, and then insert tabs as marked on Illustration A.
8. Change to Outline view.
9. Promote the six lines marked on Illustration A to Heading 1:.
10. Change back to Normal or Print Layout view and create bullet lists as marked on Illustration A.
11. Set formatting for all paragraph text (excluding lines 1 through 8, headings, and bullet lists) to double spaced, justified, first line indent, with 3 points of space before and 3 points of space after.
    ✓ Use the Format painter to copy the formatting from one paragraph to another.

12. Change margins to 1.25" top and bottom and 1.5" left and right.
13. Turn on the Track Changes feature. Make sure Track Changes is set to display and print revision marks
14. Display the document map and use it to go to the heading *Why Smart Loans?*.
15. Move the heading and the paragraph under it just before the heading *Conclusion*.
16. Print the heading and paragraph that you just moved.
17. Go to the *Risk Factors* heading and select a different bullet marker for both lists.
18. Starting at the beginning of the document, review the changes.
19. Accept all changes.
20. Turn off Track Changes.
21. Preview all pages of the document at the same time.
22. Zoom in on the bottom of page 2.
23. Insert a page break before the heading *Why Smart Loans?*.
24. Close Print Preview and close the Document Map.
25. Insert a Next Page section break before the heading *Addendum*, then change the left and right margins in the new section to 1.25".
26. Save the document.
27. Display the Web toolbar.

28. Open the Internet Simulation:

    a. Click **Go**.

    b. Click **Open**.

    c. In the Address line type the following: D:/Internet/E66/financing.htm

       ✓ *If you've copied the Internet simulation files to your hard drive or your CD-ROM drive is a letter other than D:, substitute the correct letter for D.*

    d. Click **OK**.

29. Click the *Size Standards* link.

30. Click the *121.101 What are SBA size standards?* TXT button.

31. Save the page as html only with the name **WD66-2.htm**.

32. Exit the simulation.

33. Open the **WD66-2.htm** document.

34. Arrange both documents on screen.

35. Copy the paragraph from the *121.101 What are SBA size standard?* section from **WD66-2.htm** and paste it at the end of **WD66-1.doc**.

36. Format the pasted text in 12-point serif, regular, and center it.

37. Maximize the **WD66-2.htm**.

38. Save the document and close it.

39. In **WD66-1.doc**, create a header on all but the first page. Put your name flush left and the date flush right.

40. Create a footer on all pages that has the page number centered.

41. Save the changes to **WD66-1.doc**.

42. Preview the document.

43. Print page four. It should look similar to the document shown in Illustration B.

44. Save the changes to the document, then close the file and exit Word.

Program Name
"Encouraging the Growth of Small Businesses"
A program of the Northern New England Credit Union
For more information, contact: Brian Foley

Tab ^Loan Officer *Tab*

Tab ^20 South Main Street

Tab ^Hanover, NH03755

Tab ^(603) 555-6934 ^*Insert comment. Use Foley's direct line.*

Heading 1 — Introduction

In the past 18 months, NNECU has become aware of the diverse community of small businesses springing up throughout the region. These businesses are a productive segment of the local economy, and deserve attention as such. After conducting a comprehensive study[1], NNECU has formulated a plan to help serve the financial needs of these vibrant and growing businesses.

The plan, called Program Name, is designed to encourage growth and financial success in a wide range of businesses. NNECU intends to seek out companies and individuals that can demonstrate a thoughtful and aggressive approach, and then provide the necessary financial support.

Heading 1 — Why Program Name?

Small business loans are nothing new, and NNECU has been issuing them for decades. What makes Program Name special? Program Name is a carefully managed financial program, similar in many ways to an investment fund, rather than a loan program. Program Name recipients will be responsible for more than just monthly payments. They will be required to provide constant justification of the resources received. In addition, NNECU will maintain an active role is monitoring and supervising the recipient's business operations.

Heading 1 — Target Market

The businesses most likely to benefit from the Program Name program are those that have successfully entered the business arena but are stymied by the problems encountered by growth. The particular industry segment is secondary to the business plan. That said, NNECU recognizes that certain industries are currently more suited to the Program Name program than other industries. According to a recently published report[2], Internet and Web-related businesses are experiencing strong growth and exceptional financial returns. NNECU will also focus on as other technology- and communications-driven concerns. ^ *Insert comment. Add 2 or 3 other specific industries*

Another factor that will greatly influence a company's acceptance into the Program Name program is its ability to expand outside the region. As a rapidly expanding financial institution, NNECU is interested in sponsoring this type of national, even global, vision.

Heading 1 — Risk Factors

Although NNECU expects to carefully screen and monitor all applicants to the Program Name program, some risk is inevitable. NNECU has identified the following risk factors as being of the most concern:

Bullet list

Inexperienced management at the applicant company
Misrepresentation of the applicant's current financial situation
Overestimates of applicant's growth potential ^ *Insert comment. Take this out?*
Fluctuations in regional economy

NNECU intends to take the following action to minimize risk:

Bullet list

Background checks of all management teams
Thorough audits to insure accurate financial data
Thorough market studies to insure growth potential

Heading 1 — Conclusion

Program Name is an exciting and innovative program that NNECU believes will provide a vital boost to the regional economy. To date, ten small businesses have expressed interest in the program, and two have submitted applications[3]. NNECU is looking forward to getting Program Name off and running.

Heading 1 — Addendum

NNECU complies with requirements set by the Small Business Administration.

---

[1] Brian Foley, *Program Name Loan Program Survey*, (Chicago: NNECU Research, 1999)
[2] Janice Brown, *Industries to Watch,* (New York: Business Publishing, 1999)
[3] For a list of applicants, contact Brian Foley at NNECU.

Illustration B

Your Name

5/3/99

Addendum

NNECU complies with requirements set by the Small Business Administration.

SBA's size standards define whether a business entity is
small and, thus, eligible for Government programs and preferences
reserved for "small business" concerns. Size standards have been
established for types of economic activity, or industry,
generally under the Standard Industrial Classification (SIC)
System. The SIC System is described in the "Standard Industrial
Classification Manual" published by the Office of Management and
Budget, Executive Office of the President, and sold by the U.S.
Government Printing Office, Superintendent of Documents, P.O. Box
371954, Pittsburgh, PA 15250-7954. The SIC System assigns
four-digit SIC codes to all economic activity within ten major
divisions. Section 121.201 describes the size standards now
established. A full table matching a size standard with each
four-digit SIC code is also published annually by SBA in the
Federal Register.

4

Lesson 10

Desktop Publishing and Automation

Exercise 67

◆ **Newspaper Columns** ◆ **Column Width**
◆ **Column Breaks** ◆ **Balance Columns**

On the Job

Designing a document with columns lets you present more information on a page, as well as create a visually interesting page. Newspaper-style columns are useful for creating documents such as newsletters, pamphlets, articles, or brochures.

The owner of The Sweet Tooth Candy Shop has asked you to design a newsletter. In this exercise, you will create a newsletter to send to customers.

Terms

Newspaper-style columns Columns in which text flows from the bottom of one column to the top of the next column.

Gutter The space between column margins.

Notes

Newspaper Columns

- By default, a Word document has one column, the width of the page from the left margin to the right margin.

- Use Word's Columns feature to divide a document into more than one **newspaper-style column**.

  ✓ Use tables to create-side-by side columns; use the Columns feature to create newspaper-style columns; use tabs to align data along a line in a document.

- You can apply column formatting to existing text or you can set column formatting before typing new text.

- You can apply column formatting to an entire document or to the current section.

- By dividing a document into sections, you can combine different numbers of columns within a single document.

  ✓ See Exercise 58 for information on section breaks.

- Multiple columns are not displayed in Normal view. Switch to Print Layout view or Print Preview to see the column formatting in a document.

Column Width

- By default, Word creates columns of equal width.

- You can change the width of any column. Select from Word's five preset column width arrangements or set precise column widths.

The Columns dialog box

Select a preset arrangement here

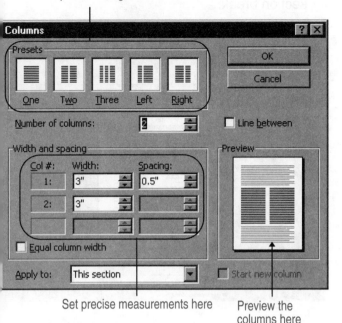

Set precise measurements here

Preview the columns here

■ You can also set the amount of space in the **gutter** between columns. Drag column margins to adjust gutter spacing.

■ You can also drag column markers on the horizontal ruler to adjust column widths.

Drag column markers to adjust columns

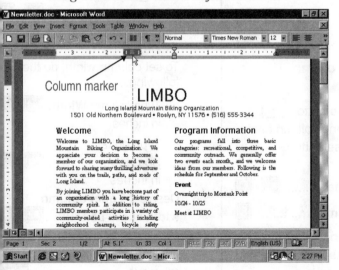

Column marker

Columns in a document

Gray area indicates width of gutter — Column margin

Dotted line shows → new location

Column Breaks

■ By default, text flows to the top of the next column when the current column is filled.

■ Use a column break to force text to flow to the top of the next column before the current column is filled.

■ Column breaks are useful for moving headings or headlines to the top of a column.

Column breaks in a document

Heading moves to the new column

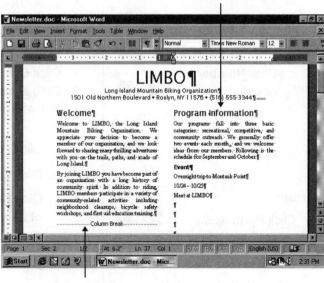

Column break

Balance Columns

- If there is not enough text to fill the last column in a document, the columns will appear uneven.

- You can balance the amount of text in multiple columns on a page by using a continuous section break.

Uneven Columns

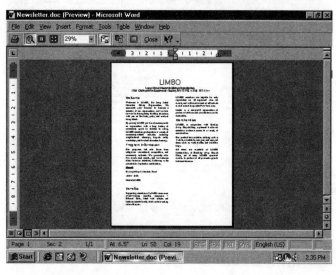

Balanced Columns

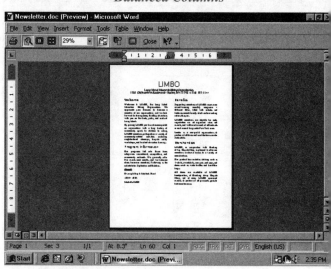

Procedures

Create Columns of Equal Width

1. Click the **Columns** button ▦.
2. Drag across the number of columns to create.
3. Release mouse button.
   OR
   a. Click **Format** .... [Alt]+[O]
   b. Click **Columns** .... [C]
   c. Click **Number of columns** .... [Alt]+[N]
   d. Type number of columns to create.
   e. Click **OK** .... [Enter]

Select a Preset Column Format

1. Click **Format** .... [Alt]+[O]
2. Click **Columns** .... [C]
3. Click desired Presets option:

   - **One**  .... [Alt]+[O]
   - **Two** ▦ .... [Alt]+[W]

   - **Three** ▦ .... [Alt]+[T]
   - **Left** ▦ .... [Alt]+[L]
   - **Right** ▦ .... [Alt]+[R]

4. Click **OK** .... [Enter]

Return to One Column Formatting

1. Click **Columns** button ▦.
2. Drag across one column only.
3. Release mouse button.
   OR
   a. Click **Format** .... [Alt]+[O]
   b. Click **Columns** .... [C]
   c. Click **Number of columns** .... [Alt]+[N]
   d. Type **1** *1*
   e. Click **OK** .... [Enter]

Create Columns of Any Width

1. Click **Format** .... [Alt]+[C]
2. Click **Columns** .... [C]
3. Click **Number of columns** .... [Alt]+[N]
4. Type the number of columns to create.
5. To set column width, do the following:
   a. Type column **Width** .. [Alt]+[I] in inches.
   b. Type gutter **Spacing** .... [Alt]+[S] in inches.
6. Deselect **Equal column width** check box .... [Alt]+[E]
7. Press **Tab** to set spacing for additional columns.
8. Click **OK** .... [Enter]

Adjust Column Width

1. Position mouse pointer on column marker.
   ✓ *When positioned correctly, the ScreenTip shows Move Column.*
2. Drag left or right.

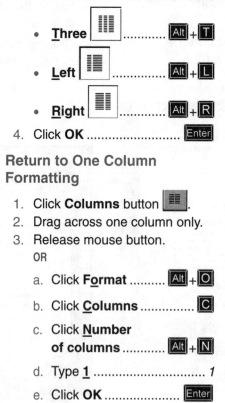

Adjust Gutter Spacing

1. Position mouse pointer on column margin marker.

   ✓ *When positioned correctly, the ScreenTip shows either Left Margin or Right Margin.*

2. Drag left or right.

Insert Column Break

1. Position insertion point where you want the break.

2. Click **Insert**.................. Alt+I

3. Click **Break**......................... B

4. Click **Column break**........... C

5. Click **OK**......................... Enter

Balance Columns

1. Position insertion point at end of last column.

2. Click **Insert**.................. Alt+I

3. Click **Break**......................... B

4. Click **Continuous**............... T

5. Click **OK**......................... Enter

Exercise Directions

1. Start Word, if necessary.

2. Open ⊙ **67NEWS**.

3. Save the document as **WD67**.

4. Format the document as follows:

   a. Center the title in 48-point serif, bold.

   b. Center lines 2 and 3 in 14-point serif.

   c. Leave 12 points of space after address.

   d. Format all four headlines in 16-point bold sans serif, flush left, with 3 points of space before and 3 points of space after.

      ✓ *You can use Outline view to promote the headlines to Heading 1 level.*

   e. Format all body text in 12-point serif, justified, with 3 points of space before and 3 points of space after.

   f. Format the five events in the *Happenings* section in 14-point serif. Make the event names bold but leave the dates regular.

   g. Use a right tab to align the dates of the events. Select all five lines and set a right tab at 2.5", then insert the tab for each line.

5. Format the entire document into three columns of equal width.

6. Preview the document.

7. Return to one column formatting.

8. Insert a continuous section break before the headline *Welcome*.

   ✓ *There are now two sections in the document.*

9. Format the second section (from the headline *Welcome* to the end of the document) into two columns of equal width.

10. Preview the document.

11. Increase the spacing between the columns to .75".

12. Preview the document.

13. Insert a column break before the headline *Happenings*.

    ✓ *This moves the headline to the top of the second column.*

14. Insert another continuous section break before the headline *School Support*.

    ✓ *There are now three sections in the document.*

15. Format the third section (from the headline *School Support* to the end of the document) using the Left Preset arrangement.

16. Preview the document.

17. Try balancing the columns in the third section by inserting a continuous section break at the end of the document.

18. Preview the document. It should look similar to the one in Illustration A.

    ✓ *If necessary, use Shrink to Fit to eliminate an extra page.*

19. Print the document.

20. Save the document.

21. Close the document and exit Word.

Sweet Talk

A Newsletter for Friends of The Sweet Tooth Candy Shop and Soda Fountain
321 Main Street Hanover, NH 03755 (603) 555-9009

Welcome

Welcome to *Sweet Talk*, the first issue of a newsletter for friends and customers of The Sweet Tooth Candy Shop. The goal if this publication is to provide interested consumers with information about activities at the Sweet Tooth as well as general information about candy and other related topics.

Please feel free to let us know which features you like and which you do not. When space permits, we will publish letters to the editor. We are also interested in story ideas.

You have received this issue because you signed the guest book at The Sweet Tooth or you ordered items from The Sweet Tooth On-line. If you do not wish to receive future issues of Sweet Talk, fill out and return the cancellation form on the last page.

Happenings

If you are a frequent visitor to The Sweet Tooth, you know that there is always something going on at 321 Main Street. From contests to cooking, to candy tasting, we try to fill the calendar with interesting and delicious activities that the whole family will enjoy.

We hope you'll stop in to see what's going on. The following events are scheduled for the coming months:

Spring Sale March 14-21

Truffle Tasting April 5

Fruit Dipping April 22

Sundae-Making May 1

Mother's Day Sale May 1-21

School Support

The Sweet Tooth Candy Shop and Soda Fountain is proud to support the local schools. In addition to contributing items for fundraising events such as raffles and auctions, The Sweet Tooth has agreed to donate a portion of all sales during the month of April to the parent/teacher organizations of the Hanover Public Schools.

The Sweet Tooth Gift Shop

In addition to candy, and ice cream, The Sweet Tooth has a large selection of gift items available for all occasions. In our gift shop you will find clothing for all ages, including T-shirts, sweatshirts, and caps. You'll also find ceramic plates and coffee mugs in a variety of styles and designs, candy-making accessories, kitchen gadgets, cards, stationery, calendars, books, and other wonderful items. Many of these items are handmade by local artisans, and are sold exclusively at The Sweet Tooth or at The Sweet Tooth On-line, our Web site.

On Your Own

1. Start Word and create a new document.

2. Save it as **OWD67**.

3. Set the document up as a newsletter. The newsletter might be about yourself, an organization of which you are a member, or about the place where you work. Include two or three articles. For example, in a newsletter about yourself you can write an article about classes you are taking, jobs you have, trips you have taken or are going to take, or movies or T.V. shows you have watched recently.

4. Use section breaks to format the newsletter with different numbers of columns. For example, use one column for the title across the top and two or three columns for the articles.

5. Use formatting such as spacing, fonts, and font effects to enhance the appearance of the document.

6. Try adjusting the width of the columns.

7. Try changing the number of columns.

8. Insert column breaks as necessary.

9. Balance the columns if necessary.

10. Print the document.

11. Save the document, close it, and exit Word.

Exercise 68

On the Job

Dropped capital letters, borders, and shading can call attention to a single word, a line, a paragraph, or an entire page. They make a document visually appealing and interesting to the reader, so the reader will be more likely to take the time to read and remember the text.

The Sweet Tooth Candy Shop wants you to create a one-page flyer that they can distribute to customers. You'll use newspaper-style columns for the flyer. You'll enhance the document with dropped capitals, borders, and shading.

Terms

Dropped capital An enlarged capital letter that drops below the first line of body text in a paragraph.

Border A line placed on one or more sides of a paragraph(s), page, or text box.

Shading A color or pattern applied to a paragraph(s), page, or text box.

3D A perspective added to a border to give the appearance of three dimensions.

Shadow An effect designed to give the appearance of a shadow behind a border.

Notes

Dropped Capitals

- **Dropped capital** letters, called drop caps, are used to call attention to opening paragraphs.

- Drop caps can be placed in the margin to the left of the paragraph, or within the paragraph.

Drop Cap dialog box

- Drop caps can be in the same font as the surrounding text or in a different font.

- Selecting a different more decorative font can enhance the drop cap effect.

  ✓ *In Normal view, drop caps will not appear exactly as they will in a printed document. Use Print Layout or Print preview to display the drop cap correctly.*

Borders and Shading

- You can apply **borders** and **shading** to a paragraph or selected paragraphs.

- You can apply page borders to the whole document or to specified section(s).

- Basic border and shading options are similar to those for tables, including line style, line width (weight), and line color.

- Additional border options include **3D** or **Shadow** effects.

A shadow border

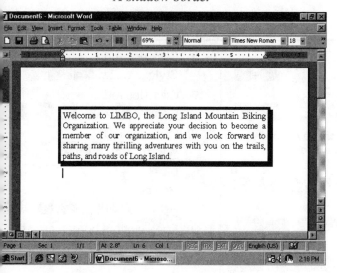

Word has a built-in list of artwork designed for page borders. Art borders are useful for stationery, invitations, and other informal, decorative documents.

Page border in a document

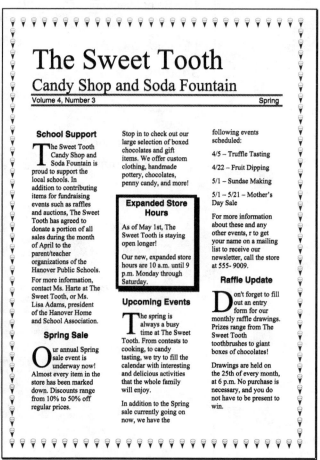

You can apply borders and shading using the Borders and Shading dialog box or using the Tables and Borders toolbar.

✓ Applying borders and shading in a table are covered in Exercise 49.

The Borders and Shading dialog box

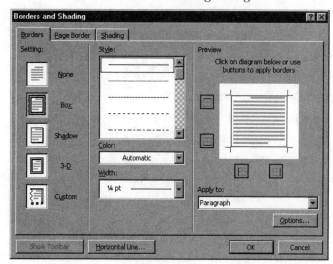

The Borders and Shading dialog box, Page Border Tab

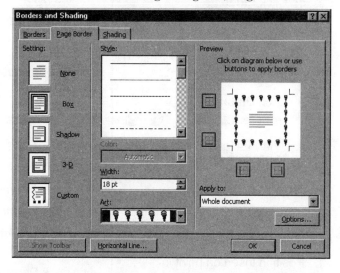

The Borders and Shading dialog box, Shading Tab

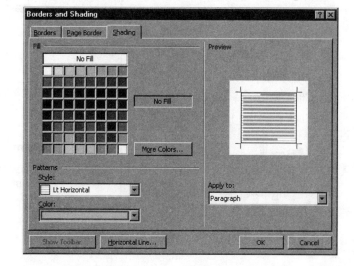

Procedures

Dropped Capital

1. Position insertion point in the paragraph.
2. Click **F**ormat .... `Alt`+`O`
3. Click **D**rop Cap .... `D`
4. Select one of the following:
   - **D**ropped .... `Alt`+`D`
   - In **M**argin .... `Alt`+`M`
     - ✓ Click *N*one to remove an existing drop cap.
5. If desired, do the following:
   a. Click **F**ont drop-down arrow .... `Alt`+`F`
   b. Select font to apply.
   c. Click **L**ines to drop .... `Alt`+`L`
   d. Type the number of lines to drop capital letter.
      - ✓ *The default is three.*
   e. Click **Distance** from te**x**t .... `Alt`+`X`
   f. Type the distance from text to position dropped capital (in inches).
      - ✓ *The default is zero.*
6. Click **OK** .... `Enter`

Paragraph Borders

1. Position insertion point in paragraph.
   OR
   Select paragraphs.
2. Click **F**ormat .... `Alt`+`O`
3. Click **B**orders and Shading .... `B`
4. Click **B**orders tab............... `B`
5. Click a Setting option:
   - Bo**x** .... `Alt`+`X`
   - Sh**a**dow .... `Alt`+`A`

   - 3-**D** .... `Alt`+`D`
   - C**u**stom .... `Alt`+`U`
     - ✓ *Click *N*one to remove existing border.*
6. Click desired St**y**le .... `Alt`+`Y`, `↓`, `↑`
7. Click desired **Color** .. `Alt`+`C`, `↓`, `↑`, `Enter`
8. Click desired **Width** ... `Alt`+`W`, `↑`, `↓`, `Enter`
9. For a custom border, click the desired button in the preview area to position border:
   - **Top** button
   - **Bottom** button
   - **Left** button
   - **Right** button
10. Click **OK** .... `Enter`

Page Borders

1. Position insertion point in paragraph.
   OR
   Select Paragraphs.
2. Click **F**ormat............... `Alt`+`O`
3. Click **B**orders and Shading .... `B`
4. Click **P**age Border tab .... `P`
5. Click **Setting** option:
   - Bo**x** .... `Alt`+`X`
   - Sh**a**dow .... `Alt`+`A`
   - 3-**D** .... `Alt`+`D`
   - C**u**stom .... `Alt`+`U`
     - ✓ *Click *N*one to remove existing border.*

---

6. Click desired St**y**le .... `Alt`+`Y`, `↓`, `↑`
7. Click desired **Color** .. `Alt`+`C`, `↓`, `↑`, `Enter`
8. Click desired **Width**.. `Alt`+`W`, `↑`, `↓`, `Enter`
   OR
   Select desired **Art**....... `Alt`+`R`, `↑`, `↓`, `Enter`
9. For a custom border, click the desired button in preview area to position border:
   - **Top** button
   - **Bottom** button
   - **Left** button
   - **Right** button
10. Select section(s) to App**ly** to .... `Alt`+`L`, `↑`, `↓`, `Ente`
11. Click **OK**........................... `Ente`

Shading

1. Position insertion point in paragraph.
   OR
   Select paragraphs.
2. Click **F**ormat............... `Alt`+`C`
3. Click **B**orders and Shading................... `E`
4. Click **S**hading tab............... `S`
5. Click **Fill**....... `Tab`, `Shift`, `↑`, `↓`
6. If desired:
   - Select Patterns St**y**le .... `Alt`+`Y`, `↑` `↓`, `Enter`
   - Select Patterns **Color** .... `Alt`+`C`, `↑` `↓`, `Enter`
7. Click **OK**................... `Tab`+`Ente`

340

Exercise Directions

1. Start Word, if necessary.

2. Open ⊘ **68SWEET**.

3. Save the document as **WD68**.

4. Format the banner (title lines) and dateline (volume, number, and date information) as follows:

   a. Use a 48-point bold serif font for *The Sweet Tooth* on the first line, and a 28-point bold serif font for *Candy Shop and Soda Fountain* on the second line.

   b. Select line 3 (the dateline) and change the font to sans serif, 12 points.

   c. Left-align the volume and number information, and use a right tab to align the date (*Spring*) on the right end of the line.

   d. Move the insertion point to the end of the third line, then change the font size to 16 points (this increases the height of the line for the border applied in the next step), and the paragraph spacing to 36 points after.

   e. Apply a ¾-point double line border above and below the paragraph.

   f. Insert a continuous section break before the first headline: *School Support*.

   g. Format the second section of the document in three columns of equal width.

5. Use 14-point bold sans serif centered text for headlines.

6. Use 12-point serif flush left text for the body text.

7. Leave 3 points before and 6 points after every paragraph (including headlines).

8. Using default settings, create dropped capitals as shown.

9. Select the three paragraphs beginning with the headline *Expanded Store Hours* and apply a 4.5 point shadow paragraph border and a 12.5% gray shading.

10. Apply the Ice Cream Cones page border (select the border from the Art drop-down list).

11. Check the spelling and grammar.

12. Preview the document. It should look similar to the one in Illustration A.

13. Print the document.

14. Close the document and exit Word, saving all changes.

The Sweet Tooth

Candy Shop and Soda Fountain

Volume 4, Number 3   Spring

School Support

The Sweet Tooth Candy Shop and Soda Fountain is proud to support the local schools. In addition to contributing items for fundraising events such as raffles and auctions, The Sweet Tooth has agreed to donate a portion of all sales during the month of April to the parent/teacher organizations of the Hanover Public Schools.

For more information, contact Ms. Harte at The Sweet Tooth, or Ms. Lisa Adams, president of the Hanover Home and School Association.

Spring Sale

Our annual Spring sale event is underway now! Almost every item in the store has been marked down. Discounts range from 10% to 50% off regular prices.

Stop in to check out our large selection of boxed chocolates and gift items. We offer custom clothing, handmade pottery, chocolates, penny candy, and more!

Expanded Store Hours

As of May 1st, The Sweet Tooth is staying open longer!

Our new, expanded store hours are 10 a.m. until 9 p.m. Monday through Saturday.

Upcoming Events

The spring is always a busy time at The Sweet Tooth. From contests to cooking, to candy tasting, we try to fill the calendar with interesting and delicious activities that the whole family will enjoy.

In addition to the Spring sale currently going on now, we have the following events scheduled:

4/5 – Truffle Tasting

4/22 – Fruit Dipping

5/1 – Sundae Making

5/1 – 5/21 – Mother's Day Sale

For more information about these and any other events, r to get your name on a mailing list to receive our newsletter, call the store at 555- 9009.

Raffle Update

Don't forget to fill out an entry form for our monthly raffle drawings. Prizes range from The Sweet Tooth toothbrushes to giant boxes of chocolates!

Drawings are held on the 25th of every month, at 6 p.m. No purchase is necessary, and you do not have to be present to win.

On Your Own

1. Open **OWD67**, the newsletter document you created in the On Your Own section of Exercise 8, or open ⊙ **68NEWS**.

2. Save the file as **OWD68**.

3. Apply dropped capitals to the first paragraph of each article.

4. Use borders to call attention to paragraphs. Try different effects, including different line styles, shadows, and 3-D. You might want to insert a border between the single column section and the multi-column section.

5. Apply a page border.

6. If necessary, adjust column breaks and balance columns to improve the appearance of the newsletter.

7. Print the document.

8. Save the document, close it, and exit Word.

Exercise 69

On the Job

Templates and Wizards help you create similar documents repeatedly. Templates include page setup and formatting settings to insure that new documents will be uniform. In many cases they include standard text and graphics as well. Wizards are automated templates that prompt you to provide information that can be used to customize the resulting document.

Tom Louris, the President of Cornerstone Graphics, is planning a business trip to Bayside Custom Clothing, a client in San Francisco. As an administrative assistant at Bayside, you are in charge of coordinating the itinerary. In this exercise, you will use a template to create a memo document. You will then use a Wizard to create a fax cover sheet.

Terms

Template A Word document on which new documents are based. Templates include formatting settings, text, and graphics used to create the new documents.

Dot extension The file extension assigned by Word to template files.

Normal.dot The default template used to create new documents in Word.

Wizard An automated template.

Notes

Templates

- All new Word documents are based on a **template**.
- Templates include formatting settings such as margins, font, and font size.
- Some templates include boilerplate text and graphics that will be part of new documents.

Memo template in Word

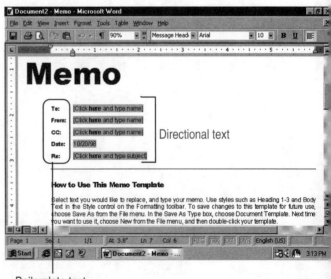

Boilerplate text

344

- All new documents based on the same template will have the same default formatting settings and will display any boilerplate text and graphics.

- Some templates include editing directions or sample text for completing the document. You replace sample text, fill in missing information, and customize the document using standard editing and formatting commands.

- Word comes with built-in templates for creating common documents such as memos, letters, and resumes.

- Built-in templates are usually available in several styles, which means different formatting settings for different situations. For example, a letter in the Professional template may be suitable for business correspondence, while the Elegant, template may be more suitable for personal correspondence.

- You can preview built-in templates in the New dialog box.

- Template files have a **.dot extension**. The default template for creating a blank document is called **Normal.dot**.

New dialog box

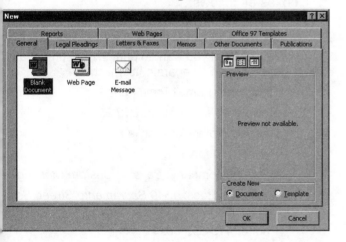

Wizards

- You can use **Wizards** to create customized new documents.

- Wizards prompt you through a series of dialog boxes to enter information that can be incorporated into the document.

  ✓ *The flowchart in the first dialog box indicates how many dialog boxes there are.*

Memo Wizard

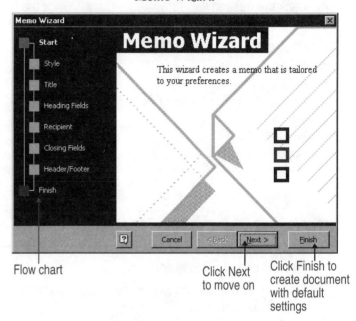

Flow chart   Click Next   Click Finish to
                    to move on   create document
                                        with default
                                        settings

- For example, a memo Wizard might prompt you for the recipient's name and the memo subject. When Word creates the document, the recipient's name and the memo subject will be entered automatically.

- You can customize documents created with a Wizard using standard editing and formatting commands.

Procedures

Create a Document Using a Template

1. Click **File** .... Alt + F
2. Click **New** .... N
3. Click the desired tab.... Ctrl + Tab
4. Click the desired template icon............... ↑, ↓
5. Click **OK** .... Enter
6. Replace directions and prompts with text.
7. Edit and format document as desired.
8. Name and save document .... Ctrl + S

Create a Document Using a Wizard

1. Click **File** .... Alt + F
2. Click **New** .... N
3. Click the desired tab ... Ctrl + Tab
4. Click the desired Wizard icon.................. ↑, ↓
5. Click **OK** .... Enter
6. Respond to prompts in dialog box.
7. Click **Next** .... Alt + N

   ✓ *Click Back to return to previous dialog box to change responses. Click Finish to create document with default settings.*

8. Repeat steps 6 and 7 until last dialog box is displayed.
9. Click **Finish** .... Alt + F
10. Edit and format document as desired.
11. **Save** document............ Ctrl + S

Exercise Directions

1. Start Word, if necessary.
2. Use the Professional Memo template to create a new document.
3. Save the file as **WD69-1**.
4. Replace the sample text with the following information as shown in Illustration A:
   Company Name: Bayside Custom Clothing
   To: Jack Shepard
   From: Your Name
   Cc: Theresa Cassell
   Date: Current date
   Re: Visit of Tom Louris
5. Replace the text *How to Use This Memo Template* and the following paragraph with the text shown in Illustration A.
6. Preview the document, and then print it.
7. Save and close the document.
8. Use the Fax Wizard to create a fax cover sheet.

9. Complete the prompts in the Wizard dialog boxes as follows:
   - In the document to fax screen, select the option to create just a cover sheet with a note.
   - Specify that you want to print the document and send it from a separate fax machine.

   Recipient's name: *Tom Louris*

   Recipient's fax number: *213-555-1112*

   Use the Professional style.

   Sender: *Your Name*

   Sender's company: *Bayside Custom Clothing*

   Mailing address: *1349 Sacramento Street, San Francisco, CA 94109*

   Phone: *415-555-0821*

   Fax: *415-555-0822*
10. Replace all remaining sample text in the document as shown in Illustration B.

    ✓ *Double-click in the Please Reply box to insert the check mark.*
11. Save the document as **WD69-2**.
12. Preview the document and then print it.
13. Close the document and exit Word, saving all changes.

Illustration A

**Bayside Custom
Clothing**

Memo

To: Jack Shepard

From: Your Name

CC: Theresa Cassell

Date: 05/03/99

Re: Visit of Tom Louris

Finalized Itinerary

We've finalized the details for Mr. Louris' visit to Bayside next week. The only major change to the original schedule is that the luncheon is now on Wednesday instead of Thursday.

I'll send along the complete final itinerary ASAP. Give me a call if you have any questions.

1

1349 Sacramento St.
San Francisco, CA 94109
Phone: 415-555-0821
Fax: 415-555-0822

Bayside Custom Clothing

To:	Tom Louris	**From:**	Your Name
Fax:	213-555-1112	**Date:**	May 3, 1999
Phone:	213-555-1002	**Pages:**	2, Including cover
Re:	Itinerary	**CC:**	Jack Shepard

☐ **Urgent**   ☐ **For Review**   ☐ **Please Comment**   ☑ **Please Reply**   ☐ **Please Recycle**

•**Comments:** Mr. Louris – Here's the itinerary for your trip to San Francisco. See you next week!

On Your Own

1. Start Word and use the Letter Wizard to create a new document.

2. Save the document as **OWD69**.

3. In the document, type a letter to a friend or relative explaining some of the documents you have learned to create with Word.

4. Use the Envelope Wizard to create an envelope for the letter

5. Add the envelope to the document, and save it as **OWD69-2**.

6. Print the documents.

7. Save the documents, close them, and exit Word.

Exercise 70

On the Job

Use styles to apply a collection of formatting settings to characters or paragraphs. Styles help ensure continuity in formatting throughout a document. You can also quickly change formatting in a document that is formatted with styles; when you modify a style, you change all text already formatted with that style.

The head of training at State-of-the-Art Solutions has asked you to prepare a document listing classes for the first three months of the year. In this exercise, you will use styles to format the document.

Terms

Style A collection of formatting settings that can be applied to characters or paragraphs.

Style sheet A list of available styles.

Notes

Styles

- **Styles** make it easy to apply a collection of formatting settings to characters or paragraphs all at once.

- Word includes built-in styles for formatting body text, headings, and other parts of documents.

- Different Word templates have different **style sheets** depending on formatting required for the document. For example, the default Normal template uses only five styles, while the Resume template includes 25 styles.

The Normal template style sheet

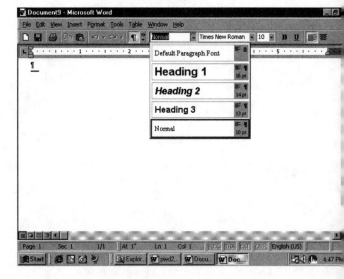

A portion of the Resume template style sheet

- You have already used styles in the exercises for working with outlines.
- You can apply a style to existing text, or select a style before you type new text.

Create a Style

- You can create new styles for formatting your documents.
- Styles can contain font and/or paragraph formatting.
- Style names should be short and descriptive.

Edit a Style

- You can modify an existing style.
- When you modify a style that has already been applied to text in the document, the formatted text automatically changes to the new style.
- If you modify a style and give it a new name, it becomes a new style; the original style remains unchanged.

Modify Style dialog box

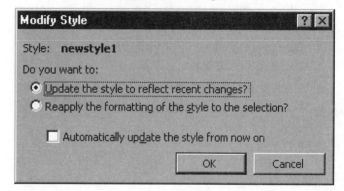

Procedures

Apply a Style

1. Click in the paragraph.
   OR
   Select the text.
2. Click the **Style** drop-down arrow `Normal` on the Formatting toolbar.
3. Select Style to apply .... `↑`, `↓`, `Enter`

Create a Style

1. Format text or paragraph.
2. Click in the Style box on the Formatting toolbar.
3. Type style name.
4. Press **Enter**..................... `Enter`

Edit a Style

1. Change formatting of text or paragraph formatted with the style.
2. Click in **Style** box `Normal` on the Formatting toolbar.
3. Press **Enter**..................... `Enter`
4. Click **Update the style to reflect recent changes?** .... `Alt`+`U`
5. Click **OK** .... `Enter`

View Style Settings *(Shift+F1)*

1. Click **Help** .... `Alt`+`H`
2. Click **What's This**............... `T`
3. Click text formatted with style.
   ✓ *Click Esc to turn off What's This pointer?*

OR

1. Click **Format**............... `Alt`+`O`
2. Click **Style** .... `S`
3. Click the name in the **Styles** list....... `Alt`+`S`, `↑`, `↓`
4. Read description.
5. View Paragraph preview.
6. Click **Cancel** .... `Esc`

Exercise Directions

1. Start Word, if necessary.

2. Open ⊙ **70COURSE**.

3. Save the document as **WD70**.

4. Apply heading styles as indicated in Illustration A.

5. Increase the font size of the title, *State-of-the-Art Solutions*, to 26 points, and center the first three lines of text.

6. Modify the Heading 1 style to include the changes made to the title, then apply the Heading 1 style to the text *Training Schedule*.

7. Change the formatting of the name of the course *Microsoft Word 1* to 12 points, bold, with a continuous underline, leaving 6 points of space after the paragraph.

8. Create a new style from the newly formatted text named *Course*.

9. Apply the *Course* style to the other two course names.

10. Format the paragraph of text under the course name *Microsoft Word 1* using 12 points justified, indented 1" from the left and the right.

11. Create a style named *Description* from the newly formatted paragraph.

12. Apply the *Description* style to the text describing the other two courses.

13. Modify the Heading 3 style to 16 points with a 3-point solid line border on the top and left side.

   ✓ *All Heading 3 headings should change.*

14. Modify the *Description* style to include a 3-point solid line border on the bottom and left, and a 20% gray shade.

15. Apply a border around the whole page.

16. Vertically justify the document.

17. Preview the document. It should look similar to the one in Illustration B.

18. Print the document.

19. Close the file and exit Word, saving all changes.

Illustration A

Heading 1 → **State-Of-The-Art Solutions**

P.O. Box 6743211, Brentwood, CA 90049
310-555-0821

Heading 2 → ***Training Schedule***

January

Microsoft Word 1
This introductory course will cover the basics of using Microsoft Word 2000 to create common business documents. By the end of the course you will know how to: create and print text-based documents such as letters and envelopes, and apply formatting.

February

Heading 3

Microsoft Word 2
A continuation of the Word I course, this introductory level class will delve into some of the more intriguing features of Microsoft Word 2000. By the end of the course you will know how to conduct a mail merge, set up a document in columns, include headers and footers, and insert pictures.

March

Microsoft Word 3
This final course in the Microsoft Word series covers the advanced features. By the end of this course you will know how to work with tables, create and modify outlines, use e-mail and Internet features in Word, and share documents with other users.

State-Of-The-Art Solutions

P.O. Box 6743211, Brentwood, CA 90049

310-555-0821

Training Schedule

January

Microsoft Word 1

This introductory course will cover the basics of using Microsoft Word 2000 to create common business documents. By the end of the course you will know how to: create and print text-based documents such as letters and envelopes, and apply formatting.

February

Microsoft Word 2

A continuation of the Word I course, this introductory level class will delve into some of the more intriguing features of Microsoft Word 2000. By the end of the course you will know how to conduct a mail merge, set up a document in columns, include headers and footers, and insert pictures.

March

Microsoft Word 3

This final course in the Microsoft Word series covers the advanced features. By the end of this course you will know how to work with tables, create and modify outlines, use e-mail and Internet features in Word, and share documents with other users.

On Your Own

1. Start Word and open **OWD33**, the one-page report you created in the On Your Own section of Exercise 33, or open ⊚ **70REPORT**.

2. Save the document as **OWD70**.

3. Set the formatting for the text in the first paragraph to the formatting that you like to use most often. For example, select a font you like in an easy to read size, set line and paragraph spacing, and set alignment options.

4. Create a style called *Report Text* from the formatted text and apply the *Report Text* style to the remaining paragraphs in the report.

5. Add a subtitle to a paragraph in the report, formatted in a different and larger font.

6. Create a style from the subtitle text, called *Sub1*.

7. Type at least one other subtitle in the report, and format it (them) using the *Sub1* style.

8. Modify the *Sub1* style.

9. If the document is now more than one page long, add a header and/or footer that includes your name, the date, and a page number.

10. Save the document, close it, and exit Word.

Exercise 71

Skills Covered:

◆ Insert a File

On the Job

Insert a file into another file to save time retyping existing text. When you insert a file, the entire contents of the file becomes part of the current document, while the original file remains unchanged.

You are in charge of responding to requests for information about sale prices at The Sweet Tooth Candy Shop. Since you already have a document listing sale prices, you can insert the list into a letter.

Notes

Insert a File

- You can insert one file into another file to incorporate the first file's contents into the second file.

- The entire contents are saved as part of the second file.

- The first file remains unchanged.

- Inserting a file is different from copying and pasting because you do not have to open the file to insert it, and the entire file contents are inserted—no selecting is necessary.

  ✓ *To see where a file is inserted into an existing document, turn on the Track Changes feature before the insertion.*

Procedures

Insert a File

1. Position the insertion point where you want file inserted.
2. Click **Insert** .... `Alt`+`I`
3. Click **File** .... `L`
4. Select file to insert .... `↓`, `↑`
5. Click **Insert**
   button `📂 Insert ▾` ... `Alt`+`S`

Exercise Directions

1. Start Word, if necessary.
2. Create a new document.
3. Save the file as **WD71**.
4. Type and format the letterhead shown in Illustration A as follows:
   a. Use a serif font.
   b. Type the store name in 28 points, centered, and apply the outline effect.
   c. Type the address in 14 points, centered; use a Wingdings symbol to separate the street address from the city.
   d. Leave 72 points of space after the address.

5. Type the letter shown in Illustration A in a 12-point serif font, using the standard block letter layout.
6. At the location marked in the Illustration, insert the file ⊘ **71SALE**.
7. Center the table on the page.
8. Check the spelling and grammar in the document.
9. Preview the document. It should look similar to Illustration B.
10. Save the document.
11. Print the document.
12. Close the file and exit Word.

The Sweet Tooth

321 Main Street ✧ Hanover, NH 03755

Insert today's date

January 31, 1999

Mr. Stephen Whittier
9066 Lee Drive
Etna, NH 03750

Dear Mr. Whittier:

Thank you for your request for information about the Valentine's Day sale currently taking place at The Sweet Tooth Candy Shop and Soda Fountain. Keep in mind that these prices are good until February 14th only.

Insert 71SALE here. →

Give me a call if you have any questions, or to place an order.

Sincerely,

Cynthia Harte
Owner

CH/yo

Illustration B

The Sweet Tooth
321 Main Street ✧ Hanover, NH 03755

January 31, 1999

Mr. Stephen Whittier
9066 Lee Drive
Etna, NH 03750

Dear Mr. Whittier:

Thank you for your request for information about the Valentine's Day sale currently taking place at The Sweet Tooth Candy Shop and Soda Fountain. Keep in mind that these prices are good until February 14th only.

Candy	Size	Regular Price	Sale Price
White Chocolate Assortment	32 ounces	$48.99	$35.00
Milk Chocolate Assortment	32 ounces	$45.99	$29.99
Assorted Truffles	16 ounces	$21.99	$15.99
Raspberry Creams	16 ounces	$16.99	$12.99
Caramels	16 ounces	$15.99	$11.99
Raspberry Creams	10 ounces	$12.99	$9.99
Caramels	10 ounces	$11.99	$8.99
Super Gift Basket	**20 pounds**	**$ 174.93**	**$115.00**

Give me a call if you have any questions, or to place an order.

Sincerely,

Cynthia Harte
Owner

CH/yo

On Your Own

1. Start Word and create a new document.

2. Save the document as OWD71.

3. Type a brief biography. The biography should be no more than two paragraphs, and it should be appropriate for inclusion in a document such as a yearbook, a team or club roster, or a theater program.

4. Save the document and close it.

5. Create another new document and save it as OWD71-2.

6. Type a letter to the yearbook editor, or the club president, or whoever is responsible for printing the collection of biographies. Leave space above the closing to insert the OWD71 document.

7. Insert the OWD71 biography into the OWD71-2 letter.

8. Save the document, close it, and exit Word.

Exercise 72

◆ Record a Macro ◆ Run a Macro

On the Job

Macros let you simplify tasks that ordinarily require many keystrokes or commands, for example, creating a header or footer, or changing line spacing and indents for a paragraph. Once you record a macro, you can run it at any time to repeat the recorded actions. You can use macros for tasks as simple as opening and printing a document, or for more complicated tasks such as creating a new document, inserting a table, entering text, and applying an AutoFormat.

The president of Cornerstone Graphics, Tom Louris, often asks you to format multi-page documents with the same header, footer, and margins. In this exercise, you will create a macro to insert a header and footer, and you will create a macro to change the margins. You will then use the macros to format a document for Mr. Louris.

Terms

Macro A series of commands and keystrokes that you record and save together. You can run the macro to replay the series.

Normal template A document that stores the default settings for new Word documents.

Shortcut key A combination of keys (including Alt, Ctrl, and/or Shift, and a regular keyboard key) that you assign to run a macro.

Notes

Record a Macro

- Record a **macro** to automate tasks or actions that you perform frequently.

- By default, new macros are stored in the **Normal template**, so they are available for use in all new documents created with the Normal template.

  ✔ *For more information about templates, see Exercise 69.*

- Macros can save time and help eliminate errors.

- A single macro can store an unlimited number of keystrokes or mouse actions.

- You can record mouse actions that select commands in menus and dialog boxes; however, you cannot record mouse actions that select text or position the insertion point.

- Recording a macro is similar to recording on a cassette tape. As soon as you start recording, everything you input into your computer is stored in the macro, just as everything you input into a cassette recorder is stored on a tape.

  ✔ *When recording a macro, the mouse pointer changes to an arrow with a cassette tape icon* 📼 *.*

- A macro is different from AutoText because a macro can store actions and commands as well as text.

- You can assign a **shortcut key** combination, including Alt, Ctrl, and/or Shift and a regular keyboard key, to a macro when you record it. Use the shortcut key combination to play the macro back at any time.

  ✓ *You can also create a toolbar button to assign to the macro.*

- If a macro doesn't work the way you want, you can delete it and record it again.

Run a Macro

- Once you have recorded a macro you can run it at any time.
- When you run a macro, Word executes the recorded commands and actions in the current document.
- Use the key combination you assigned when you recorded the macro to run the macro.
- To perform the macro on part of a document, be sure to select the relevant part first.

Procedures

Record a Macro

1. Position the insertion point where you want it to be when you start recording the macro.
2. Double-click **REC** indicator `REC` on Status bar.

   OR

   a. Click **Tools** .... `Alt`+`T`
   b. Click **Macro** .... `M`
   c. Click **Record New Macro** .... `R`
3. Type a macro name.

   ✓ *Do not use spaces in macro name.*
4. Click **Description** .... `Alt`+`D`
5. Type a description of the macro.
6. Click **Keyboard** .... `Alt`+`K`

7. Press a shortcut key combination.

   ✓ *Word displays a message indicating whether the combination is unassigned or already assigned to a Word command. If you use a combination that is already assigned, the original purpose of the combination is replaced. For example, if you assign the combination Ctrl+S, you will not longer be able to use that combination to save a file.*
8. Click **Assign** .... `Tab`, `Alt`+`A`
9. Click **Close** button

   `Close` .... `Enter`
10. Perform actions to record.

Stop Recording a Macro

- Click the **Stop** button `▼ Stop ✕` `■ ❚❚●` on the Macro Control box.

   OR

1. Click **Tools** .... `Alt`+`T`
2. Click **Macro** .... `M`
3. Click **Stop Recording** .... `R`

   OR

   Double click **REC** indicator `REC` on Status bar.

Run a Macro *(Alt+F8)*

- Press assigned key combination.

   OR

1. Click **Tools** .... `Alt`+`T`
2. Click **Macro** .... `M`
3. Click **Macros** .... `M`
4. Click the name of macro to run .... `↑`, `↓`
5. Click **Run** .... `Alt`+`R`

Delete a Macro *(Alt+F8)*

1. Click **Tools** .... `Alt`+`T`
2. Click **Macro** .... `M`
3. Click **Macros** .... `M`
4. Click the name of macro to delete .... `↑`, `↓`
5. Click **Delete** button

   `Delete` .... `Alt`+`D`
6. Click **Yes** `Yes` .... `Y`
7. Click **Close** button

   `Close` .... `Esc`

Exercise Directions

1. Start Word, if necessary.
2. In a new blank document create the following macros:
   a. Open the Record Macro dialog box.
   b. Name the macro *Header*.
   c. Include the description: *Creates a header and footer in Cornerstone documents.*
   d. Assign the macro to the key combination `Alt`+`Shift`+`H`.
   e. Click Assign and then Close to begin recording the macro keystrokes.
   f. Create a header with the company name flush left and today's date flush right.
   g. Create a footer with your name flush left and the word *Page* followed by a space then the page number flush right.
      ✓ *Close the Header/Footer dialog box. Otherwise, it will remain open when you run the macro.*
   h. Stop recording the macro.

3. Open the Record Macro dialog box and create a second macro as follows:
   a. Name the macro *Margins*.
   b. Enter the description: *Sets all margins to 1".*
   c. Assign the macro to the key combination `Alt`+`Shift`+`G`.
   d. Click Assign and then Close to begin recording the macro keystrokes.
   e. Set all page margins to 1".
   f. Stop recording the macro.
4. Close the blank document without saving any changes.
5. Open ☻**72MACROS**.
6. Save the file as **WD72**.
7. Run the Header macro.
8. Run the Margins macro.
9. Preview the document. It should look similar to the one in Illustration A.
10. Save the changes to the document.
11. Print the document.
12. Close the document and exit Word.

Cornerstone Graphics

920 Marco Place ✧ Venice, CA 90291 ✧ Phone: (213) 555-1002
www.cornerstone.com ✧ email@cornerstone.com

What is Web Page Design?

The World Wide Web is comprised of interconnected documents stored on the global network of computers known as the Internet. The documents are called Web pages. Linked pages are called Web sites. Web sites are uniquely formatted to provide information, collect information, and to capture the attention of consumers.

In today's global marketplace, a presence on the World Wide Web is vital to business success. Creating effective and appealing Web pages is both a skill and an art form that takes technical knowledge, creative abilities, and practice.

Reasons for Developing a Web Site

Studies show that millions of people have access to the Internet at home and/or at work. Forecasts predict that in the near future, Internet access will be as ubiquitous as television and telephones, and those left off the Web will be left behind in competition.

Due to the vast numbers of Internet users around the world, it is simple and cost effective to contact customers, suppliers, and others on-line. The cost of maintaining a Web site is minimal, especially in comparison to other types of marketing. Savings are made throughout the organization, including travel and entertainment costs.

Cornerstone Graphics   05/04/99

Expand Customer Base

These same contacts will lead to business expansion opportunities, with a minimum of actual travel. Another benefit is that a huge amount of information about businesses, markets, regulations, etc. is available on-line. Research can be successfully accomplished from a home office, without requiring costly travel and time spent abroad.

Flexibility

Work can be accomplished regardless of time zone differences and work habits. Not only can your staff use the Web to communicate with others, but also people around the world can contact you even in the middle of the night. Information is available 24 hours a day, seven days a week.

Web sites can be created to suit the customers' needs. Information, design, links, and other features can be developed per customer specifications. Sites can include as many or as few pages as the customer requires. Pages may include order forms, product catalogues, general information, contact names, and so on. Sites can link to existing sites, or other newly developed sites.

Web sites can dispense information and collect information. As customers access the site, demographic information can be collected. Products can be targeted to specific customers. Customers can quickly find the information and/or products they need, and respond immediately, in real time. Customer response can dictate the future development of the site.

Web sites can include graphics, video, and sound in addition to text-based information. For example, sites can be enhanced by the inclusion of video clips of sales presentations or photographs of products.

Your Name   Page 2

On Your Own

1. Start Word and open **OWD71**, the brief biography you created in the On Your Own section of Exercise 71, or open ⊘ **72BIO**.

2. Save the document as **OWD72**, and then close it.

3. Create a new blank document.

4. Create a new macro named *Insertbio* and assign it to a shortcut key combination, such as Shift + Alt + B.

5. Record the keystrokes for inserting the **OWD72** file into the open document.

6. After you stop recording the macro, close the current document without saving the changes.

7. Create a new blank document and save it as **OWD72-2**.

8. Type a document in which you can include your biography. You might type a letter to someone other than the person you wrote to in Exercise 71, or you might type part of a program or yearbook page.

9. At the appropriate location, use the Insertbio macro to insert the **OWD72** file into the **OWD72-2** document.

10. Save the document, close it, and exit Word.

Exercise 73

As director of marketing for Cornerstone Graphics, you need to create dynamic promotional documents. In this exercise, you will use a Wizard to create a memo telling Tom Louris, the company's president, about your marketing plans. You will then format a marketing document about the benefits of using the Web. Since you know that the marketing document will be included with other documents in many mailings, you will create a macro for inserting it into another file. Finally, you will use the macro to insert the marketing document into the memo document.

Exercise Directions

1. Create a new document using the Memo Wizard.

2. Provide the following information in the Wizard dialog boxes:
   - Contemporary style
   - Title: *Cornerstone Graphics*
   - Date: *Default*
   - From: *Your Name*
   - Subject: *New Documents*
   - To: *Tom Louris*
   - Cc: *Jake McNeil*
   - Include: *Attachments*
   - Header/Footer: *Defaults*

3. Save the document with the name **WD73-1**.

4. Complete the document by typing the text shown in Illustration A and applying built-in styles.
   - Use the *Body Text* style for all paragraphs.
   - Use the *Heading 1* style for the two document names.
   - Use the *Closing* style for the closing.
   - Use the *Signature Name* style for your name at the end of the document.

5. Preview the document.

6. Print the document, save all changes, and then close it.

7. Open ⊘**73WEB** and save it as **WD73-2**.

8. Format the letterhead and document title as shown in Illustration B.

9. Apply the Heading 1 style to the headline *Web Site Benefits*.

10. Modify the formatting of the headline to a different sans serif font in 14 points. Leave 6 points of space before and 3 points after the headline.

11. Use the modified text to create a new style named *New Heading*.

12. Apply the *New Heading* style to the other four headings (see Illustration B).

13. Create a new style called *Benefits Text* using the following formatting settings, and apply it to all paragraph text:
    - 12-point serif, justified
    - Leave 3 points of space before and after.

14. Insert a continuous section break before the *Web Site Benefits* headline and format the second section into two columns of equal width.

15. Increase the gutter spacing between the columns to .75".

16. Create dropped capitals as shown in Illustration B.

17. Insert a column break before the heading *Increased Visibility*.

18. Preview the document. It should look similar to the one in Illustration B.

19. Print the document.

20. Save and close the document.

21. Create a new blank document.

22. Create a macro for inserting the **WD73-2** file in another document as follows:
    - Name the new macro *InsertWeb*.
    - Type the description: Inserts Web Benefits Document.
    - Assign the key combination `Alt`+`Shift`+`W`.
    - Record the keystrokes for inserting the file, then stop recording.
23. Close the current document without saving it.
24. Open the **WD73-1** document.
25. Press Ctrl+End and insert a new blank line.
26. Insert a Next Page section break.
27. Run the *InsertWeb* macro.
28. Print the document.
29. Save and close all open documents and exit Word.

Illustration A

cornerstone graphics ← *Title*

Date: 3/2/99

To: Tom Louris

Cc: Jake McNeil

From: Your Name

RE: New Documents

Tom –

Here's the update on the two new marketing documents you've been asking about:

Web Site Benefits ← *Heading 1*

We have approved the final copy and are just working on the formatting. We want the document to really catch the attention of prospective clients. I've attached a print out of one version – I'm particularly pleased with the use of the columns. Let me know if you think the dropped capitals are too much.

Client Testimonial Web Page ← *Heading 1*

This page is also in the final stages, but I'm not ready to show it just yet. We have gathered the testimonials from the original client list and I'm going to set up the page today. I hope to have the new page ready for linking to the corporate site by the end of the week. We'll be able to update it whenever we receive new testimonials.

Let me know if you have any questions or comments.

Thanks, ← *Closing*

Your Name ← *Signature Name*

Attachments

3/2/99

1

28 pt.

12.5% gray

Cornerstone Graphics

920 Marco Place ◊ Venice, CA 90201 ◊ Phone: (213) 555-1002◊ www.cornerstone.com

10 pt.

Double line border ½ pts.

18 pt. centered

12 pt.

Maintaining A Presence on the World Wide Web

12 pt.

Web Site Benefits

In today's global marketplace, a presence on the World Wide Web is vital to business success. Creating effective and appealing Web pages is both a skill and an art form that takes technical knowledge, creative abilities, and practice.

What is the Web?

The Web is comprised of interconnected documents stored on the global network of computers known as the Internet. The documents are called Web pages. Related pages are linked into Web sites. Web sites are uniquely formatted to provide information, and to capture the attention of consumers around the world.

Increased Visibility

Studies show that literally millions of people have access to the Internet at home and/or at work and that new connections are being made by the thousands. Forecasts predict that in the near future, Internet access will be as ubiquitous as television and telephones, and those left off the Web will be left behind in competition.

Due to the vast numbers of Internet users around the world, it is simple and cost effective to contact customers, suppliers, and others on-line. Personal relationships can be established and maintained using computers, instead of scheduling expensive travel.

Increased Opportunities

These same contacts will lead to business expansion opportunities, with a minimum of actual travel. Another benefit is that a huge amount of information about businesses, markets, regulations, etc. is available on-line. Research can be successfully accomplished from a home office, without requiring costly travel and time spent abroad.

Work can be accomplished regardless of time zone differences and work habits. Not only can your staff use the Web to communicate with others, but people around the world can contact you even in the middle of the night. Information is available 24 hours a day, seven days a week.

Flexibility

Web sites can dispense information and collect information. As customers access the site, demographic information can be collected. Products can be targeted to specific customers. Customers can quickly find the information and/or products they need, and respond immediately, in real time. Customer response can dictate the future development of the site.

Lesson 11

Graphics

Exercise 74

On the Job

Use graphics, such as clip art and text boxes, to illustrate and enhance text documents. Graphics can make a document easier to read and more interesting for the reader.

The owner of The Sweet Tooth Candy Shop wants you to enhance the newsletter that you created for her. In this exercise, you will expand your desktop publishing skills using clip art and text boxes.

Terms

Graphics object A picture, chart, shape, or other element that can be inserted into a Word document.

Clip art Picture files that can be inserted into a Word document.

Text box A rectangular graphics object in which text or graphics images can be inserted and positioned anywhere on a page.

Floating object A graphics object that is positioned independently from the document text.

Bounding box A nonprinting border around the outside of an object. When the object is selected the bounding box is sometimes called the selection box, or selection rectangle.

Sizing handles Small black rectangles on the edge of a selected object, used to change the size of the object. The mouse pointer is a two-headed arrow when resting on a sizing handle.

In line A graphics object that is positioned as a text character along with other text characters in the document.

Notes

Graphics Objects

- **Graphics objects** created with other applications or with Word features can be inserted into Word documents.

- Some common graphics objects are shapes, drawings, **clip art**, charts, and **text boxes**. Horizontal lines and bullets may also be graphics objects.

Graphics objects in a document

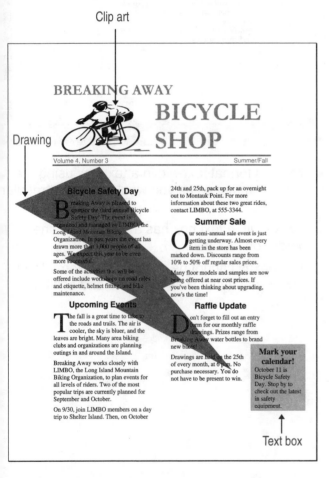

- **Floating objects** can be positioned anywhere on a page.

- Floating objects do not display in Normal view. You must use Print Layout view.

- A selected object is surrounded by a **bounding box** and **sizing handles**.

Text Wrap

- You can change the way text wraps around an object to affect the way the object is integrated into the document.

- Graphics objects can be integrated with text in five ways:

  - ***In line** with text:*   Object is positioned on a line with text characters.

  - *Wrapped square:*   Text is wrapped on all four sides of the object's bounding box.

  - *Wrapped tight:*   Text is wrapped to the contours of the image.

  - *Behind text:*   Text continues in lines over the object, obscuring the object.

  - *In front of text:*   Text continues in lines behind the object, which may obscure the text.

Select a wrapping style to integrate objects with document text.

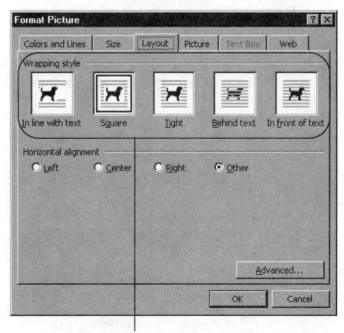

Text wrapping options

Clip Art

■ Word comes with a selection of clip art files available through the Clip Gallery feature.

Select clip art from the Clip Gallery

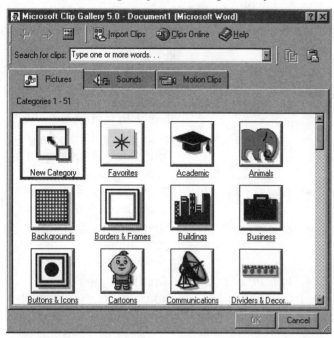

✓ *Word clip art files are stored in Windows Metafile Format, so the file extension is .wmf. Other types of graphics files can be inserted in a Word document as well.*

■ The Clip Gallery also includes sound clips, video clips, and photo clips, which can all be inserted in a document.

■ Additional clip files can be purchased or downloaded from the Web and inserted as graphics files.

✓ *Downloading clip art from the Web is covered in Exercise 76.*

■ When you select a clip art object, the Picture toolbar is displayed. Use the Picture toolbar buttons to format the object.

Picture toolbar

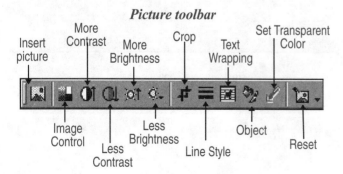

Text Boxes

■ You can draw a text box in the location and size you want.

✓ *Moving and resizing text boxes and other objects are covered in Exercise 75.*

Text box with default border

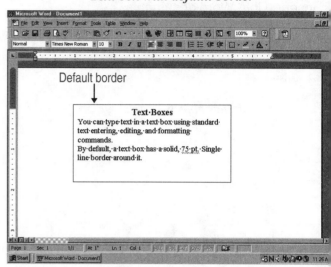

■ You can format text within a text box using the same commands as you would to format regular text.

■ By default, a text box has a solid single line border on all sides.

■ Text boxes cannot be displayed in Normal view. Use Print Layout view to create and edit text boxes.

Procedures

Insert Clip Art

Use Clip Gallery:

1. Click **Insert** .... `Alt`+`I`
2. Highlight **Picture** .... `P`
3. Click **Clip Art** .... `C`

   ✓ *The Clip Gallery opens. The clips available in the Clip Gallery depend on the options you have installed.*

4. Click desired category .... `↕`, `Enter`
5. Click desired clip art image .... `↕`
6. Click **Insert Clip** button 🖼.
7. Click dialog box **Close** button to return to document.

Insert graphics file:

1. Click **Insert** .... `Alt`+`I`
2. Highlight **Picture** .... `P`
3. Click **From File** .... `F`
4. Select disk/folder where desired file is stored.
5. Select desired file.
6. Click **Insert** .... `Alt`+`S`

Create Text Box

1. Click **Insert** .... `Alt`+`I`
2. Click **Text Box** .... `X`

   ✓ *The mouse pointer changes to a cross hair.*

3. Position the mouse pointer where you want the upper left corner of the text box to be.
4. Click and drag diagonally to draw the text box.
5. Release the mouse button.
6. Type text.

Wrap Text around an Object

1. Click object.
2. Click the **Text Wrapping** button 🖼 on the Picture toolbar.
3. Click desired wrapping option.

OR

1. Click object.
2. Click **Format** .... `Alt`+`O`
3. Click **Picture** .... `I`

   OR

   Click **Object** .... `O`

   OR

   Click **Text Box** .... `O`

4. Click **Layout** tab .... `Ctrl`+`Tab`
5. Click desired Wrapping style:
   - **In line with text** ..... `Alt`+`I`
   - **Square** .... `Alt`+`Q`
   - **Tight** .... `Alt`+`T`
   - **Behind text** .... `Alt`+`B`
   - **In front of text** .... `Alt`+`F`
6. Click **OK** .... `Enter`

Delete an Object

1. Click the object to select it.
2. Press **Del** .... `Del`

Exercise Directions

1. Start Word, if necessary.

2. Open ⊚ **74SWEET**.

3. Save the document as **WD74**.

4. Format the banner (title lines) and dateline (volume, number, and date information) as shown in Illustration A:

   a. Use a 48-point bold serif font in dark blue to format *The Sweet Tooth*, and a 28-point bold serif font in dark blue to format *Candy Shop and Soda Fountain*.

   b. Format the volume, number, and date information in 12-point sans serif, then left-align the volume and number information, and use a right tab to align the date (Spring).

   c. Move the insertion point to the end of the line and change the font size to 16 points.

   d. Apply a ¾-point double line border above and below the paragraph, in dark blue.

   e. Set the paragraph spacing to 36 points after.

   f. Insert a continuous section break before the first headline, *School Support*.

5. Format the second section of the document in two columns of equal width.

6. Use 12-point serif flush left text for the body text.

7. Use 14-point bold sans serif, centered text for headlines.

8. Leave 3 points before and 3 points after every paragraph in the second section (including headlines).

9. Using default settings, create dropped capitals as shown in Illustration A.

10. Preview the document. It should look similar to Illustration A.

11. Use the Clip Gallery to locate a clip art of an ice cream cone and insert it at the end of the first line of text as shown in Illustration B.

    ✓ If the clip art file used in the illustration (cone2.wmf) is not available, select a different one.

12. Set the clip art object in-line with the text.

13. Insert a text box approximately 1.5" wide by 1" high within the *School Support* information, as shown in Illustration B.

14. Select the Square wrapping style.

15. Type and format the text in the text box as shown:

    a. Set the headline to 12-point bold serif, centered.

    b. Set the body text to 12-point regular serif, flush left.

16. Create another text box of approximately the same size in the *Raffle Update* information, as shown in Illustration B.

17. Select the Square wrapping style.

18. Type and format the text as shown, using the same formatting as for the first text box.

    ✓ If necessary, use a smaller font so that all of the text is visible in the text box.

19. Preview the document. It should look similar to Illustration B.

    ✓ If the document extends on to two pages, use Shrink to Fit to reduce it to one page.

20. Print the document.

21. Close the file and exit Word, saving all changes.

The Sweet Tooth
Candy Shop and Soda Fountain

Volume 4, Number 3   Spring

School Support

The Sweet Tooth Candy Shop and Soda Fountain is proud to support the local schools. In addition to contributing items for fundraising events such as raffles and auctions, The Sweet Tooth has agreed to donate a portion of all sales during the month of April to the parent/teacher organizations of the Hanover Public Schools.

For more information, contact Ms. Harte at The Sweet Tooth, or Ms. Lisa Adams, president of the Hanover Home and School Association.

Spring Sale

Our annual Spring sale event is underway now! Almost every item in the store has been marked down. Discounts range from 10% to 50% off regular prices.

Stop in to check out our large selection of boxed chocolates and gift items. We offer custom clothing, handmade pottery, chocolates, penny candy, and more!

Upcoming Events

The spring is always a busy time at The Sweet Tooth. From contests to cooking, to candy tasting, we try to fill the calendar with interesting and delicious activities that the whole family will enjoy.

In addition to the Spring sale currently going on now, we have the following events scheduled:

4/5 – Truffle Tasting

4/22 – Fruit Dipping

5/1 – Sundae Making

5/1 – 5/21 – Mother's Day Sale

Raffle Update

Don't forget to fill out an entry form for our monthly raffle drawings. Prizes range from The Sweet Tooth toothbrushes to giant boxes of chocolates!

Drawings are held on the 25th of every month, at 6 p.m. No purchase is necessary, and you do not have to be present to win.

The Sweet Tooth
Candy Shop and Soda Fountain

Volume 4, Number 3   Spring

School Support

The Sweet Tooth Candy Shop and Soda Fountain is proud to support the local schools. In addition to contributing items for fundraising events such as raffles and auctions, The Sweet Tooth has agreed to donate a portion of all sales during the month of April to the parent/teacher organizations of the Hanover Public Schools.

> **April Fundraiser**
> A portion of all sales during the month of April will go to the Hanover Home and School Association.

For more information, contact Ms. Harte at The Sweet Tooth, or Ms. Lisa Adams, president of the Hanover Home and School Association.

Spring Sale

Our annual Spring sale event is underway now! Almost every item in the store has been marked down. Discounts range from 10% to 50% off regular prices.

Stop in to check out our large selection of boxed chocolates and gift items. We offer custom clothing, handmade pottery, chocolates, penny candy, and more!

Upcoming Events

The spring is always a busy time at The Sweet Tooth. From contests to cooking, to candy tasting, we try to fill the calendar with interesting and delicious activities that the whole family will enjoy.

In addition to the Spring sale currently going on now, we have the following events scheduled:

4/5 – Truffle Tasting

4/22 – Fruit Dipping

5/1 – Sundae Making

5/1 – 5/21 – Mother's Day Sale

Raffle Update

Don't forget to fill out an entry form for our monthly raffle drawings. Prizes range from The Sweet Tooth toothbrushes to giant boxes of chocolates!

> **New Store Hours!**
> The Sweet Tooth is now open from 10:00 a.m. until 9:00 p.m. Monday through Saturday!

Drawings are held on the 25th of every month, at 6 p.m. No purchase is necessary, and you do not have to be present to win.

On Your Own

1. Open **OWD68**, the newsletter document you used in the On Your Own section of Exercise 68, or open ⊙ **74NEWS**.

2. Save the file as **OWD74**.

3. Insert a text box between the two columns and type in a headline, quotation, or other important information you want to stand out in the document.

4. Select a text wrapping option that enhances the appearance of the document.

5. Insert a clip art image in the newsletter title.

6. Try different text wrapping options.

7. Preview the document.

8. Adjust column breaks and balance columns as necessary.

9. Print the document.

10. Save the document, close it, and exit Word.

Exercise 75

◆ Select Objects ◆ Resize Objects ◆ Move Objects

On the Job

You can manipulate graphics objects to make sure they are positioned the way you want in a document. You can make objects larger or smaller and move them to a new position on the page.

The president of Cornerstone Graphics has asked you to enhance the marketing flyer using graphics. In this exercise, you will insert a clip art picture and a text box in the flyer. You will resize and position the objects to achieve the best effect.

Terms

AutoShape A predefined graphics object created using Word's drawing tools.

Scale To change the size of an object by a percentage of the original size. For example, to double the size of an object, the scale would be set to 200%.

Notes

Select Objects

- You must select objects in order to change them.
- Sizing handles are displayed around selected objects.
- You can select more than one object at a time; changes will affect all selected objects.

Select objects in a document

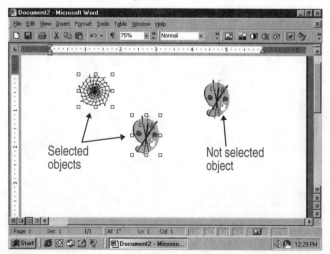

Selected objects

Not selected object

Resize Objects

- You can make existing objects larger or smaller.
- Objects can be resized using the sizing handles or using the appropriate Format dialog box.
  - Most Clip Art objects use the Format Picture dialog box, although some use the Format Object or Format AutoShape dialog box.
  - Text boxes use the Format Text Box dialog box.
  - **AutoShapes** use the Format AutoShape dialog box.
    - ✓ *AutoShapes are covered in Exercise 77.*

Format Picture dialog box

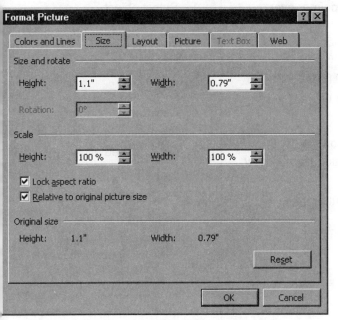

Scale objects

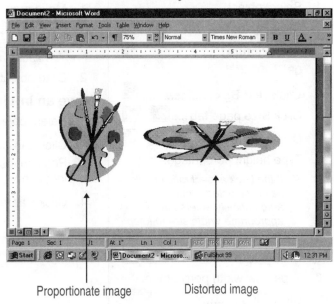

Proportionate image   Distorted image

■ Objects can be **scaled** so the height and width remain proportional, or they can be resized unevenly, distorting the image.

Move Objects

■ Floating objects can be positioned anywhere on the page.

■ In-line objects can be moved like regular text characters.

■ You can use alignment options to right-align, left-align or center an object on the page.

Procedures

Select Object

• Click desired object.

Select Multiple Objects

1. Click first object to select.
2. Press and hold **Shift**.......... `Shift`
3. Click next object to select
4. Repeat until all objects are selected.
5. Release **Shift**..................... `Shift`
   OR
   a. Click **Select Object** button ![pointer] on Drawing toolbar.
   b. Click and drag to draw a box around all objects to select.
   c. Release mouse button.
   d. Click **Select Object** button ![pointer] to turn feature off.

Resize Object

Use Resizing handles:

1. Select object to resize.
2. Move mouse pointer over desired sizing handle:
   • Use side handle to change width.
   • Use top or bottom handle to change height.
   • Use corner handle to change height and width proportionately.
     ✓ *Mouse pointer changes to double-headed arrow.*
3. Drag handle in to decrease size
   OR
   Drag handle out to increase size.

Set a precise size:

1. Select object to resize.
2. Click **Format**.............. `Alt`+`O`
3. Click **Picture**..................... `I`
   OR
   Click **Text Box**.................... `O`
4. Click **Size** page tab `Ctrl`+`Tab`
5. Click **Height**................. `Alt`+`E`
6. Type new height measurement.
   ✓ *If the Lock aspect ratio check box is selected, Word automatically enters the appropriate Width measurement to keep the object proportioned.*
7. Click **Width**................. `Alt`+`D`
8. Type new width measurement.
9. Click **OK** .... `Enter`

Scale an object:

1. Select object.
2. Click **Format** .... Alt+O
3. Click **Picture** I

   OR

   Click **Text Box** .... O
4. Click **Size** page tab ..... Ctrl+Tab
5. Click **Height** .... Alt+H
6. Type height percentage.

   ✓ *If the Lock aspect ratio check box is selected, Word automatically enters the appropriate Width size to keep the object proportioned.*
7. Click **Width** .... Alt+W
8. Type new width percentage.
9. Click **OK** .... Enter

Move a Floating Object

1. Move mouse pointer over object.

   ✓ *Mouse pointer changes to four-headed arrow.*
2. Drag object to new location.

Move an In-Line Object

1. Select object
2. Click **Cut** button .
3. Position insertion point in new location
4. Click **Paste** button 📋.

Align an Object

1. Select object.
2. Click **Format** .... Alt+C
3. Click **Picture** I

   OR

   Click **Text Box** C
4. Click **Layout** page tab .... Ctrl+Tab
5. Click desired alignment setting
   • **Left** .... Alt+L
   • **Center** .... Alt+C
   • **Right** .... Alt+F

   ✓ *Other is selected by default when object is manually positioned on page by dragging. Note that these alignment options are not available if the text wrapping is set to In line.*

Exercise Directions

1. Start Word if necessary.
2. Open 💿 **75FLYER**.
3. Save the document as **WD75**.
4. Insert a clip art picture of an artist's palette in the heading at the top of the page (see Illustration A).

   ✓ *If the file used in the illustration (Palette3.wmf) is not available, select a different picture.*
5. Set the text wrapping around the object to Square.
6. Resize the object so it is approximately 1.5" high and 1.1" wide.
7. Left-align the object (see Illustration A).
8. Insert a clip art picture of a spider web into the paragraph under the heading *What is the Web?* (see Illustration A).

   ✓ *If the file used in the illustration (Spiweb.wmf) is not available, select a different picture.*
9. Set the text wrapping around the object to Tight.
10. Scale the object to 225% of its original height. With the aspect ratio locked, the width adjusts automatically to 226%.
11. Move the object into the right-hand column, next to the paragraph under the heading *What is the Web?* (see Illustration A).
12. Preview the document. It should look similar to the one in Illustration A.
13. Print the document.
14. Close the document and exit Word, saving all changes.

Illustration A

Cornerstone Graphics

920 Marco Place ✧ Venice, CA 90201 ✧ Phone: (213) 555-1002✧
www.cornerstone.com

Maintaining A Presence on the World Wide Web

Web Site Benefits

In today's global marketplace, a presence on the World Wide Web is vital to business success. Creating effective and appealing Web pages is both a skill and an art form that takes technical knowledge, creative abilities, and practice.

What is the Web?

The Web is comprised of interconnected documents stored on the global network of computers known as the Internet. The documents are called Web pages. Related pages are linked into Web sites. Web sites are uniquely formatted to provide information, and to capture the attention of consumers around the world.

Increased Visibility

Studies show that literally millions of people have access to the Internet at home and/or at work and that new connections are being made by the thousands. Forecasts predict that in the near future, Internet access will be as ubiquitous as television and telephones, and those left off the Web will be left behind in competition.

Due to the vast numbers of Internet users around the world, it is simple and cost effective to contact customers, suppliers, and others on-line. Personal relationships can be established and maintained using computers, instead of scheduling expensive travel.

Increased Opportunities

These same contacts will lead to business expansion opportunities, with a minimum of actual travel. Another benefit is that a huge amount of information about businesses, markets, regulations, etc. is available on-line. Research can be successfully accomplished from a home office, without requiring costly travel and time spent abroad.

Work can be accomplished regardless of time zone differences and work habits. Not only can your staff use the Web to communicate with others, but people around the world can contact you even in the middle of the night. Information is available 24 hours a day, seven days a week.

Flexibility

Web sites can dispense information and collect information. As customers access the site, demographic information can be collected. Products can be targeted to specific customers. Customers can quickly find the information and/or products they need, and respond immediately, in real time.

On Your Own

1. Start Word and open the document **OWD74**, the newsletter that you used in the On Your Own section of Exercise 75, or open ⊘**75NEWS**.

2. Save the document as **OWD75**.

3. Resize the objects in the document.

4. Move the objects to new locations on the page. If you don't like the look, move them back.

5. Change the way the text in the document wraps around the objects. Select the text wrapping option that you think works best for the document.

6. Save the document.

7. Close the document and exit Word.

Exercise 76

Skills Covered:

◆ Download Graphics Objects from the Web

On the Job

Download graphic objects from the World Wide Web to supplement the objects in the Clip Gallery. You can download clip art, sounds, photos, and videos suitable for regular Word documents as well as for Web page documents.

The owner of The Sweet Tooth Candy Shop has hired you to create an on-line version of the store newsletter. You will create the newsletter document using a Web page template. You will download graphics objects from the Web to insert in the document including clip art and a dividing line.

Terms

Download Copy a file from the Internet and store it locally on your computer.

Notes

Download Graphics from the Web

- Microsoft maintains a Web site called Microsoft Clip Gallery Live where you can locate graphics objects not available on the Word 2000 CD.

- If you cannot find an object you like in the Clip Gallery, you can go directly to the Microsoft site and **download** a file(s).

- You can download clip art, photos, sounds, and video clips from the Clip Gallery Live site.

- Word stores downloaded objects in the Downloaded Clips category of the Clip Gallery.

Download clip art

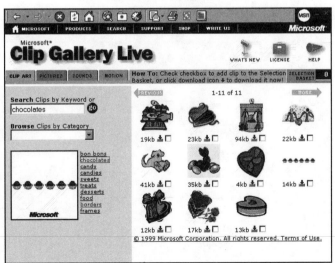

Procedures

Download Graphics Objects from the Web

1. Click **Insert**................. `Alt`+`I`
2. Click **Picture** .... `P`
3. Click **Clip Art** .... `C`
4. Click **Clips Online** button
   `Clips Online` .... `Alt`+`C`
5. Click **OK** .... `Enter`
6. Log on to Internet.
7. Read license agreement.
8. Click **Accept** button `Accept` .
9. Click **Browse Clips by Category** drop-down arrow.

10. Click desired category.
    OR
    a. Click in Search Clips by Keyword text box.
    b. Type keyword.
    c. Click **Go** 🔵 .... `Enter`
11. Click **Download** icon under desired picture ⬇.
12. Disconnect from Internet.

Download Multiple Objects at One Time

1. Click **Insert**................. `Alt`+`I`
2. Click **Picture**...................... `P`
3. Click **Clip Art**..................... `C`
4. Click **Clips Online** button
   `Clips Online` .... `Alt`+`C`
5. Click **OK** .... `Enter`

6. Log on to Internet.
7. Read license agreement.
8. Click **Accept** button `Accept`
9. Click **Browse Clips by Category** drop-down arrow.
10. Click desired category.
    OR
    a. Click in Search Clips by Keyword text box.
    b. Type keyword.
    c. Click **Go** 🔵 .... `Ente`
11. Click checkbox under desired items.
12. Click *Selection Basket* link.
13. Click *Download* link.
14. Click *Download Now* link.
15. Disconnect from Internet.

386

Exercise Directions

1. Start Word, if necessary.

2. Create a new document based on the Right-aligned Column Web Page Template.

3. Save the file as **WD76**, with the Web Page title *Sweet Talk On-Line*.

4. Replace the sample text with the text shown in Illustration A.
   - Use default formatting unless otherwise marked on the illustration.
   - Delete unnecessary sample text.
   - Leave the sample picture in place for now.

5. Use Web Page preview to preview the document. It should look similar to the one in Illustration A.

6. Save the document.

7. Display the Web toolbar.

8. Open the Internet Simulation:
   a. Click **Go**.
   b. Click **Open**.
   c. In the Address line type the following: D:/Internet/E76/ClipGlry.htm
   ✓ *If you've copied the Internet simulation files to your hard drive or your CD-ROM drive is a letter other than D:, substitute the correct letter for D.*

   Click **OK**.

9. Type *chocolates* in the VIEW CLIPS by type text box and click *Go*.

10. Click the check box below the line of bon bons (second row, fourth column) to add it to the Selection Basket.

11. Do a search on the words *ice cream*.

12. Click the check box below the banana split (third row, first column) to add it to the Selection Basket.

13. Click *Download 2 Clips!*.

14. Click *Download Now!* to download the items to the Clip Gallery.

15. If the Clip Gallery opens on-screen, close it.

16. Exit the simulation.

17. Insert a blank line under the second line of the document.
    ✓ *The blank line will be in the cell across the top of the table.*

18. Insert the downloaded line of bon bons on the blank line.
    ✓ *Open the Glip Gallery and select the Downloaded Clips category.*

19. Center the line horizontally.

20. Resize the object to .33" high.

21. Select the sample picture in the document.

22. Insert the downloaded picture of the banana split.

23. Resize the picture to approximately 3" high by 3" wide.

24. Replace the sample caption with the text: *Access Recipes for Ice Cream Treats*.

25. Apply the Sweets Theme to the document.

26. Save the changes to the document.

27. Use Web Page Preview to preview the document. It should look similar to Illustration B.

28. Close Web Page Preview.

29. Close all open documents and exit Word.

Sweet Talk On-Line ←— *20-pt. serif*

A Newsletter for Friends of The Sweet Tooth Candy Shop and Soda Fountain ←— *12-pt. serif*

Welcome

Welcome to the first edition of Sweet Talk On-Line, a Web-based version of our monthly newsletter. Access this page to read about what's happening at The Sweet Tooth Candy Shop, to find out about contests and on-line specials, and for links to other sites we think you might find interesting.

Upcoming On-Line Events

Visit The Sweet Tooth Calendar Page to see a complete list of activities taking place at the store.

Join us this month on-line for the following:

- Chat with Cynthia Harte, Sweet Tooth owner
- Questions and Answers with Master Candy Maker Jeanne LaBelle.
- Access on-line recipes for ice cream treats.
- Enter to win a trip to Hershey, PA.

Monthly Specials

This month sale prices are in effect for all gift boxes of assorted chocolates.

Visit The Sweet Tooth on-line shopping page for more information and to place an order.

Caption goes here

Illustration B

Sweet Talk On-Line

A Newsletter for Friends of The Sweet Tooth Candy Shop and Soda Fountain

Welcome

Welcome to the first edition of Sweet Talk On-Line, a Web-based version of our monthly newsletter. Access this page to read about what's happening at The Sweet Tooth Candy Shop, to find out about contests and on-line specials, and for links to other sites we think you might find interesting.

Upcoming On-Line Events

Visit The Sweet Tooth Calendar Page to see a complete list of activities taking place at the store.

Join us this month on-line for the following:

   ❀ Chat with Cynthia Harte, Sweet Tooth owner.

   ❀ Questions and Answers with Master Candy Maker Jeanne LaBelle.

   ❀ Access on-line recipes for ice cream treats.

   ❀ Enter to win a trip to Hershey, PA.

Monthly Specials

This month sale prices are in effect for all gift boxes of assorted chocolates.

Visit The Sweet Tooth on-line shopping page for more information and to place an order.

Access Recipes for Ice Cream Treats

On Your Own

1. Start Word and open the file **OWD64**, the event announcement you used in the On Your Own section of Exercise 64, or open ⊚ **76EVENT**.

2. Save the file as **OWD76**.

3. Insert clip art objects to illustrate the document.

4. If you have access to the Internet, download at least one object and insert it in the document.

5. Set the text wrapping to integrate the object(s) into the document.

6. Position and size the objects so they look good in the document.

7. Preview the document.

8. Save the document.

9. Close the document and exit Word.

Exercise 77

Skills Covered:

◆ **Drawing Objects** ◆ **AutoShapes**

On the Job

Use Word's drawing tools to create original artwork in Word documents, or to enhance and modify existing graphics objects. Word's drawing toolbar provides tools for creating basic shapes, such as circles, squares, and rectangles, which can be combined to create pictures. You can also use the drawing tools to insert AutoShapes such as hearts or lightning bolts into your documents to add excitement or emphasize text.

Cornerston Graphics is having a company picnic. In this exercise, you will create a flyer announcing the picnic. You will combine text, drawing objects, and AutoShapes to complete the document.

Terms

Drawing objects Graphics objects you create in a document using Word's drawing tools.

AutoShapes Predesigned shapes you select from a palette to insert in a Word document.

Notes

Drawing toolbar

Drawing Objects

- Word's drawing toolbar provides the tools you need to create and format **drawing objects** in your Word documents.
- There are two basic types of drawing objects:
  - Closed shapes. Closed shapes include rectangles and ovals as well as more complex shapes such as hexagons, hearts, stars, and lightning bolts.
  - Lines. Lines include straight lines, curved lines, freeform lines, and arrows.

- To draw objects you simply select the type of shape, then drag the mouse pointer to draw the shape in the document.
- You must work in Print Layout view to use the drawing tools.
- Use the Format AutoShape dialog box to set text wrapping and size options for drawing objects.

AutoShapes

- You can use Word's drawing tools to draw your own objects, or you can insert **AutoShapes** selected from one of the AutoShapes palettes:
  - Lines
  - Basic Shapes
  - Block Arrows
  - Flowchart
  - Stars and Banners
  - Callouts

The Basic Shapes palette

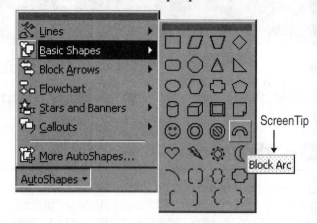

- Rest your mouse pointer on any AutoShape button to display the button name in a ScreenTip.
- All AutoShapes are closed shapes except those created with tools on the Lines palette.
- Use the Format AutoShape dialog box to set text wrapping and size options for AutoShapes.

Procedures

Display the Drawing Toolbar

- Click **Drawing** button ![] on Standard toolbar.

OR

1. Click **View** .... Alt + V
2. Click **Toolbars** .... T
3. Click **Drawing.**

   ✓ *If you are not working in Print Layout view, Word automatically switches to it.*

Draw Closed Shapes

Draw rectangle:

1. Click **Rectangle** button ![] on Drawing toolbar.

   ✓ *Mouse pointer changes to a cross hair.*

2. Click in document where you want shape to begin.
3. Drag diagonally to draw shape.
4. Release mouse button when shape is desired size.

Draw square:

1. Click **Rectangle** button ![] on Drawing toolbar.

   ✓ *Mouse pointer changes to a cross hair.*

2. Press and hold **Shift** key ... Shift
3. Click in document where you want shape to begin.
4. Drag diagonally to draw shape.
5. Release mouse button when shape is desired size.

Draw oval:

1. Click **Oval** button ![] on Drawing toolbar.

   ✓ *Mouse pointer changes to a cross hair.*

2. Click in document where you want to begin shape.
3. Drag to draw shape.
4. Release mouse button when shape is desired size.

Draw circle:

1. Click **Oval** button ![] on Drawing toolbar.

   ✓ *Mouse pointer changes to a cross hair.*

2. Press and hold **Shift** key ... Shift
3. Click in document where you want shape to begin.
4. Drag to draw shape.
5. Release mouse button when shape is desired size.
6. Release **Shift** key .... Shift

Draw Lines

Draw straight lines:

1. Click **Line** button ![] on Drawing toolbar.

   ✓ *Mouse pointer changes to a cross hair.*

2. Click in document where you want line to begin.
3. Drag to point where you want line to end.
4. Release mouse button.

Draw arrows:

1. Click **Arrow** button ![arrow] on Drawing toolbar.
   - ✓ *Mouse pointer changes to a cross hair.*
2. Click in document where you want arrow to begin.
   - ✓ *This end will not have an arrowhead.*
3. Drag to point where you want arrow to end.
4. Release mouse button.
   - ✓ *Word adds an arrowhead to end of line.*

Draw AutoShapes

Select AutoShapes:

1. Click **AutoShapes** button `AutoShapes ▾` on Drawing toolbar .... `Alt`+`U`
2. Click desired palette:
   - **Lines** .... `L`
   - **Basic Shapes** .... `B`
   - **Block Arrows**................. `A`
   - **Flowchart**....................... `F`
   - **Stars and Banners**........ `S`
   - **Callouts**.......................... `C`
3. Click desired button.

Insert any AutoShape closed object:

1. Click **AutoShape** button `AutoShapes ▾` .... `Alt`+`U`
2. Click desired palette.
3. Click desired closed shape button.
   - ✓ *Mouse pointer changes to a cross hair.*
4. Click in document where you want shape displayed
   OR
   Click and drag to draw shape.

Insert AutoShape line, arrow, or double arrow:

1. Click **AutoShape** button `AutoShapes ▾` .... `Alt`+`U`
2. Click **Lines** .... `L`
3. Click desired button.
   - ✓ *Mouse pointer changes to a cross hair.*
4. Click in document where you want line to begin.
5. Drag to point where you want line to end.
6. Release mouse button.

Insert AutoShape curve line:

1. Click **AutoShape** button `AutoShapes ▾` .... `Alt`+`U`
2. Click **Lines** .... `L`
3. Click **Curve** button `S`.
4. Click in document where you want line to begin.
5. Release mouse button.
6. Click in document at point where you want line to curve.
7. Repeat step 6 at each point where you want line to curve.
8. Double-click to end line.

Insert AutoShape freeform line:

1. Click **AutoShape** button `AutoShapes ▾` .... `Alt`+`U`
2. Click **Lines** .... `L`
3. Click **Freeform** button.
   - ✓ *Mouse pointer changes to pencil icon.*
4. Click in document where you want line to begin.
5. Drag to draw freehand as if you were using a pencil.
   OR
   Release mouse button and click to draw straight lines.
   - ✓ *Mouse pointer changes to cross hair.*
6. Double-click to end line.

Insert AutoShape scribble line:

1. Click **AutoShape** button `AutoShapes ▾` .... `Alt`+`U`
2. Click **Lines** .... `L`
3. Click **Scribble** button.
   - ✓ *Mouse pointer changes to pencil icon.*
4. Click in document where you want line to begin.
5. Drag to draw freehand as if you were using a pencil.
6. Release mouse button to end line.

Set Text Wrapping for AutoShapes

1. Select object.
2. Click **Format**............... `Alt`+`O`
3. Click **AutoShape**................. `O`
4. Click **Layout** tab .... `Ctrl`+`Tab`
5. Click desired text wrapping option.
   OR
   a. Select object.
   b. Click **Draw** button `Draw ▾` on Drawing toolbar .... `Alt`+`R`
   c. Click **Text Wrapping**...... `T`
6. Click desired text wrapping option.

Exercise Directions

1. Start Word, if necessary.

2. Type and format the document shown in Illustration A, or open the file ⊙ **77PICNIC** and format it as indicated.

   a. Use an 18-point sans serif font except where noted.

   b. Use spacing and alignment options as marked.

3. Save the document as **WD77**.

4. Use Word's Drawing tools to draw the house shown in Illustration B:

   a. Draw a rectangle for the main building.

   b. Draw two straight lines for the roof.

   c. Draw a small rectangle for the door.

   d. Draw three perfect circles for the windows.

   e. Draw one curve or scribble line for the left side of the walkway.

   f. Draw a second curve or scribble line for the right side of the walkway.

   g. Draw a third curve or scribble line for the bottom of the walkway.

5. Set text wrapping around the house for Top and Bottom

   a. Use Select Objects tool on Drawing toolbar to select all of the objects used to draw the house.

   b. Click Draw button on Drawing toolbar and select Top and Bottom from Text Wrapping menu

6. Insert the lightning bolt AutoShape found on the Basic Shapes palette to the left of the rain date information. Refer to Illustration B.

7. Size the AutoShape to approximately 1" high by 1.25" wide.

8. Left align the lightning bolt AutoShape, and set the text wrapping around it to Tight.

9. Draw an arrow pointing to the phone number information. Refer to Illustration B.

10. Preview the document. It should look similar to Illustration B.

11. Print the document.

12. Close the document and exit Word, saving all changes.

Illustration A

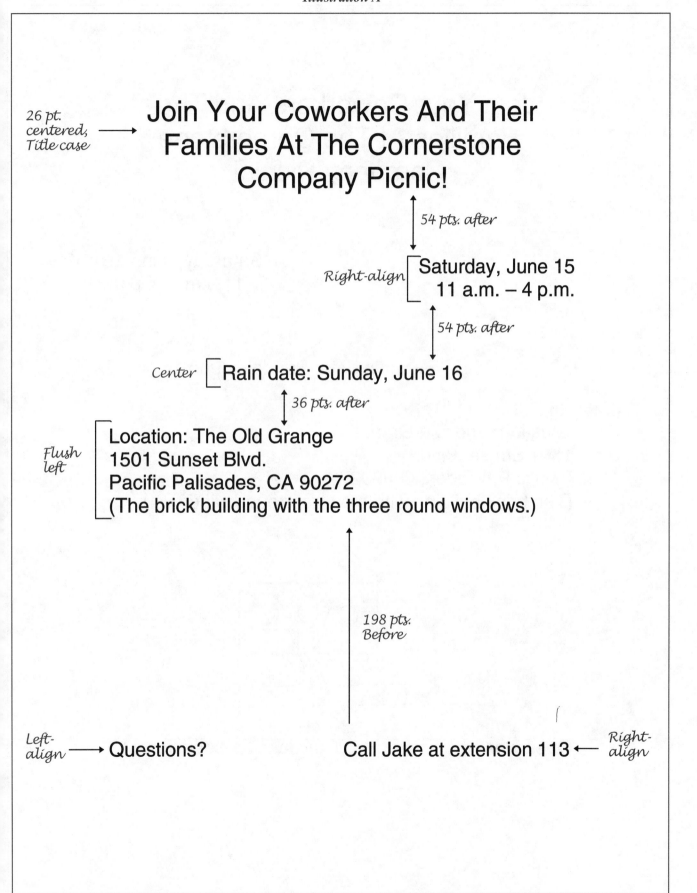

Join Your Coworkers And Their Families At The Cornerstone Company Picnic!

Saturday, June 15
11 a.m. – 4 p.m.

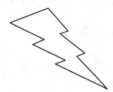

Rain date: Sunday, June 16

Location: The Old Grange
1501 Sunset Blvd.
Pacific Palisades, CA 90272
(The brick building with the three round windows.)

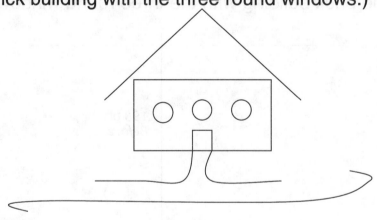

Questions? ⟶ Call Jake at extension 113

On Your Own

1. Start Word and create a new document.
2. Save the document as **OWD77**.
3. Display the Drawing toolbar.
4. Use the drawing tools to draw a simple picture. For example, draw a person, a tree, or a flower.
5. Insert AutoShapes in the document. For example, insert a lightning bolt, the sun, the moon, or stars.
6. Save the document.
7. Close the document and exit Word.

Exercise 78

On the Job

You can manipulate objects to make sure they are positioned the way you want in a document. You can rotate objects around an axis and flip them horizontally or vertically. Many drawing objects have adjustment handles, which you can use to alter the most prominent feature of the object. For example, you can change the mouth on a smiley face from a smile to a frown.

You've been hired to design a logo for the Northern New England Credit Union's Smart Loans program for small business. You will use two AutoShapes to create the logo, combined with a slogan typed as document text. To correctly position the AutoShapes you will resize them and move them, use the rotate and flip commands. One shape will need to be adjusted to achieve the most effective appearance. Finally, you will select a text wrapping option to integrate the shapes with the slogan text.

Terms

Adjustment handle A small yellow diamond used to alter the most prominent feature of an AutoShape. The mouse pointer is an arrow point when resting on an adjustment handle.

Rotate Shift the position of an object in a circular motion around its axis, or center point.

Rotation handle Small, green circles used to drag an object around in a circle. The mouse pointer looks like a circular arrow when resting on a sizing handle.

Flip Reverse the position of an object.

Notes

Adjust Objects

- Some AutoShapes have an **adjustment handle** that looks like a small yellow diamond.
- You can drag the adjustment handle to alter the most prominent feature of the shape.

Adjust objects

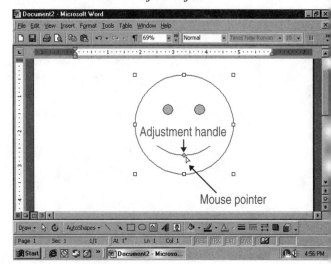

Rotate and Flip Objects

- You can **rotate** an object to the left or right around its center point, or axis.

- Word lets you rotate an object by 90 degrees in either direction, or to use the Free Rotate command to rotate the object any amount.

- When you select free rotate, Word displays **rotation handles**, which you drag to rotate the object around its axis.

- Free rotate remains active until you turn it off.

Rotate and flip objects

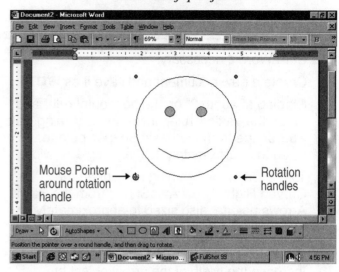

- You can **flip** an object horizontally (left to right) or vertically (top to bottom).

Procedures

Adjust Object

1. Select object to adjust.
2. Move mouse pointer over adjustment handle.
   - ✓ *Mouse pointer changes to arrowhead.*
3. Drag adjustment handle to change feature's shape.

Rotate Object

Rotate left or right:

1. Select **object** to rotate.
2. Click **Draw** button Draw ▾ on Drawing toolbar........... Alt+R
3. Click **Rotate or Flip** .... P
4. Click **Rotate Left** to rotate object 90 degrees to left....... L
   OR
   Click **Rotate Right** to rotate object 90 degrees to right .... R

Free rotate:

1. Select **object** to rotate.
2. Click **Free Rotate** button 🔄 on Drawing toolbar.
   OR
   a. Click **Draw** button Draw ▾ on Drawing toolbar .... Alt+R
   b. Click **Rotate or Flip** .... P
   c. Click **Free Rotate**........... T
3. Move mouse pointer over rotation handle.
   - ✓ *Mouse pointer changes to circular arrow.*
4. Drag rotation handle in the desired direction.
5. Release mouse button when object is in desired position.
6. Click **Free Rotate** button 🔄 to turn feature off.

Flip Object

1. Select **object** to flip.
2. Click **Draw** button Draw ▾ on Drawing toolbar .... Alt+R
3. Click **Rotate or Flip**............. P
4. Click **Flip Horizontal** to flip object left to right .... H
   OR
   Click **Flip Vertical** to flip object top to bottom V

Exercise Directions

1. Start Word if necessary.
2. Create a new document and save it as **WD78**.
3. Starting at about 3" on the horizontal ruler and .5" on the vertical ruler, insert the Lightning Bolt AutoShape from the Basic Shapes palette, sized to approximately 1.5" high by 1.5" wide.
4. To the left of the lightning bolt, insert the Curved Right Arrow AutoShape from the Block Arrows palette, also sized to approximately 1.5" high by 1.5" wide.
5. Flip the lightning bolt vertically.
6. Increase the width of the arrow object by dragging the sizing handle in the middle of the right side to the right approximately .5".
7. Decrease the size of the arrowhead by dragging the adjustment handle below the right tip of the arrowhead toward the arrow point.

    ✓ *The arrow has three adjustment handles. The one closest to the right tip adjusts the size of the arrowhead; the other two adjust the width of the arrow body.*

8. Using Free Rotate, rotate the arrow to the left until it is pointing up and to the right, along a similar line as the lightning bolt.

9. Turn off Free Rotate.
10. Move the lightning bolt so that it begins at the tip of the arrow (see Illustration A).
11. On the first line of the document, use a 28-point serif font and type the text: *Smart Loans*.

    ✓ *Don't worry if the text goes behind or in front of the objects. You will adjust the text wrapping after all of the text is entered.*

12. On the second line of the document, using the same font and font size, type the text: *"Because Lightning Only Strikes Once"*
13. Select both drawing objects.
14. Set text wrapping to Square.
15. Preview the document. It should look similar to the one in Illustration A.
16. Make any adjustments necessary to the size and position of the objects.
17. Print the document.
18. Close the document and exit Word, saving all changes.

Illustration A

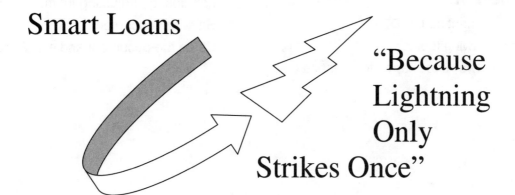

On Your Own

1. Start Word and open the document **OWD76**, the event announcement that you created in the On Your Own section of Exercise 76, or open ⊙ **78EVENT**.

2. Save the document as **OWD78**.

3. Display the Drawing toolbar.

4. Insert at least two AutoShapes to enhance the document.

5. Rotate and flip the AutoShape(s) in the document.

6. If any of the AutoShapes have adjustment handles, try adjusting them.

7. Save the document.

8. Close the document and exit Word.

Exercise 79

◆ **Line Color and Styles** ◆ **Fill Color** ◆ **Shadows and 3-D Effects**

On the Job

Use color and special effects with drawing objects to create professional-looking graphics and pictures. You can change the color and style of the lines used to draw both closed shapes and lines, and you can enhance closed shapes by filling them with color or patterns. Shadows behind an object give a document the appearance of depth, while 3-D effects give depth to the object itself.

The owner of The Sweet Tooth Candy Shop has hired you to design a flyer advertising a grand opening sale. To make the flyer look really great, you've decided to use variety of line styles, line colors, and fill colors. You also want to apply shadows and 3-D effects to some of the objects.

Terms

Line style The width and appearance of a line used to draw an object.

Fill Color or patterns used to fill a closed shape.

Shadow An effect applied to objects to make it look as if the object is casting a shadow.

3-D Effect An effect applied to objects to make them look as if they are three dimensional.

Notes

Line Color and Styles

- You can select the width, appearance, and color of lines used to draw closed shapes, lines, and arrows.
- You can select the style of arrowheads used for arrow objects.
- **Line styles** are applied to objects after they have been drawn.
- Combine line color and style effects to achieve the desired result.

Change line color and styles

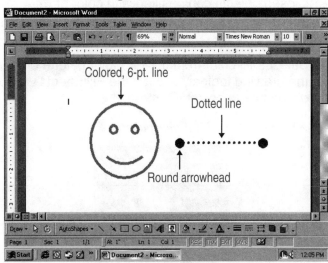

- Select line color and style from the palettes on the Drawing toolbar, or open the Format AutoShape dialog box for additional options.

Drawing toolbar

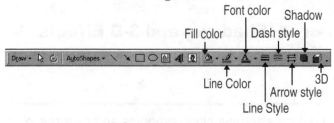

Format AutoShape dialog box

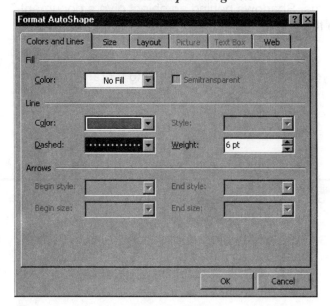

Fill Color

- Closed objects can be filled with color or patterns.
- You apply a **fill** to an existing object.
- Select a fill color from the Fill Color palette on the drawing toolbar, or open the Fill Effects dialog box to select a pattern.

Fill Color palette

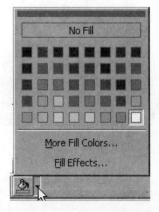

Fill Effects dialog box

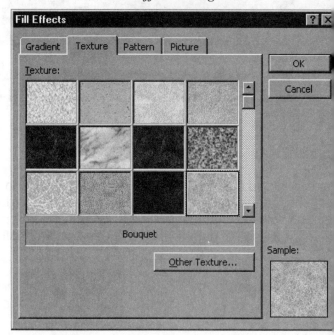

- Remember that color is best used in documents designed to be viewed on screen, such as Web pages, or documents that will be printed on a color printer.

Shadows and 3-D Effects

- **Shadows** and **3-D effects** can be applied to any drawing object.
- Word comes with a palette of shadows and a palette of 3-D Effects from which you select the options you want.

Shadow palette

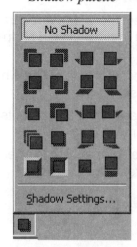

3-D palette

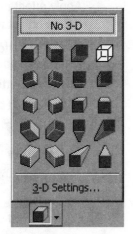

Shadow Settings toolbar

■ You can customize the 3-D effect by changing the color, lighting, depth, direction, angle, and/or surface of the object.

3-D Settings toolbar

■ You can customize the shadow effect by changing the shadow color and/or by adjusting the position of the shadow.

Procedures

Line Color and Style

Select line color:

1. Select object.

2. Click **Line Color** button drop-down arrow on Drawing toolbar.

3. Click desired color.

   ✓ Click No Line to remove existing line.

   OR

   a. Click **Patterned Lines** .... P

   b. Click desired pattern.

   c. Click **OK** .... Enter

   ✓ To apply the color currently displayed on Line Color button, click the Line Color button.

Select line style:

1. Select object.

2. Click **Line Style** button on Drawing toolbar.

3. Click desired line style.
   OR

   a. Click **More Lines** .... M

   b. Click **Style** drop-down arrow .... Alt + S

   c. Click desired line style.

   d. Click **OK**.

Select dash style:

1. Select object.

2. Click **Dash Style** button on Drawing toolbar

3. Click desired dash style.

Select arrow style:

1. Select object.

2. Click **Arrow Style** button on Drawing toolbar.

3. Click desired arrow style.
   OR

   a. Click **More Arrows** .... M

   b. Click **Begin style** ... Alt + B

   c. Click desired arrow style for beginning of arrow.

   d. Click **Begin size** ..... Alt + I

   ✓ For double-headed arrows only.

   e. Click **End style** ...... Alt + E

   f. Click desired arrow style for end of arrow.

   g. Click **End size** .... Alt + Z

   h. Click desired size for end of arrow.

   i. Click **OK**.

Fill Color

1. Select object.

2. Click **Fill Color** button drop-down arrow on Drawing toolbar.

3. Click desired color.

   ✓ Click No Fill to remove existing fill color.

   OR

   a. Click **Fill Effects** .... F

   b. Click desired tab .... Ctrl + Tab

   c. Click desired option.

   d. Click **OK** .... Enter

   ✓ To apply the color currently displayed on Fill Color button, click the Fill Color button.

Shadows

Apply shadows:

1. Select object.

2. Click **Shadow** button on Drawing toolbar.

3. Click desired effect.

   ✓ Click No Shadow to remove existing shadow.

Shift shadow position:

1. Apply shadow to object.
2. Select object to change.
3. Click **Shadow** button 🔲 on Drawing toolbar.
4. Click **S**hadow Settings ...... Ⓢ
5. Click button as necessary:
   - **Nudge Shadow Up** 🔲
   - **Nudge Shadow Down** 🔲
   - **Nudge Shadow Left** 🔲
   - **Nudge Shadow Right** 🔲

Change shadow color:

1. Apply shadow to object.
2. Select object to change.
3. Click **Shadow** button 🔲 on Drawing toolbar.
4. Click **S**hadow Settings ...... Ⓢ
5. Click **Shadow Color** button 🔲 drop-down arrow.
6. Click desired color.
   - ✓ *To apply the color currently displayed on Shadow Color button, click the Shadow Color button.*

Close Shadow Settings toolbar:

- Click **Close** button ✖ on Toolbar title bar.

OR

1. Click **Shadow** button 🔲 on Drawing toolbar.
2. Click **S**hadow Settings ...... Ⓢ

3-D Effects

Apply 3-D effects:

1. Select object.
2. Click **3-D** button 🔲 ▾ on Drawing toolbar.
3. Click desired effect.
   - ✓ *Click No 3-D to remove existing effect.*

Shift 3-D angle:

1. Apply effect to object.
2. Select object to change.
3. Click **3-D** button 🔲 ▾ on Drawing toolbar.
4. Click **3**-D Settings .... ③
5. Click button as necessary:
   - **Tilt Up** 🔲
   - **Tilt Down** 🔲
   - **Tilt Left** 🔲
   - **Tilt Right** 🔲

Change 3-D color:

1. Apply effect to object.
2. Select object to change.
3. Click **3-D** button 🔲 ▾ on Drawing toolbar.
4. Click **3**-D Settings .... ③
5. Click **3-D Color** button 🔲 ▾ drop-down arrow.
6. Click desired color.
   - ✓ *To apply the color currently displayed on 3-D Color button, click the button.*

Change other 3-D settings:

1. Apply effect to object.
2. Select object to change.
3. Click **3-D** button 🔲 ▾ on Drawing toolbar.
4. Click **3**-D Settings .... Ⓚ
5. Click desired button:
   - **Depth** 🔲
   - **Direction** 🔲
   - **Lighting** 🔲
   - **Surface** 🔲
6. Click desired option.

Close 3-D Settings toolbar:

- Click **Close** button ✖ on toolbar title bar.

OR

1. Click **3-D** button 🔲 ▾ on Drawing toolbar.
2. Click **3**-D Settings .... Ⓚ

Exercise Directions

1. Start Word, if necessary.

2. Open ⊙ **79SALE** or create the document shown in Illustration A.

3. Save the document as **WD79**.

4. In the upper left of the document, below the first line of text, insert the Explosion 1 AutoShape from the Stars and Banners palette, as shown in illustration B.
   - Size the shape to approximately 1.75" high by 2.5" wide.

5. Format the AutoShape as shown in Illustration B.
   a. Use the 2 ¼-point line style.
   b. Use the Round Dot dash style (second from the top in the Dash style palette).
   c. Fill the shape with Yellow.
   d. Apply the Shadow Style 1 shadow effect to the AutoShape.

6. Modify the shadow settings to move the shadow up from the AutoShape.
   a. Click Shadow Settings on the Shadow palette to display the Shadow Settings toolbar.
   b. Click the Nudge Shadow Up button four times.

7. In the upper right of the document, below the first line of text, insert the Explosion 2 AutoShape from the Stars and Banners palette, as shown in illustration B.
   - Size the shape to approximately 1.75" high by 2.5" wide.

8. Format the AutoShape as shown in Illustration B.
   a. Use the 2 ¼-point line style.
   b. Use the Round Dot dash style (second from the top in the Dash style palette).
   c. Fill the shape with Blue.
   d. Apply the Shadow Style 2 shadow effect to the AutoShape.

9. Modify the shadow settings to move the shadow away from the AutoShape.
   a. Click Shadow Settings on the Shadow palette to display the Shadow Settings toolbar.
   b. Click the Nudge Shadow Right button four times.

10. Insert the Heart AutoShape from the Basic Shapes palette to the left of the text: *You'll Love the Great Values on,* as shown in Illustration B.

11. Format the AutoShape as shown in Illustration B.
    a. Fill the shape with the color Rose.
    b. Apply the 3-D Style 16 effect.

12. Insert the Heart AutoShape from the Basic Shapes palette to the right of the text: *You'll Love the Great Values on*, as shown in Illustration B.

13. Format the AutoShape as shown in Illustration B.
    a. Fill the shape with the color Rose.
    b. Apply the 3-D Style 19 effect.

14. Draw an arrow to point at the item *Gift Baskets*, as shown in Illustration B.

15. Draw the same arrow to point at the other items: *Truffles, Penny Candy, Assorted Chocolates*, as shown in Illustration B.

16. Select all four arrows.

17. Format the arrows as shown in Illustration B.
    a. Change the line color to Dark Blue.
    b. Change the line style to 2 ¼-point.
    c. Change the arrow style to Arrow Style 9.

18. Save the changes.

19. Preview the document. It should look similar to the one in Illustration B.

20. Print the document.

21. Close the document and exit Word, saving all changes.

Grand Opening Sale

To celebrate the opening of our new store
The Sweet Tooth Candy Shop
is slashing prices!

You'll Love
the Great Values on:

Gift Baskets
Truffles
Penny Candy
Assorted Chocolates

Sale Prices Effective Sunday April 15 through Saturday April 21

Grand Opening Sale

To celebrate the opening of our new store
The Sweet Tooth Candy Shop
is slashing prices!

You'll Love
the Great Values on:

Gift Baskets
Truffles
Penny Candy
Assorted Chocolates

Sale Prices Effective Sunday April 15 through Saturday April 21

On Your Own

1. Start Word and open the document **OWD78**, the event announcement that you created in the On Your Own section of Exercise 78, or open ⊙ **59EVENT**.

2. Save the document as **OWD79**.

3. Display the Drawing toolbar.

4. Change the line color and style of some of the objects in the document. Feel free to insert new objects if you think they will enhance the document.

5. Fill the objects with color.

6. Apply shadows and 3-D effects to the objects.

7. When you achieve the look you want, save the document.

8. Close the document and exit Word.

Exercise 80

On the Job

Integrate drawing objects with text to illustrate and enhance documents. Objects can be layered with each other and with text to create different effects. For example, you can design a letterhead with text layered on top of a logo created from drawing objects. You can group objects together to create one complete picture, and ungroup objects to edit them individually.

The Sweet Tooth Candy Shop is sponsoring a fund raising event for the local parent/teacher organization. In this exercise, you will create a flyer for HSTPO, the Hanover Schools Parent/Teacher Organization, advertising the event. You will first design a letterhead for the organization using an AutoShape and text. You will then create the rest of the document using AutoShapes and other drawing objects. You will add text to some of the AutoShapes. You will also group some of the objects so you can move them as a single unit, and you will layer the objects with each other.

Terms

Group Select multiple objects and combine them into a single object.

Ungroup Separate a grouped object into individual objects.

Layer Position objects and/or text so they overlap on the page.

Notes

Group and Ungroup Objects

- You can **group** objects together when you want to create a single unified object.
- Sizing handles are displayed around the entire grouped object, not around the individual objects.

Multiple selected objects

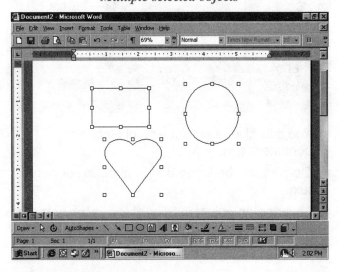

411

A grouped object

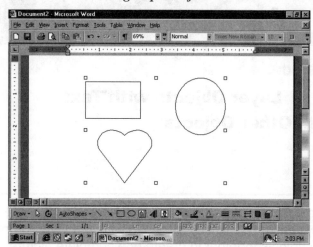

A grouped object

- All changes are made to the entire group.
- You must **ungroup** the objects in order to edit them individually.
- You can ungroup pictures such as clip art images created with other programs in order to modify the individual elements.

Layer Objects with Text

- You can add text to any drawing object.
- When you add text to an object, Word creates a text box around the object's perimeter; text is displayed within the borders of the object.

Text on an object

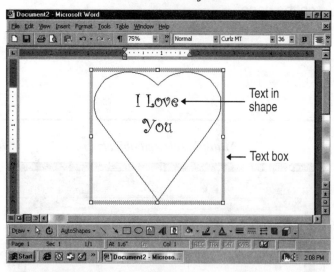

- You can also **layer** drawing objects with document text.
- Objects can be layered in front of text or behind text.
- Layering an object in front of text is the same as setting the text wrapping for the object to the In front of text setting.

- Layering an object behind text is the same as setting the text wrapping for the object to the Behind text setting.

Layer Objects with Other Objects

- Two or more objects may be overlapping in a document.
- You can insert a new object on top of an existing object, or move an object into a new position overlapping another.
- Objects in layers can be rearranged layer-by-layer using the Bring Forward command to move an object forward one layer at a time or the Send Backward command to move an object backward one layer at a time.
- The Send to Back command lets you move the selected object in back of all other objects.
- The Bring to Front command lets you bring an object in front of all other objects.

Stacked objects

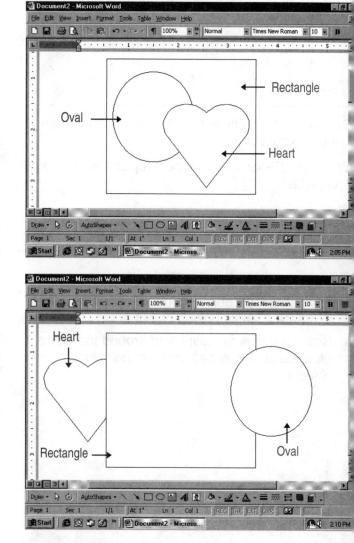

Procedures

Group Objects

1. Select all objects to group.
2. Click **Draw** button `Draw ▾` on Drawing toolbar............`Alt`+`R`
3. Click **Group** ....`G`

Ungroup Objects

1. Select grouped object.
2. Click **Draw** button `Draw ▾` on Drawing toolbar............`Alt`+`R`
3. Click **Ungroup** ....`U`

Add Text to Object

1. Right-click object.
2. Click **Add Text** ....`X`
3. Type and format text
4. Click outside object.

Layer Objects with Text

1. Select object.
2. Click **Draw** button `Draw ▾` on Drawing toolbar ....`Alt`+`R`
3. Click **Order**.........................`R`
4. Click desired option:
   - **Bring in Front of Text**... `R`
   - **Send Behind Text** ....`H`

Layer Objects with Other Objects

1. Select object.
2. Click **Draw** button `Draw ▾` on Drawing toolbar ....`Alt`+`R`
3. Click **Order**.........................`R`
4. Click desired option:
   - **Bring to Front** ....`T`
   - **Send to Back**................`K`
   - **Bring Forward**.............`F`
5. **Send Backward**.................`B`

Exercise Directions

1. Start Word, if necessary.
2. Create a new document and save it as **WD80**.
3. Using a 28-point sans serif font in bold, type: *HSPTO*
4. Change the font to 12 point, and on the next line type: *The Hanover Schools Parent/Teacher Organization.*
5. Change the font to 10 point, and on the third line type: *1501 South Main Street; Hanover, NH 03755*
6. Start the fourth line and type: *(603) 555-3344; http://www.hspto.org.*
7. Insert the Sun AutoShape from the Basic Shapes palette.
   a. Size the shape to approximately 2" by 2".
   b. Move the shape to the upper-left corner of the document so it overlaps the acronym *HSPTO*.
   - ✓ *Try to align the vertical point with the .5" mark on the horizontal ruler, and the horizontal ray with the .5" mark on the vertical ruler.*
8. Fill the sun AutoShape with the color yellow.
9. Layer the sun AutoShape behind the text. The letterhead should look similar to the letterhead in Illustration A.
10. Use the Oval drawing tool to draw three balloons in the upper right corner of the document under the letterhead.
    a. Make two balloons ovals, sized approximately 1" high by .75" wide.
    b. Make one balloon a circle, sized approximately 1" by 1".
11. Fill one balloon with red, one with blue, and one with dark green.
12. Use the Curve line tool on the Lines AutoShapes palette to draw three strings starting from each balloon and coming together into a bunch.
13. Format the three line objects using the 2 ¼-point line style.
14. Layer the three lines behind the oval balloon shapes.
15. Select the three ovals and the three lines, and group them together.
16. Drag the grouped balloons and strings down to the lower left corner of the document (refer to Illustration A).
17. Insert the 16-point star AutoShape from the Stars and Banners palette into the middle of the document.

18. Size the star approximately 5.5" by 5.5".

19. Using a 24-point sans serif font in bold, add the text shown in Illustration A to the star.
    - Left align the first three lines and center the last two.

20. Fill the star with light yellow.

21. Apply the 3-D style 6 to the Star AutoShape.

22. Layer the star AutoShape behind the grouped balloons.

23. Insert the Wave AutoShape from the Stars and Banners palette into the document above the star.

24. Size the wave at approximately 2.5" high by 4.25" wide, and center it on the page.

25. Change the line style to Square Dot.

26. Fill the wave shape with yellow.

27. Using a 24-point sans serif font, centered, add the text: *Sponsored by The Sweet Tooth Candy Shop* to the wave AutoShape.

28. Rotate the wave shape to the left so the top right corner of the shape points up vertically (refer to Illustration A).

29. Layer the wave behind the star AutoShape.

30. Preview the document. It should look similar to Illustration A.

31. Print the document.

32. Close the document and exit Word, saving all changes.

Illustration A

On Your Own

1. Start Word and create a new document.
2. Save the document as **OWD60**.
3. Display the Drawing toolbar.
4. Use drawing objects and text to create an invitation to your next birthday party, or to another event.
5. Use different text formatting such as fonts and alignments.
6. Layer the objects and the text in the document.
7. Make use of line styles, color, fills and effects to achieve the look you want. Group objects to apply formatting to all of them.
8. If necessary, rotate, flip, and adjust objects so they look good on the page.
9. Save the document.
10. Close the document and exit Word.

Skills Covered:

◆ **Create WordArt** ◆ **WordArt Text** ◆ **WordArt Shapes and Formatting**

On the Job

Use WordArt to transform text into artwork for letterheads, logos, brochures, and other documents. WordArt lets you create special effects using any text that you type. You can stretch characters, rotate them, reverse direction, and even arrange the text in shapes such as circles, waves, or arcs.

The owner of The Sweet Tooth Candy Shop has liked the work that you've done for her. She's opening a new store and has asked you to design a flyer announcing the grand opening.

Terms

WordArt A feature of Word used to transform text into a drawing object.

WordArt text The text included in a WordArt object.

WordArt style The shape and formatting characteristics of a WordArt object.

Notes

Create WordArt

- **WordArt** is a Word feature that you use to transform text into a drawing object.
- The WordArt Gallery includes a selection of styles you can quickly apply to any text.

The WordArt Gallery

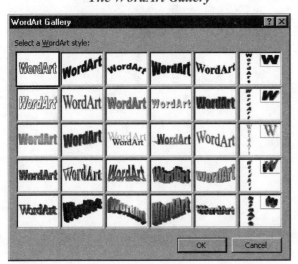

- You can customize WordArt objects to achieve the specific results you want.

WordArt Text

- You enter **WordArt text** when you create the WordArt object.

- The default text is: Your Text Here, which is replaced by any text you type.

- You can select text already typed in the document to use as the WordArt text.

    ✓ *The selected text will remain unchanged in the document, independent of the new WordArt object.*

- You can edit the text displayed in a WordArt object at any time.

- You can change the font, font size, and font style used for WordArt text.

The Edit WordArt Text dialog box

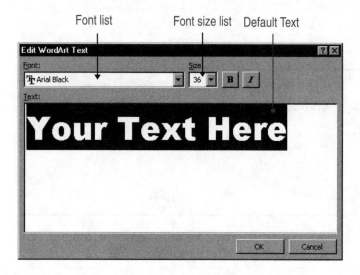

WordArt Shapes and Formatting

- The **WordArt styles** in the WordArt Gallery include shape and formatting characteristics.

- When you select a WordArt object, the WordArt toolbar is displayed. Use the buttons on the WordArt toolbar to edit and format the object.

The WordArt toolbar

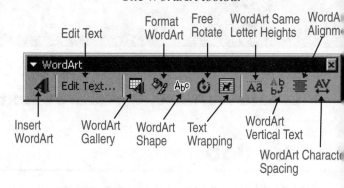

- You can change the shape of a WordArt object by selecting a different shape from the WordArt Shape palette.

- Rotate the WordArt object using the Free Rotate button.

- Select a text wrapping option to integrate the WordArt object with existing document text.

- Stretch lowercase letters to the same height as uppercase letters using the WordArt Same Letter Heights button.

- Align WordArt text vertically using the WordArt Vertical Text button.

- Align the entire WordArt object on the page using the WordArt alignment button.

- Adjust the spacing between characters in a WordArt object using the WordArt character spacing button.

- In addition to the commands on the WordArt toolbar, WordArt objects can be edited and modified using the same techniques used to edit other drawing objects, including moving and resizing, adjusting, rotating, flipping, shadow and 3-D effects, and layering.

Procedures

Create WordArt

1. Display Drawing toolbar.
2. Click the **WordArt** button  on the Drawing toolbar.
   OR
   a. Click **Insert** .... `Alt`+`I`
   b. Click **Picture** .... `P`
   c. Click **WordArt** .... `W`
3. Click desired WordArt style.
4. Click **OK** .... `Enter`
5. Type WordArt text.
6. Click **OK** .... `Enter`

WordArt Text

Edit WordArt text:

1. Select WordArt object.
2. Click **Edit text** button
   on WordArt toolbar .... `Alt`+`X`
3. Type new text.
4. Click **OK**.

Format WordArt text:

1. Select WordArt object.
2. Click **Edit text** button
   WordArt toolbar .... `Alt`+`X`
3. Click **Font** drop-down
   arrow .... `Alt`+`F`
4. Click desired font.
5. Click **Size** drop-down
   arrow .... `Alt`+`S`
6. Click desired size.
7. Click Font style buttons as
   desired:
   - **Bold** **B**
   - **Italic** *I*
8. Click **OK** .... `Enter`

WordArt Shapes and Formatting

Change WordArt style:

1. Select WordArt object.
2. Click **WordArt Gallery** button
   on WordArt toolbar.
3. Click desired style.
4. Click **OK** .... `Enter`

Change WordArt shape:

1. Select WordArt object.
2. Click **WordArt Shape** button
   on WordArt toolbar.
3. Click desired shape.

Rotate WordArt object:

1. Select WordArt object.
2. Click **Free Rotate** button
   on WordArt toolbar.
3. Drag rotation handle to rotate
   object.
4. Release mouse button when
   object is in desired position.
5. Click **Free Rotate** button
   on WordArt toolbar to turn Free
   Rotate off.
   ✓ You can rotate and flip WordArt
     objects using the commands
     on the Drawing toolbar.

Wrap text around a WordArt object:

1. Select WordArt object.
2. Click **Text Wrapping** button
   on WordArt toolbar.
3. Click desired text wrapping
   option.

Adjust letter height:

1. Select WordArt object.
2. Click **WordArt Same Letter
   Heights** button on
   WordArt toolbar

Align WordArt text vertically:

1. Select WordArt object.
2. Click **WordArt Vertical Text**
   button on WordArt toolbar.
   ✓ Repeat to return text to
     horizontal alignment.

Align WordArt object:

1. Select WordArt object.
2. Click **Format** .... `Alt`+`O`
3. Click **WordArt** .... `O`
4. Click Layout tab.
5. Click desired alignment option.
6. Click **OK** .... `Enter`

Adjust character spacing:

1. Select WordArt object.
2. Click **WordArt Character
   Spacing** button on
   WordArt toolbar.
3. Click desired option.

Exercise Directions

1. Start Word, if necessary.
2. Create a new document.
3. Save the document as **WD81**.
4. Display the Drawing toolbar.
5. Start WordArt.
6. Select the style in the fourth row of the second column (refer to Illustration A).
7. Using a 40-point sans serif font, enter the WordArt text: *The Sweet Tooth.*
   - ✓ *Click OK to create the WordArt object.*
8. Resize the WordArt object to approximately 1" high and 5.5" wide.
   - ✓ *You can resize the object using the sizing handles, or by entering precise measurements in the Format WordArt dialog box.*
9. Position the WordArt object so the highest point starts at about .5" on the vertical ruler, and center it horizontally on the page.
   - ✓ *To position the object vertically, try increasing the zoom so you can better align the top of the object against the ruler.*
10. Make all of the characters in the object the same height.
11. Position the insertion point approximately 1" below the bottom of the WordArt object.
12. Using a 36-point script font, type the five lines of text shown in Illustration A.
13. Center the five lines of text horizontally.
14. Create another WordArt object using the arc style that is in the first row of the third column.
15. Using a 28-point serif font, type the following address and URL information on three separate lines, and then insert the object into the document:

    1010 North Quail Drive
    Etna, NH
    http://www.thesweettooth.com
    - ✓ *Click OK to create the WordArt object.*

16. Change the shape of the WordArt object to Button (curve).
    a. Select the object.
    b. Click the WordArt Shape button on the WordArt toolbar.
    c. Click the Button (curve) shape (4th column, 2nd row in the Shape palette).
       - ✓ *Use ScreenTips to identify the names of the shapes.*
17. Position the WordArt object so the top starts at approximately 6" on the vertical ruler.
18. Set the size of the WordArt object to approximately 2.5" by 3.25", and center it horizontally on the page.
19. Insert the Explosion 1 AutoShape in the upper left corner of the document.
20. Resize it to approximately 2.5" by 2.5".
21. Fill it with 25% gray.
22. Position it over the beginning of the first WordArt object.
23. Send it back behind the text.
24. Preview the document. It should look similar to Illustration A.
25. If necessary, make adjustments to the size and position of all objects in the document.
26. Print the document.
27. Close the document and exit Word, saving all changes.

Illustration A

Announces
the
Grand Opening
of its
Newest Store

1010 North Quail Drive

Etna, NH

http://www.thesweettooth.com

On Your Own

1. Start Word and create a new document.

2. Save the document as **OWD81**.

3. Use WordArt to create a logo for a business, club, or organization to which you belong.

4. Try different WordArt Shapes.

5. Try different formatting such as Same Letter Heights, Character Spacing, or Vertical Text.

6. Try applying effects such as 3-D or Shadows to the WordArt object.

7. See how rotating or adjusting the WordArt object affects its appearance.

8. When you are satisfied with the result, save the document.

9. Close the document and exit Word.

Exercise 82

On the Job

Place a watermark on almost any document to make an impression on readers, convey an idea, or provide a consistent theme. For example, a watermark on corporate stationery can create a corporate identity. Watermarks can be fun or serious, barely noticeable or strikingly bold. You can save a watermark as part of a template and use it on new documents.

Your boss has asked you to create a notice announcing a job fair open house for State-of-the-Art Solutions and Cornerstone Graphics. You will use a Clip Art image to create a watermark on the document.

Terms

Watermark Text or graphics positioned behind text in a document.

Notes

Watermarks

- Insert text or graphics objects as a **watermark** to provide a background image for text-based documents.

- You can create a watermark from a picture object, such as clip art or a photograph file.

- You can also use drawing objects such as AutoShapes or WordArt.

- When you use text as a watermark, it should be inserted as a drawing object using a text box or WordArt.

- A watermark is usually sized to fill the document page and set to a light shade so it doesn't interfere with the text.

- Watermarks can be inserted before or after text is entered in a document.

- Watermarks are not displayed in Normal view. Use Print Layout view or Print preview to see the watermark.

Watermark in a document

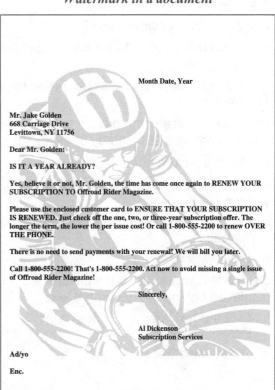

423

Procedures

Create Watermark Using a Picture Object

1. Insert picture.
2. Position and size picture as desired.
3. Click **Image Control** button ▧ on Picture toolbar.
4. Click **Watermark**................. W
5. Click **Text Wrapping** button ▦ on Picture toolbar.
6. Click **Behind Text**.............. D

   ✓ *If the picture doesn't move behind the text, try, selecting Behind Text from the text Wrapping drop-down menu again.*

OR

a. Insert picture.
b. Position and size picture as desired.
c. Click **Format** .... Alt + O
d. Click **Picture** I
e. Click **Picture** tab ... Ctrl + Tab
f. Click **Color** drop-down arrow .... Alt + C
g. Click Watermark.
h. Click **Layout** tab.... Ctrl + Tab
i. Click **Behind text** .. Alt + B
j. Click **OK** .... Enter

Create Watermark Using a Drawing Object

1. Insert object.
2. Select light colors or gray shades for fill and/or line colors.

   ✓ *For black and white printing, use 25% gray; for color printing, use light yellow, light green, rose, tan, light turquoise, pale blue, or lavender.*

3. Position and size object as desired.
4. Click **Draw** button [Draw ▾] on Drawing toolbar........... Alt + R
5. Click **Text Wrapping** .... T
6. Click **Behind Text**............... D

Exercise Directions

1. Start Word, if necessary.
2. Create a new document as save it as **WD82**.
3. Insert the clip art file ⊚ **Eagle.wmf** supplied with this book.

   ✓ *Alternatively, select any clip art picture from the clip gallery.*

4. Increase the size of the picture to fill the page (approximately 8.25" high by 6" wide).
5. Center the picture horizontally and vertically.
6. Change the image control for the picture to watermark.

   a. Click the Image Control button on the Picture Toolbar.
   b. Click Watermark.

7. Set the text wrapping so the picture is displayed behind the document text.

   a. Click the Text Wrapping button on the Picture toolbar.
   b. Click Behind Text.

8. Deselect the picture and then type and format the text as shown in Illustration A.

   a. Center align all text, and vertically center the text on the page.
   b. Unless otherwise marked, use a 20-point bold, sans serif font
   c. Where space is left after a paragraph, leave 36 point.

9. Preview the document. It should look similar to the one in Illustration A.

   ✓ *If the image appears too dark, select it and click the More Brightness button on the Picture toolbar.*

10. Print the document.
11. Save the document and exit Word.

Illustration A

SOAR

To New Heights With
State of the Art Solutions
And
Cornerstone Graphics

**For information about
career opportunities in**
Public Relations, Marketing,
And
Web Design

**Please Come to Our
Open House/Career Fair**
Saturday April 15th and Sunday April 16th
10:00 a.m. – 3:00 p.m.

920 Marco Place
Venice, CA 90291
Call 213-555-1002 for more information

On Your Own

1. Start Word and open the document **OWD32**, the resume you created in the On Your Own section of Exercise 32, or open the document ⊘**82RESUME**.

2. Save the document as **OWD82**.

3. Create a Watermark for the resume. Use Clip Art or use the drawing tools.

4. Make sure the watermark is correctly sized and positioned on the page.

5. Preview the resume with the Watermark.

6. Save the document.

7. Save the document, close it and exit Word.

Exercise 83

You've been asked to design an invitation to a luncheon honoring the employee of the year at Cornerstone Graphics. The invitation will include AutoShapes, WordArt, and a watermark. You will integrate text with the objects to create an effective, eye-catching document.

Exercise Directions

1. Start Word, if necessary.
2. Create a new document and save it as **WD83**.
3. In a 16-point script font, centered, type the following lines of text:

   You are cordially invited
   To attend a luncheon
   In honor of
   Cynthia Coynes
   Friday, October 19
   12:30 in the afternoon
   Café Bon Vivant
   2023 Marco Place
   Venice, CA 90291
   RSVP (213) 555-1002

4. Format the first paragraph to leave 36 points of space before the first line.
5. Create a WordArt object as follows:
   a. Select the style in the first row of the fourth column.
   b. Use a script font in 36 points.
   c. For the WordArt text, type *Cornerstone Graphics*.
6. Size the WordArt object to approximately 2" high by 7.5" wide.
7. Position the WordArt object so the top is approximately .5" from the top of the page on the vertical ruler, and center it horizontally on the page.

8. Create a second WordArt object as follows:
   a. Select the style in the second row of the fourth column.
   b. Use a serif font in 28 points.
   c. Type Employee of the Year as the WordArt text.
9. Size the new WordArt object to approximately .75" high by 4.5" wide.
10. Change the font color of the WordArt object to Pale Blue.
11. Change the shadow color of the WordArt object to Dark Blue.
12. Position the object so the top is at approximately 2" on the vertical ruler, and center it horizontally on the page.
13. Select both WordArt objects and set text wrapping to Top and Bottom
14. Insert the Down Ribbon AutoShape from the Stars and Banners palette.
15. Size it to 2.75" high by 5.75" wide.
16. Position it so its top starts at approximately 7.5" on the vertical ruler (move it up if it causes the document to spread onto two pages), and center it horizontally on the page.
17. In a 20-point serif font, centered and in bold, add the following text to the AutoShape:

    Cornerstone Graphics
    Employee of the Year
    Ms. Cynthia Coynes

18. Leave 12 points of space before and after the first line, and leave 12 points of space before the third line.

19. Fill the AutoShape with Pale Blue.

20. Create a Watermark using the Sun AutoShape from the Basic Shapes palette as follows:

   a. Insert the Sun AutoShape.

   b. Size it to approximately 7.5" high by 7" wide.

   c. Center it horizontally on the page.

   d. Center it vertically as well.

      ✓ *Center it vertically by estimating, or open the Format AutoShapes dialog box, click the Layout tab, click the Advanced button, select the Alignment option button, select Centered from the Alignment drop down list and select Page from the relative to drop down list. Click OK twice.*

   e. Change the line color to 25% gray.

   f. Layer the AutoShape behind the document text.

21. Preview the document. It should look similar to the one in Illustration A.

22. Print the document.

23. Close the document and exit Word, saving all changes.

Illustration A

Cornerstone Graphics

Employee of the Year

*You are cordially invited
To attend a luncheon
In honor of
Cynthia Coynes
Friday October 19
12:30 in the afternoon
Café Bon Vivant
2023 Marco Place
Venice, CA 90291
RSVP (213) 555-1002*

Cornerstone Graphics

Employee of the Year

Ms. Cynthia Coynes

Lesson 12

Integration

Exercise 84

Skills Covered:

◆ **Microsoft® Office 2000** ◆ **Run Multiple Programs at the Same Time**
◆ **Arrange Multiple Program Windows** ◆ **Switch Among Open Programs**

On the Job

If you use Microsoft Office 2000, you may find it necessary to work with more than one application at a time. For example, you might want to create a report detailing your department's decreased costs by combining a Word document with an Excel spreadsheet. Or, you might want to illustrate a Word letter using an Excel Chart. You can open multiple applications at the same time and easily switch among them. You can also arrange the open applications on the screen so you can quickly find the information you need.

The training director at State-of-the-Art Solutions has taken a position at Cornerstone Graphics. You have been promoted to take his place. He left some unfinished documents created with different applications stored on his computer. In this exercise, you will start Word and open a document. You will then start other Office applications, arrange the applications on screen, and switch among open applications.

Terms

Software suite A group of software applications sold as a single unit. Usually, the applications have common features that make it easy to integrate and share data among documents.

Spreadsheet A program used to organize data in columns and rows. Spreadsheets are often used for performing calculations, such as financial or budget analysis.

Presentation application A program used to create presentations, such as slide shows.

Personal information manager (PIM) A program that keeps track of such items as addresses and phone numbers, appointments and meetings, and things to do.

Database An organized collection of records, such as client records, a personal address book, or product inventory.

Tile Arrange open windows on-screen so they do not overlap.

Cascade Arrange open windows on-screen so they overlap, with the active window displayed on top.

Alt +Tab switching A keyboard method of switching among open windows.

Notes

Microsoft® Office 2000

- Microsoft Office 2000 is a **suite** of software applications.

- The Standard edition of the Microsoft Office 2000 suite includes Word (a word processing program), Excel (a **spreadsheet** program), PowerPoint (a **presentation** program), and Outlook (a **personal information manager** and e-mail program).

- The Professional version of the Microsoft Office 2000 suite includes the same programs, plus Access (a **database** program) and Publisher (a publishing program).

Run Multiple Programs at the Same Time

- You can run multiple programs at the same time.

- Use the Windows Start Menu to start any program with a blank document open, or to start the program and open a document at the same time.

  - You can open any Office 2000 document using the Open Office Document dialog box accessed directly from the Windows Start menu.

  - Click the Documents menu to open one of 15 most-recently used files.

  - Locate and open any document using Windows Explorer.

- Each open application window is represented by a button on the Windows taskbar.

- If multiple documents are open in an application, each open document is represented by a button on the Windows taskbar.

Arrange Multiple Program Windows

- You can arrange open program windows on the screen in a number of ways:

  - **Tile** windows when you want to see all windows at the same time. Tiled windows are arranged so they do not overlap.

    ✓ *You can tile windows horizontally across the screen or vertically up and down.*

Windows tiled horizontally

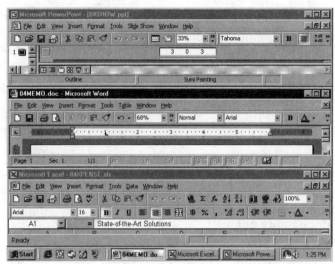

- Cascaded windows overlap like a fanned deck of cards. The active window is displayed on top.

- **Cascade** windows when you want to see the active window in its entirety, as well as the title bars of all other open windows.

Cascaded windows

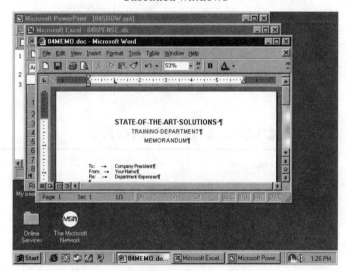

Switch Among Open Programs

- You switch among open programs to make a different window active.

- In any application, the active window appears with a darker title bar, and its taskbar button appears pressed in.

- Use taskbar buttons or **Alt**+**Tab Switching** to change the active window.

Procedures

Start Multiple Programs

Start programs with blank documents open:

1. Click **Start** button

    .... Ctrl + Esc

2. Click **Programs**.................. P

3. Click name of program you want to start.

4. Repeat steps 1 through 4 for each program to open.

Start programs with existing documents open:

1. Click **Start** button

    .... Ctrl + Esc

2. Click **Documents**............... D

3. Click document name.

OR

1. Right-click **Start** button

   Start .

2. Click **Explore** .... E

3. Select drive where folder/file is located.

4. Open folder.

5. Double-click name of document to open.

Arrange Program Windows

1. Right-click on blank area of Windows taskbar.

2. Select desired option:

   a. **Cascade** .... A

   b. **Tile Horizontally**.................. H

   c. **Tile Vertically** .... E

   d. **Minimize All Windows** .... M

   ✓ *Maximize active window to display active window only.*

Switch Between Programs

- Click taskbar button of desired window.

OR

- Click in desired window if it is visible on screen.

  OR

  a. Press and hold Alt

  b. Press **Tab** to cycle through open windows.

  c. Release Alt when desired window is selected.

Close Programs

1. Click **File**..................... Alt + F

2. Click **Exit** .... Alt + X

   OR

   Click **Close** if Exit command is not available........................ C

3. If prompted, click **Yes** .... Y
   to save changes to open document(s).

   OR

   Click **Application Close** icon X .

Exercise Directions

1. Start Word.

2. Open the file 📀**84MEMO.doc**.

3. Start Excel.

4. Open the file 📀**84XPENSE.xls**.

5. Start PowerPoint.

6. Open the file 📀**84SHOW.ppt**.

   ✓ *Opening, saving, and closing files in Excel and PowerPoint are the same as in Word.*

7. Tile the windows vertically on-screen. They should look like Illustration A.

8. Make the Word document 📀**84MEMO.doc** active.

9. Tile the windows horizontally.

10. Make the Excel document 📀**84XPENSE.xls** active.

11. Cascade the windows.

12. Make the PowerPoint file 📀**84SHOW.ppt** active.

13. Maximize the PowerPoint window.

14. Exit PowerPoint.

    ✓ *Do not save any changes.*

15. Exit Excel.

    ✓ *Do not save any changes.*

16. Exit Word.

    ✓ *Do not save any changes.*

Illustration A

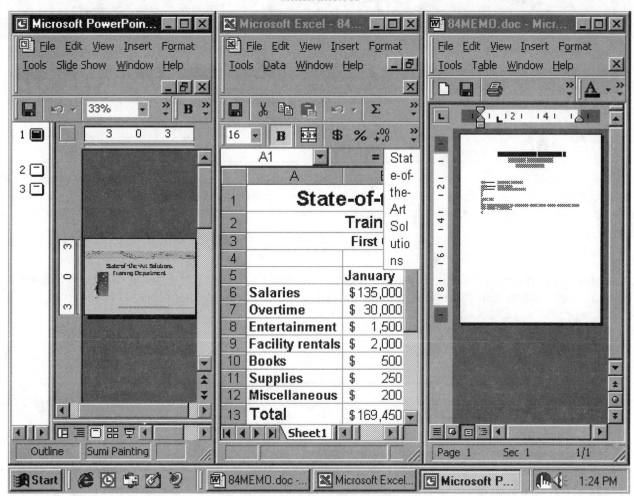

On Your Own

1. Start Word and open the document **OWD82**, that you created in the On Your Own section of Exercise 82, or open ⊚ **84RESUME**.

2. Start Excel with a blank workbook open.

3. Start PowerPoint with a blank presentation open.

4. Arrange the open windows in a cascaded fashion.

5. Arrange the windows in a tiled fashion.

6. Practice switching from window to window.

7. Maximize the Excel window.

8. Close the PowerPoint window without saving any changes.

9. Close the Excel window without saving any changes.

10. Exit Word without saving any changes.

Exercise 85

Skills Covered:

◆ Copy/Move Data from One Application to Another

On the Job

You can use the standard copy and move commands to copy or move data from a document created with one application—such as an Excel worksheet—into a document created with a different application – such as a Word report. Copying or moving data from one application to another saves you the time and trouble of retyping.

As the new training director at State-of-the-Art Solutions, you must complete some of the unfinished work left by your predecessor. In this exercise, you will complete a memo to the president of the company by copying data from an Excel worksheet into a Word document.

Terms

Source file The file that contains the data to be copied.

Destination file The file where the data is pasted

Notes

Copy/Move Data from One Application to Another

- You can use the Windows Clipboard or drag-and-drop editing to copy or move data from one application to another.

- The procedures for copying or moving data from one application to another are similar to copying or moving data from one Word document to another.

  - ✓ See Exercise 61 for information on copying and moving data between Word documents.

- The **source file** contains the original data and the **destination file** is where the data is pasted

- Data pasted into a destination file becomes part of the destination file. No connection to the source file is retained.

- Word may automatically format pasted data. For example, Excel data pasted into a Word document is displayed as a table.

- You edit pasted data using standard commands for the destination application.

Procedures

Copy Data Between Applications

Use Clipboard:

1. Open applications and appropriate source and data files.
2. Select data to copy.
3. Click **Copy** button 📋.
   OR
   a. Click **E**dit .... `Alt`+`E`
   b. Click **C**opy .... `Ctrl`+`C`
   OR
   • Press **Ctrl+C** .... `Ctrl`+`C`
4. Switch to destination file.
5. Position insertion point in the desired location.
6. Click **Paste** button 📋.
   OR
   a. Click **E**dit .... `Alt`+`E`
   b. Click **P**aste .... `P`
   OR
   • Press **Ctrl+V** .... `Ctrl`+`V`

Use drag-and-drop editing:

1. Open applications and display source and destination files.
2. Right-click taskbar.
3. Choose **Tile Vertically** .... `V`

4. Scroll source document to display data to copy.
5. Scroll in destination document to display desired new location.
6. Select data to copy.
7. Move pointer to edge of selection.
   ✓ *Pointer changes to display selection arrow.*
8. Press and hold down **Ctrl**.... `Ctrl`
9. Drag selected data to correct position in destination file.
   ✓ *Gray vertical bar that moves with pointer indicates new location. The + symbol attached to pointer indicates selected data is being copied, not moved.*
10. Release mouse button.
11. Release **Ctrl** .... `Ctrl`

Move Data Between Applications

Use the Clipboard:

1. Open applications and appropriate source and data files.
2. Select data to move.
3. Click **Cut** button ✂.
   OR
   a. Click **E**dit .... `Alt`+`E`
   b. Click **Cu**t .... `T`
   OR
   • Press **Ctrl+X** .... `Ctrl`+`X`

4. Switch to destination file.
5. Position insertion point in the desired location.
6. Click **Paste** button 📋.
   OR
   a. Click **E**dit .... `Alt`+`E`
   b. Click **P**aste .... `P`
   OR
   • Press **Ctrl+V** .... `Ctrl`+`V`

Use drag-and-drop editing:

1. Open applications and display source and destination files.
2. Right-click taskbar.
3. Choose **Tile Vertically** .... `V`
4. Scroll source document to display data to move.
5. Scroll in destination document to display desired new location.
6. Select data to move.
7. Move pointer to right edge of selection.
   ✓ *Pointer changes to display selection arrow.*
8. Drag selected data to correct position in destination file.
   ✓ *Gray vertical bar that moves with pointer indicates new location.*
9. Release mouse button.

Exercise Directions

1. Start Microsoft Word.

2. Open the document ⊙ **85MEMO.doc**.

3. Save the document as **WD85**.

4. Replace the text *Your Name* with your own name.

5. Insert a new blank line at the end of the document.

6. Start Microsoft Excel.

7. Open the worksheet ⊙ **85XPENSE.xls**.

8. Select cells A5 through E13.

9. Copy the selected range of cells to the last line of the **WD85** document.

10. Apply the 3D Effects 3 AutoFormat to the table.

11. Center the table horizontally on the page.

12. Save the changes to the **WD85** document.

13. Preview the document. It should look similar to Illustration A.

14. Print the **WD85** document.

15. Close the ⊙ **85XPENSE.xls** worksheet and exit Excel.

16. Save and close the **WD85** memo.

17. Exit Word.

STATE-OF-THE-ART SOLUTIONS

TRAINING DEPARTMENT

MEMORANDUM

To: Company President
From: Your Name
Re: Department Expenses

Dear Sir:

Per your request, here are the expense figures for the training department for the
first quarter of the year.

	January	February	March	Total
Salaries	$135,000.00	$135,000.00	$135,000.00	$405,000.00
Overtime	$ 30,000.00	$ 32,000.00	$ 29,000.00	$ 91,000.00
Entertainment	$ 1,500.00	$ 1,750.00	$ 1,200.00	$ 4,450.00
Facility rentals	$ 2,000.00		$ 1,500.00	$ 3,500.00
Books	$ 500.00	$ 250.00	$ 500.00	$ 1,250.00
Supplies	$ 250.00	$ 150.00	$ 375.00	$ 775.00
Miscellaneous	$ 200.00	$ 175.00	$ 300.00	$ 675.00
Total	$169,450.00	$ 575.00	$167,875.00	$337,900.00

On Your Own

1. Start Word and create a letter addressed to your friends and/or family telling them that you have made up a list of books and/or CDs that you would like to receive as birthday or holiday gifts.

2. Save the letter as **OWD85**.

3. Start Excel and create a worksheet listing the names and prices of CDs and/or books you would like to own, or open the file **85GIFTS.xls**.

4. Save the worksheet as **OWD85-2**.

5. Select the Excel worksheet data and copy it to the Word document.

6. Copy the Excel worksheet data to the Word letter.

7. Format the data in the Word letter to improve its appearance and make it easier to read.

8. Save the Word and Excel files, close both, and then close Word and Excel.

Exercise 86

On the Job

Link files when you have existing data in one file that you want to use in one or more other files. Whenever the original data is changed, the link ensures that it will be updated in all other files. Linking lets you maintain data in a single location, yet use it in other locations as well.

As the new training director at State-of-the-Art Solutions, you have been asked to submit the department's expenses for the first quarter to the company president. However, you only have preliminary data available. In this exercise, you will link the preliminary data stored in an Excel worksheet into a Word memo. You will then change the data to reflect actual expenses, and update the data in the Word document.

Terms

OLE Object Linking and Embedding enables many Windows applications to share data.

Link To insert an object in a destination file. When the source file is edited, the linked object in the destination file is updated to reflect the change.

Embed Insert an object in a file. The embedded object is not linked to a source file, but it is linked to the source application. You edit the object using the source application, but changes do not affect the source file data.

Notes

Object Linking and Embedding (OLE)

- Object Linking and Embedding (**OLE**) is the feature that enables you to **link** or **embed** objects between Windows applications.
- OLE makes it easier to integrate data among documents created with different applications.

Link Files

- Use linking to create a dynamic connection between two files. Linking enables you to keep files that include the same data up to date, without having to edit the data in every file.
- The source file contains the original data and the destination file contains the linked object.
- Source data can be linked to many destination files. For example, data in an Excel worksheet can be linked to multiple Word documents, and to a PowerPoint slide.

- When you edit the source file, the linked object in the destination file(s) is changed as well.
- Use the Paste Special command to link files.

Paste Special dialog box

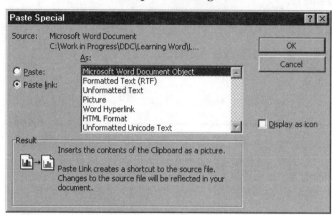

Edit a Linked Object

- You use the source application to edit a linked object. For example, if Excel data is linked to a Word memo, you must use Excel to edit the data.
- When you double-click a linked object, the source application and file open.
- Changes made to the original source file are reflected in the linked object when the link is updated.

- Although you cannot edit a linked object using the destination application, linked objects can be formatted, moved, and resized using many techniques you learned for working with graphics objects.

  ✓ See Lesson 11 for information about working with graphics objects.

Update Links

- By default, links update automatically
- When both the source and destination files are open, the linked object must be selected for the update to occur.
- When only the source file is open, the linked object is updated when you open the destination file.
- If there are many links in a file, automatic updating can slow down your system.
- You can turn off automatic updates and manually update links.

Links dialog box

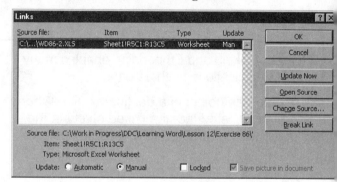

Procedures

Link Files

1. Open source and destination and files.
2. Highlight data to be linked from source file.
3. Click **Edit**..................... `Alt`+`E`
4. Click **Copy** .... `C`
   OR
   Click **Copy** button .
5. Switch to destination file.
6. Position insertion point.
7. Click **Edit**..................... `Alt`+`E`
8. Click **Paste Special** .... `S`
9. Click **As** box to choose format............................ `↑` `↓`

10. Click **Paste Link**.......... `Alt`+`L`
11. Click **OK** .... `Enter`

Edit Linked Object

1. Open destination file.
2. Double-click linked object.
   ✓ *Source application and file open.*
3. Edit source file.
4. **Save** changes .... `Ctrl`+`S`
5. Close source file and application.

Update Links

Turn off automatic updating:

1. Click **Edit** .... `Alt`+`E`
2. Click **Links**......................... `K`
3. Click **Manual** option button............................ `Alt`+`M`
4. Click **OK**........................ `Enter`

Update links manually:

1. Select object.
2. Press **F9** .... `F9`
   OR
1. Click **Edit** .... `Alt`+`E`
2. Click **Links**......................... `K`
3. Click **Update Now** .... `U`

Exercise Directions

✓ *The steps in this exercise assume you know how to select and enter data in an Excel worksheet. If necessary, ask your instructor for more information.*

1. Start Word, if necessary.

2. Open ⊚ **86MEMO.doc**.

3. Save the document as **WD86-1.doc**.

4. Replace the sample text *Your Name* with your own name.

5. Insert a new blank line at the end of the document.

6. Start Excel.

7. Open the file ⊚ **86XPENSE.xls**.

8. Save the file as **WD86-2.xls**.

   ✓ *Use the File, Save As command just as you would in Word.*

9. Link the Excel worksheet data on the last line of the **WD86-1.doc** memo.

   a. Select cells A5:E13 in the **WD86-2.xls** worksheet.

   b. Copy the selected range to the Clipboard.

10. Switch to the **WD86-1.doc** memo.

   • Use the Paste Special command to link the Microsoft Excel Worksheet Object into the Word document.

11. Center the object in the memo horizontally on the page.

   ✓ *Use the Format Object dialog box.*

12. Save the memo document.

13. Double-click the object in the Word document.

   ✓ *The WD86-2.xls worksheet is displayed.*

14. In cell C9—February Facility rentals—type 1,500 and then press Enter.

15. Close the **WD86-2.xls** worksheet, saving the changes, and exit Excel.

16. The **WD86-1.doc** memo is displayed with the new data in place.

17. Edit the link so it will update manually instead of automatically.

18. Double-click the Excel object in the Word memo.

   ✓ *The WD86-2.xls worksheet is displayed.*

19. Edit cell D12—March Miscellaneous expenses—from 300 to 150, and then press Enter.

20. Close the **WD86-2.xls** worksheet, saving the changes, and exit Excel.

21. Notice that the change is not reflected in the linked object in the **WD86-1.doc** memo.

22. Update the link manually

23. Preview the **WD86-1** document. It should look similar to Illustration A.

24. Save the document and close it.

25. Exit Word.

STATE-OF-THE-ART SOLUTIONS
TRAINING DEPARTMENT
MEMORANDUM

To: Company President
From: Your Name
Re: Department Expenses
Date: May 7, 1999

Dear Sir:

Per your request, here are the preliminary expense figures for the training department for the first quarter of the year. I will update the figures as soon as I receive the actuals.

	January	February	March	Total
Salaries	$135,000.00	$135,000.00	$135,000.00	$405,000.00
Overtime	$ 30,000.00	$ 32,000.00	$ 29,000.00	$ 91,000.00
Entertainment	$ 1,500.00	$ 1,750.00	$ 1,200.00	$ 4,450.00
Facility rentals	$ 2,000.00	$ 1,500.00	$ 1,500.00	$ 5,000.00
Books	$ 500.00	$ 250.00	$ 500.00	$ 1,250.00
Supplies	$ 250.00	$ 150.00	$ 375.00	$ 775.00
Miscellaneous	$ 200.00	$ 175.00	$ 150.00	$ 525.00
Total	$169,450.00	$ 575.00	$167,725.00	$337,750.00

On Your Own

1. Start Word and open **OWD85**, the letter you created in the On Your Own section of Exercise 85, or open ⊙ **86LETTER.doc**.

2. Save the document as **OWD86**.

3. Delete the table from the document.

4. Start Excel and open the **OWD85-2**, the worksheet containing the list of books or CDs you created in the On Your Own section of Exercise 85, or open ⊙ **86GIFTS.xls**.

5. Save the worksheet as **OWD86-2**.

6. Link the worksheet data to the Word document.

7. Change some of the data in the Excel worksheet.

8. Make sure the data updates in the Word document.

9. Save and close the Excel worksheet and exit Excel.

10. Save and close the Word document and exit Word.

Exercise 87

Skills Covered:
◆ Embed Objects ◆ Edit Embedded Objects

On the Job

Embed data when you do not want a link between the source data and the embedded object. You can edit embedded data without the changes affecting the source. This is useful for illustrating changes that might occur, or for submitting information that might vary depending on the recipient, such as a proposal bid, or a contract.

At the new training director at State-of-the-Art Solutions, you are planning a weekend training retreat for upper level management. Your boss has asked you to submit a preliminary budget for the event. In this exercise, you will embed an existing budget in a Word memo. You will then edit and format the object using Excel.

Terms

Embed To insert an object in a file without maintaining a link to the source file.

Office links A feature of Office 2000 that facilitates integration between the Office 2000 applications.

Notes

Embed Objects

- **Embedding** inserts an object into a destination file.
- There is no link between the original data in the source file and the embedded object, however, you can use all of the source application's commands to edit, format, and manipulate the embedded object.
- Use the Paste Special command to create an embedded object from existing data.
- Use **Office links** to create a new embedded object.
- You can embed an entire file as an object in a destination file.

Edit Embedded Objects

- Edit embedded objects using the source application. Changes do not affect the source data.
- Format embedded objects using the source application as well.
- When you edit embedded objects in Word, the source application commands and toolbars are displayed in the Word window.

Edit embedded object

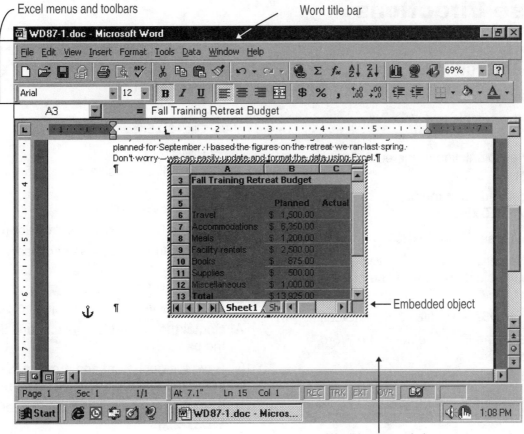

Excel menus and toolbars

Word title bar

Embedded object

Word document window

Procedures

Embed Selected Data

1. Open source file.
2. Select data to be copied.
3. Click **Edit** .... Alt + E
4. Click **Copy** C
5. Open destination file.
6. Position insertion point.
7. Click **Edit** .... Alt + E
8. Click **Paste Special** .... S
9. Select object type from **As** list .... Alt + A , ↑ ↓
10. Click **Paste** .... Alt + P
11. Click **OK** .... Enter

Embed Entire File

1. Open destination file.
2. Position insertion point.
3. Click **Insert** .... Alt + I
4. Click **Object** .... O

5. Click **Create from File** tab .... Alt + F
6. Click **Browse** .... Alt + B
7. Click **Look in** drop-down list box .... Alt + I
8. Type or select drive letter containing file to insert. .... Tab , ↑ ↓ , Enter
9. Double-click folder in Directories list box containing file to insert.
10. Click file name .... ↑ ↓
11. Click **Insert** .... Alt + S
12. Click **OK** .... Enter

Embed a New Object

1. Open destination file.
2. Position insertion point
3. Click **Insert** .... Alt + I
4. Click **Object** .... O
5. Click **Create New** tab .. Alt + C

6. Click **Object type** list box .... Alt + O
7. Select object type. ... Tab , ↑ ↓
8. Click **OK** to create new object. .... Enter

   ✓ *Selected application opens.*

9. Type desired information.
10. Click outside of object to return to close source application and display object in destination file.

Edit Embedded Object

1. Open file containing embedded object.
2. Double-click embedded object.

   ✓ *Source application menus and toolbars are displayed within destination application.*

3. Edit embedded data using source application commands.
4. Click outside embedded object to close source application.

Exercise Directions

1. Start Word, if necessary.
2. Open ⊙ **87RETREAT.doc**.
3. Save the document as **WD87-1**.
4. Replace the sample text *Your Name* with your name.
5. Insert a new blank line at the end of the document.
6. Start Excel and open the file ⊙ **87BUDGET.xls**.
7. Save the file as **WD87-2.xls**.
8. Embed the cells A3:C13 as an Excel Worksheet Object on the last line of the Word document.
9. Close the **WD87-2.xls** file and exit Excel.
10. Double-click the Excel object in the Word document.
    ✓ *Excel commands become available in Word.*
11. Edit the worksheet title from Spring Training Retreat Budget to Fall Training Retreat Budget.
    a. Click cell A3 in the embedded object.
    b. In the Formula bar, replace the text *Spring* with the text *Fall*.
    c. Press Enter.
12. Delete all of the data from the Actual column.
    a. Select cells C6:C13.
    b. Press Delete.
13. Apply the 3D Effects 2 AutoFormat to the object.
    a. Click Format.
    b. Click AutoFormat.
    c. Click 3D Effects 2.
    d. Click OK.
14. Increase the font size in the entire worksheet object to 12 points.
    a. Select cells A3:C13.
    b. Select 12 from Font Size drop-down list.
15. Adjust column widths as necessary.
    • Double-click borders between columns on worksheet frame.
16. Click outside embedded object to close Excel.
17. Center the embedded object horizontally on the page.
18. Save the document and preview it. It should look similar to the one in Illustration A.
19. Start Excel and open the worksheet **WD87-2.xls**.
20. Notice that the worksheet has not been changed.
21. Close the worksheet and exit Excel.
22. Close the **WD87-1.doc** document and exit Word.

Illustration A

STATE-OF-THE-ART SOLUTIONS
TRAINING DEPARTMENT
MEMORANDUM

To: Director of Training
From: Your Name
Re: Training Retreat Budget
Date: August 16, 1999

Boss:

Per your request, here are the preliminary budget figures for the training retreat planned for September. I based the figures on the retreat we ran last spring. Don't worry – we can easily update and format the data using Excel.

Fall Training Retreat Budget		
	Planned	Actual
Travel	$ 1,500.00	
Accommodations	$ 6,350.00	
Meals	$ 1,200.00	
Facility rentals	$ 2,500.00	
Books	$ 875.00	
Supplies	$ 500.00	
Miscellaneous	$ 1,000.00	
Total	$ 13,925.00	

On Your Own

1. Start Word and open **OWD86**, the letter you created in the On Your Own section of Exercise 86, or open ⊙ **87LETTER.doc**.

2. Save the document as **OWD87**.

3. Delete the linked object from the document.

4. Start Excel and open the **OWD86-2**, the worksheet containing the list of books or CDs you created in the On Your Own section of Exercise 86, or open ⊙ **87GIFTS.xls**.

5. Embed the worksheet data into the Word document.

6. Close the Excel worksheet and exit Excel.

7. Use Excel to edit the data in the embedded object.

8. Apply formatting to the embedded object.

9. If you want, check to see that the original data has not changed.

10. Save and close the Word document and exit Word.

Exercise 88

Skills Covered:

◆ Merge a Word Document with an Access Database

On the Job

Creating a data source document in Word for a mail merge is unnecessary if you already have a database stored in a database application, such as Microsoft Access. You can easily merge the Access data with a Word main document.

The training director at State-of-the-Art Solutions has asked you to send out a letter to people who attended the Business on the Web Seminar asking them to evaluate the event. The name and address information is already entered in an Access database. In this exercise, you will create a form letter document in Word, and then merge it with the data in an Access database table. Finally, you will use the Access table to create envelope documents as well.

Terms

Database A file used to store records of data.

Access table An object organized in rows and columns and used to store data in an Access database.

Access query An object containing a subset of records in an Access database.

Notes

Merge a Word Document with an Access Database

- If you have an Access **database** file, you can merge it with a Word main document.

- You can merge with Access **tables** or **queries**.

- The Word main document is set up the same way as it is when merging with a Word data source document.

  ✓ See Exercise 52 for information on setting up a form letter main document and Exercise 55 for setting up envelopes and mailing labels.

- The merge fields in the Word document must match the fields used in the Access table.

- The procedure is similar to merging with an existing data source, however, you must select the specific Access object to use for the merge.

  ✓ You can also start a merge from Access using the Tools, Office Links, Merge It with MS Word command. Office 2000 starts the Mail Merge Wizard to prompt you through the necessary steps.

This Access table can be used as a merge data source

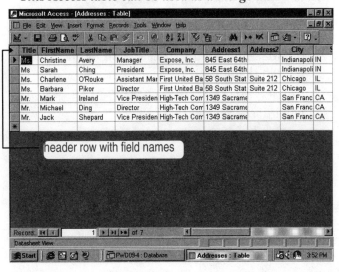

451

Procedures

Merge Word Document with Access Database

1. Open a main document in Word, or create a new document.
   - ✓ *For a refresher on creating a main document, see Exercise 52.*
2. Click **Tools**.................. `Alt`+`T`
3. Click **Mail Merge**................ `R`
4. Click **Get Data** button

   `Get Data ▾` .... `Alt`+`G`
   - ✓ *If the Get Data button is not available, you do not have a main document open.*

5. Click **Open Data Source**..... `O`
6. Click **Files of type**....... `Alt`+`T`
7. Click **MS Access Databases (*.mdb, *.mde)**.
8. Select database file ...... `↓`, `↑`
   - ✓ *Use the Look-in drop-down list to locate the file, if necessary.*
9. Click **Open** .... `Alt`+`O`
   - ✓ *Word starts Access and displays a list of available tables.*

10. Select table to use.
    OR
    - Click Queries tab and select query to use.
11. Click **OK**.......................... `Enter`
    - ✓ *Word displays a message asking you to insert merge fields in your main document.*
12. Click **Edit Main Document**.................. `Alt`+`M`
13. Insert merge fields in main document as necessary.
14. Merge documents when ready.

Exercise Directions

1. Make a copy of the Access database file ⊙**88MERGE**, and name the copy **WD88-1**.
   - ✓ *To copy an Access database, right-click the file in the Window's Explorer window, and select Copy. Then go to where you wish to copy the file. Right-click on the destination folder, and select Paste. Right-click on the copied file and select Rename to rename the file.*

2. Open the document ⊙**88SURVEY** and save it as **WD88-2**.
   - ✓ *This will be used as the main document.*

3. Use the Mail Merge helper to make **WD88-2** a form letter main document.

4. Use the Attendees table in the **WD88-1** Access database file as the data source for the **WD88-2** main document.

5. Edit the main document (**WD88-2**) as shown in Illustration A.
   a. Type the document text.
   b. Insert the merge fields.

6. Preview the merge documents.

7. Merge to a new document.

8. Print the merge documents.

9. Save the merge document form letters file as **WD88-3**.

10. Close all open files.

11. Create a new document that you can use to create an envelopes main document.

12. Use the Mail Merge Helper to create an envelopes main document.

13. Again, use the Attendees table in the **WD88-1** Access database file as the data source.

14. Insert the necessary merge fields to set up the envelopes Main document the way you want the addresses to appear.

15. Preview the merge document.

16. Merge the envelopes to a new document and save it as **WD88-4**.

17. Print the merge documents.

18. Save the envelope main document as **WD88-5**, then close it.

19. Close all open files and exit all open applications, saving all changes.

Illustration A

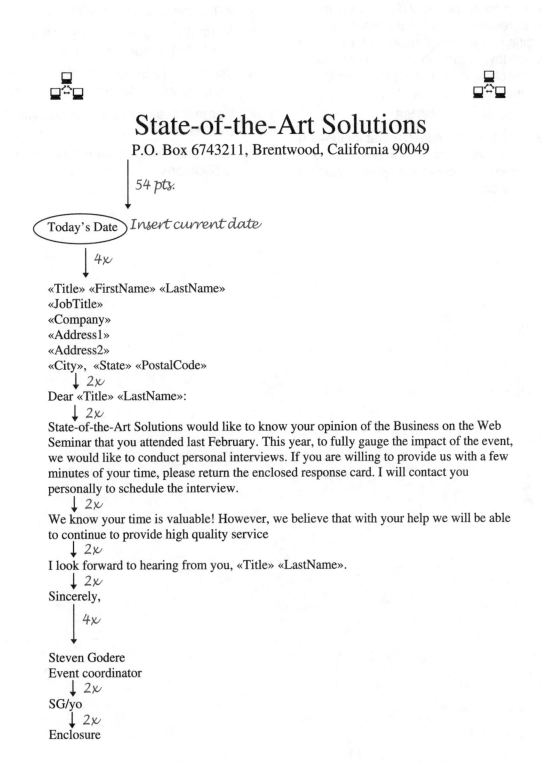

State-of-the-Art Solutions
P.O. Box 6743211, Brentwood, California 90049

54 pts.

(Today's Date) *Insert current date*

4x

«Title» «FirstName» «LastName»
«JobTitle»
«Company»
«Address1»
«Address2»
«City», «State» «PostalCode»
2x
Dear «Title» «LastName»:
2x
State-of-the-Art Solutions would like to know your opinion of the Business on the Web Seminar that you attended last February. This year, to fully gauge the impact of the event, we would like to conduct personal interviews. If you are willing to provide us with a few minutes of your time, please return the enclosed response card. I will contact you personally to schedule the interview.
2x
We know your time is valuable! However, we believe that with your help we will be able to continue to provide high quality service
2x
I look forward to hearing from you, «Title» «LastName».
2x
Sincerely,

4x

Steven Godere
Event coordinator
2x
SG/yo
2x
Enclosure

On Your Own

1. Create a form letter main document that you can send to relatives and friends thanking them for gifts you received recently for a birthday, holiday, or graduation. You can use graphics objects and formatting to make the document interesting to look at.

2. Save the document as **OWD88**.

3. Create an Access database file that includes a table listing the names and addresses of the people you want to receive the letter. Include at least five records.

4. Name the database **OWD88-2**.

5. Alternatively, make a copy of the ⊙**88GIFTS.mdb** file and name it **OWD88-2**.

6. Use the table in the **OWD88-2** database file as the data source for the **OWD88** form letter.

7. Merge the letters to a new document named **OWD88-3**.

8. Save and close all open files, and exit all open applications.

Exercise 89

Skills Covered:

◆ **Embed a PowerPoint Slide in a Word Document**

◆ **Export PowerPoint Slides and Notes to a Word Document**

◆ **Export PowerPoint Text to a Word Document**

On the Job

Share information between two applications to save yourself work and to provide consistency between documents. If you have a PowerPoint presentation, for example, you can use the information in a Word document. You can embed PowerPoint slides in a Word Document as graphics objects, and you can export text and graphics from a PowerPoint presentation into a Word document.

An intern in the training department at State-of-the-Art Solutions has started creating a presentation about the current course offerings using PowerPoint. You can use pieces of the presentation to create other documents for the department. In this exercise, you will create a cover for the new course guide using a slide from the PowerPoint presentation. You will then export the entire presentation to a Word document that you can use as a handout with information about the courses, leaving blank lines for writing notes. Finally, you will export the text from the presentation into a Word document so you can use it to create a document listing the names and main topics of courses.

Terms

Export To send text or data from one application to another application. The original data remains intact.

Notes

Embed a PowerPoint Slide in a Word Document

- You can embed a slide in a Word document.
- The slide appears in Word in full color with graphics and text.
- Embedding a slide is similar to embedding an Excel object in a Word document.
  - ✓ *See Exercise 87 for information on embedding an Excel object in a Word document.*

Export PowerPoint Slides and Notes to a Word Document

- You can **export** PowerPoint slides and notes to a Word document.
- When you export slides, miniatures of your slides are inserted in a table in the Word document.

- You can print slide notes with the slides, or leave blank lines for entering handwritten notes or comments.
- You can link the slides in the Word document to the source document so when you change the source document the linked document in Word updates automatically.

Export PowerPoint Text to a Word Document

- You can export PowerPoint text to a Word document.
- Text will be saved as an RTF file.
- The text will be formatted using Outline heading levels.
- When you open the RTF file in Word, you can save it as a Word file.

Procedures

Embed a PowerPoint Slide in Word

1. Open presentation in PowerPoint.
2. Go to Slide Sorter view.
3. Select slide to copy.
4. Click **Copy**
   button 🖻 ....`Ctrl`+`C`
5. Switch to Word document and position cursor.
6. Click **Paste**
   button 🖻 ....`Ctrl`+`V`

Export PowerPoint Slides and Notes to Word

1. Open presentation in PowerPoint.
2. Click **File** ....`Alt`+`F`
3. Click **Send To**....................`D`
4. Click **Microsoft Word** ....`W`
5. Select option for page layout in Word.
6. Select one of the following:
   - **Paste**....................`Alt`+`P`
   - **Paste link** ....`Alt`+`I`
7. Click **OK** ....`Enter`

Export PowerPoint Text to Word

1. Open presentation in PowerPoint.
2. Click **File**....................`Alt`+`F`
3. Click **Save As**....................`A`
4. Click **Save as type** ......`Alt`+`T`
5. Select **Outline/RTF (*.rtf)**.
6. Click **Save**....................`Alt`+`S`

Open RTF File in Word

1. Click **File**....................`Alt`+`F`
2. Click **Open**....................`O`
3. Select **All Files** from **Files of type** drop-down list.
4. Select file in list
5. Click **Open**....................`Alt`+`O`

Exercise Directions

✓ *The steps in this exercise assume you know how to use a PowerPoint presentation file. If you do not, ask your instructor for more information.*

1. Start Word if necessary and create a new blank document.
2. Insert four blank lines at the top of the document and then save the document as **WD89-1**.
3. Start PowerPoint.
4. Open ⊙ **89TRAIN.ppt**.
5. Save it as **WD89-2.ppt**.
6. Click the Slide Sorter view button to change to Slide Sorter view.
7. Click slide 2 to select it.
8. Copy the selected slide to the Clipboard.
9. Switch to the **WD89-1** document in Word.
10. Paste the slide from the Clipboard into the Word document.
11. Enter and format the text shown in Illustration A.
12. Select the slide and center it.
13. Preview the document. It should look similar to Illustration A.
14. Save the document and close it.
15. Switch back to the **WD89-2.ppt** PowerPoint presentation, and export the slides to a new Word document using the Send To command. Paste the slides, and select the option to leave blank lines next to slides, as shown in Illustration B.
16. Save the document as **WD89-3.doc**.
17. Preview the document. The first page should look similar to Illustration B.
18. Save the document and close it.
19. Switch back to the **WD89-2.ppt** PowerPoint presentation, and save the file in RTF format with the name **WD89-4.rtf**.
20. Close the **WD89-2.ppt** presentation file and exit PowerPoint. Do not save any changes.
21. Switch to Word and open the **WD89-4.rtf** file.
22. Change to Outline view
23. Preview the document.
24. Close the document and exit Word, saving all changes.

Illustration A

State-of-the-Art Solutions
Training Department

Course Guide
Spring/Fall

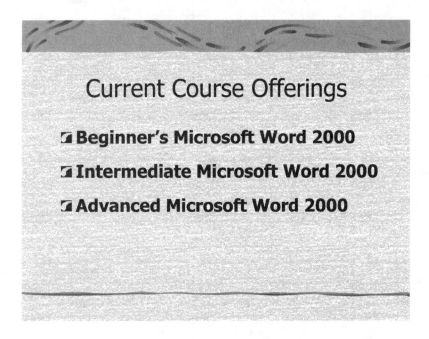

Slide 1

Slide 2

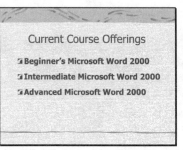

Slide 3

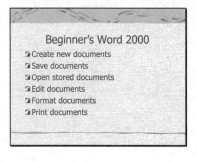

On Your Own

1. Create a PowerPoint presentation about yourself or about a club or organization to which you belong, or open the presentation ⊙**89MYLIFE**.

2. Save the presentation with the name **OWD89**.

3. Create a report in Word by exporting the entire presentation to a new Word document. Include notes if there are any, or leave blank lines for hand writing notes.

4. Save the document with the name **OWD89-2**.

5. Create another new blank Word document to use as a cover for the report. Enter and format text for a title.

6. Save the document with the name **OWD89-3**.

7. Embed a slide from the presentation in the report cover document.

8. Save all documents, close them, and exit both PowerPoint and Word.

Exercise 90

◆ Critical Thinking

The owner of The Sweet Tooth Candy Shop has asked you to create a fundraising letter to send to contributors for the store's scholarship fund. In this exercise, you will create a letter including an embedded Excel worksheet object that displays financial information, and an embedded slide as an example of a presentation. Finally, you will use an Access database as a data source to create mailing labels so you can mail the documents to the contributors.

Exercise Directions

✓ *The steps in this exercise assume you know how to use Excel, Access, and PowerPoint files. If you do not, ask your instructor for more information.*

1. Start Word if necessary and create a new blank document.

2. Save the document as **WD90-1.doc**.

3. Enter and format the text as shown in Illustration A.

   ✓ *Leave blank lines as marked.*

4. Save the changes.

5. Start Excel and open the document ⊙ **90MONEY.xls**.

6. Save the document as **WD90-2.xls**.

7. Select the range A3:D8.

8. Copy the range to the Clipboard.

9. Embed the range as a worksheet object into the **WD90-1.doc** file, on the blank line above the third paragraph (refer to illustration A).

10. Close the **WD90-2.xls** file, and exit Excel.

11. Center the embedded object in the **WD90-1.doc** file.

12. Double-click the object and use Excel commands to format the object with a solid black border and an ice blue shading fill.

   ✓ *Use the Format, Cells command. Click the Border tab to apply a border, then click the Pattern tab to select a fill.*

13. Save the changes to the document.

14. Start PowerPoint and open the document ⊙ **90SWEET.ppt**.

15. Save the document as **WD90-3.ppt**.

16. Select slide 1 and copy it to the clipboard.

17. Paste the slide into the **WD90-1.doc** file on the middle blank line between the third and fourth paragraphs.

18. Close the **WD90-3.ppt** file and exit PowerPoint.

19. Resize slide to approximately 1" high by 1.33" wide.

20. Center the slide object in the Word document.

21. Preview the **WD90-1.doc** file. It should look similar to the one in Illustration B.

22. Save the document and close it.

23. Create a new blank document.

24. Use Mail Merge to make the blank document a mailing labels main document.

25. Use the Donors table in the Access database ⊙ **90NAMES.mdb** as the data source for the mail merge.

26. Set up the main document.

27. Merge the labels to a new document.

28. Save the merge document as **WD90-4**.

29. Save the main document as **WD90-5**.

30. Save and close all documents and exit Word.

Illustration A

The Sweet Tooth Scholarship Fund

321 Main Street ✧ Hanover, NH 03755

72 pts.

Dear Contributors:

2x

Last year your generosity enabled us to provide funding for six highly qualified motivated students to pursue academic goals. We hope we can count on you again.

2x

Below is a table listing our projected expenses for the coming year. As you can see, they have increased considerably. Please take this into account when making your pledges.

3x

Embed Excel object here

On a lighter note, we are in the process of developing a slide show to help spread the word about our activities. We hope to have it completed in time for the annual dinner next month. This sample slide is representative of the look and feel of the presentation.

4x

Embed PowerPoint slide here

Again, thank you for your support. We couldn't do it without you!

2x

Sincerely,

3x

The Sweet Tooth Scholarship Fund Officers

The Sweet Tooth Scholarship Fund

321 Main Street ✧ Hanover, NH 03755

Dear Contributors:

Last year your generosity enabled us to provide funding for six highly qualified motivated students to pursue academic goals. We hope we can count on you again.

Below is a table listing our projected expenses for the coming year. As you can see, they have increased considerably. Please take this into account when making your pledges.

Annual Expenses		
Salaries	$	150,000
Overhead	$	84,000
Marketing	$	175,000
Grants	$	250,000
Total	**$**	**659,000**

On a lighter note, we are in the process of developing a slide show to help spread the word about our activities. We hope to have it completed in time for the annual dinner next month. This sample slide is representative of the look and feel of the presentation.

Again, thank you for your support. We couldn't do it without you!

Sincerely,

The Sweet Tooth Scholarship Fund Officers

Lesson 13

Challenge Exercises

Exercise 91

Skills Covered:

◆ **Create a Document Using a Template**

◆ **Retrieve Data From an Internet Web Site** ◆ **Send Document Via E-mail**

You are a tour guide employed by Adventures in Travel, a package travel tour operator specializing in unique travel experiences. The company owner, Natalie Chaves, has agreed that you need a notebook computer to bring with you on tours. She has asked you to research the current features and prices and then forward the information to him so he can authorize the purchase. You will use the CNET Web site to locate information about notebook computers. You will copy the information into a Word document, edit the document, and then e-mail the document to the shop owner.

✓ *If you do not have access to the Internet, use the CD-ROM simulation that accompanies this book to complete the exercise.*

Exercise Directions

1. Start Word, if necessary, and use the Professional Memo template to create a new document.

2. Save the document as **WD91**.

3. Enter the text shown in Illustration A. Delete the CC: field.

4. Display the Web toolbar.

5. Open the Internet Simulation:

   a. Click **Go**.

   b. Click **Open**.

   c. In the Address line type the following: D:/Internet/E91/cnet.htm

   ✓ *If you've copied the Internet simulation files to your hard drive or your CD-ROM drive is a letter other than D:, substitute the correct letter for D.*

   Click **OK**.

6. On the CNET home page, click the *Hardware* link.

7. Click the *Notebooks* link.

8. Click the *Ultralight Notebooks* link.

9. Click the *Comparison Chart* link.

10. Select the chart (8 columns and 9 rows) and copy it to the Clipboard.

11. Switch to the **WD91** document and paste the selection on the last line of the document.

12. Exit the simulation.

13. Select the table in the **WD91** document and s the font size to 8 points.

14. Apply the Grid 4 AutoFormat to the table.

15. Preview the document. It should look similar t the one in Illustration B.

    ✓ *If necessary, adjust the size of the table so the document fits on one page.*

16. Send the document via e-mail to: learn@ddcpub.com.

    ✓ *You may be prompted to connect to the Internet.*

17. Disconnect from the Internet.

18. Save and close the **WD91** document, and exit Word.

Illustration A

Enter company name ——————→ **Adventures in Travel**

Memo

Delete CC: line

To: Natalie Chaves
From: (Your Name) *Insert your own name*
Date: 05/10/99
Re: Notebook Computer Prices

Nat – ←—— *Heading 1 style*

Body text style

I did some research about notebook computer prices on the Internet. Here's a comparison chart from the CNET Web site. I like the Toshiba model at the bottom of the list. For more information, you can click any notebook name and go right to the site yourself. Let me know if I can go ahead and order something. I can do that on-line, too.

↓ *2x leave a blank line*

● Page 1

Memo

To: Natalie Chaves

From: Your Name

Date: 05/10/99

Re: Notebook Computer Prices

Nat –

I did some research about notebook computer prices on the Internet. Here's a comparison chart from the CNET Web site. I like the Toshiba model at the bottom of the list. For more information, you can click any notebook name and go right to the site yourself. Let me know if I can go ahead and order something. I can do that on-line, too.

	Est. price	Processor	RAM installed	Hard disk size/type	Screen size	Modem	Traveling weight
Acer TravelMate 313T	$1,799	Intel Pentium MMX-266	32MB	3.2GB/EIDE	8.4 in.	56-kbps K56flex V.90	4.28 lb.
Mag TinyNote 200TNS	$999	Cyrix Media GXm-200	32MB	2.1GB/EIDE	8.2 in.	56-kbps V.90	6.34 lb.
MetroBook SLT	$1,495	Intel Pentium MMX-200	64MB	4.3GB/EIDE	8.4 in.	56-kbps K56flex V.90	6.1 lb.
NEC Ready 120LT	$899	Cyrix Media GXm-200	64MB	2.1GB/EIDE	8.2 in.	56-kbps V.90	6.34 lb.
Ricoh Magio 4G	$2,299	Intel Pentium MMX-266	64MB	4.3GB/EIDE	9.2 in.	none	4.3 lb.
Sharp Actius PC-A150	$1,999	Intel Pentium MMX-266	64MB	4.3GB/EIDE	11.3 in.	56-kbps K56flex V.90	4.64 lb.
Sony VAIO PCG-505TX	$2,499	Intel Pentium MMX-300	64MB	6.4GB/EIDE	10.5 in.	56-kbps K56flex V.90	4.78 lb.
Toshiba Portégé 3020CT	$1,999	Intel Pentium MMX-300	32MB	6.4GB/EIDE	10.4 in.	56-kbps V.90	4.0 lb.

● Page 1

Exercise 92

Skills Covered:

◆ **Link a Worksheet into a Word Document**

◆ **Locate Data on the Internet** ◆ **Edit Excel Worksheet**

◆ **Update Linked Object in a Word Document**

You have been asked to organize a five-day bicycle tour of Nova Scotia for Adventures in Travel. You have an Excel worksheet listing lodging costs in Canadian dollars. In this exercise, you will link the worksheet to a Word memo, then locate current exchange rates on the Web and edit the Excel worksheet to convert the costs to U.S. dollars. Finally, you will update the link to the Word document.

Exercise Directions

1. Start Word, if necessary, and create the document shown in Illustration A, or open ⊙ **92BIKING.doc**.

2. Save the file as **WD92-1.doc**.

3. Start Excel and open the workbook ⊙ **92COSTS.xls**.

4. Save the file as **WD92-2.xls**.

5. Copy the range A1:D10 to the Clipboard.

6. Switch back to Word and link the worksheet object on the last line of the **WD92-1** document.

7. Set the link for manual updating.

8. Display the Web toolbar.

9. Open the Internet Simulation:

   a. Click **Go**.

   b. Click **Open**.

   c. In the Address line type the following: D:/Internet/E92/currencytable.htm

   ✓ *If you've copied the Internet simulation files to your hard drive or your CD-ROM drive is a letter other than D:, substitute the correct letter for D.*

   Click **OK**.

10. In the list of base currencies, select *CAD Canada Dollars*.

11. Click the *Generate Currency Table* button.

12. Locate the *USD (American Dollars)* exchange rate, select the rate for the number of Canadian dollars per one U.S dollar, and copy it to the Clipboard.

    ✓ *The first column lists the number of Canadian dollars per one U.S. dollar; the second column lists the number of U.S. dollars per Canadian dollar.*

13. Switch to the **WD92-2.xls** worksheet in Excel.

14. Paste the data from the Clipboard into cell C5, then copy it to cells C6, C7, and C8.

    ✓ *If necessary, ask your instructor for information about working with Excel.*

15. Exit the CD simulation.

16. Select the cells C5, C6, C7, and C8 and increase the font size to 12.

17. In the Excel worksheet, create a formula in cell D5 to calculate the current cost in U.S. dollars of lodging in a four star hotel.

    ✓ *Hint: Divide the CAD cost by the exchange rate.*

18. Copy the formula to cells D6:D8.

19. Switch to the **WD91-1.doc** document in Word.

20. Update the link.

21. Preview the document. If should look similar to Illustration B.

22. Save and close all open documents and exit all open applications.

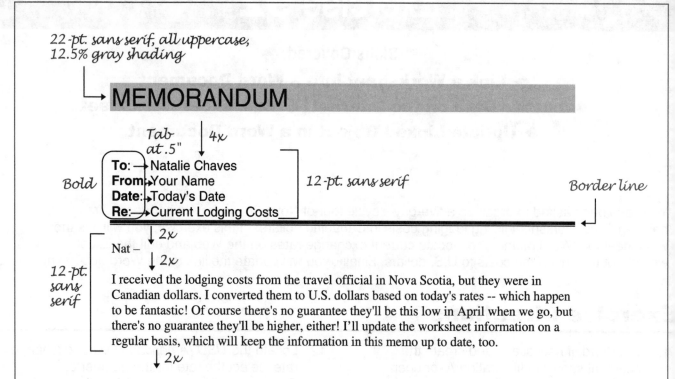

22-pt. sans serif, all uppercase, 12.5% gray shading

MEMORANDUM

Tab at .5" ↓ *4x*

Bold

To: → Natalie Chaves
From: → Your Name
Date: → Today's Date
Re: → Current Lodging Costs

12-pt. sans serif

Border line

↓ *2x*

12-pt. sans serif

Nat –

↓ *2x*

I received the lodging costs from the travel official in Nova Scotia, but they were in Canadian dollars. I converted them to U.S. dollars based on today's rates -- which happen to be fantastic! Of course there's no guarantee they'll be this low in April when we go, but there's no guarantee they'll be higher, either! I'll update the worksheet information on a regular basis, which will keep the information in this memo up to date, too.

↓ *2x*

Illustration B

MEMORANDUM

To: Natalie Chaves
From: Your Name
Date: Today's Date
Re: Current Lodging Costs

Nat –

I received the lodging costs from the travel official in Nova Scotia, but they were in Canadian dollars. I converted them to U.S. dollars based on today's rates -- which happen to be fantastic! Of course there's no guarantee they'll be this low in April when we go, but there's no guarantee they'll be higher, either! I'll update the worksheet information on a regular basis, which will keep the information in this memo up to date, too.

Lodging Packages; Four Nights, Five Days*
Nova Scotia

Accommodations	Cost (CAD)	Exchange Rate	Cost (USD)
Four Star	$ 575.00	1.50939	$ 380.95
Three Star	$ 515.00	1.50939	$ 341.20
Economy	$ 465.00	1.50939	$ 308.07
Budget	$ 350.00	1.50939	$ 231.88

*Rates Based on Double Occupancy

Exercise 93

Skills Covered:

Save a Word Document as a Web Page
Download Clip Art and Insert it on a Web Page
Link Excel Data with a Web Page   Update linked Data

The owner of Adventures in Travel wants you to provide information about the bike trip to Nova Scotia on the company's Web site. In this exercise, you will create a Word document about the trip and save it as a Web page. You will download clip art from the Web and insert it on the Web page. You will also link worksheet information about lodging costs to the Web document, so if the conversion rate changes, the information on the Web site will remain current.

Exercise Directions

1. Start Word if necessary and create the document shown in illustration A, or open ☞ **93BIKING**.

2. Save the document as **WD93-1.doc**.

3. Save the document as a Web page with the title *Bike Trips* and the file name **WD93-2.htm**.

4. Apply the Maize theme to the Web page.

5. Use the Clip Gallery Live Web site to locate a clip art image of a bicycle and a photo of the ocean (refer to illustration B).

6. Download the graphics into your Microsoft Clip Gallery.

7. Insert the graphics into the **WD93-2.htm** Web page.

8. Resize the graphics so they are each 1.5" high.

9. Set the text wrap around both graphics to Square.

10. Position the graphics as shown in Illustration B.

11. Save the changes.

12. Start Excel and open the workbook ☞ **93COSTS.xls**.

13. Save the file as **WD93-3.xls**.

14. Copy the range A1:D10 to the Clipboard.

15. Switch back to the **WD93-2.htm** Web page in Word and link the worksheet object on the last line of the document.

16. Switch back to the **WD93-3.xls** file in Excel.

17. Change the exchange rate in cells C5, C6, C7, and C8 to 1.506.

18. Switch back the Word to see if the link is updated in **WD93-2.htm**.

19. Use Web Page Preview to preview the document. It should look similar to Illustration B.

20. Close Web Page Preview.

21. Save and close all open documents, and exit all open applications.

Illustration A

28-pt. sans serif,
Centered ——→ # Bike Nova Scotia

72 pts.

Join Adventure in Travel's knowledgeable and experienced guides on an exciting five-day bicycle excursion to delightful
↓*2x*
NOVA SCOTIA
↓*2x*
Contact: Natalie Chaves for more information.
↓*2x*
Highlights include:
↓*2x*

14 pts.

- Five days/four nights including transportation and lodging
- Fine dining
- Quaint seaside villages
- Exciting natural wonders
↓*2x*
Exchange rates are highly favorable right now. Check out the current cost of lodging:
↓*2x*

Bike Nova Scotia

Join Adventure in Travel's knowledgeable and experienced guides on an exciting five-day bicycle excursion to delightful

NOVA SCOTIA

Contact: Natalie Chaves for more information.

Highlights include:

- Five days/four nights including transportation and lodging
- Fine dining
- Quaint seaside villages
- Exciting natural wonders

Exchange rates are highly favorable right now. Check out the current cost of lodging:

Lodging Packages; Four Nights, Five Days*
Nova Scotia

Accommodations	Cost (CAD)	Exchange Rate	Cost (USD)
Four Star	$ 575.00	1.506	$ 381.81
Three Star	$ 515.00	1.506	$ 341.97
Economy	$ 465.00	1.506	$ 308.76
Budget	$ 350.00	1.506	$ 232.40

*Rates Based on Double Occupancy

Exercise 94

Skills Covered:

◆ **Create a Home Page Using a Table**

◆ **Link the Home Page to Presentation Web Sites**

◆ **Link the Home Page to an Internet Site**

◆ **Add a Web Page to Your Favorites Folder**

◆ **Print a Web Page off the Internet**

You are a Web site designer for Cornerstone Graphics. The Adventures in Travel tour group has hired you to improve its Web site. They have already created two presentation Web sites from PowerPoint presentations about a bicycle tour in Nova Scotia and a canoe trip on the Saco River in Maine, but they need you to design a Home page and set up necessary links. In this exercise, you will create a Home page in Word using tables. You will link the home page to the existing presentation Web sites. You will also provide links from the Home page to a site on the Internet about touring Nova Scotia. When you test the links, you will print a Web page off the Internet, and add a Web page to your Favorites folder for future reference.

Exercise Directions

1. Start Word, if necessary, and create the document shown in Illustration A, or open the file ⊙ **94TRAVEL.doc**.

   a. Create a table with nine rows and two columns.

   b. Set the height of rows 1, 2, 5 and 7 to at least 1.5".

   c. Set the height of rows 4, 6, 8, and 9 to at least .25".

   d. Set the height of row 3 to at least .5".

   e. Merge the cells in row 2, and then the cells in row 3.

   f. In row 1, set column 1 to approximately 4" wide and column 2 to approximately 2" wide.

   g. In the remaining rows with two columns, set column 1 to approximately 3.5" wide and column 2 to approximately 2.5" wide.

   h. Type the text as shown using a sans serif font in the specified size.

   i. Apply the specified alignments.

   j. Use the Clip Gallery to locate the three clip art pictures shown in Illustration A and insert them in the appropriate cells.

   ✓ *If you cannot locate the same pictures, select others, or try using the on-line Clip Gallery Live.*

   k. Set the height of each clip art picture to 1.5". Leave the aspect ratio locked so the width will adjust automatically.

   l. Center each picture horizontally and vertically within its cell.

   m. Apply borders as shown in Illustration A.

2. Save the document as a Web Page with the name **WD94.htm** and the Web page title *Adventures in Travel Home Page*.

3. Apply the Willow theme to the page.

4. Select the text *Tour Nova Scotia* and insert a hyperlink to the PowerPoint Web presentation file ⊙ **94BIKE.htm**.

   ✓ *If you are using a browser that does not support frames, you may have a problem accessing the PowerPoint Web presentation. Ask your instructor for more information.*

5. Select the clip art picture of the bicyclists and insert another hyperlink to ⊙ **94BIKE.htm**.

6. Link the text *Paddle the Saco* with the PowerPoint Web presentation file ⊙ **94CANOE.htm**.

7. Link the clip art picture of the canoeists to the ⊙ **94CANOE.htm** file, as well.

8. Use the text Virtual Nova Scotia to create a hyperlink to the Virtual Nova Scotia tourism Web site, at the URL address: D:/Internet/E94/welcome.htm

   ✓ *If you've copied the Internet simulation files to your hard drive or your CD-ROM drive is a letter other than D:, substitute the correct letter for D.*

9. Use Web Page Preview to check the **WD94.htm** Home page.

10. Test each link to the presentation Web sites.

    ✓ *While in Web Page Preview, browse the presentation sites using the Outline on the left side of the screen or the Forward and Back buttons. Use the Back button on the Web toolbar or the Home link on the title slide of either presentation to return to the Home page.*

11. From the **WD94.htm** Home page, test the link to the Virtual Nova Scotia tourism Web site

12. Click the *Jump to Website* link.

13. Click the *Great Outdoors* link.

14. Add the Great Outdoors page to your Favorites folder.

15. Click the *Scenic Travelways* link.

16. Print the *Scenic Travelways* page.

17. Return to the *Virtual Nova Scotia Home* page.

18. Exit the simulation.

19. Close Web Page Preview.

20. Save and close all open documents and exit Word.

Illustration A

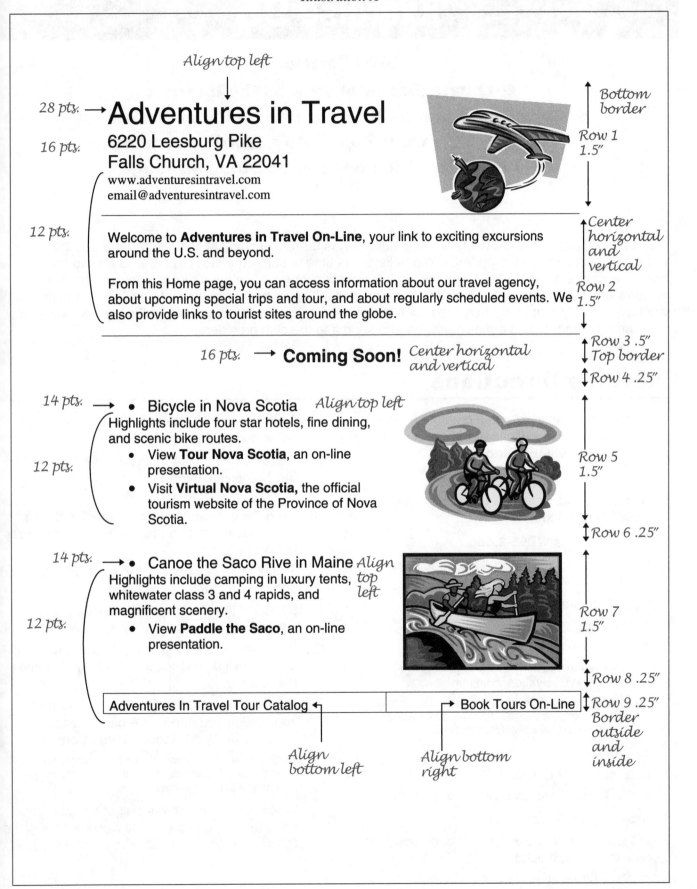

Align top left

28 pts. → **Adventures in Travel**

16 pts. 6220 Leesburg Pike
Falls Church, VA 22041

www.adventuresintravel.com
email@adventuresintravel.com

Bottom border

Row 1 1.5"

12 pts. Welcome to **Adventures in Travel On-Line**, your link to exciting excursions around the U.S. and beyond.

From this Home page, you can access information about our travel agency, about upcoming special trips and tour, and about regularly scheduled events. We also provide links to tourist sites around the globe.

Center horizontal and vertical

Row 2 1.5"

16 pts. → **Coming Soon!** *Center horizontal and vertical*

Row 3 .5" Top border

Row 4 .25"

14 pts. → • Bicycle in Nova Scotia *Align top left*
Highlights include four star hotels, fine dining, and scenic bike routes.

12 pts. • View **Tour Nova Scotia**, an on-line presentation.
• Visit **Virtual Nova Scotia,** the official tourism website of the Province of Nova Scotia.

Row 5 1.5"

Row 6 .25"

14 pts. → • Canoe the Saco Rive in Maine *Align top left*
Highlights include camping in luxury tents, whitewater class 3 and 4 rapids, and magnificent scenery.

12 pts. • View **Paddle the Saco**, an on-line presentation.

Row 7 1.5"

Row 8 .25"

Adventures In Travel Tour Catalog ← → Book Tours On-Line

Row 9 .25" Border outside and inside

Align bottom left

Align bottom right

Exercise 95

Skills Covered:

◆ **Locate Financial Data on the Internet**

◆ **Copy Data from the Internet Into an Excel Worksheet**

◆ **Copy Data from Excel into a Word Document**

◆ **Attach the Document to an E-mail Message**

A group of employees at State-of-the-Art Solutions has formed an investment club. As the club treasurer you have been tracking the portfolio. You believe it is time to sell some stock in order to spread the investments into other market segments. In this exercise you will use the Internet to look up the ticker symbols and current market prices of the stocks. You will copy the information into an Excel worksheet you have already prepared, then copy the entire worksheet into a Word document. Finally, you will attach the Word document to an e-mail message and send it to the club president.

Exercise Directions

1. Start Word if necessary and create the memo document shown in Illustration A, or open the document ⊚ **95MEMO.doc**.

2. Save the file as **WD95-1.doc**.

3. Start Microsoft Excel and open the workbook ⊚ **95STOCKS.xls**.

4. Save the file as **WD95-2.doc**.

5. Switch back to Word and display the Web toolbar.

6. Open the Internet Simulation:

   a. Click **Go**.

   b. Click **Open**.

   c. In the Address line type the following: D:/Internet/E95/yahoo_com.htm

   ✓ *If you've copied the Internet simulation files to your hard drive or your CD-ROM drive is a letter other than D:, substitute the correct letter for D.*

   d. Click **OK**.

7. Click the *Stock Quotes* link.

   ✓ *The Yahoo! Finance page displays on your screen.*

8. Click the *symbol lookup* link.

9. In the Lookup text box, type *Amazon.com*, then click the *Lookup* button.

   ✓ *The ticker symbol for Amazon.com is AMZN.*

10. Switch to the **WD95-2.xls** file and type the ticker symbol in cell B6.

11. Switch back to your Internet browser and click the *Home* link at the top of the page to return to the Yahoo! Finance page.

12. Type the company's ticker symbol in the Get Quotes text box and then click the *Get Quotes* button.

13. Select the stock price in the Last Trade column and copy it to the Clipboard.

14. Switch to the Excel worksheet it past it into cell F6.

15. Switch back to your Internet browser and click the *Home* link to display the Yahoo! Finance home page.

16. Repeat steps 10 through 15 to gather the information you need for America On Line, Lycos, MCI WorldCom, and Intel Corp.

   ✓ *Enter the ticker symbol data into the appropriate cells in Column B and enter the last trade data into the appropriate cells in column F*

17. When you have gathered all of the data you need to complete the Excel worksheet, exit the CD simulation.

18. In the **WD95-2.xls** worksheet, copy the range A1:H10 to the clipboard.

19. Switch to the **WD95-1.doc** Word document and paste the worksheet on the last line of the memo.

20. Apply the Professional AutoFormat to the table in the Word document.

21. Close the Excel file and exit Excel.

22. Preview the Word document. It should look similar to Illustration B.

    ✓ *The current market prices will vary depending on whether you are working on line, or using the CD simulation.*

23. Use the File, New command to create a new e-mail message document.

24. Enter the following header information (leave the CC: field blank):

    To: Learn@ddcpub.com

    Subject: Stock Prices

25. Type the message: Here's the information I promised. Get back to me ASAP – these stocks are volatile and we have to act fast.

26. Attach the **WD95-1.doc** document to the message and send it.

    ✓ *You will be prompted to log on to the Internet.*

27. Save the **WD95-1.doc** file and close it.

28. Exit Word.

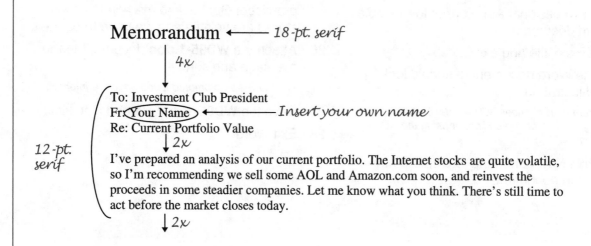

Illustration B

Memorandum

To: Investment Club President
Fr: Your Name
Re: Current Portfolio Value

I've prepared an analysis of our current portfolio. The Internet stocks are quite volatile, so I'm recommending we sell some AOL and Amazon.com soon, and reinvest the proceeds in some steadier companies. Let me know what you think. There's still time to act before the market closes today.

State-of-the-Art Solutions							
Investment Club							
Date:	3/26/99						
Company	Ticker Symbol	Shares Owned	Price When Purchased	Original Investment	Current Market Price	Current Value	Return on Investment
Amazon.com	AMZN	100	85 3/8	$ 8,537.50	142	$ 14,200.00	$5,662.50
America On Line	AOL	200	92 5/16	$18,462.50	125 7/8	$ 25,175.00	$6,712.50
Lycos	LCOS	75	77 1/2	$ 5,812.50	90 9/16	$ 6,792.19	$ 979.69
MCI WorldCom	WCOM	150	64 3/8	$ 9,656.25	90 3/8	$ 13,556.25	$3,900.00
Intel Corp	INTC	100	100	$10,000.00	118 1/8	$ 11,812.50	$1,812.50

Exercise 96

Skills Covered:

◆ **Record a Macro for a Mail Merge**

◆ **Use an Access Database as a Merge Data Source** ◆ **Run a Macro**

As a tour guide for Adventures in Travel, you are leaving on a ten-day climbing trip in the Canadian Rocky Mountains. While you are gone, you want the person covering for you to send out a mailing to past customers about the upcoming bike trip to Nova Scotia and the canoe trip in Maine. You already have the address information stored in an Access database table, but your replacement is not comfortable using Access. In this exercise, you will record a macro for creating mailing labels from the Access database table so that your replacement will be able to complete the task. You will then run the macro to make sure it works.

Exercise Directions

1. Use Windows to make a copy of the 🔗 **96MERGE.mdb** Access database.

   ✓ *To copy an Access database, right-click the file in the Window's Explorer window, and select Copy. Then go to where you wish to copy the file. Right-click on the destination folder, and select Paste. Right-click on the copied file and select Rename to rename the file.*

2. Name the copied database file **WD96-1.mdb**.

3. Start Word if necessary and create a new blank document.

4. Save the file as **WD96-2.doc**.

5. Create a new macro named Labels.

6. Enter the description: *Use Mail Merge to create mailing labels from Access database.*

7. Assign the macro to an unassigned key combination, such as Alt+L.

8. Start recording the macro.

9. While the macro is recording, use Mail Merge to create mailing labels.

   a. Use **WD96-2.doc** as the Mailing Labels main document.

   b. Use the Addresses table in the **WD-96-1.mdb** database as the data source.

   c. Use the default label style (Avery Standard 2160 Mini-Address).

   d. Set up the main document so the address appears correctly on the labels.

   e. Merge to a new blank document.

10. When the merge document is displayed on-screen, stop recording the macro.

11. Close the merge document without saving it.

12. Close the main document (**WD96-2.doc**) without saving it.

13. Reopen **WD96-2.doc**.

    ✓ *The document should be blank.*

14. Run the Labels macro to make sure it works.

15. When the merge document is displayed on screen, save it as **WD96-3.doc**. The first page should look similar to Illustration A.

16. Close **WD96-3.doc**.

17. Save and close **WD96-2.doc**.

18. Exit Word.

19. Exit Access, if necessary.

Illustration A

Mr. Anthony Anzio
75 Auburn Ave.
Auburn, ME 04210

Mr. Alex Daniels
1031 Roosevelt Parkway
Suite 52D
W. Hempstead, NY 11552

Ms. Angela DiMarco
6220 Leesburg Pike
Jenkintown, PA 19046

Mr. Thomas Gomez
P.O. Box 1033
Bethesda, MD 20814

Exercise 97

Skills Covered:

◆ **Create a Double-Sided Flyer**
◆ **Attach Two Documents to an E-mail Message**
◆ **Run a Macro to Create Mailing Labels**

You are covering the office for a tour guide at Adventures in Travel. While the guide is gone, you must send out a mailing, advertising two upcoming trips. In this exercise, you will create two documents that can be printed as a double-sided flyer, folded in half, stapled, and mailed. To set up the document you will use columns, sections, text boxes, and clip art. When the flyer is complete, you will attach both documents to an e-mail message and send them to the tour guide for approval. Finally, you will use a macro the tour guide left you to create mailing labels.

Exercise Directions

1. Start Word if necessary and create a new blank document.

2. Save the document as **WD97-1.doc**.

3. Create the document shown in Illustration A. This will be one side of the flyer.

   a. Insert a text box for entering the return address.

   b. Size the text box to .75" high and 2.25" wide.

   c. Make sure there is no border around the box.

   d. Position the text box in the upper left corner of the page, as shown in Illustration A.

   e. Enter the text shown in Illustration A. Use a sans serif font. Type the company name in 14 points and the address in 12 points.

   f. Insert another text box to mark where the mailing label will go, as shown in Illustration A.

   g. Size the second text box to accommodate your mailing labels. For the default label (Avery Standard 2160 Mini-Address) make the box 1.25" high by 2.75" wide, and apply a dotted border (refer to Illustration A).

   h. Position the text box so that its top is aligned with 2.5" on the vertical ruler, and center it horizontally.

   i. Enter the text shown in Illustration A. Use a 12-point serif font, centered.

   j. Insert a clip art picture below the return address box, as shown in Illustration A.

   k. Size the picture to 2.5" high and 3.25" wide.

   l. Insert the Explosion 2 AutoShape.

   m. Format the AutoShape in the 3-D Style 2, with a Light Turquoise fill.

   n. Size the AutoShape to 4.5" high by 6.5" wide.

   o. Position the AutoShape starting approximately .5 inches from the bottom of the page, and centered horizontally.

   p. Add the text shown in Illustration A, using a 24-point bold, sans serif font, centered.

4. Save the document.

5. Preview the document. It should look similar to Illustration A.

6. Create a new blank document, or open the document ⊚ **97SIDEB**.

7. Save the document as **WD97-2.doc**.

8. Create the document shown in Illustration B. This will be the other side of the flyer.

   a. Type the text as shown, using a sans serif font in the sizes indicated on the Illustration.

   b. Center the first three lines, the two headlines, and the last paragraph, and leave all other paragraphs flush left.

   c. Apply a border under the second line, as shown in the Illustration.

   d. Leave 6 points of space after the second line, then 3 points of space after all other paragraphs.

e. Insert a continuous section break between the third and fourth lines.

f. Insert a continuous section break before the last paragraph on the page.

g. Leave 12 points of space before the last paragraph on the page.

h. Format Section 2 into two columns of equal width.

i. Apply bullet lists as shown in Illustration B.

j. Apply dropped capitals as shown in Illustration B.

k. Insert a column break after the first bulleted list.

l. Insert clip art pictures as shown in Illustration B.

   ✓ *If you cannot locate the shown clip art in the Clip Gallery, select any clip art you like.*

m. Set text wrap for the clip art to Tight.

n. Size both pictures to 1.25" high, and leave the aspect ratio locked so the width will adjust automatically.

o. Position the clip art pictures as shown in Illustration B.

9. Save the document.

10. Preview the document. It should look similar to the one in Illustration B.

11. Print **WD97-1.doc**.

12. Reload the printed document in the printer so that you can print on the other side.

   ✓ *Ask your instructor for information on loading paper into the printer for double-sided copying.*

13. Print **WD97-2.doc**.

14. Save and close **WD97-1.doc** and **WD97-2.doc**.

15. Create a new e-mail message.

16. Fill in the message header as follows (Leave the CC: field blank):

   TO: learn@ddcpub.com

   Subject: Flyer

17. Type the following message: I've attached the two documents I created for the flyer. As soon as you approve them, I'll print and mail. Thanks.

18. Attach both the **WD97-1.doc** and **WD97-2.doc** documents to the message.

19. Save the message with the name **WD97-3.doc**.

20. Send the message.

   ✓ *You may be prompted to log on to the Internet.*

21. Create a new blank document and save it as **WD97-4.doc**.

22. Run the Labels macro you created in Exercise 96 to create mailing labels.

23. Save the merge document as **WD97-5.doc**.

24. Save and close all open documents.

25. Exit Word.

26. Exit Access, if necessary.

Adventures in Travel
6220 Leesburg Pike
Falls Church, VA 22041

Attach mailing label here

REGISTER NOW
FOR ONE OF
OUR EXCITING,
NEW
ADVENTURES!

Illustration B

46 pts. # Adventures In Travel

14 pts. "Specializing in Exciting Excursions Around the Globe"

20 pts. ## Announcing our two newest adventures!

18 pts. ### Bike Nova Scotia

Join us for a four-night/five-day bicycle tour of scenic Nova Scotia. This exciting adventure begins in Halifax, and includes a circular route that

covers many of the major attractions of the beautiful and friendly Canadian province. The cycling is moderate, with no major elevation changes. Enrollment is limited, so register now!

Highlights include:

- Four-star accommodations
- Fine dining
- Natural wonders
- Experienced guides

Canoe the Saco River

This wet and wild adventure is sure to attract a lot of interest among everyone who loves running the rapids! Although the Saco River is gentle and calm for most of the year, the spring runoff provides an exiting surge of white water!

This three-day trip covers nearly thirty miles of river and includes class 3 and 4 rapids.

Canoeing experience is recommended, although whitewater experience is not required.

Highlights include:

- Sturdy, aluminum canoes
- Large, comfortable tents
- Gourmet cooking around the campfire

14 pts.

For more information about these or any of our adventures, call: 1-800-555-1270. *12 pts.*
Or visit our website at: www.adventuresintravel.com.

Index

Fast-teach
Learning Books

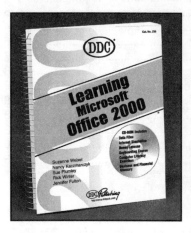

How we designed each book

Each self-paced hands-on text gives you the software concept and each exercise's objective simple language. Next to the exercise we provi the keystrokes and the illustrated layout; step b simple step—graded and cumulative learning.

Did we make one for you?

Titles *$27 each* — Cat. No.

Title	Cat. No.
Creating a Web Page w/ Office 97	Z23
Corel Office 7	Z12
Corel WordPerfect 7	Z16
Corel WordPerfect 8	Z31
DOS + Windows	Z7
English Skills through Word Processing	Z34
Excel 97	Z21
Excel 5 for Windows	E9
Excel 7 for Windows 95	Z11
Internet	Z30
Internet for Business	Z27
Internet for Kids	Z25
Keyboarding/Word Processing with Word 97	Z24
Keyboarding/Word Processing for Kids	Z33
Lotus 1-2-3 Rel. 2.2–4.0 for DOS	L9
Lotus 1-2-3 Rel. 4 & 5 for Windows	B9
Microsoft Office 97	Z19
Microsoft Office for Windows 95	Z6
PowerPoint 97	Z22
Windows 3.1 – A Quick Study	WQS1
Windows 95	Z3
Windows 98	Z26
Word 97	Z20
Word 6 for Windows	1WDW6
Word 7 for Windows 95	Z10
WordPerfect 6 for Windows	Z9
WordPerfect 6.1 for Windows	H9
Works 4 for Windows 95	Z8

Microsoft® OFFICE 2000

Titles *$29 each* — Cat. No.

Title	Cat. No.
Accounting Applications with Excel 2000	Z41
Access 2000	Z38
Create a Web Page with Office 2000	Z43
Desktop Publishing with Publisher 2000	Z47
Excel 2000	Z39
Office 2000	Z35
Office 2000 Deluxe Edition $34	Z35D

• Includes advanced exercises and illustrated solutions for most exercises

Title	Cat. No.
Office 2000: Advanced Course	Z45
PowerPoint 2000	Z40
Web Page Design with FrontPage 2000	Z49
Windows 2000	Z44
Word 2000	Z37

 each with CD-ROM

Preview any of our books at ou Web site: http://www.ddcpub.co

to order call: 800-528-3897 or fax 800-528-3862

The Visual Reference Series

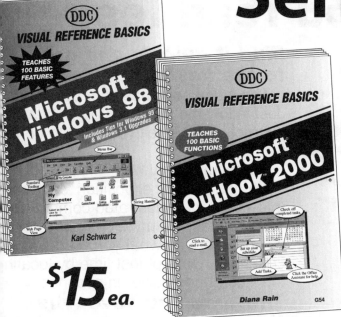

Each book shows you the 100 most important functions of your software programs

We explain your computer screen's elements—icons, windows, dialog boxes—with pictures, callouts, and simple, quick "Press this—type that" illustrated commands. You go right into software functions. *No time wasted.* The spiral binding keeps the pages open so you can type what you read.

$^\$15$ ea.

Did we make one for you?

CAT. NO. TITLE

G29 .. **Microsoft® Access 97**
G21 .. **Microsoft Excel 97**
G33 .. **The Internet**
G37 .. **Internet Explorer 4.0**
G19 .. **Microsoft Office 97**
G23 .. **Microsoft Outlook 97**
G50 .. **Microsoft Outlook 98**
G22 .. **Microsoft PowerPoint 97**
G20 .. **Microsoft Word 97**
G36   **Microsoft Windows 98**
G43 .. **Access 2000**
G58 .. **ACT! 4.0**
G46 .. **Excel 2000**
G40 .. **Office 2000**
G54 .. **Outlook 2000**
G44 .. **PowerPoint 2000**
G45 .. **Word 2000**
G70 .. **Upgrading to Office 2000**

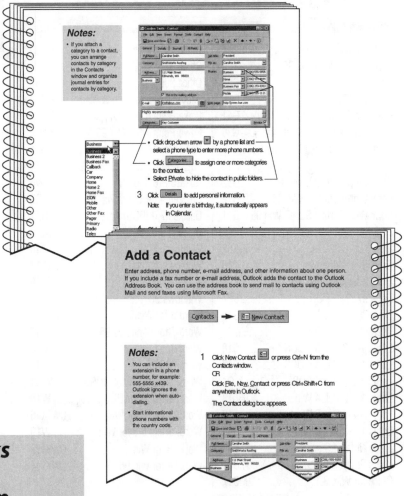

**Preview any of our books
at our Web site
http://www.ddcpub.com**

To order call 800-528-3897
or fax 800-528-3862

99 V

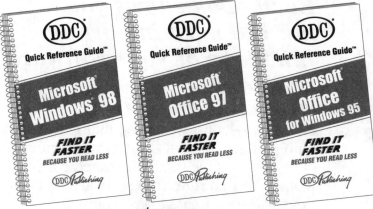
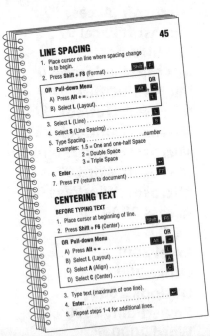

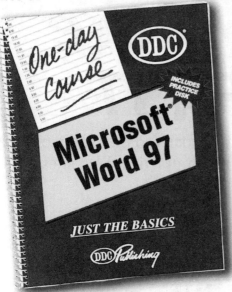

FREE CATALOG
AND
UPDATED LISTING

We don't just have books that find your answers faster; we also have books that teach you how to use your computer without the fairy tales and the gobbledygook.

We also have books to improve your typing, spelling and punctuation.

Return this card for a free catalog and mailing list update.

275 Madison Avenue,
New York, NY 10016

☐ Please send me your catalog
and put me on your mailing list.

Name

Firm (if any)

Address

City, State, Zip

Phone (800) 528-3897   Fax (800) 528-3862

SEE OUR COMPLETE CATALOG ON THE INTERNET @: http://www.ddcpub.com

---

FREE CATALOG
AND
UPDATED LISTING

We don't just have books that find your answers faster; we also have books that teach you how to use your computer without the fairy tales and the gobbledygook.

We also have books to improve your typing, spelling and punctuation.

Return this card for a free catalog and mailing list update.

275 Madison Avenue,
New York, NY 10016

☐ Please send me your catalog
and put me on your mailing list.

Name

Firm (if any)

Address

City, State, Zip

Phone (800) 528-3897   Fax (800) 528-3862

SEE OUR COMPLETE CATALOG ON THE INTERNET @: http://www.ddcpub.com

---

FREE CATALOG
AND
UPDATED LISTING

We don't just have books that find your answers faster; we also have books that teach you how to use your computer without the fairy tales and the gobbledygook.

We also have books to improve your typing, spelling and punctuation.

Return this card for a free catalog and mailing list update.

DDC *Publishing*

275 Madison Avenue,
New York, NY 10016

☐ Please send me your catalog
and put me on your mailing list.

Name

Firm (if any)

Address

City, State, Zip

Phone (800) 528-3897   Fax (800) 528-3862

SEE OUR COMPLETE CATALOG ON THE INTERNET @: http://www.ddcpub.com